EASTERN MONACHISM:

AN ACCOUNT OF THE

ORIGIN, LAWS, DISCIPLINE, SACRED WRITINGS,

MYSTERIOUS RITES,

RELIGIOUS CEREMONIES, AND PRESENT CIRCUMSTANCES

OF THE

ORDER OF MENDICANTS

FOUNDED BY

GOTAMA BUDHA

EASTERN MONACHISM:

AN ACCOUNT OF THE

ORIGIN, LAWS, DISCIPLINE, SACRED WRITINGS,

MYSTERIOUS RITES,

RELIGIOUS CEREMONIES, AND PRESENT CIRCUMSTANCES

OF THE

ORDER OF MENDICANTS

FOUNDED BY

GOTAMA BUDHA

(COMPILED FROM SINGHALESE MSS AND OTHER ORIGINAL SOURCES OF INFORMATION);
WITH COMPARATIVE
NOTICES OF THE USAGES AND INSTITUTIONS OF THE WESTERN ASCETICS
AND A
REVIEW OF THE MONASTIC SYSTEM

BY

R. SPENCE HARDY,

MEMBER OF THE CEYLON BRANCH OF THE ROYAL ASIATIC SOCIETY.

GYAN

Published by

GYAN

Gyan Publishing House
5, Ansari Road
Daryaganj, New Delhi-110002
Phone: 011-47034999, 9811692060
E-mail: books@gyanbooks.com

Distribution Network
gyanbooks.com
India, USA, Canada, UK, Australia, France

ISBN : 978-81-212-2382-9 (PB)
First Published, 1860

2nd Impression 2021

Printed at: Gyan Press, Delhi.

Eastern Monachism
Author: R. Spence Hardy

EASTERN MONACHISM:

AN ACCOUNT OF THE

ORIGIN, LAWS, DISCIPLINE, SACRED WRITINGS, MYSTERIOUS RITES, RELIGIOUS CEREMONIES, AND PRESENT CIRCUMSTANCES

OF THE

ORDER OF MENDICANTS

FOUNDED BY

GÓTAMA BUDHA,

(COMPILED FROM SINGHALESE MSS. AND OTHER ORIGINAL SOURCES OF INFORMATION);

WITH COMPARATIVE

NOTICES OF THE USAGES AND INSTITUTIONS OF THE WESTERN ASCETICS

AND A

Review of the Monastic System.

BY

R. SPENCE HARDY,

MEMBER OF THE CEYLON BRANCH OF THE ROYAL ASIATIC SOCIETY.

Τὸ γεγεννημένον ἐκ τῆς σαρκὸς, σάρξ ἐστι·
I. H. S.

WILLIAMS AND NORGATE,
14, HENRIETTA STREET, COVENT GARDEN, LONDON;
AND
20, SOUTH FREDERICK STREET, EDINBURGH.
1860.

PREFACE.

It has been computed by Professor Neumann that there are in China, Tibet, the Indo-Chinese countries, and Tartary, THREE HUNDRED AND SIXTY-NINE MILLIONS of Budhists. The laws and regulations of the priesthood belonging to a religion so extensively professed as the system of Gótama, must necessarily be an object of great interest. But whilst Brahmanism has been largely elucidated, comparatively little is yet known of Budhism by Europeans.

In the month of September, 1825, I landed in the beautiful island of Ceylon as a Wesleyan Missionary, and one of the first duties to which I addressed myself was, to acquire a knowledge of the language of the people among whom I was appointed to minister. After reading the New Testament in Singhalese, I began the study of the native books, that I might ascertain, from authentic sources, the character of the religion I was attempting to displace. From the commencement, I made notes of whatever appeared to me to be worthy of remembrance in the works I read; and about ten years ago determined to pursue my researches with more of method, from the intention I then formed of publishing the result, if permitted to return to my native land.

In preparing the present work, it has been my principal aim to afford assistance to the missionaries who are living in

I would not, for a moment, depreciate the more honourable labours of those who have chosen the arduous task of studying the system in the language in which it was originally promulgated. I am like one who has met with individuals that have visited some Terra Incognita, and are able to describe it; they have presented before me their stores of information, and I have examined them with all the accumen I possess; and the result of my scrutiny is recorded in these pages. But they who study the original canon may be regarded as actually entering the land, and winning here and there a portion of territory more or less extensive; and by and bye the whole region will be gained; when the initiatory labours I am now pursuing will be forgotten, as they will have been succeeded by more authoritative investigations. Nevertheless, in the present state of our knowledge of Budhism, authentic translations from the more modern languages are of great importance; and they have an additional interest, peculiar to themselves, as they reveal the sentiments, and illustrate the manners, of the present race of priests. The writings of the Singhalese authors abound with quotations from the Pali, of which language they have a competent knowledge; and as they regard the works they translate or paraphrase as a divine record, we have every reason to believe that a correct idea of the original code may be gained through this medium.

As some of the names herein inserted have never previously been printed in English, I trust that the oriental scholar will forgive a want of uniformity in the spelling. It will be noticed that some of the words have a Sanskrit, and others a Pali or a Singhalese, form. I have endeavoured to avoid this confusion, but have not succeeded to the extent that is to be desired.* There are slight discrepancies in some of the dates; but in each case I have followed the author whose work I was translating.

I send forth my treatise to the world, aware of its numerous imperfections, but cheered by the consciousness of integrity in its preparation; and I ask for no higher reward than to be an humble instrument in assisting the ministers of the cross in their combats with this master error of the world, and in preventing the spread of the same delusion, under another guise, in regions nearer home.

R. SPENCE HARDY.

HEBDEN BRIDGE, NEAR HALIFAX,
May 1st, 1850.

* I have been under the necessity of reading some of the proof-sheets in the railway carriage, which will account for some oversights. The reader is requested to correct the following, in addition to the errors inserted in the errata:—Page 190, *line* 18, *for* Tabular Raica *read* Tabula Ilaica; page 292, *line* 40, for nirwáwa *read* nirwána, *and dele the space between* dharmmá *and* bhisamaya; page 308, *line* 4, *for* facultives *read* faculties; page 379, *line* 28, *for* by *read* of; page 386, *line* 16, *for* intelligibiles *read* intelligibilis; page 387, *line* 18, *for* interiorum *read* interiorem; page 388, *after the word* things, *line* 3, *insert as a note*, "Morell's History of Modern Philosophy;" page 389, *lines* 27 and 28, *for* delusion *read* illusion; *and for* anhatamisra *read* andhatamisra.

CONTENTS.

EASTERN MONACHISM.

I. GOTAMA BUDHA.

About two thousand years before the thunders of Wycliffe were rolled against the mendicant orders of the west, Gótama Budha commenced his career as a mendicant in the east, and established a religious system that has exercised a mightier influence upon the world than the doctrines of any other uninspired teacher, in any age or country. The incidents of his life are to be found in the sacred books of the Budhists, which are called in Páli, the language in which they are written, Pitakattayan, from pitakan, a basket or chest, and táyo, three, the text being divided into three great classes. The instructions contained in the first class, called Winaya, were addressed to the priests; those in the second class, Sútra, to the laity; and those in the third class, Abhidharmma, to the déwas and brahmas of the celestial worlds. There is a commentary, called the Atthakathá, which until recently was regarded as of equal authority with the text. The text was orally preserved until the reign of the Singhalese monarch Wattagamani, who reigned from B. C. 104 to B. C. 76, when it was committed to writing in the island of Ceylon. The commentary was written by Budhagósha, at the ancient city of Anurádhapura, in Ceylon, A. D. 420. In this interval there was ample space for the invention of the absurd legends that are inserted therein relative to Budha and his immediate disciples, as we may learn from the similar stories that were invented relative to the western saints, in a period less extended.

The father of Gótama Budha, Sudhódana, reigned at Kapilawastu, on the borders of Nepaul; and in a garden near that city the future sage was born, B. C. 624. At the moment of his birth he stepped upon the ground, and after looking around towards the four quarters, the four half-quarters, above, and below, without seeing any one in any of these ten directions who was equal to himself, he exclaimed, "Aggo hamasmi lókassa; jettho hamasmi lókassa; settho hamasmi lókassa; ayamantimájáti; natthidáni punabbhawo; I am the most exalted in the world; I am chief in the world; I am the most excellent in the world; this is my last birth: hereafter there is to me no other existence." Upon his person were certain signs that enabled the soothsayers to foretell that he would become a recluse, preparatory to his reception of the supreme Budhaship. Five days after his birth he received the name of Sidhártta, but he is more commonly known by the name of Sákya or Gótama, both of which are patronymics. When five months old he sat in the air, without any support, at a ploughing festival. When sixteen years of age he was married to Yasódhará, daughter of Suprabudha, who reigned at Kóli. The father of the predicted Budha having heard that it would be by the sight of four signs—decrepitude, sickness, a dead body, and a recluse—he would be induced to abandon the world, commanded that these objects should be kept away from the places to which he usually resorted; but these precautions were all in vain. One day, when proceeding to a garden at some distance from the palace, he saw an old man, whose trembling limbs were supported by a staff. Attracted by the sight, he asked his charioteer if he himself should ever be similarly feeble, and when he was told it was the lot of all men, he returned to the palace disconsolate. Four months afterwards he saw a leper, presenting an appearance utterly loathsome. Again, after the elapse of a similar period he saw a dead body, green with corruption, with worms creeping out of the nine apertures.* And a year after the sight of the aged man he saw a recluse proceeding along the road in a manner that indicated the possession of an inward tranquillity; modest in his deportment, his whole appearance was strikingly decorous. Having

* The text is almost a literal parallelism to the words of the old ballad.

"On looking up, on looking down,
She saw a dead man on the ground;
And from his nose, unto his chin,
The worms crawl'd out, the worms crawl'd in.

"Then she unto the parson said,
Shall I be so when I am dead,
Oh yes! oh yes! the parson said,
You will be so when you are dead."

learnt from his charioteer the character of this interesting object, he commanded him to drive on rapidly to the garden, where he remained until sunset, in unbounded magnificence, a vast crowd of attendants ministering to his pleasure, amidst strains of the most animating music. In the course of the day a messenger arrived to announce that the princess had been delivered of a son. This was the last occasion on which he engaged in revelry. On his return to the city, the most beautiful attendants at the palace took up their instruments, upon which they played in their most skilful manner, but the mind of the prince wandered away to other objects; and when they saw that they could not engage his attention they ceased to play, and fell asleep. The altered appearance of the sleeping courtesans excited additional contempt for the pleasures of the world; as some of them began to gnash their teeth, whilst others unwittingly put themselves in unseemly postures, and the garments of all were in disorder, the splendour of the festive hall seemed to have been at once converted into the loathsomeness of a sepulchre. Roused by these appearances, Sidhârtta called for his favourite charger, and having first taken a peep at his son from the threshold of the princess's apartment, who was asleep at the time with her arm around the babe, he retired from the city, and when he had arrived at a convenient place assumed the character of a recluse. In the forest of Uruwela he remained six years, passing through a course of ascetic discipline; but as the austerities he practised led to no beneficial result, he reduced his daily allowance of food to a pepperpod, or some equivalent minimum, until his body was greatly attenuated, and one night he fell senseless to the ground from exhaustion. After this he went to another part of the forest, and under a bó-tree, near which Budha Gaya was afterwards built, received the supreme Budhaship.

In births innumerable, previous to his present state of existence as a man, he had set the office of a budha before him as the object of his ambition; and in all the various states of existence through which he passed, animal, human and divine, had accomplished some end, or exercised some virtue, that better fitted him for its reception. Whilst under the bó-tree he was attacked by a formidable host of demons; but he remained tranquil, like the star in the midst of the storm, and the demons, when they had exerted their utmost power without effect, passed away like the thunder-cloud retiring from the orb of the moon, causing it to appear in greater beauty. At the tenth hour of the same night, he attained the wisdom by which he knew the exact circumstances of all the beings that have ever existed in the infinite worlds; at the twentieth hour he received the divine eyes by which he had the power to see all things within the space of the infinite systems of worlds as clearly as if they were close at hand; and at the tenth hour of the following morning, or the close of the third watch of the night, he attained the knowledge by which he was enabled to understand the sequence of existence, the cause of all sorrow and of its cessation. The object of his protracted toils and numerous sacrifices, carried on incessantly through myriads of ages, was now accomplished. By having become a Budha he had received a power by which he could perform any act whatever, and a wisdom by which he could see perfectly any object, or understand any truth, to which he chose to direct his attention.

At this time he began the exercise of his ministry, announcing himself as the teacher of the three worlds, wiser than the wisest, higher than the highest. The places near which he principally resided were Benares, Rajagaha, Wésáli, and Sewet; but he visited many other parts of India, and is said to have proceeded as far as Ceylon. The déwas and brahmas were also included among his auditors, as he occasionally visited the celestial worlds in which they reside. The wonders that he performed were of the most marvellous description; but in those days the possession of supernatural power was a common occurrence, and there were thousands of his disciples who could, with the utmost ease, have overturned the earth or arrested the course of the sun. At the age of eighty years he died, near Kusinára, which is supposed by some to be in Assam, and by others near Delhi. After the burning of his body, his relics were preserved, and became objects of worship to his disciples.

According to the doctrines propounded by Gótama Budha, there are innumerable systems of worlds, called sakwalas, which attain their prime, and then decay and are destroyed, at periods regularly recurring, and by agencies that are equally regular in the manner of their operation. Upon the earth there are four great continents, which do not communicate with each other, except in specified cases. In the centre of the earth is an immense mountain, called Maha Méru, around and above the summit of which are the déwa and brahma lókas, the abode of those beings who in their different states of existence have attained a superior degree of merit. Within the earth is a material fire, the abode of those who possess a decided preponderance of demerit. Neither the one state nor the other is of permanent duration; though it may extend to a period immensely great, it is not infinite.

The Budhas are beings who appear after intervals of time inconceivably vast. Previous to their reception of the Budhaship, they pass through countless phases of being; at one time receiving birth as a déwa, and at another as a frog, in which they gradually accumulate a greater degree of merit. In this incipient state they are called Bódhisatwas. In the birth in which they become Budha they are always of woman born, and pass through infancy and youth like ordinary beings, until at a prescribed age they abandon the world and retire to the wilderness, where, after a course of ascetic observance, at the foot of a tree they receive the supernatural powers with which the office is endowed. But their greatest distinction and highest glory is, that they receive the wisdom by which they can direct sentient beings to the path that leads to nirwána, or the cessation of existence. At their death, they cease to exist; they do not continue to be Budhas, nor do they enter upon any other state of being. Expositions of the doctrines of Budha, whether orally delivered or written in books, are called bana, or the Word; and the system itself is called dharmma, or the Truth.

According to Budhism, there is no Creator, no being that is self-existent and eternal. All sentient beings are homogeneous. The difference between one being and another is only temporary, and results from the difference in their degrees of merit. Any being whatever may be a candidate for the Budhaship; but it is only by the uniform pursuit of this object throughout innumerable ages that it can be obtained.

The power that controls the universe is karma, literally action; consisting of kusala and akusala, or merit and demerit. There is no such monad as an immaterial spirit, but at the death of any being, the aggregate of his merit and demerit is transferred to some other being, which new being is caused by the karma of the previous being, and receives from that karma all the circumstances of its existence. Thus, if the karma be good, the circumstances are favourable, producing happiness, but if it be bad, they are unfavourable, producing misery.

The manner in which being first commenced cannot now be

ascertained. The cause of the *continuance* of existence is ignorance, from which merit and demerit are produced, whence comes consciousness, then body and mind, and afterwards the six organs of sense. Again, from the organs of sense comes contact; from contact, desire; from desire, sensation; from sensation, the cleaving to existing objects; from this cleaving, reproduction; and from reproduction, disease, decay, and death. Thus, like the revolutions of a wheel, there is a regular succession of death and birth, the moral cause of which is the cleaving to existing objects, whilst the instrumental cause is karma. It is therefore the great object of all beings who would be released from the sorrows of successive birth to seek the destruction of the moral cause of continued existence, that is to say, the cleaving to existing objects, or evil desire. It is possible to accomplish this destruction, by attending to a prescribed course of discipline, which results in an entrance to one of the four paths, with their fruition, that lead, by different modes, to the attainment of nirwána. They in whom evil desire is entirely destroyed are called rahats. The freedom from evil desire ensures the possession of a miraculous energy. At his death the rahat invariably attains nirwána, or ceases to exist.

But this review must be regarded as containing only a brief summary of some of the principal doctrines of Budhism, intended to assist the reader of the following pages; the system is so vast and complicated, that many volumes must be written before it can receive a perfect elucidation.

II. THE LAWS AND REGULATIONS OF THE PRIESTHOOD.

About two months after the prince Sidhártta had attained the dignity of a supreme Budha, he went to the city of Benares, and there delivered a discourse, by which Kondanya, and afterwards four other ascetics, were induced to become his disciples. From that period, whenever he preached, multitudes of men and women embraced his doctrines, and took upon themselves certain obligations, by which they declared themselves to be prawarjita, or to have renounced the world. From time to time rules were made, and afterwards enlarged or modified, and exceptions allowed, by which the code was gradually completed. It is evident that all laws referring to untried situations and circumstances must arise in this manner; and though the Budhists maintain that their founder declared at an early period in his career that this would be his rule, the statement was most probably invented to avoid the imputation that might otherwise have been made against his omniscience. It is necessary to remember that these modifications took place, or the student of Budhism will meet with many anomalies for which he cannot account.

Milinda, the king of Ságal, when conversing with the priest Nágaséna, objected to the mode in which Budha instituted the priestly discipline, and said, "If the rishis, by their own intuitive knowledge, were able to tell at once the nature of all diseases, and to prescribe remedies for them, why did not Budha, who by his divine eyes must have seen beforehand the faults of his disciples, forbid the commission of such and such things previous to their occurrence?" Nágaséna replied that it was forseen by Budha, at the commencement, that there were 150 precepts it would be proper to enforce; but he reflected thus, "If I at once enforce the observance of all these precepts, the people will say, 'In this religion there are a great number of things that it is necessary to observe; it is indeed a most difficult thing to be a priest of Budha,' and be afraid; those who might think of becoming priests will hesitate; they will not listen to my words; they will not learn my precepts; they will despise them, and thus be born in a place of torment. It will therefore be better, when a fault has been committed, to issue a precept forbidding it to be repeated." At subsequent periods, nine kelas (each kela containing ten millions), one hundred and eighty-five lacs, and thirty-six precepts, were promulgated by Budha.*

The manner in which the code was gradually perfected may be learnt from the circumstances under which the precept relative to continence arrived at the state in which it was promulgated in its complete form. There was a priest named Sudinna, who was solicited by his mother-in-law to lie with the woman who was his wife previous to his embracing the life of an ascetic, that there

* Milinda Prasna: a work in Pali, of which there is a Singhalese translation, that contains an account of conversations that took place between Milinda, king of Ságal, supposed to be the Sangala of the Greeks, and Nágaséna, a Budhist priest, a short time previous to the commencement of the Christian era. In the following chapters, whenever the name of Nágaséna, is introduced, it is to be understood that the information is taken from this work.

might be a rightful heir to the family possessions. At that time there appears to have been no law prohibiting such a course; but when Sudinna yielded to the solicitations by which he was assailed, and was afterwards led, from a conviction that he had done wrong, to declare to his fellow priests what had taken place, Budha, after reproving him for his conduct, enacted the following law, and declared that it was universally binding upon those who would renounce the world. "Yo pana bhikkhu méthunan dhamman patiséweyya párájikó hóti asanwáso: What priest soever shall have intercourse with a woman is overcome and excluded." Under the plea that intercourse with women alone was prohibited by this law, another priest acted improperly in a forest frequented by monkeys, so that it became necessary to introduce the clause "antamaso tiratchánagatáyapi: Even with an animal." At a subsequent period, some priests of Wajji, without a formal renunciation of asceticism, were guilty of improper conduct. Though they then laid aside their robes, yet, as they met with many afflictions in the world, such as the loss of relatives, they requested readmission to the priesthood. This request was not granted; but a clause was added to the form of prohibition, by which any priest who was unable to maintain a state of continence might receive permission to become a laic, without any bar to his readmission to the priesthood at a future period, if he so willed it. The entire prohibition was then to this effect: "Any bhikkhu who has engaged to live according to the laws given to the priesthood, if he shall, without having made confession of his weakness and become a laic, hold intercourse with a female of what kind soever, is overcome and excluded." *

Of the five sections into which the Winaya Pitaka is divided, the first and second, Párájiká and Páchiti, contain a code of ordinances relative to priestly crimes and misdemeanors; the third and fourth, Maha Waga and Chula Waga, miscellaneous rules and regulations, relative to ordination, the ceremony called wass, &c.; and the fifth, Pariwánapáta, contains a recapitulation of the preceding books.

The precepts and prohibitions contained in the Párájiká and Páchiti, 227 in number, are collected together, apart from the details and explanations by which they are accompanied, in a work called Pátimokkhan, or in Singhalese, Prátimóksha, which is to be recited twice every month in an assembly of priests consisting of

* Gogerly's Essay on Budhism, Journ. Ceylon Branch Royal As. Soc. i. 85.

not fewer than four persons. The subjects of investigation are arranged in the following order:—1. Párájiká, four in number, referring to crimes that are to be punished by permanent exclusion from the priesthood. 2. Sanghádisésá, thirteen in number, that require suspension and penance, but not permanent exclusion. 3. Aniyatá-dhammá, two in number, that involve exclusion, suspension, or penance, according to circumstances. 4. Nissagiyá-páchittiyá-dhammá, thirty in number, requiring forfeiture of such articles as the priests are permitted to possess. 5. Páchittiyá-dhammá, ninety-two in number, requiring confession and absolution. 6. Pátidésani-dhammá, four in number, involving reprimand. 7. Sékhiyá-dhammá, seventy-five in number, containing various prohibitions, and inculcating certain observances and proprieties. 8. Adhikarana-samatá-dhammá, seven in number, the rules to be observed in conducting judicial investigations relative to the conduct of the priests.*

The four crimes that involve permanent exclusion from the priesthood are sexual intercourse, theft, murder, and a false profession of the attainment of rahatship; but as the whole of the rules contained in the Pátimokkhan appear in thefollowing chapters, under the heads to which they respectively belong, it will not be necessary to insert them in the order in which they are recited in the bi-monthly convention of ecclesiastics. The various rules and obligations of the priest have been divided into an almost numberless array of classes; but their tedious minuteness must ever tend to deter any one from prosecuting their examination, who does not trust in the three gems as an object of religious confidence.

There is, however, one division, called the Teles-dhútanga, from teles, thirteen, dhúṭa, destroyed, and anga, ordinance, meaning the thirteen ordinances by which the cleaving to existence is destroyed, too important to be omitted. These ordinances enjoin the following observances on the part of the priest by whom they are kept. 1. To reject all garments but those of the meanest description. 2. To possess only three garments. 3. To eat no food but that which has been received under certain restrictions. 4. To call at all houses alike when carrying the alms-bowl. 5. To remain on one seat, when eating, until the meal be finished. 6. To eat only from

* Gogerly's Essay on the Laws of the Priesthood, Ceylon Friend, 1839. Nearly the whole of my information relative to the contents of the Pátimokkhan has been derived from this source.

one vessel. 7. To cease eating when certain things occur. 8. To reside in the forest. 9. To reside at the foot of a tree. 10. To reside in an open space. 11. To reside in a cemetery. 12. To take any seat that may be provided. 13. To refrain from lying down under any circumstance whatever. The three principal observances are the 4th, 5th, and 10th; and he who observes these three may be said to practise the whole series. The entire number may be kept by priests, eight by priestesses, twelve by novices, seven by female novices, and two by the lay devotees called upásakas, whether male or female. Thus there are in all forty-two divisions. The five observances that the priestesses are forbidden to keep are the 7th, 8th, 9th, 10th, and 11th; the last three cannot be observed by them under any circumstances, as it would be highly improper for the priestess to remain in a solitary place. The novice may keep all except the 2nd. The lay devotee can keep only the 5th and 6th.*

Nearly the whole of these observances are included in the code that is known among the Chinese by the name of Chi eul theou tho king, or The Sacred Book of the Twelve Observances, quoted in the San tsang fă sou, lib. xliv. p. 10. Cf. Vocabulaire Pentaglotte, sect. xlv.†

III. NAMES AND TITLES.

The priests of Budha have received various names, of which the following are the principal:—1. Sráwakas, from the root sru, to hear, answering to the ακουστικοι of the Greeks. 2. Sarmanas, from srama, the performance of asceticism, answering to the ἀσκηται, exercisers, of the ancient church. By the Chinese the word is written Cha men and Sang men, and is said by Klaproth to mean "celui qui restreint ses pensées, ou celui qui s'efforce et se restreint." It is probable that the epithet Samanean, as applied to the religious system of Tartary, is derived from the same word. It is to the priests of Budha that Strabo (lib. xv. cap. i.) refers,

* Milanda Prasna: Wisudhi Margga Sanné.

† Foë Kouĕ Ki, ou Relation des Royaumes Bouddhiques: Voyage dans la Tartarie, dans l'Afghanistan et dans l'Inde, exécuté a la fin du IVe Siècle, par Chў fă hian. Traduit du Chinois et commenté par M. Abel Remusat. Ouvrage posthume, revu, complété, et augmenté d'éclaircissements nouveaux, par MM. Klaproth et Landresse: Paris, 1836.

when he speaks of the Garmanas of India. By Clemens Alexandrinus (Stromat. lib. i.) they are called Sarmanas, though he afterwards mentions the followers of Butta (Budha) as belonging to a separate community. In other works of the fathers they are called Semnoi. Porphyrius (De Abst. lib. iv.) calls them Samanacani. 3. Théros, or elders, answering to the זקנים* of the Old Testament and the πρεσβυτεροι of the New. 4. Bhikshus, or in Pali, bhikkhu, from bhiksha, to beg, literally a mendicant. The bhikshu is said to be so called "because of the fear he manifests of the repetition of existence; because he goes to seek his food as a mendicant; because he is arrayed in shreds and rags; and because he avoids the practice of whatever is evil." The eastern etymologists, with their usual ingenuity, find all these ideas in the root of the word, either by addition, elision, or transposition. When Budha addressed the priests, it was usually by this appellation. It is said by M. Abel Remusat that the Chinese word Pi khicou "is the equivalent of the Sanskrit bhikchou, mendiant." They are called in Tibetan, dGe slong. "When the four rivers fall into the sea they no longer retain the name of river: when men of the four castes become Samaneans, they receive the common name of sons of Sákya (synonymous with bhikchou). The Tsun ching king calls them Pi thsiu (the name of a shrub that grows upon the Himalayas)." †

In Ceylon, the novices, as well as the priests who have not received ordination, are called ganinnansés, from gana, an assemblage or association; and the superior priests are called térunnánsés, from the Pali théro, an elder. Their collective name is mahunánsé, literally, the great one. In the books they are represented as being addressed by the name of áyusmat, ancient, venerable. When any one embraced the priesthood he was said to be prawarjika, from wraja, to abandon, one who has abandoned the world, answering to a name of the ancient monks, ἀποταξαμενοι, apotactates, renouncers. In Nepaul the priests are called bandaya (whence also the Chinese bonze), which, in Sanskrit signifies a person entitled to reverence, from the word bandana. They are there divided into

* In like manner, Arab. Sheikh, an old man, and then "chief of a tribe;" also Ital. Signor, Fr. Seigneur, Span. Señor, Engl. Sir, all of which come from the Lat. Senior, elder; also, Germ. Graf. count, is pp. i. q. graw, krawo, grey-headed. Gesenius, sub voce.

† Relation des Royaumes Bouddhiques, p. 60, quoted from San tsang fă sou, liv. xxii. p. 9.

four orders; bhikshu, or mendicants; sráwaka, or readers; chailaka, or scantily robed; and arhanta, or arhata, adepts.* Among the Burmese the priests, or talapoins, of the superior order, are called ponghis, and of the inferior pazens; they are all subordinate to the zaradó, who resides in the capital.†

It has been doubted whether Budhism allows of any such distinction as that which is inferred in the use of the words clerus and laicus; but all arguments founded upon the meaning of terms, when these terms can be used in a sense different to their primitive signification, or when that signification has not been authoritatively defined, are inconclusive. Thus the word clergy, though we allow that it is derived from κληρος, may either mean that the ministers of the church were chosen by lot, or that they were the lot and heritage of the Lord. The word priest is generally supposed to be derived, through the Saxon preost, from the Greek πρεσβυτερος, an elder, but by others it is said to be an ancient Saxon word, in use before the introduction of Christianity; and if we look away from its original meaning to its conventional use, it may represent the sacerdos of the Latins, the ιερευς of the Greeks, the כהן of the Hebrews, or the minister of any other religion; and its signification will be altered according to the office that it represents. The rites of religion could only be performed among the Greeks and Romans by members of the sacerdotal class; but these persons were not thereby incapacitated, by any positive law, from engaging in duties and offices that by ourselves would be regarded as utterly unsuited to the clerus. But this is the less remarkable when other circumstances are taken into the account; as their duty consisted principally in the performance of certain ceremonies, or the instructing of others in their proper mode of observance, whilst no traces are presented of their publicly addressing the people upon moral subjects. Hence the importance of the position maintained by the philosophers, who in some measure supplied this defect; but their auditors were comparatively few; and as he who appeared to understand the deepest mysteries would be regarded as the most wise, there was a continual tendency in all the schools to dwell upon subjects that bewilder, rather than upon those that are connected with practical instruction. The sramanas of Budha unite

* Hodgson's Illustrations of the Literature and Religion of the Buddhists: Serampore, 1841.

† Sangarmano's Burmese Empire: Rome, 1833.

the characters of priest and philosopher, as they were presented among the nations of classic antiquity; but, from their possession of a record that they consider to be divine, the reverse of that which took place among the ancients of the west is presented; individual speculation is almost entirely discountenanced, and the bare reading of the record too commonly usurps the place of hortatory teaching.

The apostle Paul tells us that the priest is "one who is ordained for men in things pertaining to God, that he may offer both gifts and sacrifices for sins," Heb. v. 1; but this definition is confessedly inapplicable to any order of men among the Budhists, as the system knows nothing whatever of "sacrifices for sins."

When compared with the priest of Romanism there is a greater resemblance between the two orders. Both are separated from the world; both profess to instruct the people; and both perform ceremonies that are supposed to confer merit upon those in whose name, or in whose presence they are conducted. I have therefore retained the word priest to designate the sramanas of Budha; they are monks as to the economy of their own lives, but priests as to the world without; clerici regulares.

The innovations made by St. Francis in the monastic institute were of great importance. Until that period the monks had been insulated from the world. Even the pastoral duties were forbidden them. It was ordained by Conc. Pictav. c. 11, that no monk should perform the work of a parochial minister, i. e. "to baptise, to preach, and to hear confession." He was not allowed (Conc. Lat. I.) to visit the sick. But when Francis received the impression that it was his duty to renounce the possession of gold, silver, and money; to have neither wallet, nor satchel, nor bread; to travel without a staff, and without shoes, and with a simple tunic; he was at the same time moved to the resolution to preach repentance and the kingdom of God. When monachism commenced, the ascetic renounced all trust in the vicarious acts of a more favoured order; he himself worked out his own salvation; he was himself a priest, though without investiture or ordination; and it was not until the monks had degenerated that individuals sought admission to the priesthood, and combined two offices that were at first distinct. But the rule of Francis did not contemplate merely the occasional election of a monk to the pastorate or episcopate, or the appointment of an ordained abbot to rule over "the church in the house" of some separate fraternity; his mendicant followers were thrown upon the world; from it they were to receive their subsistence; and it was only by the personal activity of each individual member that the order could be preserved in its integrity. In the history of Budhism there are evidences of a similar departure from the first principles of asceticism; but when it commenced, or in what manner it was effected, cannot now be ascertained. It appears to have been the original intention that the sramana, during the greater part of the year, should reside in solitude; but the injunction to carry the alms-bowl to the houses of the people would tend to produce an unfavourable consequence, as it would continually present to his mind the advantages of social existence, and tempt him to take up his residence as near the dwellings of men as was possible without an entire change of the system. Then, as he was dependent upon the people for every comfort he enjoyed, it was natural that he should endeavour to magnify his office, and place as immense a distance as possible between himself and his supporters, by convincing them that whilst he received from them the temporal aid that he needed they were indebted to him, and the power with which he was officially clothed, for their present prosperity and for their expectation of a future reward. Thus, although he offered no sacrifice in the literal sense of the term, he became virtually invested with the character of a priest. This change in the economy of Budhism has been carried to so great an extent, that the true ascetic, or one who renounces the world for his own soul's good, without regarding the souls of others, is now almost unknown.

There is undoubtedly a great difference between the sramana and the grahapati; the receiver of alms, who by that reception confers merit, and the giver of alms, who by that gift expects to gain merit: the man who lives (to use a distinction of Pythagoras) ὑπερ φυσιν, above nature, and him who lives κατα φυσιν, according to nature; and the higher attainments of the systemcan only be acquired by one who has abandoned the world either in the present or some previous birth; but the householder is not rejected as being without the pale of privilege, and is far from being classed among unbelievers. Even at the commencement of Budhism the bana was publicly recited, so that from the beginning a distinction must have existed between the teacher and the taught, which would cause the priest to be regarded as a mediator, or intervenient instrumentality, between the householder and the consequences of his demerit. The benefits received from listening to the bana were not prospective or conditional; they were not dependent upon some new course of action that was to be pursued in consequence of this instruction: it was an opus operatum; and the householder retired to his home, after listening to the word, with the consciousness that he had thereby acquired merit, and that if he continued in the wise exercise of the privileges placed within his reach, without taking upon himself the more arduous practices of the ascetic, he would be enabled to attain a reward that was worthy of his ambition. We therefore conclude that Budhism has always recognised the two classes of mendicant and householder; and that both the one and the other is regarded as recipient of the blessings it imparts to its disciples.

In the gospel there is a distinction between the clerus and laicus as to matters of discipline; but the child, the woman, the slave, the lowest member of the church, whatever his condition, has an equal freedom of access to the throne of the heavenly grace with the mitred ecclesiastic or the most privileged priest, and may aspire to an equal inheritance of glory in the world to come. But in Budhism the distinction is more essential, as no one who has not in some state of existence, either present or past, observed the ordinances of asceticism, can obtain nirwána. This may be learnt from a conversation that took place between the king of Ságal and Nágaséna. One day, when Milinda was reclining upon his royal couch, reflecting upon religious subjects, he wondered how it was that, if householders could enter the paths leading to nirwána, any one should take the trouble to observe the Thirteen Ordinances, the practice of which is so exceedingly difficult; and he therefore went to Nágaséna, that his doubts upon the subject might be removed. "Can the householder," said he, "attain nirwána; he whose mind is occupied by (panchakáma) that which is apparent to the five senses; who lives in a fixed habitation, procreates children, enjoys possessions, uses ointments and perfumes, receives money, and puts on the crown adorned with jewels and gold?" Nágaséna replied, "Not only one hundred but myriads of householders have attained nirwána. But as to the Thirteen Ordinances, it is a subject most extensive; however many things I might say relative to the religion of Budha they would all belong to them. As all the rain that falls runs into the rivers, and thence into the sea, so all that the most learned person might say relative to religion would be directed to them. All the knowledge I possess is included in them; they are, in the most eminent degree, profitable, beautiful, and complete. At Sewet there were many myriads of upásakas, both male and female, who entered the paths, of whom 356,000 entered the third path; and at other places, when Budha preached different sútras, countless companies of men and déwas received the same privilege, all of whom were gihi, householders, and not prawarjita, those who have abandoned or renounced the world." Milinda:—"Then to what purpose is it that men observe with so much strictness the Thirteen Ordinances, if they can enter the city of peace without it? If a sick man can be cured by simples, he does not torture his body by taking emetics or violent purgatives; if the enemy can be warded off by a slight blow we do not use clubs or formidable weapons; the high ladder is of no use if the tree can be ascended without it; when a man can sleep soundly on the ground he need not seek a splendid couch and coverlets; when the fearless man can traverse the wilderness alone he does not require an armed escort; he who can swim across the river or lake does not look out for rafts, boats, or bridges; he who has food of his own need not, in order to satisfy his hunger, go begging from his friends or the rich, flattering them and running hither and thither; if water can be procured from a natural fountain, it is to no purpose to dig wells or tanks: in like manner, if the householder, who enjoys worldly possessions, can also enjoy the prospect of nirwána, of what benefit are the Thirteen Ordinances?" Nágaséna:—"The Budhas have set forth twenty-eight advantages as connected with the observance of these rites: such as fearlessness, protection, freedom from evil desire, the patient endurance of affliction, confirmed attachment to religion, an entrance into the paths, &c. When the Thirteen Ordinances are observed, there are eighteen virtues that are brought into exercise, such as, that the thought is extinguished, that this is mine, or me; hatred is avoided; much sleep is shunned; no fixed habitation is required; solitary meditation is exercised; and there is opposition to all evil. There are also ten other virtues that must be possessed: such as faith or purity, great diligence, freedom from all that tends to deceive, respect for the precepts, equanimity, &c. When the householder attains nirwána, it is because he has kept the Thirteen Ordinances in some former state of existence: just as the bowman, after learning the science of archery in the hall of instruction and becoming perfect, then goes to the king and receives the reward of his skill. No one who has not observed the Thirteen Ordinances, either in the present birth or a former one, can enter the path that leads to the city of peace. . . . Men eat food that they may receive strength, take medicine that they may drive away disease, exercise friendship that they may secure assistance, enter a ship that they may cross the sea, and use flowers and perfumes that a fragrant smell may be emitted: the pupil who would receive instruction places himself under a preceptor; he who would have honour seeks it from the king; and he who would have anything that he can wish for, gains possession of the magical jewel: in like manner, he who would receive the full benefit of asceticism, practises the Thirteen Ordinances. As water for the nourishment of grain, fire for burning, food for imparting strength, withs for binding, women for contention, water for removing thirst, treasure for independence, a ship for navigation, medicines for imparting health, a couch for repose, a place of refuge for safety, the king for protection, weapons for giving confidence, the preceptor for instruction, the mother for rearing children, the mirror for seeing the countenance, jewels for ornament, garments for clothing, scales for equality, the mantra for spells and charms, the lamp for dispelling darkness, and the precept for restraining the disobedient; so is an attention to the Thirteen Ordinances for the nourishing of asceticism, the burning up of evil desire, &c."*

IV. THE NOVICIATE.

For the rapidity of its early extension, and its subsequent popularity, Budhism is in a great measure indebted to the broad basis upon which admission to the priesthood has been placed; and in this respect it stands in perfect contrast with the system to which it is the greatest antagonist. No one can become a Brahman, except by birth; but the privileges of the ascetic are offered to all who will receive them upon the condition implied in their acceptance, unless the candidate be diseased, a slave, a soldier, or unable to obtain the permission of his parents. This comprehensive rule has been disregarded; but the system itself is not to be charged

* Milinda Prasna.

with the innovations that have been made in its original constitution. The slave is inhibited from becoming a recluse; but the name is not to be taken in its modern acceptation, as implying a state of degradation. The bar to admission does not arise from the inferiority of the condition, as even the outcast is received; but as the peculium belongs to another, no slave is thought to have the right to place himself in a situation that may for ever deprive his master of his services. In the reign of Justinian (Nov. v. c. 2) slaves were allowed to enter convents without leave of their masters; but among the Anglo-Saxons the candidate for ordination was required to prove that he was not of spurious or servile birth. That the priest should be free from disease has been generally insisted on in all ages. The Jews, in their comments upon Levit. xxi. 17, have enumerated 142 blemishes that produced unfitness to minister before the Lord. "Sacerdos integer sit," was a law of the Romans; but among the ancients the disease or the blemish was not a bar to the reception of the office from its unsightliness alone; it was regarded as unpropitious, and it was therefore said, "vitandus est," as it was supposed that it would render the sacrifice coming from such a source of no avail. This idea, though not expressed in the ritual, is entirely consonant with the Budhistical system.

The novice is called a sámanéra, from sramana, an ascetic. He must be at least eight years of age, and must have received the consent of his parents to his abandonment of the world. He cannot receive upasampadá, or ordination, until he is twenty years of age; were even the office to be conferred on him by the proper authorities, and the ceremony to be performed according to the ritual, the proceedings would be invalid if the stipulated age was not attained. The novice is not regarded as a member of the sangha, or chapter; he can perform any religious rite, but is not allowed to interfere in matters of discipline or government. But in China, ordination must be granted at an earlier period, as Bishop Smith states that he saw a little priest, about nine years of age, a pet of the abbot, who looked forward to the age of sixteen, "when he would have his head entirely shaven, and be inducted into the full privileges of the priesthood." *

The necessity of some law, imperatively stating the earliest age at which the obligations of the recluse can be taken, must be at

* Smith's China.

once apparent. Leo I. required the age of forty in monks before their consecration, and the same age was ordered by several councils. Pius I. recommended the twenty-fifth year, which was confirmed by the third council of Carthage. Synods of a more recent date have allowed vows of virginity to be taken as early as fourteen years of age in males, and twelve in females. The council of Trent recognises sixteen years as the age before which vows should not be taken.* Among the Anglo-Saxons, the vows of the nun were retarded until she had reached her twenty-fifth year. In the monasteries of the Greek church belonging to the rule of St. Basil, the male novices are not allowed to take the vows before the thirtieth, nor females before the fiftieth year. The mendicant orders are accused by Wycliffe of endeavouring to seduce young children into their "rotten habit;" and it was decreed by the parliament that no scholar under eighteen years of age should be received into the community. †

There are many circumstances that make the yoke of the sámanéra less onerous than that of the stricter communities among the western celibates. The vows are not in any case irrevocable; and the constant intercourse that is of necessity kept up with the people, affords opportunities of communion with the exterior world that are denied to the inmate of the high-walled monastery or the iron-barred convent. It must often cause the deepest sorrow, only passing away with the utter searing of every right affection or with life itself, when the recluse has to reflect that by the step he has taken he has sent the barbed arrow into the heart of an affectionate mother, or stricken to premature age a father whose eye is ever filled with the gushing tear, as he looks around upon the social circle and sees that the place is vacant where the object of his brightest hopes once sat. Yet it was accounted as an additional merit by the Nicene doctors when the vow of celibacy was taken against the wish or advice of parents, or against their knowledge. ‡ It was also regarded as an act of merit when the mother devoted her unconscious child to the service of the sanctuary, as in the case of Gregory Nazianzen, who, before his birth, was devoted to God by his mother Nonna. This was usually done by taking the child before the altar, and placing in its hands the book of the gospels; but at a later period the parents wrapped the hands of their children

* Elliott's Roman Catholicism. † Vaughan's Wycliffe.

‡ Taylor's Ancient Christianity.

in the altar-cloth. By Cod. Just. i. 3, 55, parents were forbidden to hinder their children from becoming monks, if they so wished. Even among the Budhists, it sometimes occurs that a woman vows she will dedicate her son to the temple, should the reproach of her unfruitfulness be taken away; and when the child afterwards received puts on the robe of a recluse, he may at first, and in his youth, be charmed by the honour he receives, so as to be more than reconciled to his situation; and should there be, at a subsequent period, a painful sense of the constraint under which he lives, from a feeling of pride he may never utter to another the story of his woe, or take the liberty that is presented by the institute of returning for a time to the state of a laic. But in all such cases there will be the bearing of a burden that must greatly embitter existence; and the spirit will become moody or morose, that under other circumstances might have been cheerful as the lark at matins, or gentle as the lamb as it crops the grass of the mead.

The sámanéra usually begins his connexion with the monastery by becoming a pupil in the school kept by the priest; and by this means he gains an insight into the duties he will afterwards be required to perform. The priesthood is to be sought in order that existence may be overcome, and that nirwána, or the cessation of existence, may be obtained. It was declared by Nágaséna that the benefits to be derived from embracing the priesthood are, the destruction of present and the avoiding of future sorrow, the preventing of the occurrence of the birth arising from evil desire and scepticism, and the attainment of nirwána. "This," said he, "is the end for which the priesthood ought always to be sought; but it is sometimes sought from a different intention, as the fear of kings or of robbers, or because of debt, or to obtain a livelihood." Whoever would enter upon the course of discipline necessary for the attainment of this great object, must be assured that by the observance of the prescribed rules of asceticism, the cleaving to existence, which is regarded as the source of all evil, will be extinguished. If possible, the novice must live in the same monastery as his preceptor, but if not convenient, he may live in another place, at the distance of four, eight, or sixteen miles. When he thus lives at a distance, he must rise early in the morning, perform what is necessary to be done at his own dwelling, then go to the monastery of his preceptor, and return the following day to his own abode. And when he cannot live within the distance of sixteen miles, he must learn as well as he can from his preceptor, and afterwards meditate at his leisure on the instruction he has received. In Ceylon, there are not at present any instances in which this privilege is accepted, as the sámanéra invariably resides at the monastery; and from the commencement of his noviciate he is regarded as a priest.

When the pupil becomes an accepted novice, it is required of him that he be careful as to the character of the monastery in which he intends to reside. There are eighteen kinds of places that it will be well for him to avoid: 1. A large wihára (the monastery or temple in which the priests reside), as in such a place many persons will meet together, and there will be much talking; the enclosure round the bó-tree not being swept, and no water brought either to drink or for bathing, these things will have to be done, and thus time will be lost; the novice, after performing this, must go with the alms-bowl, but as he will have been preceded by others, the food intended for the priesthood will all have been given away. In a large wihára, the noise of the novices repeating their lessons will cause a disturbance. But if all the work be properly attended to, and there be nothing to distract, a large wihára may be chosen. 2. A new wihára, as there will be much work to do, which if not done may cause the displeasure of the senior priests; but if there should be others to do the work, so as to leave the novice free, he may remain in a new residence. 3. An old wihára, as it will require much reparation; if this be not attended to, it will bring down the rebuke of the senior priests; and if it be, it will leave no time for meditation. 4. A wihára near a high road, as stranger priests will be continually calling, who will require attention. 5. A wihára near which there are many tanks and much water, as people will resort thither, and the disciples of the learned men connected with the court will come from the city to dye their garments, and will want fuel, vessels, and other things. 6. A wihára near which there is an abundance of herbs, as women will come to gather them, singing all kinds of foolish songs, the hearing of which is as poison; and though they should even not be singing, the voice of a woman heard in any way is an enemy to the ascetic. 7. A wihára near which there are many flowers, as there will be the same danger. 8. A wihára near which there are many fruit-trees, such as mango, jambu, and jack, as people will come to ask for them, and if not given they will become angry or take them by force; and when the priest walks to and fro at night, to subdue the mind, they will see and ridicule him. 9. A wihára that persons are accustomed to visit, such as Dakkhina-giri, Attikuchi-léna, Chétiya-giri, and Chittala-pabbata; to these places the faithful resort that they may worship, because they were formerly the residences of rahats; but the priest may dwell near these places, if he can make such arrangements as will enable him to be absent during the day, and return to them only at night. 10. A wihára near a city, as there will be many things to attract the eyes; the women will not leave the road when they are met, and they will make a noise with their earthen vessels; and the place will be resorted to by great men. 11. A wihára near which there is much fuel or timber for building, as women will come to gather the firewood and artisans to fell the trees; at night, when they see the priest walking in the place of ambulation they will ridicule or otherwise molest him. 12. A wihára near a rice-field, as the cultivators will have to make the platform on which the oxen tread out the rice, and a disturbance will be caused. 13. A wihára near which cattle are accustomed to graze, as they will break into the rice-fields, and the owners will accuse the priests, and make complaints to the magistrates. 14. A wihára in which the resident priests are not on friendly terms with each other; they will quarrel, and if told to be at peace, they will say that they never prospered since this rigid ascetic came who now gives his advice. 15, 16, 17. A wihára near a seaport, a river, or a forest; the mariners will request assistance, and these men are not believers in the truth. 18. A wihára on the borders of a country,* as the resident will be exposed to wars, will be now under one king, and then under another, and will be liable to be accounted as a spy. †

All these places are to be avoided, as though they were inhabited by so many demons; and the dangers arising from these non-human beings are represented as being by no means small. There was a priest residing in a forest, who one day hearing a female demon sing near the door of his residence was (improperly) attracted to the place; but when he came near she caught him and hurried him away that she might eat him. The priest insisting upon knowing

* The monks of Christendom, on some occasions, manifested a different spirit to that which is here inculcated. On the edge of Spalding Moor, in Yorkshire, there was a cell for two monks, whose employment was to guide travellers over the dreary waste upon which they here entered. Whilst one acted as a conductor, the other implored by prayer the protection of heaven for those who were exposed to the dangers of the road.

† Wisudhi Margga Sanné.

what she was about to do, she said that she had eaten many such priests as he, and that she should reckon it to be a great misfortune if the time should come when she would be unable to secure some member of the sacred community.

The novice must choose a residence that is not far from the village to which he has to go to procure alms. Budha has said that it must not be more than four miles distant, nor nearer than the length of 500 bows. It must be a place easy of access; free from dangers; where the people offer no interruption; at night subject to no noise; at a distance from the hurry of the multitudes; not infested by flies, musquitoes, or snakes, nor subject to an excess of wind or sun; where the requisites of the priest can be obtained without difficulty; and where there are superior priests to whom he can resort, that he may ask questions, and have his doubts solved.

The place of residence having been chosen, the novice must declare his intention to a superior priest; or he must take a robe, and after having shaved his head and bathed, give it to a priest, requesting to receive it from him again, that he may thus be able to commence his noviciate. He must then ask the priest to impart to him the tun-sarana, or three-fold protective formulary, which is as follows:—

Budhang-saranang-gach'hámi	I take refuge in Budha.
Dhammang-saranang-gach'hámi	I take refuge in the Truth.
Sanghang-saranang-gach'hámi	I take refuge in the Associated Priesthood.

or the same formulary may be repeated by himself; but in that case he must change the *ng* at the end of each word into *m*, and say Budham saranam, instead of Budhang saranang, &c.* He must then repeat the dasa-sil, or the ten obligations.

1. Pánátipátáwéramanísikkhápadangsamádiyámi.
2. Adinnádánáwéramanísikkhápadangsamádiyámi.
3. Abrahmachariyáwéramanísikkhápadangsamádiyámi.
4. Musáwádáwéramanísikkhápadangsamádiyámi.
5. Surámérayamajjapamádatthánáwéramanísikkhápadangsamádiyámi.
6. Wikálábhójanáwéramanísikkhápadangsamádiyámi.
7. Nachagítawáditawisúkadassanáweramanísikkhápadangsamádiyámi.

* Wisudhi Margga Sanné.

8. Málágandhawilépanadháranámandanawibhúsanattánáwéramanísikkhápadangsamádiyámi.

9. Uch'hasayanamahásayanáwéramanísikkhápadangsamádiyámi.

10. Játarúparajatapatiggahanáwéramanísikkhápadangsamádiyami.

---

1. I will observe the precept, or ordinance, that forbids the taking of life.

2. I will observe the precept, or ordinance, that forbids the taking of that which has not been given.

3. I will observe the precept, or ordinance, that forbids sexual intercourse.

4. I will observe the precept, or ordinance, that forbids the saying of that which is not true.

5. I will observe the precept, or ordinance, that forbids the use of intoxicating drinks, that lead to indifference towards religion.

6. I will observe the precept, or ordinance, that forbids the eating of food after mid-day.

7. I will observe the precept, or ordinance, that forbids attendance upon dancing, singing, music, and masks.

8. I will observe the precept, or ordinance, that forbids the adorning of the body with flowers, and the use of perfumes and unguents.

9. I will observe the precept, or ordinance, that forbids the use of high or honourable seats or couches.

10. I will observe the precept, or ordinance, that forbids the receiving of gold or silver.

The principal duties that are to be attended to by the novice are set forth in a manual called Dina Chariyáwa, or the Daily Observances of the Priest:—"He who, with a firm faith, believes in the religion of truth, rising before day-light, shall clean his teeth, and shall then sweep all the places that are proper to be swept, such as the court-yard, the platform near the bó-tree, and the approaches to the wihára; after which he shall fetch the water that is required for drinking, filter it, and place it ready for use. When this is done, he shall retire to a solitary place, and for the space of three hours* meditate on the obligations, considering whether he has kept them or not. The bell will then ring, and he must reflect that greater than the gift of 100 elephants, 100 horses, and 100 chariots, is the reward of him who takes one step towards the place where worship

* There are sixty hours in one day.

is offered. Thus reflecting, he shall approach the dágoba (a conical erection under which some relic is placed) or the bó-tree, and perform that which is appointed; he shall offer flowers, just as if Budha were present in person, if flowers can be procured; meditate on the nine virtues of Budha, with a fixed and determined mind; and having worshipped, seek absolution for his negligences and faults, just as if the sacred things (before which he worships) had life. Having risen from this act of reverence, he shall proceed to the other places where worship is offered, and spreading the cloth or skin that he is accustomed to place under him, he shall again worship (with his forehead to the ground, and touching the ground with his knees and toes). The next act that he is required to perform is to look at his lita, or calendar, in order that he may learn the awach'háwa (the length of the shadow, by which according to rules regularly laid down, varying with the time of the year, the hour of the day may be known), the age of the moon, and the years that have elapsed since the death of Budha; and then meditate on the advantages to be derived from the keeping of the obligations, carrying the alms-bowl, and putting on the yellow robe. It will now be time for him to take the alms-bowl, and when going his round, he is to bear in mind the four karmasthánas, not to go too near, nor to keep at too great a distance from, his upádya or preceptor; at a convenient distance from the village, having swept a small space clean, he is properly to adjust his robe. If going with his upádya or preceptor, he is to give the bowl into his hands, and accompany him to the village, carefully avoiding the sight of women, men, elephants, horses, chariots, or soldiers. According to the rules contained in the Sékhiyá, he is to proceed along the road; and after the alms have been received he is to retire from the village in the manner previously declared. Taking the bowl and outer robe of his superior, he shall then proceed to the wihára. If there be a place appointed for the robe, he shall put it there after folding it; then place a seat, wash his feet, enquire if he is thirsty, place before him the tooth-cleaner, and bring the alms-bowl, or if this be refused, a small portion of rice. The stanzas must be repeated that are appointed to be said before eating, after eating, and when the things are received that may be used as sick diet; and the food is to be eaten in the manner laid down in the Sékhiyá. Then taking the bowl of his superior he shall wash it, put it in the sunshine to dry, and deposit it afterwards in its proper place. This being done he is to wash his own face, and putting on his robe, he is first to worship his superior, and then Budha. The next act is to go again to some solitary place, and there repeat the appointed stanzas, considering whether he has omitted the practice of any obligation, or in any way acted contrary to them, after which he must exercise maitri-bháwaná, or the meditation of kindness and affection. About an hour afterwards, when his weariness is gone, he is to read one of the sacred books, or write out a portion of one; and if he has anything to ask from his preceptor, or to tell him, this is the time at which it should be done. In some convenient place the bana is to be read; and when this is concluded, if there be time before the setting of the sun, he is again to sweep the court-yard, &c. as before.

"One by one each day, in regular order, the sámanéra novices shall kindle a fire, light a lamp, make all ready for the reading of the bana, call the priest who is appointed to recite it, wash his feet, sit down in an orderly manner and listen to the bana, and then repeat the pirit, or ritual of priestly exorcism. Having done whatever is necessary to be done for the guru, and offered him worship, if the novice has doubts respecting any matter he must ask to have them solved; or if accustomed to read the sacred books as a lesson, it must now be done, and he must repeat the Sékhiyá and Chatu-párasudhi-síla. If there be in the same wihára a priest older than himself, he is to render him all necessary assistance, such as to wash his feet, and anoint them with oil, and after offering to him worship, he must ask permission to retire. Reclining in the place where he intends to sleep, he is again to repeat the four stanzas and the four karmasthánas, as before, and reflect that in the morning he will have to rise. Having slept, he is to rise in the morning before day-break, and after again repeating the four stanzas and the four karmasthánas, he must repeat the pirit taken from the Ratana-sútra, exercise maitri-bháwaná, and do all that is required to be done. In the morning, as well as at night, he is to reflect on the eight things that produce sorrow, on the infirmities of the body, on death, and on all that is declared in the Dasa-dharmma-sútra. Not giving his mind to the four things that lead to hell, viz. evil desire, anger, fear, and ignorance, should he know that any priest in the community has committed an error, he must go and declare it to him in a friendly manner, by which he will derive the benefit that follows right speech. If there be a priest who lives according to the precepts, and is obedient thereto, he is like one who does personal service to Budha; he honours Budha, acknowledges that he is supreme, and offers to him that which is the most excellent pújá, or oblation. The sámanéra is then to reflect whether he has rightly attended to the Dina Chariyáwa; if he has done so, he must remain silent upon the subject, saying nothing about it; but if he finds that he has neglected obedience in any one particular, and is examined by the guru, he shall confess his fault. When anything has been done without due consideration, inadvertently, he is to bring a measure of sand, and sprinkle it in the sacred court. He must at all times be ready to do that which is necessary to be done for his preceptor, and to the more aged priests he must be respectful and obedient, washing their feet without any pride. With the four articles that he has received as a novice, of what kind soever they may be, whether good or bad, he must rest contented; nor must he covet to have anything more than the allowed requisites of the priesthood. Maintaining a course of good behaviour, he must keep under the five senses, with matured wisdom, and without any haughtiness of either body, speech, or mind. He must not associate with those who are not ascetics, nor follow their customs; and he must be careful to avoid the commission of the least crime. By this means he will render an oblation worthy of Budha, the ruler of the world. This is the Dina Chariyáwa."

In addition to the works read by the lay student, which will afterwards be enumerated, the following formularies are to be learnt by the sámanéra novice.

1. Heranasikha: from herana, a novice, and sikha, rule or precept. It is written in Elu, a dialect of the ancient Singhalese, and contains the dasa-sil, the dasa-sikha, the dasa-pariji, the dasa-násaná, and the dasa-dandu. The dasa-sil, or the ten obligations, have already appeared. The dasa-sikha relate to the same rules as the dasa-sil, as do also the first five of the dasa-pariji, with the addition of the word "knowingly" to each; and the other five forbid—1. The speaking disrespectfully of Budha. 2. The speaking disrespectfully of the truth. 3. The speaking disrespectfully of the associated priesthood. 4. The entertaining of heretical notions. 5. Sexual intercourse with a priestess. The dasa-násaná make known that after expulsion for committing any of the first five of the pariji there may be restoration to the priesthood, but after expulsion for any of the second five there can be no restoration.

The dasa-dandu forbid—1. The eating of food after mid-day. 2. The seeing of dances or the hearing of music or singing. 3. The use of ornaments or perfumes. 4. The use of a seat or couch more than a cubit high. 5. The receiving of gold, silver, or money. 6. Practising some deception to prevent another priest from receiving that to which he is entitled. 7. Practising some deception to injure another priest, or bring him into danger. 8. Practising some deception in order to cause another priest to be expelled from the community. 9. Speaking evil of another priest. 10. Uttering slanders, in order to excite dissension among the priests of the same community. The first five of these crimes may be forgiven, if the priest bring sand and sprinkle it in the court yard of the wihára, and the second five may be forgiven, after temporary expulsion.

2. Dina Chariyáwa. This work is also written in Elu.

3. Satara-kamatahan, in Pali and Elu, from satara, four, and kamatahan, abstract meditation, contains rules for meditation on the four important subjects, Budha, kindness, evil desire, and death.

4. Dammapadan, or the Footsteps of Budha, in Pali. This work contains a number of moral precepts, apparently selected from various parts of the Tun-Pitakas. It is one of the fifteen books belonging to the fifth or last section of the discourses of Budha. It contains 423 verses, in each of which there are four or six lines of eight syllables each; but other measures are occasionally used. It is divided into chapters, with such names as Yamaka, or double-answering Verses; Appamádo, or Religion; Chittan, or Mind; and Puppham, or Flowers. There is a paraphrase of this work in Singhalese, called Dhampiyáwa, which is much valued by the people. About 350 of the verses have been translated by the Rev. D. J. Gogerly (Ceylon Friend, vol. iv. Aug. 1840, &c.); and the selection gives a more favourable idea of the morality of Budhism (though its principal defects are equally apparent) than any other work I have seen. The first chapter is thus rendered in Mr. Gogerly's translation:—

"Mind precedes action. The motive is chief: actions proceed from mind. If any one speak or act from a corrupt mind, suffering will follow the action, as the wheel follows the lifted foot of the ox.

"Mind precedes action. The motive is chief: actions proceed from mind. If any one speak or act with a pure intention, enjoyment will follow the action, as the shadow attends the substance.

"Their anger is not subdued who recal to mind—he abused me, he struck me, he conquered me, he plundered me—

"But their anger is subdued who do not recal to mind—he abused me, he struck me, he conquered me, he plundered me.

"Anger will never be appeased by anger, but by gentleness. This is the doctrine of the ancients.

"Persons do not reflect, We shall speedily die; if any do thus reflect, their quarrels speedily terminate.

"He who lives regarding the pleasures of existence, with unrestrained passions, immoderate in food, indolent, unpersevering, Máraya (lust) will certainly subdue him, as the feeble tree is overturned by the blast.

"He who lives meditating on the evils of existence with restrained passions, temperate in food, religious, and persevering, Máraya will certainly not overpower him, as the solid rock stands unmoved by the storm.

"He who wears the yellow garment with a polluted mind, regardless of true doctrine, and destitute of a subdued spirit, is unworthy of the yellow robe.

"He is worthy of the yellow robe who is purified from lusts, established in virtue, of a subdued spirit, and conversant with true doctrine.

"Those who regard evil as good, or good as evil, will never attain to excellence, but are nurtured in error.

"Those who know good to be good, and evil to be evil, will attain to excellence, being nourished by truth.

"As the rain completely penetrates the ill-thatched roof, so will lust completely subdue the unmeditative mind.

"As the rain cannot penetrate the well-covered roof, so lust cannot overcome the contemplative mind.

"The sinner mourns in this world, and he will mourn in the next world. In both worlds he has sorrow; he grieves, he is tormented, perceiving his own impure actions.

"The virtuous man rejoices in this world, and he will rejoice in the next world. In both worlds he has joy; he rejoices, he exults, perceiving his own virtuous deeds.

"The sinner suffers in this world, and he will suffer in the next world. In both worlds he suffers; he suffers, knowing—sin has been committed by me; and dreadfully will he suffer in the regions of torment.

"The virtuous man is happy in this world, and he will be happy in the next world. In both worlds he is happy; he is happy, knowing—I have acted virtuously, and greatly will he rejoice in heaven.

"The worldly-minded man, who understands much of religion, and talks much concerning it, without keeping its precepts, is like a herdsman of other men's cattle, who is not a partaker of the flock he tends.

"The pious man, who though he understands but little, and talks but little of religion, is an observer of its precepts; who removes lust, wrath, and folly far from him; who is considerative, possessed of a mind free from evil and without attachments; he, in this world and that to come, is a partaker of the fruits of piety.

"End of the Yamaka, or the chapter of double-answering Verses."

5. Piruwáná-pota. This work contains a Manual of Exorcism. It is written in Pali, and consists of extracts from the sacred books, the recital of which, with certain attendant ceremonies, called in Singhalese, pirit, is intended to ward off evil and bring prosperity. The whole of it has been translated by the Rev. D. J. Gogerly, and appears in the Ceylon Friend, vol. ii. April, 1839, &c.

6. Sékhiyá. In this work, which is also written in Pali, there are seventy rules, by which the priest is to be guided in such matters as the putting on of his robes, the manner in which he enters a house or village, &c. The rules are incorporated in the following chapters. The work is referred to in an inscription at Mihintala, near Anurádhapura, recorded about the year A.D. 262: "The priests resident at this wihára shall make it a constant practice to rise at the dawn, meditate on the four preservative principles, perform the ablution, and then, having attired themselves with the chíwara (robes), in the manner prescribed in the Sékhiyá, they shall resort to the Æt wihára, and having there performed the religious offices, afterwards partake of rice-gruel and rice, and shall duly administer to the priests who could not attend on account of sickness, such things, at their respective cells, as the physicians had prescribed."

7. Pilikul-bháwaná. This Manual, written in Pali, contains information relative to the manner in which the priest is to meditate on the corruption of his own body. It is divided into thirty-two parts, corresponding with the principal members.

8. Satara-sangwara-síla, from satara, four, sangwara, self-control, and silá, precepts. They are—1. Prátimóksha, the observance of all the precepts contained in the Prátimóksha, from the fear of breaking even the least of them. 2. Indriya, the entire freedom from any affection for sensible objects, as when the beautiful figure is seen, it is as though it were not seen: when the pleasant sound is heard, it is as though it were not heard. 3. Ajíwapárisudhi, the keeping of such precepts, as that when the priest goes to receive alms he must not by word or gesture make known that food or raiment is desired by him. 4. Prat'yasannisrata, the observance of such precepts as those that inculcate that when the robe is put on, it is not for beauty or ornament, but to ward off the heat and cold, musquitoes, flies, snakes, the rays of the sun, and the wind.

These treatises are to be learnt by the novice; and in the works that he is afterwards required to read, he is frequently reminded that great diligence and exertion must be used, if he would succeed in effecting the object for which he has become a recluse. On one occasion, Budha said to the priests by whom he was accompanied, "Were a man, who wishes to make a small fire into a large one, to take wet grass, wet cow-dung, and wet fuel, and blow it with a wet winnowing fan, you would say that he is unskilful. In like manner, the mind of the being who is idle and indifferent cannot be brought into the paths that lead to nirwána simply by abstract meditation; he must investigate causes and exercise energy even as the fire is increased by applying to it fuel that is dry." It is said again, "The bowman seeks out good weapons, plants his foot carefully, and when he has succeeded in cleaving a hair with the arrow, marks the manner in which it was done, and tries the same method on other occasions. The skilful cook seeketh out condiments that are savoury, and makes such food as he thinks will be agreeable to his master; and when he finds that his master has enjoyed this dish or eaten plentifully of that, he prepares the same kind of food again, and so gains credit with his master, receiving many presents, In like manner, the priest who would enter the paths meditates carefully on the precepts, puts them to the test, and repeats the practice of those by which he is assisted."*

The novice is taught that there are eight benefits to be derived from becoming a recluse:—1. Deliverance from wastu-káma, the love of wealth, and klésa-káma, the love of pleasure. 2. The re-

* Wisudhi Margga Sanné

ception of food in a proper manner. 3. The custom of eating any food that comes to hand, of what kind soever it may be. 4. Deliverance from the oppression of wicked men and of kings. 5. Freedom from all anxiety about such things as gardens, fields, and cattle. 6. Deliverance from the dread of thieves. 7. Deliverance from the dread of persons in authority, and release from the necessity of rising up when they approach. 8. Deliverance from fear, in whatever place.*

There are also ten things that cause men to neglect the assumption of the yellow robe, or tempt them to cast it off after it has been assumed:—1. The mother. 2. The father. 3. The wife. 4. Children. 5. Poor relations. The thought will come that these relatives ought to be provided for, which cannot be done by the recluse. 6. Friends. 7. Property. 8. The desire of obtaining wealth. 9. The desire of worldly honour. 10. The love of pleasure.†

The precepts must be obeyed from a pure motive. Were any one to practise the Ten Obligations merely "to fill the belly," this man, deceiving the laity, greedy of fame, destitute of virtue, and unworthy to enjoy the privileges of the priesthood, will receive a double punishment; after death he will be born in the Awíchi hell, where he will have to reside myriads of years, in the midst of flames, hot, fierce, and overpowering, in which he will be turned upside down, and in every possible direction, covered with foam. When released from this hell, he will be born in the hell of sprites, where he will have a body extremely attenuated, and most loathsome in its appearance, whilst he will have to endure the severest privations, and will have to walk upon earth in misery, the spectre of a priest. Just as when a man of ignoble appearance and inferior family, by some deception succeeds in being anointed king: but he is afterwards punished: his arms, legs, nose, and ears are cut off; the scalp is torn away, and boiling gruel poured on his head; his skull is rubbed with gravel until it is white as a sea-shell; a lighted brand being put in his mouth, his body is rubbed with oil and set on fire; his frame is hacked; he is thrown down, and a spike being driven from ear to ear he is pinned to the ground; his flesh is torn with hooks, and cut with small pieces of metal like coins; the body is transfixed to the ground, and turned round and round by the legs, the pin serving as a pivot; he is flogged, until his body is of the consistence of a whisp of straw; he is eaten by hungry-dogs; his

* Pújáwaliya.

† Milinda Prasna.

tongue is fastened to a stake, and he remains there until he dies; or he is beheaded.* By these terrible allusions the novice is warned against becoming a recluse merely that he may secure a livelihood; and they may be received as illustrative of the modes of punishment then used.

The priest who does not obey the precepts is represented as being like a man who daubs himself all over with the most disgusting filth in order to render himself beautiful: he is like an ass among cattle; he is shunned by all; he is like the fire of a cemetery where bodies are burnt, or like one blind, or an outcaste.†

Upon another occasion it was declared by Budha, in the Aggikkhanda-pariyá-sútra, that it is better for a priest to embrace the flame than to approach a woman, however exalted her rank; that the consquence of the one act would be only temporary pain, or at most death; whilst the consequence of the other would be long-continued torment amidst the flames of hell. He said further, that it were better for the priest who does not keep the precepts to be bound with a cord made of hair, and dragged from place to place until his flesh is torn off, and his bones are laid bare, even to the marrow, than for such a one to receive worship from the faithful of any of the three great castes: that it were better for him to be cruelly pierced in the body than to receive service from the well-disposed among the laity: that it were better for him to have molten metal poured down his throat, until his lips, teeth, tongue, stomach, and intestines were all burnt, than for him to receive an offering of food given as alms: that it were better for him to be put in a red-hot iron chair or bed, or to be put into a caldron of molten metal with his head downwards, than for him to receive the gift of a residence. The misery in the one case is merely temporary, but in the other case it will endure long. The receiving of honour or assistance by the priest who breaks the precepts is like the eating of food upon which the serpent has left its poison: it is no benefit to him, and will be attended by intense suffering.‡

The course of asceticism upon which the novice enters is intended, not only to overcome the evils of the passing moment, but also to prevent the afflictions of the future. This is he taught from one of the conversations that took place between Milinda and Nágaséna. The king said to the sage, "Are the pains that you take intended to drive away past sorrow?" and when he answered that

* Wisudhi Margga Sanné † Ibid. ‡ Ibid.

they were not, the king again asked, "Are they to drive away present sorrow?" but the answer was the same. Milinda:—"Then if it be neither to drive away past sorrow nor present, why do you take pains at all?" Nágaséna:—"We thus exert ourselves that we may destroy present sorrow and drive away future sorrow." Milinda:—"Is there future sorrow?" Nágaséna:—"No." Milinda:—"You are wise and learned, and yet do you take pains to destroy a sorrow that does not exist?" Nágaséna:—"When the kings that are your enemies come to fight against you, do you just at that time dig the ditches of your fortifications, build the walls, place the guards in the watch-towers, and lay in provisions for the siege?" Milinda:—"No: I should prepare all these things before the day came." Nágaséna:—"Would you on that day begin to train the elephants, the horses, the charioteers, the archers, the swordsmen, and the mace-men?" Milinda:—"No: all this is done beforehand." Nágaséna:—"Why?" Milinda:—"To ward off future fear (or fear of the future.)" Nágaséna:—"Is there future fear?" Milinda:—"No." Nágaséna:—"You are a wise and prudent king, and do you prepare all things necessary for the battle in order that you may drive away a fear that in reality has no existence?" The king requested further information. Nágaséna proceeded and said, "When you are thirsty, and wish to drink water, do you tell your servants to dig the well or open the fountain? Do you not cause these places to be prepared beforehand? And thus you give orders relative to a thirst that has no existence. Again, when you are hungry, and wish to eat rice, do you tell your servants to plough the field and sow the grain? Do you not cause the rice to be cultivated beforehand? And yet you, a wise and prudent king, do all this relative to the driving away of a hunger that is still future, and has therefore no existence. In like manner the priest acts in relation to the future; that which he does is in order to drive away future sorrow."

It excited the wonder of Milinda that the priests should have any regard whatever to the body; but the novice is to bear in mind that this is done, not from complacency or pride, but that it may be the better adapted to carry into effect the ascetic rites he is called upon to exercise. The king said to Nágaséna, "Do the priests respect the body?" and when the sage replied in the negative, he again asked, "Then why do they take so much pains to preserve it? Do they not by this means say, this is me, or mine?" Nágaséna:—

"Were you ever wounded by an arrow in battle?" Milinda:—"Yes." Nágaséna:—"Was not the wound anointed? Was it not rubbed with oil? And was it not covered with a soft bandage?" Milinda:—"Yes." Nágaséna:—"Was this done because you respected the wound, or took delight in it?" Milinda:—"No; but that it might be healed." Nágaséna:—"In like manner, the priests do not preserve the body because they respect it; but that they may have the power required for the keeping of the precepts."

There are some priests who throw off the robe and return to the state of a laic. This might be brought as a charge against the system of Budha; it may be said that it is without power, or they would not have acted in such a manner. But the novice is taught to reason thus. There is a tank full of water; now if a man have his body covered with dirt and dust, and his garments all soiled, where is the fault? Can it be charged upon the water? Again, there is a skilful physician; now if a man labour under a severe disease, and does not apply to the physician, the disease may increase in malignity, but is the skill of the physician thereby impeached? Is it not rather the fault of the man? Again, there is plenty of food provided, and plenty of water, and men are invited to partake of them; but if they refuse, and will rather suffer hunger and thirst than come, can blame be attached to the food or the water? In like manner, when the priest, without attaining nirwána, leaves his robe and becomes a laic, it is not the fault of the system but of the man; he is not sincere; therefore the system has no hold upon him, as the lotus does not allow the water to adhere to its petals, or as the sea casts upon the shore any body that may be thrown into its waves. When the warrior sees that he has to encounter an armed host, he becomes afraid, and runs away; he cannot face the enemy; so the priest who does not keep the precepts, by which he might be preserved, is overcome by evil desire, as he is without any defence or protection. When there are flowers upon a tree, those that are worm-eaten fall down and rot; whilst those that are not thus eaten continue to flourish, and send forth their perfume on every side; and again, there may be grass and rushes in the field where the best rice is sown, but whilst the rice ripens, the grass and rushes will wither and die. Now the priest who does not keep the precepts is like the worm-eaten flower, or the grass of the rice field.*

* Milinda Prasna.

Respecting some of the advantages that are expected to be gained by embracing the priesthood, the teachings of Budhism are not uniform. It is sometimes said that the sins of the man are to the priest as the sins that have been committed in a former state of existence, and are no bar to the reception of nirwána. Thus Anguli-mála, a student, who at the instigation of his preceptor committed 999 murders, became a rahat. But on another occasion it is said by Nágaséna that certain priests were prevented from attaining nirwána by the sins they had unknowingly committed before they abandoned the world. Milinda said to him, "There is a laic who unwittingly commits one of the five deadly sins; he afterwards embraces the priesthood, and still unaware that he has committed the sin, endeavours to become a rahat; can such a one succeed in attaining nirwána?" Nágaséna replied, "No; if even previously to the commission of the crime he had the merit whereby he might have attained nirwána, it would be destroyed, cut off, by his sin." Milinda:—"You have said on a previous occasion that when a man knows he has committed a deadly crime, he is in doubt; when he is in doubt his mind is prevented from rightly attending to the obligations and the other ordinances; and because his mind is thus agitated, he is unable to attain nirwána; but in this instance the crime is not known, and there is therefore no doubt." Nágaséna:—"A man takes good seed, and sows it in the fertile soil of a field that has been ploughed and prepared for its reception; he takes the same kind of seed, and sows it upon the bare rock; in the one case it is productive; in the other it is not: for this reason; that upon the rock there is no hétu, that which is necessary for the fructifying of the seed is not there. Again, when sticks and stones are thrown upon the ground, there they remain; but when the same things are thrown into the sky, they do not remain there; they fall down; for this reason, that in the sky there is no hétu, nothing by which they can be supported. Again, when a fire is lighted upon the earth, it burns; but a fire cannot be kindled upon the water; for this reason: the water is ahétu as to fire, there is nothing in it upon which the fire can lay hold." Milinda:—"But explain to me how it is that when the crime is committed unwittingly, and there is therefore no doubt, no agitation, arising from it, still nirwána should not be obtained?" Nágaséna:—"When a man takes poison unknowingly, does it not injure him? When he treads upon fire unknowingly, does it not burn him? When a nayá bites him during sleep, or when in any other way unconscious, will he not die? There was a chakrawartti (a universal emperor, who also possesses preternatural powers), who with his army was one day passing through the sky; unknowingly he happened to approach the bó-tree near which the prince Sidhártta became a supreme Budha; but he was not able to pass over the sacred place; his progress was arrested, though he knew not from what cause. In like manner, when a priest who during the time he was a laic has committed any of the five deadly sins, attempts to attain nirwána, he is unable to accomplish the object at which he aims."

It will be said by the Budhist that though Anguli-mála committed so many murders, he did not commit any of the five deadly sins; which are, 1. Matricide. 2. Patricide. 3. The murder of a rahat. 4. Wounding the person of a supreme Budha (his life cannot possibly be taken). 5. Causing a schism among the priesthood. But though this reply may seem to prove the uniformity of the system, it lays it open to a serious charge upon moral grounds. In the arguments brought forward by Nágasēna, the dangerous extent to which imagery may be carried, and the manner in which the operation of moral causes is confounded with that of physical causes, are too apparent to require specific indication. The advantages that may be gained by the sincere novice are, however, here represented as very great; by becoming a recluse the way to nirwána is opened before him, and there can be no barrier to its attainment, if he be free from the five sins.

That considerable attention is yet paid to the conduct of the novices may be learnt from what is said in an epistle sent by the sangha rája of Burma to the priests of Ceylon in 1802. "As some erroneously think," he says, "that certain observances are not enacted for the novices, but are only obligatory on the ordained priests, I quote the following passage from the commentary on the Mahawaggo, to show how unfounded is their assertion—'As long as a priest is ignorant of the discipline to be observed by him; unskilful in the adjusting of the robes, in the manner in which he ought to carry the alms-bowl, in the modes of standing and sitting, eating and drinking; he ought not to be sent to any of the alms-houses where food is distributed to the priesthood at large, nor to any place where food is daily distributed to a select number of priests, nor to the forest, nor to any public assembly; but he should be kept near the senior priests; he should be nourished like a little child; he should constantly be informed of what is allowed and what is not; and he should be duly trained up in the modes of wearing and covering the robes, and in the other parts of the discipline he is required to observe.' . . . . Some assert that whatever is sanctioned by the preceptor becomes binding upon the novices, and is legalised by his dictum alone. But hear what is said upon this point in the Sanghiti Khandaka. 'It is allowable to a pupil to observe some things, saying, My preceptor has enjoined it, or, My teacher has enjoined it; therefore I observe it;—but of the matters thus sanctioned some may be legal and some may not.' The commentary explains the expression, 'some are legal,' by saying that of course it is meant of those things that are in themselves good, and do not militate against the laws of Budha." *

The difficulties that have sometimes to be encountered by the youth who wishes to renounce the world, and the reasons that are supposed to induce him to take this important step, may be inferred from the legend of Rathapála, as it appears in the Rathapála-sútra-sanné. Though somewhat long, as it abounds with illustrative incidents, and contains a moral from which even the wisest may receive instruction, I insert it in its original form, with scarcely any abridgement.

When Gótama Budha visited the different places in the province of Kuru, that he might confer benefits upon the people, he came to the brahman village of Thullakotthitan, so called on account of the numerous castles it contained, that were filled with all kinds of treasures. The people of the village had embraced the doctrines of Budha. Among the rest there was a brahman of a respectable family called Rathapála, who came to Gótama when he visited the village, and requested that he might be admitted to the priesthood, as he said that it was difficult for him to act aright so long as he continued a laic. Budha enquired if his parents had given their consent, and when Rathapála said that he had not requested their permission, the sage made known to him that it was not his custom to receive any into the priesthood who had not gained the consent of their parents. The brahman then went to his parents, and told them that since he had heard the discourses of Budha it was his wish to become a priest; and he now requested their permission to carry this wish into effect. But his parents replied, "You are our

* The Sandésa of the Sangha Rája of Burma, translated by L. de Zoysa. Ceylon Friend, vol. viii. 1845.

beloved son, our only son; we have none older than you, none younger; you have lived in all happiness; you have enjoyed yourself; you know nothing of sorrow; remain contented; eat and drink whatever is cherishing or delicious; take to yourself a retinue of beautiful maidens; have dancing girls to amuse you; remain a householder; and gain merit by giving alms to the three gems. We cannot give you permission to embrace the priesthood; we do not wish you to become a priest even after we are dead, and cannot therefore give our consent whilst we are alive." Rathapála then said, "Unless I receive your permission, I will die here;" and having said this, he lay down upon the bare ground. The parents repeated their former declarations three several times, and entreated him to rise; but as he still continued silent, they went to some of his friends, informed them of the determination of their son, and asked them to come and try to persuade him to change it. The friends accordingly came to the place where he was, and thrice urged the same reasons as his parents to induce him to remain a laic; but he still remained silent. They then went to his parents, and telling them it was in vain to attempt to alter his resolution, said it would be better to give their consent; they would then be able to see him at intervals; but if they still refused their permission he would die. To this advice they agreed, on condition that the person who ordained him would allow him to pay them a visit from time to time. When the friends informed Rathapála that his parents gave their consent, he arose, took some refreshment, and went to the residence of Budha, who admitted him to the priesthood on learning that his parents had granted their permission.

Not long after Rathapála had thus renounced the world, he attained rahatship, and became indeed one of the chief of the rahats; after which he went to Budha, who was now resident at Rajagaha, and requested permission to go and see his parents according to the promise he had given. As his request was granted, he went to his native village, near which he remained in a garden called Migachíra, belonging to the king Kórawya. At the proper time, taking his alms-bowl, he went to the village to receive alms, after putting on his robe in such a way as to conceal his person. As he approached his own residence, in going regularly from house to house, his father was standing in the central door-way of the mansion, which had in all seven doors. When his father saw him in the distance he said, "This is one of the priests who took away from us our only and beloved son." No attentions were paid to him by any of the family; nor were any alms presented; abuse was all that he received. At that time the female slave of one of his relatives was taking some food made of barley, which had been boiled the previous night and become stale, in order to throw it away. When Rathapála perceived her intention, he told her it would be better to put it in his bowl. She accordingly did so; but when he held out his bowl to receive it, she had the opportunity of seeing his hands and feet, and from this, as well as from his voice, she knew that it was Rathapála. At once she went and informed his mother, who was overjoyed at receiving this intelligence, and promised the slave that if it were true she should receive her freedom. The mother went and imparted the news to his father; and in the mean time Rathapála eat the stale food he had received. The father went to the place whither he had retired, and said to him, "Would it not be better to come and reside at your own house, than to eat food that has become stale?" Rathapála replied, "Householder, the priests are houseless; we do not reside in houses; I have already been to your house; no alms were given me; not even a kind word did I receive." The father again entreated his son to return; but he said it was needless, as he had already partaken of food. He was then invited to come on the following day; and though he remained silent, his father knew his intention. The mansion was fitted up for his reception in the most splendid manner, and the wife of Rathapála was commanded to put on her most beautiful ornaments.

The next day, Rathapála was informed that all was ready and he went to his former dwelling. His father displayed before him all his wealth, and said to him, "This is the property of your mother; this belongs to your father; the rest was inherited from our ancestors. Illustrious Rathapála, take possession of all this, become a laic once more, and gain merit by the giving of alms." But he replied, "If my advice were followed, all this gold, and all these jewels, and this wealth, would be placed upon waggons, taken to the Ganges or the Yamuna, and thrown into the stream; for they cause only sorrow, lamentation, grief, distress, and disappointment." His wife then held him by the feet and said, "Have you abandoned the world for the sake of some celestial nymph? If so, tell me, what is the manner of her appearance?" He replied, "Yes; it is for the sake of a celestial nymph that I have abandoned the world." On hearing this she fell down in a fit, from the excess of her grief.

Rathapála then said to his father, "If I am to receive food, let it be given; do not distress me by showing me wealth, or by the approach of women." His father informed him that all was prepared, and presented the food with his own hand, until he was satisfied. He then took the bowl, and preparing to depart, said, "The body is arrayed in garments and ornamented by jewels; it is like an image beautifully painted; it has hands, feet, and various members, is built about with flesh, and is subject to disease and decay; think about it well; if it were not for the manner in which it is ornamented, it would be loathsome; men and women have affection for this vile and perishing body, and none for nirwána. The body is washed in perfumed water; the hair is braided in eight different ways, and ornamented with coronets; and the eyes are anointed with collyrium; but nirwána is despised. Householder! you are like a man who places a gin made of withs to catch deer; you have displayed before me this wealth that I might be ensnared; but I am like the deer that eats the grass and escapes the snare; I have partaken of your food, and now depart." Having spoken these words he went away.

About this time Kórawya, the king, called Migawa, the gardener, and commanded him to prepare the Migachíra garden for his reception. When the gardener was about to carry this command into effect, he saw Rathapála at the foot of a tree; upon which he went to inform the king, who said that he would visit the place without delay. When leaving the palace, he sat in his chariot; but when at a proper distance he alighted therefrom, and approached the priest on foot. The king requested him to mount the royal elephant; but he refused, saying that they had both better remain as they then were, each on his own proper seat. "There are four causes of affliction;" the king proceeded to say; "on account of one or other of these causes men most frequently embrace the priesthood; they are, decay, disease, the loss of property, and the loss of friends. A man becomes old; all his powers have begun to fail; he thinks thus: I am now old; I can acquire no more property, or if I acquire it I cannot keep it; it will be better for me to become a recluse. But you, most noble Rathapála! are not old; you are yet a youth; your hair is like that of Krishna: you are yet in the beginning of your strength; what, then, did you learn, or see, or hear, that induced you to become a priest? There is the affliction arising from disease; men are subject to coughs, asthma, diabetes, and other discases; and they therefore embrace the priesthood. But you are in perfect health; the digestive faculty is unimpaired; why then did you embrace this ascetic course? There is the affliction arising from the loss of property; men lose their possessions and wealth; they therefore embrace the priesthood. But you belong to a respectable family in this brahman village; you have not suffered any loss of property; then why do you endure these privations? There is the affliction arising from the loss of friends; men lose their children and other relatives; they therefore embrace the priesthood. But you are a stranger to this affliction. Then, tell me, why did you become a priest?"

Rathapála replied, "O king! four aphorisms have been declared by Budha, and it was because I understood them, saw and heard them, that I became a priest. They are: 1. The beings in this world are subject to decay, they cannot abide long. 2. They have no protection, no adequate helper. 3. They have no real possessions; all that they have they must leave. 4. They cannot arrive at perfect satisfaction or content; they are constantly the slaves of evil desire." The king enquired what was the meaning of these aphorisms, and Rathapála explained them thus: "When you, Kórawya, were twenty or twenty-five years of age, were you not able to subdue the horse, drive the chariot, and bend the bow; and were you not then a powerful warrior?" The king replied in the affirmative; but when Rathapála asked him if he was the same now, he confessed that his former energy had passed away; and when the priest further enquired how this had come to pass, he said, "I am now old; I am eighty years of age; if I think to place my foot here, it goes there; I am feeble." "It was on this account," said Rathapála, "that Budha declared: the being who is resident in this world is carried away by decay, or old age; he cannot remain long." The king said, "What Budha has declared is true; but he has also said that though there may be an army to defend the monarch against his enemies, there is no protection against the approach of sickness; what is the meaning of this?" The priest enquired, "Are you subject to any incurable disease?" and the king said, "Yes; I am subject to such a disease; sometimes my sons and other relatives assemble around me and exclaim: The king Kórawya will now die." "Well then," asked the priest, "if at such a time you were to say to your relatives, or to the nobles in attendance, Help me to endure my pain; divide it among yourselves, and take part of it in my stead;—would they be able thus to assist you?" The king declared that they would not. "Therefore," said the priest, "Budha has declared that man has no protection, no adequate helper." The king again said, "Budha has declared that though a man may have much wealth, it is not his own; though he may possess it for a time, he must leave it; what is the meaning of this?" "You, O king," said Rathapála, "have abundance; much wealth and many attendants; when you enter the other world, will you still possess them, or will they be the property of another?" The king confessed that he must leave them, and that they would belong to another. "It was on this account," Rathapála said, "Budha declared that man has no real possessions." The king continued, "You have told me that Budha has said: The mind is not satisfied, or contented; it still covets more; what does this mean?" "Suppose" said the priest, "a man worthy of all credence were to come from the eastern part of Kuru, and say that in that part of the country he had seen many nations, with cities, armies, wealth, and maidens beautiful as the celestial déwís, what would you do?" The king said, he should go and conquer them. The priest put the same question relative to each of the other quarters; and upon receiving the same reply he said, "It was on this account Budha has declared that the mind is never satisfied; it is always wanting more; and it was because I learnt these truths that I embraced the priesthood."

Rathapála then repeated these stanzas:—"There are some men who have much property; but on account of the false medium through which all things appear to them, it seems as if it were little; they are covetous of more, and are continually trying to add to their possessions. There are kings who subdue the whole of the four quarters, even to the borders of the sea; but they are still not content; they wish to cross the ocean, that they may find out more worlds to conquer, but they are never satisfied with what they acquire, and the craving continues until death. There is no means of satisfying the desire of the worldling. When he dies, his friends go about with disordered hair, and weep; they exclaim, He is gone, he is dead,—and they then enwrap the body in cloth, and burn it upon the pyre. He cannot take with him either property or wealth; even the cloth in which he is enwrapped is burnt. When about to die, neither relatives, friends, nor companions, can afford him any protection. He who dies is accompanied only by his merit and demerit; nothing else whatever goes with him; he cannot take with him children, or women, or wealth, or lands. Decay is not prevented by wealth, nor is old age; the life continues only for a little time. The rich and the poor, the wise and the unwise, men of every condition, must equally encounter death; there is no one to whom its embrace does not come. The unwise man trembles at the approach of death; but the wise man is unmoved. Wisdom is therefore better than wealth; of all possessions it is the chief; it is the principal means by which evil desire is destroyed, and purity is attained. The cleaving to sentient objects is the cause of many dangers, and prevents the reception of nirwána. For these reasons I have embraced the priesthood."

V. ORDINATION.

It has been said that "ordination is nothing but a word borrowed from the Roman empire, in which it is the legitimate and customary mode of designating the institution of a person to some honourable office; and this was the original church meaning, as both Eichhorn and Rothe have shown." * The act by which admission into the priesthood is received among the Budhists may therefore not improperly be termed ordination. It binds the recipient to observe certain ordinances or rules; but it is to be regarded as conveying an obligation to refrain from certain usages, rather than as imposing a class of duties that he is to perform. On the part of the candidate it is an acknowledgment of the excellence of asceticism, with an implied declaration that its obligations shall be observed; and on the part of the priests by whom the ceremony is conducted, it is an acknowledgment that the candidate is eligible to the reception of the office, and that, so long as he fulfils its duties, he will be received as a member of the ascetic community, and be entitled to partake in all its rights and privileges.

The mode in which the ceremony is conducted is extremely simple, as appears from the formulary of admission contained in the work called Kammawáchan, of which there is a Singhalese translation. A sangha, or chapter, having been called, the candidate is asked if the requisites of the priest (as the alms-bowl, robes,

* Bunsen's Church of the Future.

&c. that have been previously prepared and deposited in the place of assembly) belong to him. On answering in the affimative, he is commanded to remain in a place that is pointed out; and he is then asked if he is free from certain diseases that are named, including the leprosy, epilepsy, &c.; if he is a human being, a man, and a freeman; if he is out of debt; if he is free from the king's service; if he has the consent of his parents; if he has attained the age of twenty years; and if he is provided with the priestly requisites. He is then asked his own name, and the name of his upádya (the priest by whom he is presented for ordination). These things being ascertained, the moderator commands him to advance; and the candidate, addressing the assembly, says respectfully, thrice, "I request upasampadá." The moderator then makes known that he is free from the impediments that would bar his admission to the priesthood, that he possesses the requisites, and that he requests upasampadá; and thrice calls out, "Let him who assents to this request be silent; let him who dissents, now declare it!" If the assembly be silent the moderator infers that consent is given; upon which he repeats to the candidate the more important of the rules by which he will have to abide—relating to the food he may receive, the garments he may wear, the place in which he may reside, the medicaments he may use in case of sickness, and the crimes that involve expulsion from the priesthood. It is declared that these ordinances are worthy to be kept unto the end of life; to which the candidate assents, without, however, making any promise or taking any vow. From this time he is regarded as an upasampadá, from upa, exceeding, and sampadá, gain, advantage.

It is not unusual for the candidate to put off the robe he had worn as a novice, and to reassume for the nonce the dress of a layman; his body is anointed with sandal and other fragrant substances; and with banners and music his friends accompany him to the place of ordination. It is said that upon some occasions the monarch of Ceylon, the two adigars, and the four nobles next in rank, accompanied the procession through the principal streets of Kandy. In like manner, the nun is arrayed in her gayest attire on the day when she finally abandons the world, and becomes what is called, though the name is too often a solemn mockery, "The spouse of Christ."

The ceremony of upasampadá is sometimes called by Europeans the superior ordination, implying that there are two orders in the

Budhist priesthood; but this mode of speaking is incorrect, as the sámanéra is regarded only as a candidate or novice, and requires no other permission for the wearing of the yellow robe than the sanction of an upasampadá priest.

In Ceylon, ordination is seldom conferred by the established community in any place but the city of Kandy, where the maha-náyaka, or arch-priest, and the anu-náyaka, his deputy, reside; but this is an innovation similar to the taking away of the power of ordination from "the hands of the presbytery," and confining it to hands episcopal, and has no sanction whatever from the earlier usages of Budhism.

Upasampadá confers no mystic power, nor is it regarded as an indelible order. The instances are numerous in which the priest returns to the state of a laic, frequently remaining in this state until death; but at other times returning to the profession; which he is permitted again to assume without being regarded as having committed a breach of the law by his temporary retirement. Indeed, it must be evident, upon a consideration of the subject, that no office or authority conferred by man, in that which relates to matters that demand the consent of the will, and righteousness of life, for their right fulfilment, can be properly indelible. The master may coerce his slave; and the liege lord, his subjects; and an unwilling service or a constrained obedience may as effectually carry into effect the command of an earthly superior as the most affectionate submission; but the bad man, or the man who after ordination has received conscientious scruples relative to the ministry, cannot be coerced into a right discharge of the duties of this sacred office. This conclusion does not at all affect the case of man's responsibility to God; when "a dispensation of the gospel" has been committed to any one, it is at his peril if he "entangleth himself with the affairs of this life;" he may not be imperatively confined to any particular course of discipline; he may modify his creed or change his community; but the work of the Lord is not to be neglected, nor the ministry of the word forsaken, so long as there is the ability to fulfil the exercise in an efficient manner.

By an express ordinance of Budha his disciples are permitted to retire from the priesthood under certain circumstances; such as their inability to remain continent; impatience of restraint; a wish to enter upon worldly engagements; the love of parents or friends; or doubts as to the truth of the system propounded by Budha. This permission would, however, open the way for the practice of all kinds of evil, as the priest might do wrong under the supposition that, if detected, he had only to declare that he had renounced the obligations; by which means he would be saved from the penalty that must otherwise be enforced, and his character be preserved. But to prevent these perversions it is ordained that no priest shall be allowed to throw off the robe without express permission had and obtained from a legal chapter.

VI. CELIBACY.

In all ages, and among all nations, in which men have broken away from the laws of the Lord, and attempted to establish their own righteousness, the practice of celibacy has been enjoined upon those who are called upon to perform the more sacred rites of religion. The echo of the voice of God, "It is not good that man should be alone;" first heard by man in innocence, was still carried on when the visions of Paradise had faded from his sight; and its tones were sufficiently distinct many centuries after his expulsion from that scene of beauty, to exercise an influence the most powerful. The divine revelations with which he was afterwards favoured, as we may clearly learn from the comparatively few of these interpositions that are recorded in sacred writ, contributed to produce the same effect; with the caution, however, that the help-meet should not be taken promiscuously from among women; "the daughters of men," the maidens of Heth, were to be avoided. But still the wife was to be sought; and domestic relations were entered into by the most holy of the patriarchs, not excepting even the one who "was not, for God took him." At what period a different opinion began to prevail we have no evidence; but it probably commenced at the same time as polytheism, and spread co-extensively with that error. When the idea has gone forth that man possesses the power to offer a sacrifice, that as a natural consequence, irrespective of any ulterior arrangement, will bring to him merit, it is thought that in proportion to the value of the sacrifice will be the increase of the treasure of righteousness acquired by its presentation; and as it is only an expansion of the same thought, that the giving up of the will must be equally meritorious with the resignation of the substance, it follows that the more rigid the course of self-denial that is entered upon, and the more cruel and comprehensive its requirements, the greater will be the amount of gain to the ascetic. The same consequences have been produced by another error, of separate origin but correlative effect. It has been supposed that in all matter there is an evil principle, and that the body of man is an avatár, or impersonation of this principle in its most malignant type; hence all that ministers to its gratification must be avoided; the appetites and passions must be overcome; and the man who neither eats, nor drinks, nor sleeps, who has no covering to his nakedness, no wife, and no home, is in a high state of preparation for extinguishing his existence for ever, or becoming absorbed in the ocean of the divine essence.

It were needless to multiply instances in proof of the prevalence of these sentiments. The priests of Isis were obliged to observe perpetual chastity. The persons who were initiated into the Eleusinian mysteries were obliged to keep themselves unpolluted during nine days; and the high priest was never permitted to marry at all, as he was regarded as being given up entirely to the service of the gods. The neophytes admitted to the Bacchic mysteries were obliged to abstain from sexual intercourse during the ten days of initiation. The vestal virgins were bound by a solemn vow to preserve their chastity for the space of thirty years. The more strict of the Essenes avoided marriage, and extolled the virtue of continence; in this, as in other instances, being opposed to the religion that their forefathers had received from God.

At an early period of the church, celibacy was represented as the principal of the Christian virtues; and it seemed to be the general supposition that no corporeal shrine desecrated by marriage was worthy of receiving the inhabitation of the Holy Spirit, according to the promise granted to the elect of God. Hence such declarations as that of Jerome (Adv. Jov. i. 4): "Qamdiu impleo mariti officium, non impleo Christiani;" and such ordinances as that of Con. Carthag. iv. 13, that the newly married "cum benedictionem acceperint, eadem nocte pro reverentia ipsius benedictionis in virginitate permaneant." At first the clergy were only forbidden to marry a second time; then they were not allowed to marry at all after their ordination, unless at the time they put in a special claim to be exempted from the law, from having a previous engagement. After this no clergyman was allowed to marry, under any circumstances; and last of all, ordination was conferred upon no one who had previously entered into the marriage state. By the ancient canons no priest was allowed to have any female in his house, unless she were his mother, his sister, his aunt, or some person above suspicion. But the celibacy of the clergy, though first prescribed by law in the western church A.D. 385, was never enjoined in the eastern church; and even some of the boldest advocates of monachism rejected the notion that it was necessary for the clergyman to be unmarried. It was openly declared at the Council of Constance that no remedy could be devised for stopping the licentiousness of the clergy but that of granting them permission to marry. Not long afterwards it was proposed that each church should have two married priests who were to do duty upon alternate weeks, and during the week of their ministration to preserve continence. Even at the Council of Trent, when the stroke fell that so welded the mighty fetter as to have rendered it hitherto proof against all attempts to break it asunder, the question was agitated, that if settled in a different manner would have brought a sweet serenity into many a circle that has only been brooded over by the worst passions of hell. By the 10th canon of the 24th session it was decreed, "Si quis dixerit, statum conjugalem anteponendum esse statui virginitatis, vel caelibatus, et non esse melius ac beatius manere in virginitate, aut caelibatu, quam jungi matrimonio; anathema sit:" i. e. "Whoever shall affirm that the conjugal state is to be preferred to a life of virginity or celibacy, and that it is not better and more conducive to happiness to remain in virginity or celibacy, than to be married, let him be accursed."

The legends of the Budhists agree with the records of the western historians in presenting the existence of a sect of religionists in India called gymnosophists, who were either literally naked, or had no clothing worthy of the name. One of the epithets by which they are designated is equivalent to "air-clad." Some of these ascetics retired to the woods, whilst others resided among men, in order that they might give the most convincing proof that their passions were entirely subdued. In the age of Gótama they appear to have been held in high honour, and to have been regarded as possessing a virtue that raised them to superhuman pre-eminence. They could only perpetuate these honours by a strict observance of their professions; but at times there were individuals who disregarded the precepts of the community, and emulated the extravagancies of the Gnostics; teaching, like them, that as everything outward is utterly and entirely indifferent to the inward man, the outward man may give himself up to every kind of excess, provided the inward man be not thereby disturbed in the tranquillity of his contemplation; and representing themselves as like the ocean, that receives everything, but is still, from its own greatness, free from pollution, whilst other men are like the small collection of water that is defiled by a single earth-clod. The Brahmanical system could only be kept up by procreation, and it was therefore expressly ordained (Manu, v. 45) that "if a brahman have not begotten a son, yet shall aim at final beatitude, he shall sink to a place of degradation. "By the procreation of children (Inst. ii. 28) the human body is rendered fit for a divine state." In more mature age a course of asceticism was commenced; and then he who could most completely assimilate himself to the denizens of the forest around him was the most exalted sage.

In the dasa-sil binding upon the priest of Budha, the precept that enjoins the practice of celibacy is the third in order, The depravity of the people among whom it was promulgated is seen in the stringency of its requirements. It was not an intact virginity that was held up to honour; but true continence during the period in which any one professed to be prawarjita, or to have renounced the world. Gótama was a married man, and had a son, Ráhula, previous to his entrance upon the course of asceticism by which he became a supreme Budha. This feature of the system opened the privileges of the priesthood to a greater number of postulants; but it must often have brought deep sorrow into the domestic circle. Yet in this it was only in consistence with the habitudes of a more recent period, as we see in the instance of Paul the Simple, who resigned his wife and children to another with a smile, when he departed to embrace the monastic life. By Justinian (Novell. cxxiii. c. 40) it was ordained that when a married person, whether it were the husband alone or the wife alone, entered a monastery, the marriage was dissolved; but this law did not meet with universal approval.

Among the practices forbidden in the Pátimokkhan* the following are included:—Sexual intercourse with any being of whatever kind, or in whatever form; wilful pollution; contact with the person of a woman; impure conversation with a woman; the commendation of acts of impurity in the presence of a woman; acting the

* Gogerly's Translation of the Pátimokkhan, Ceylon Friend, Oct. 1839, &c.

part of a procurer; sitting on the same seat as a woman in any private place; giving the robe to a priestess, who is not a relation, to be smoothed or washed; receiving a robe from a priestess; procuring a fleece of wool to be prepared by a priestess who is not a relation; sleeping with any one not a priest more than two or three times; reclining on the same place as a woman; preaching more than five or six sentences to a woman, except in the presence of a man who understands what is said; delivering exhortations to the priestesses, without permission of the chapter, or when permitted, after sunset; except in case of sickness, going to the residence of the priestesses to deliver exhortations; giving a robe to a priestess who is not a relation; sewing, or causing to be sewed, the robe of a priestess who is not a relation; except in a caravan, and when danger is apprehended, travelling in company with a priestess; sailing on the water with a priestess by appointment, except in passing from one bank to another; receiving food given on the request of a priestess; sitting in private with a priestess; sitting with a woman on a couch in a secluded place; being alone with a woman; tickling with the fingers; sporting in the water; accompanying a woman on a journey, though it be only to the end of the village; entering the harem of a king without giving previous notice; taking food from a priestess, unless she be a relation; and allowing a priestess to prescribe what food shall be given at a public meal.

The priest is told at his ordination that when the head is taken off it is impossible that life can be retained in the body; and that in like manner the priest who holds sexual intercourse with any one, is thereby incapacitated from continuing to be a son of Sákya, or a sramana.*

In addition to the ordinances that refer to the outward conduct, the priests are directed to live in a state of entire abstraction from the world, so that when in the midst of enticements to evil, all impurity may be avoided. The door of the eye is to be kept shut. When the outer gates of the city are left open, though the door of every separate house and store be shut, the enemy will enter the city and take possession; in like manner, though all the ordinances be kept, if the eye be permitted to wander, evil desire will be produced. . . . It is better to have a red-hot piece of iron run through the eye, than for the eye to be permitted to wander, as by this

* Kámawáchan.

means evil desire will be produced, and the breaking of all the precepts will follow. The mind will then be like a field of grain that has no hedge, or a treasure-house with the door left open, or a dwelling with a bad roof through which the rain continually falls. The same may be said of all the other senses; and it is therefore requisite that they be kept under strict restraint.

Numerous examples are given of priests who are said to have attended to these advices, and gained therefrom the benefits they are intended to impart. On a certain day, when Maha Tissa resided in the rock Chétiya, he went to the city of Anurádhapura to receive alms, and in the way met a female who had quarrelled with her husband, and was returning in consequence to her parents. She was a beautiful woman, and arrayed in a very splendid manner. Wishing to attract the attention of the priest, she smiled; but by so doing she showed her teeth, and on seeing them he thought only of the impermanence of the body; by which means he attained rahatship. Soon afterwards he met her husband in the street, who asked him if he had seen a woman; but he replied that he had seen only a loathsome skeleton; whether it were that of a male or female he could not tell.

A priest who had recently taken the obligations, on going to receive alms saw a beautiful female, by the sight of whom his mind was agitated. On this account he went to Ananda, a relative of Gotama Budha, and informed him of what had occurred. Ananda told him that he must reflect upon the subject in a proper manner, and that he would then see that the form he had looked upon was in reality utterly destitute of beauty; that it was filthy, defiled, unreal, and impermanent; by this means the agitation of his mind would pass away. This evil arose from the want of caution, as the priest had not kept a guard over the sense of sight.

There was another priest, Chittagutta, who resided in the Karandu-léna, a cave in the southern province of Ceylon, upon the walls of which were painted, in a superior manner, the stories of the Budhas. The cave was visited by some priests, who greatly admired the paintings, and expressed their admiration to Chittagutta; but he replied that he had lived there sixty years and had never seen them, and that he should not now have known of their existence if it had not been for their information. There was near the door of the cave a large ná-tree; but he only knew that the tree was there from the fall of the pollen and flowers. The tree itself he never saw, as he carefully observed the precept not to look upwards or to a distance. The king of Mágam having heard of his sanctity, invited him to come to his palace that he might worship him; but though he sent three messages, the priest was not willing to leave his cave. The king therefore bound up the nipple of a woman who was giving suck to her child, sealed it with the royal seal, and declared that it should not be broken until the priest came. When Chittagutta heard of what the king had done, out of compassion he went to the palace. The monarch worshipped him on his arrival, and told him that a transient sight of him was not sufficient, as he wanted to keep the precepts another day. This he did in order that he might detain the priest; and in this way seven days passed over. At his departure the king and his queens worshipped him, and the king carried his alms-bowl some distance; but he merely said in return, " May you prosper!" When some other priests expostulated with him, for not being more respectful, and told him that he ought to have said, " May you prosper, great king! May you prosper, illustrious queens!" he replied that he knew not to whom he was speaking; he had not even noticed that they were persons of rank. On arriving at the cave, he walked at night to exercise the rite of meditation, when the déwa of the ná-tree caused a light to shine, by which the greatness of his abstraction was perceived, and the deities of the rocks around called out in approval. During the same night he became a rahat. From this may be learnt the benefit of keeping the eyes from wandering; they must not be permitted to roll about, like those of a monkey, or of a beast of the forest when in fear, or of a child; they must be directed downwards.*

The monks of the Greek and Roman churches have seen, in a similar manner, the necessity of placing a guard over their eyes, and of being circumspect in their intercourse with women. Aphraates, the Persian anchoret, would never speak to a woman but at a distance, and always in as few words as possible. When the sister of Pachomius, the Egyptian ascetic, went to his monastery to see him, he sent her word that no woman could be allowed to enter the enclosure, and that she ought to be contented by hearing that he was alive. The Roman anchoret, Arsenius, would seldom see strangers who came to visit him, saying that he would only use his eyes to behold the heavens. Bernard is said to have walked a whole day

* Wisudhi Margga Sanné.

along the lake of Lausanne without perceiving it. In the rules laid down by Augustin he ordains that no one shall ever steadfastly fix her eyes upon another, even of the same sex, as this is a mark of immodesty; he would never suffer a woman to converse in his house, not even his sister, as he said that she might sometimes be attended by other females, or be visited by them; and he never spoke to a woman, unless some of his clerks were near. Simeon Stylites never suffered a woman to come within the enclosure in which his pillar stood. It was Basil's rule never to speak to, to touch, or to look at, a woman, unless in case of necessity; after a year's noviciate he did not know whether the top of his cell had any ceiling; nor whether the church had more than one window, though it had three. Theodorus enjoined his monks not to open the gate of the monastery to any woman, nor ever to speak to a female, except in the presence of two witnesses. The sainted founder of the Franciscans kept so strict a watch over his eyes, that he scarcely knew any woman by sight. When some one fixed his eye too steadily, and for too long a time, upon Ignatius Loyola, he was enjoined to make the government of his eyes the subject of particular examination, and to say every day a short prayer for fifteen months. The Jesuits were not permitted by their founder to visit women, even of the highest quality, alone; and when they conversed with them, or heard their confessions, it was to be so ordered that a companion might see all that passed, though he did not hear what was said. The monks of La Trappe usually keep their eyes cast down, and never look at strangers. Women are not only excluded from the second enclosure of the Carthusians, but even their church; and no one is permitted to go out of the bounds of the monastery, except the prior and procurator, and they only upon the necessary affairs of the house. In some of the monasteries it was the almoner's office either to enquire himself, or procure proper persons to enquire for him, where any sick or infirm persons resided who had not a sufficient support; but if he himself undertook this office, he was to take two servants with him, and before he entered any house, he was to cause the women, if there were any in it, to leave the house; nor was he allowed to enter any house in which sick or infirm women lay.

As we approach our own times, this state of abstractedness from all things earthly, or these precautionary measures against the entrance of evil, appear to have been carried to the greatest excess; but to assimilate more to the practices of the Budhists. Peter, of Alcantara, who died in 1562, in order that his eyes might be "more easily kept under the government of reason, and that they might not, by superfluous curiosity, break in upon the interior recollection of his mind, put them upon such restraint that he had been a considerable time a religious man before he knew that the church of his convent was vaulted. After having had the care of serving the refectory for half a year, he was chid by the superior for having never given the friars any of the fruit in his custody, to which the servant of God humbly answered that he had never seen any. The truth was, he had never lifted up his eyes to the ceiling where the fruit was hanging upon twigs, as is usual in countries where grapes are dried and preserved. He lived four years in a convent, without taking notice of a tree that grew near the door." He told St. Teresa that he had lived three years in a house of his order without knowing any of the friars but by their speech, as he never lifted up his eyes; if he did not follow the other friars, he was unable to find his way to many places that he frequented. It is said of Lewis Gonzaga, 1591, that although he every day waited on the infant of Spain, James, and had to pay his respects to the empress, he never looked at her face, or took notice of her person.*

The permission to retire from the priesthood under certain circumstances was an important feature in the monastic institutions of Budhism. In this it resembled the usages of the church when celibacy was first enjoined among Christians. Even Cyprian (Epist. 62), after extolling the merit of the virgins who had taken the vows, says, "but if they are unwilling to persevere, it is better that they marry." They who broke the vow were commanded (Conc. Ancyran. can. 19) to fulfil the same term as the bigamist. "Wherever (at the commencement of monachism) there dwelt a monk of superior reputation for sanctity," says Lingard, "the desire of profiting by his advice and example induced others to fix their habitations in his neighbourhood: he became their abbas or spiritual father, they his voluntary subjects; and the group of separate cells which they formed around him was known to others by the name of his monastery (so that the word which originally signified the single mansion of one solitary, now denoted a collection of such mansions). To obtain admission into their societies no

* Alban Butler's Lives of the Fathers, Martyrs, and other principal Saints, passim. Whitaker's History of Whalley. Tindal's History of Evesham.

other qualification was required in the postulant than a spirit of penitence and a desire of Christian perfection. As long as this spirit continued to animate his conduct, he was exercised in the several duties of the monastic profession; if he repented of his choice, the road was open, and he was at liberty to depart . . . It was not till a much later period, and after the decline of the original fervour, that irrevocable vows were enjoined by the policy of subsequent legislators."* It was by Benedict (Reg. c. 58) that the law was first peremptorily made that all who entered a convent should remain for life. This system was soon adopted in other convents besides the monasterium Cassinense in which he resided; and these several convents, becoming united under one form of discipline, gave rise to the first monastic order.† In some instances among the Romanists the abbots have retired upon pensions, become monks deraigne, and then quitted their profession and married.‡ Among the Nestorians there are monks who are forbidden to marry whilst they remain in the fraternity, but they are at liberty to leave the convent when they wish to enter into the marriage state.§ In the Abyssinian church the monks are generally married, except the abbot. They do not live in regular monasteries, but in solitary places near the church. They maintain themselves and their families by agriculture, and their only duty as monks is to read certain passages and psalms, so that the monastic life is properly speaking one of ascetic rustics.

In some countries where Budhism is professed it is usual for all persons to take upon themselves, during some period of their lives, the obligations of the priest; but this is probably only an entrance into the noviciate. In Ceylon it is less common for any one thus to assume the yellow robe who does not intend to devote his whole life to the profession. Nearly every male inhabitant of Siam enters the priesthood once in his life. The monarch of this country every year, in the month of Asárha, throws off his regal robes, shaves his head, adopts the yellow sackcloth of a novice, and does penance in one of the wiháras, along with all his court. At the same time slaves are brought to be shaved and initiated, as an act of merit in their converter. The same practice prevails in Ava. Among the Burmans, instead of the expensive mode of putting away a husband

* Lingard's History of the Anglo-Saxon Church, cap. iv.
† Giesler's Text-Book of Ecclesiastical History, § 34.
‡ Fosbroke's British Monachism.
§ Conder's Analytical View of all Religions.

or wife, which the common law furnishes, a much easier is often resorted to with complete success. The parties aggrieved merely turn priests or nuns, and the matrimonial bond is at once dissolved. They may return to a secular life at any time, and marry another; but, for the sake of appearance, their return to the world is usually deferred some months.* It is the custom in China to serve three years as abbot, and after this period to retire into privacy.

The true ascetic is enjoined to renounce all carnal indulgences; but this is only an inferior requirement of the institute. There must be a complete annihilation of the affections; he must forget, so far as the most determined effort can accomplish this object, that he has now, or ever has had, any connexion with the world of men. Regarding himself as if thrown into existence immediately from the hand of God, without the intervention of any material instrumentality, or looking upon himself as the temporary incarnation of some seraph, whose native abode is the blue empyrean, he retires within the mystic circle of his own purity; and though the affection manifested by his parents will at times start up in vivid imagery, and the cadence of the hymn with which his sweet sister was wont to soothe him in his little troubles will sometimes seem to be repeated in the wind's low tone as it passes in its softer mood, it is only like the dip of the swallow's beak into the water of the placid lake, or the gentle falling of the withered leaf upon its surface, a slight impression, in a moment gone. Intercessory prayer is a practice that he disdains to follow, as such an exercise would be a confession of weakness; a spectre of earth in the shrine where angels only ought to enter. And if we were to question the correctness of this course, the advocates of the system would probably reply, that he prays for none but himself on earth, in order that he may have the more power to pray for others when he enters heaven.

These reprehensible sentiments have prevailed, with more or less intensity, in all places where monachism has been established; as they are a legitimate, and almost necessary, result of its institutions. The Essenes were forbidden to assist any of their relatives who might be in need, unless under the inspection of others, lest they should favour them above that which was their due. Alipius, bishop of Adrianople, forbade the nuns to receive visits from their parents, even though they might be at the point of death.† When

* Howard Malcolm's Travels in South-Eastern Asia.
† Hospin. De Monachis.

Fulgentius, procurator of Byzacena, embraced the monastic profession, his mother went to the convent, and, in transports of grief, cried out to the abbot to restore her son, and not rob a desolate widow; but the son was deaf to her cries, and refused to return to his paternal residence. When Paula, a Roman lady in whom was the blood of the Scipios and the Gracchi, had resolved upon taking a similar step, and for this purpose took her passage for Syria, her relations attended her to the water-side, striving with tears to induce her not to leave them. Even when the vessel was ready to sail, her little son Toxotius, with uplifted hands and bitterly weeping, begged her not to leave him. The rest, who were scarcely able to speak from the poignancy of their grief, entreated her at least to delay her departure a little time; but the mother "turned her dry eyes to heaven," and was soon away from this touching scene. One of the works written by Chrysostom, entitled "On Providence," was addressed to Stagirius, who had exasperated his father by turning monk, and was afterward seized (as well he might) with a dreadful melancholy that the usual palliatives were unable to subdue. In another of his works, entitled "Against the Impugners of the Monastic State," he addresses first a pagan father whose son had irritated him by becoming a monk, and afterwards a Christian father, whom he threatens with the judgment of Eli, if he withdrew his children from the monastery, telling him that in this profession "they would have become suns in heaven; whereas, if they were saved in the world, their glory would probably be only that of the stars."*

It was demanded of the monk by Basil, though he did not permit the novice to be received without the consent of his parents, that after reception he should, as far as possible, break connexion with his nearest relatives, and literally cease henceforward to know his parents, brethren, and sisters, according to the flesh. "It is the devil's craft," said he, "to keep alive in the mind of the monk a recollection of his parents and natural relatives, so as that, under cover of rendering them some aid, he may be drawn aside from his heavenly course." A monk when urgently entreated to visit a dying sister, at last consented; but as he had vowed never to see any of his relatives, and, in common with others, never to look upon a woman, he, after a long journey, presented himself at the door, and, resolutely shutting his eyes, called to his sister, "Here

* Alban Butler, passim.

am I, your brother, look at me!" and then, refusing to enter, returned to his wilderness.* "According to the scriptural declaration, He that hath said to his father and mother, I know ye not, and to his brethren, I know ye not, and hath not known his children, they have kept thy word. The monks were to forget filial affections, and this not of any stiffness or hardness of heart; for if a mere stranger with them be in misery, they mourn as easily for him as for another; but the sword is it that we spake of that is in their heart, and hath cut them away from their wonted acquaintance and affinity, not for that they have to love them still, that love also their very enemies, but because they have cast away all carnal love which groweth to mere dotage, and have converted the same wholly to spiritual charity." † The monks of La Trappe never write to their friends in the world after their profession, nor hear anything respecting them; they only know that there is a world in order that they may pray for it. When the parent of any monk dies, the news is sent to the superior only, who tells the community that the father of one of them is dead, and enjoins them to pray for his soul. It is at present a rule in Italy, that when a monk meets any of his relatives in the street, he is not to raise his eyes to their countenances, but to give them a slight token of recognition, by raising the hat from the head.

There were, however, some exceptions to this general disregard of filial duty. There was a regulation of St. Augustine's Abbey, at Canterbury, that "if it should so happen that the father, the mother, the sister, or brother of any monk in the monastery should come to such great want and indigency as that (to the reproach of any of the brethren) he or she be forced to ask at the gates the alms of the fraternity, then, such of them so asking should be provided for in the hospital attached to the monastery of sufficient sustentation, according to the ability of the house." ‡ There is a sentence written by the stern Jerome (Epist. ad Eustoch.) relative to the monks of Egypt, that speaks volumes, wherein he tells us that the sick monk was well attended to, "ut nec delitias urbium, nec *matris* quaerat *affectum*."

We shall perhaps be reminded, in defence of the monastic usages, of the command of Christ, Luke xiv. 26; but we think that these

* Taylor's Ancient Christianity.
† Fosbroke's British Monachism, quoted from the Harleian MS.
‡ Somner's Antiquities of Canterbury.

words refer to the situation of the individual who must either displease his relatives or commit sin; and that they have no reference whatever to the vows of the monk. Hence we admire rather than condemn the resolution of Phileos, an Egyptian nobleman, whose martyrdom is recorded in the same work as many of the preceding narratives.* As he refused to offer sacrifice, the governor, Culcion, endeavoured to overcome him by appealing to the grief of his wife, children, brother, and other relations, who were present at the trial; but he, like the rock unshaken by the impetuous waves that dash around it, stood unmoved, and raising his heart to God, protested aloud that he owned no other kindred but the apostles and martyrs; and that he would die for Christ rather than deny him.

The eastern ascetic presents a similar insensibility to the important duties that are disregarded by the western monk. It is said by Manu (Inst. ii. 205), "Let not the Brahman student, unless ordered by his spiritual father, prostrate himself, in his presence, before his natural father." The writings of the Budhists abound with maxims and legends illustrative of the same type of character. Kula, the family or relationship, is called a hindrance to the exercise of sámadhi, which consists in the collecting of the thoughts, and the fixing of them upon one object, so as to be free from all wandering or perturbation of mind. The sramana recluse who enters into an intimacy with any other person, though it should even be a priest, will be prevented from acquiring the tranquillity at which he ought constantly to aim. He will be indisposed, by other calls upon his attention, to enter upon the exercises it is necesary for him to perform. But there are some priests who are superior to the attractions that would ensnare them, and are even indifferent respecting their parents, so that, when communicating with them, the relationship is entirely disregarded. We have seen that Rathapála called his father merely "Householder," and that he paid no regard to his wife or mother when in their presence. A priest who resided at Koranakara had a nephew who was a priest in the same wihára; but in the course of time the nephew went to reside at Ruhuna (the southern province of Ceylon, whilst the uncle's village must have been somewhere in the north). After this his parents were continually asking the older priest if he had heard any news of their son. At last, as they were so importunate, he set out for Ruhuna, that he might enquire after the welfare of his

* Alban Butler, Feb. 4.

nephew, and be able to satisfy the wishes of his parents. By this time the nephew thought it would be well to go and see his uncle, as he had been absent from him a considerable period. The two priests met on the borders of the river Mahaweli; and, after mutual explanations, the uncle remained near the same place to perform a certain ceremony, and the nephew proceeded onward to his native village. The day after his arrival his father went to invite him to perform wass at his house, as he had heard that a stranger had come to the monastery. The priest accordingly went every day, for the space of three months, to his father's house to say bana; but he was not recognized by any of his relatives. When the ceremony was concluded, he informed his parents that he was about to depart; but they entreated him to come the next day, and they then gave him a cruse of oil, a lump of sugar, and a piece of cloth nine cubits long. After giving them his blessing, he began his journey to Ruhuna. The two priests again met on the borders of the river, when the nephew informed his uncle that he had seen his parents, and at the same time washed his feet with the oil, gave him the sugar to eat, and presented him with the piece of cloth. He then proceeded on his journey, and his uncle set out to return to Koranakara. From the time that the son began to perform wass at his parent's house, his father went out every day in the direction of Ruhuṇa, to see if the priest was returning with his child; but when he saw him alone, as he concluded at once that his son was dead, he threw himself at the feet of the priest, wept, and lamented aloud. The priest saw the error into which the father had fallen, and made known to him what had taken place, convincing him of the reality of what he said by showing him the cloth he had received. The father then went in the direction his son had gone, fell on his face and worshipped, saying that his son was without an equal, as he had visited his parents' house every day during three months, and yet never ḍiscovered himself to any of his relatives. To such a priest even parents are no palibhóda or hindrance to the reception of tranquillity.*

* Wisudhi Margga Sanné.

VII. POVERTY.

The vow of poverty is a natural result of asceticism, so that we expect to meet with it as a matter of course wherever men have been taught that to save their souls it is necessary for them to abandon the world. The monks of Christendom suppose that they have an additional motive for this rule in the example of Christ and his apostles. Thus, Chaucer's Wife of Bath, v. 6761, exclaims,

> "And ther as ye of poverte me repreve,
> The highe God, on whom that we beleve,
> In wilful poverte chese to lede his lif:
> And certes, every man, maiden, or wif
> May understond, that Jesus heven king,
> He wold not chese a vicious living."

The universal tendency there is among all ascetics to the breaking of this law, as well as the difficulty of framing regulations that may not be set aside by the ingenuity of those who wish to transgress them, may be seen in the fact, that nearly every order has been intended at its commencement to repress the style of luxury in which the preceding communities have lived; whilst it has only required the elapse of a reasonable time before the new order has been drawn into the vortex of the very extravagancies it was intended to put down, and for which purpose it was originated. By Jerome (Ep. 95) complaint is made that some who called themselves solitarii lived in the midst of a crowd, and had the attendance of servants; they had all the conveniences requisite for a carousal; and their food was eaten from vessels of glass or some other costly material. The same author relates (Ep. 18) that a certain anchoret left a hundred crowns at his death. When the monks resident in the same desert met together to enquire what was to be done with the money, some proposed that it should be given to the poor, but it was finally resolved that the whole sum should be thrown into his grave, with the malediction, "May thy money pass with thee to perdition." Until the rise of the mendicants, the individual members of the various orders were regarded as denying themselves the enjoyment of personal property, though the community to which they belonged might itself possess ample revenues. Even Dominic, though he prescribed the most severe poverty, did not forbid the houses of his order to enjoy in common small rents in money. But Francis prohibited his monks from possessing a collective revenue, and the vow of poverty was absolute. The rule was as follows:—"Fratres sibi nihil approprient, nec domum, nec locum, nec aliquam rem; sed sicut perigrini et advenae in hoc seculo, in paupertate et humilitate famulantes Domino, vadant pro eleemosynâ confidenter." The bishop of Acco, 1220, writing of the Franciscans, says, "They have neither monasteries nor churches; neither fields, nor vineyards, nor cattle; nor houses, nor any possessions; nor where to lay the head." When a church was bestowed upon Francis by the Benedictines of Monte Sonbazo, he refused to accept the property or dominion, and would only have the use of the place; in token of which he sent the monks annually a basket of fish. He would not allow any property to be invested in his order, that he might say more perfectly that he had neither house, food, nor clothes. When asked which of all the virtues he thought was the most agreeable to God, he replied, "Poverty is the way to salvation, the nurse of humility, and the root of perfection. Its fruits are hidden, but they multiply themselves in ways that are infinite," Yet a division broke out among his followers as to the precise interpretation of his rule, in consequence of which a mitigation of the requirement as to the total abrogation of all worldly possessions was made by Gregory IX. in 1231; and in 1245 the bull of Innocent IV. allowed them to possess certain articles of furniture, with a few utensils, books, &c. About a century afterwards a dispute arose between the Franciscans and Dominicans respecting the poverty of Christ and his apostles; it being argued by the followers of Francis that they had no possessions of any kind whatever, either as private property or as a common treasure, whilst the followers of Dominic asserted most strenuously a contrary opinion. The pope decided in favour of the Dominicans; and it is recorded that many of the Franciscans perished in the flames of the inquisition for persisting in their opposition to this decree. It was enjoined by Ignatius Loyola that the professed Jesuits should not possess any real estates or revenues, either in particular or in common; but that colleges might enjoy revenues and rents for the maintenance of students of the order. It is said* to be peculiar to this society, that the religious, after their first vows, retain some time the dominion or property of their patrimony, without the administration (the latter condition being essential to a religious vow of poverty) till they make their renun-

* Alban Butler, July 31.

ciation. Francis of Sales did not allow the nuns belonging to the order of the Visitation to have the propriety or even the long use of anything whatever, even their chambers, beds, crosses, beads, and books, were to be changed every year.

The monastic churches were, however, sometimes adorned in a costly manner, even when the rule of poverty was personally regarded with all strictness. Benedict long used wooden, and afterwards glass or pewter chalices at the altar, and if any presents of silk ornaments were made to him, he gave them to other churches; but he afterwards effected a change in this practice, and built a stately church, furnished with silver chalices and rich ornaments. It was a rule among the Cistertians that in their places of worship all unnecessary display should be avoided; they had neither gold nor silver crosses, nor candelabras, except one of iron; nor a chalice, except it were one of copper or iron; and they reproached the monks of Clugny with having churches "immensely high, immoderately long, superfluously broad, sumptuously furnished, and curiously painted;" so that men were led to admire more that which was beautiful than that which was sacred. There were individual monks who carried out these ideas to their utmost extent. All the furniture in the little cell of John, the Carmelite, consisted of a paper image and a cross made of rushes, and his beads and breviary were of the meanest description.

The words fakir and dervish, so commonly met with in all accounts of Mahometan countries, are said to mean, the one in Arabic, and the other in Persian, poor. These devotees ask alms in the name of God, and are restricted to a life of poverty, relying for their support upon the charity of the faithful. Some of them are independent, whilst others are associated together in communities like the monastic orders of Christendom. The monks endeavour to trace the origin of their system to the first year of the Hegira; and it is said that there are now thirty-two different orders existing in the Turkish empire. They found the reason of the ascetic life upon a saying of Mahomet—Poverty is my glory.

The priest of Budha, previous to his ordination, must possess eight articles, called ata-pirikara. 1, 2, 3. Robes, of different descriptions. 4. A girdle for the loins. 5. A pátara or alms-bowl. 6. A razor. 7. A needle. 8. A perahankada, or water-strainer. The robes will form the subject of a separate section. The bowl is for the purpose of receiving the food presented in alms by the faithful. The razor is for the shaving of the hair. The needle, which is for the repairing of the priest's robes, is not to have a case made of bone, ivory, or horn; if he is found to possess one, it is to be broken, and the fault requires confession and absolution. In this respect some of the monks carried their vow of poverty to greater excess than the Budhists, as Theodorus forbade his followers to have even as much property as a needle. Among the later monks, however, every one had a table-book, knife, needle, and handkerchief. It was formerly common for men to carry needle-cases about their persons, in order that they might be able to mend their clothes. In the time of Chaucer the needle was of silver.* The water-strainer is considered to be a necessary article, as "if any priest shall knowingly drink water containing insects, it is a fault that requires confession and absolution;" it is to be a cubit square, without a single thread broken. Even the laic who takes upon himself the five obligations is required to possess a strainer, and to use it whenever he drinks water. The Jaina priests, in addition to the strainer, carry a broom, in order that they may sweep the insects out of their way as they walk, as they fear to tread on the minutest being.†

These articles can be given to a single priest; but as other descriptions of property can only be given to a chapter, they are the only things he can possess in his own individual right. When taking upon himself the last of the ten obligations, the priest declares, "I will observe the precept that forbids the receiving of gold or silver." But some other articles, such as chairs, couches, curtains, umbrellas, sandals, and staves, may be received by the chapter. If the priest receives coined gold or silver, or causes it to be received, or uses it if deposited for him; or if he uses any kind of bullion; it is a fault involving forfeiture. He is also expressly forbidden to engage in mercantile transactions. When the priest sees money, jewels, or ornaments in any place, he is not to touch them, though they may appear to be lost, unless it be in a house or garden, in which case it may be picked up and given to the owner.

It was supposed by the late James Prinsep, from the absence of any of the titles of sovereignty on many coins that are evidently of Budhist origin from the symbols that they bear, that the Budhist

* Fosbroke's British Monachism.
† Colebrooke's Miscellaneous Essays, ii. 194.

coinage was struck in the monasteries of the priesthood; but as the priest was forbidden to touch money, under any circumstances, the supposition must be incorrect. It has been doubted whether any native coin, properly so called, was circulated in India anterior to the incursion of Alexander, as none of the ancient books of the Hindus mention coined money;* but in the most ancient laws of the Budhists, the distinction is recognised between coined money and bullion. The monks of Britain were less scrupulous in this matter than their eastern compeers. The monastic mint was not unfrequently an establishment of great importance, and if we may judge from the number of their coins yet in existence, the issues must have been extensive. The abbey of Bury had the following officers:—custos cunci, or keeper of the mint; monetarius, the moneyer or mint-master; cambiator, or exchanger; duo custodes, or keepers; and duo assaisiatores, or assayers.†

Among the easterns generally, the most valuable personal property is that which can be corrupted by "the moth and the rust;" or garments, and ornaments fabricated of the precious metals; and as the priest can only possess three robes, and these of a particular kind, and is not allowed to have rich furniture, or to possess gold or silver, it is not in his power to accumulate that which alone would in India be regarded as wealth. Even when articles of a more valuable description are presented to the community, they cannot be used by the priest without being previously disfigured. Thus the priest may have a carpet or coverlet, but it must not be made with a mixture of silk; nor of woollen of a black colour, but two parts black, one white, and one brown; it is to be used six years, and then not given away or renewed, without the consent of the other priests; and the sitting carpet is to be disfigured by having part of an old carpet attached to it of a span in size.‡

The second of the three great ecumenical convocations that at an early period were held by the Budhists, was assembled in consequence of the unauthorised practices of some of the priests in the city of Wésáli. Among other things it was their custom upon the lunar festivals to fill a golden basin with water, and placing it in the midst of the assembly, to say to their followers, "Beloved! bestow upon the priesthood a kahapanan coin, or half, or a

* Journal Bengal As. Soc. Aug. 1843.
† Taylor's Index Monasticus.
‡ Gogerly's Translation of the Pátimokkhan.

quarter of one, or even the value of a mása; to the priesthood it will afford the means of providing themselves with the sacerdotal requisites!" *

But the rule of poverty, as among the monks of the west, was in a great degree nullified by the specious distinction between the priest and the priesthood, the individual and the community, the sramana and the sangha. The community is allowed to be rich in lands, and to have splendid edifices dedicated to its use, whilst the individual priest is regarded as having renounced all worldly possessions. That which is given to the general fund is not to be appropriated as private property by any member of the community, nor given to a laic. No stool or couch belonging to the chapter is to be carelessly left out in the open air; by which is to be understood that the property of the community is to be taken care of in a proper manner. In an inscription cut in the rock near Mihintala in Ceylon, it is directed that the lands which belong to the wihára shall be enjoyed by the priesthood in common, and not divided into separate parcels. We learn from the same inscription, that exact accounts, regularly audited, were kept of the revenues of the temple. After paying the prescribed wages to those who were entitled to receive them, the rest of the revenues proceeding from the lands belonging to the wihára were to be entered in books by the proper officers, that the same might be under inspection. The daily expenditure on account of the public alms-bowl, and of the hired servants, and for repairs, was to be written in books; and an account was to be kept of the contents of the store-room. Every month these several accounts were to be collected into one; and at the end of the year the monthly accounts were again to be formed into one list or register, to be produced before a chapter of the priests.

When passing through the interior of Ceylon, amidst scenery so beautiful that it almost appears to give reality to the legend that it once was Paradise, and my attention has been attracted by the sight of lands teeming with more than usual fertility, it has almost invariably happened that on enquiring to whom these rich domains belonged, I have been told that they were the property of the priests. Their possessions must therefore be very extensive; though perhaps not equal to those of the clergy in England, who in the

* Turnour's Examination of the Pali Budhistical Annals: Journ. Bengal As. Soc. Sept. 1837.

thirteenth century are said to have had in their hands 28,000 out of the 53,000 knights' fees connected with the landed property of the realm. Though the monarch of Ceylon was considered to have been originally the sole possessor of the soil, there were in all times of which we have any statistical accounts a large proportion of lands appropriated to private individuals and to the priests. The temple lands were principally royal donations, but not in every instance. It is not very clear how lands came into the possession of private individuals, so as to be alienable; but we may infer that they were originally granted by the kings for some signal services performed, and that the families thus rewarded, afterwards falling into decay, found themselves obliged to look out for some more powerful protection. They might either become retainers of the crown or the church; but as the temple service was nearer their own homes, was less arbitrary and oppressive, and had moreover the recommendation that by this means they might benefit their souls, it was natural that they should dedicate their lands to the priest, rather than to the king. Lands that were newly cleared might also be considered as liable to no compulsory custom; and from a similar motive, to ensure protection, they would sometimes be given over to the temple; then, in return for the protection received, certain services would be promised on the part of the individual who presented the gift, as it would be understood that his family was to retain possession of the lands, though the proprietorship was nominally in the temple. Of this mode of the transmission of property we have many parallel instances in the history of the feudal times. When lands were dedicated by the kings of Ceylon, the services that were to be rendered by the cultivator of the soil to the priesthood were very minutely set forth, as is testified by many inscriptions still to be traced upon slabs of stone, and occasionally in the solid rocks, near the temples to which the lands were given.

The temple lands were invariably free from royal custom or duty, the services which in the royal villages were paid to the king being here paid to the temple. This system existed in very ancient times, some of the grants being nearly as old as the time of Christ. An extract from the Account of Ceylon, published by Robert Knox, will illustrate the usages as they prevailed during his captivity in Kandy, which commenced in the year 1659 :—" Unto each of the pagodas there are great revenues of land belonging; which have been allotted to them by former kings, according to the state of the kingdom: but they have much impaired the revenues of the crown, there being rather more towns belonging to the church than to the king. These estates of the temples are to supply a daily charge they are at, which is to prepare victuals or sacrifices to set before the idols. They have elephants also, as the king has, which serve them for state. Their temples have all sorts of officers belonging to them, as the palace hath. . . . Many of the vehars (wiháras) have farms belonging to them, and are endowed. The tirinanxes (priests who have received ordination) are the landlords, unto whom the tenants come at a certain time, and pay their rents. These farmers live the easiest of any in the land, for they have nothing to do but at these set times to bring in their dues and so depart, and to keep in repair certain little vehars in the country. So that the rest of the Chingulais envy them and say of them, Though they live easy in this world, they cannot escape unpunished in the life to come, for enjoying the Buddou's land and doing him so little service for it."

It is said, in an official report published in 1831:—"The possessions of the temples constitute a large proportion of the cultivated lands in the Kandyan provinces. In the several temples and colleges there are registers of the lands dependent on them, but these registers not having been examined, their extent has not been accurately ascertained. At my request, translations were made of the registers of the principal temples of Kandy; and from these it appears that the tenants and proprietors of what are called Temple Lands in the several provinces, are liable, on the requisition of the chiefs and priests, to render services and contributions of various kinds. These are minutely detailed in the registers, and the occupier of each allotment of land has a special duty assigned to him, or a special contribution to make, either for the repairs of the temples, the subsistence of the chiefs and priests, and their attendants, or on occasion of the annual festivals."*

From these documents it is evident that the situation of the priests of Ceylon is at present very different to that which was intended at the commencement of their order by Gótama Budha, as they must have degenerated therefrom in proportion to the extent of their lands and of their social and political privileges. Professedly

* Report of Lieut. Col. Colebrooke, one of His Majesty's Commissioners of Enquiry upon the Administration of the Government of Ceylon, dated Dec. 24, 1831.

mendicants, and possessing only a few articles that are of no intrinsic value, they are in reality the wealthiest and most honoured class in the nation to which they belong. In other countries where Budhism is professed, it is probable that they are less wealthy: but in no place can we find the recluse of the primitive institution.

VIII. MENDICANCY.

The priest of Budha is not allowed to bring within the door of his mouth any food not given in alms, unless it be water, or some substance used for the purpose of cleaning the teeth; and when in health the food that he eats must be procured by his own exertions in carrying the alms-bowl from house to house in the village or city near which he resides. When going to receive alms, the bowl is slung across his shoulder, and is usually covered by the outer robe. It may be made of either iron or clay, but not of any other material. It must first be received by a chapter, and then be officially delivered to the priest whose bowl, after examination, is found to be in the worst condition. No priest is allowed to procure a new bowl so long as his old one has not been bound with five ligatures to prevent it from falling to pieces; and he is not allowed to use an extra bowl more than ten days without permission from a chapter. When passing from place to place, the priest must not look to a greater distance before him than the length of a yoke; nor must he look on one side, or upwards, nor bend his body to look at anything upon the ground; he is not to look at elephants, chariots, horses, soldiers, or women; nor is he allowed to put out his arms or feet in a careless manner. He may not call a woman by her name, nor ask what kind of victuals there are in the house, or what kind will be presented. He may not say that he is hungry in order that food may be given him. Should he see a child driving calves, he may not ask if they still suck, in order that the child may tell its mother, and the mother be induced to give him milk. A certain priest, who was suffering from hunger, went to a house to receive food. The woman of the house said that she had nothing to give him, but she pretended that she would go and ask something from her neighbour, for which purpose she left the house and went to a little distance. The priest took the opportunity of looking to see what was in the house; and in the corner near the door he saw a piece of sugar-cane; he also saw some sugar-candy, salted meat, rice, and ghee, in different vessels; after which he again retired to the outer court. When the woman returned, she said that she had not succeeded in obtaining any rice. The priest replied, "It is not a fortunate day for the priesthood; I have seen an omen." She asked what it was; and he proceeded, "I saw a serpent, like a piece of sugar-cane; on looking for something to strike it with, I saw some stones like pieces of sugar-candy; the hood of this snake was like a piece of salted meat; its teeth were like grains of rice; and the poisonous saliva falling from its gums was like ghee in an earthen vessel." The woman on hearing this, was unable to deny the truth of the inference; so she presented the priest with the whole of the articles he had seen. But in this manner to speak of what is near is forbidden; it is sámanta jappana.

It is forbidden to the priest to proclaim his purity, or attainments, to the householder, in order that he may gain honour or gifts. When persons come to the temple, he may not go up to them and address them, asking them why they have come; and when he has ascertained that they have come to make offerings, tell them that his name is so and so, and that he is the religious teacher of such a noble or such a king; he may not address them with high titles and flatter them; he may not say that during seven generations the members of their family have been generous to the priests, and ask why they do not follow the same excellent example; nor is he allowed to be continually pressing them and urging them to give. Should he meet any one with a piece of sugar-cane in his hand, he may not ask from what garden it has been procured, in order that it may be given him. When two priests enter a village, they may not call for some noble female, and when she has come, say to each other that in such a way her mother assisted them, in order that she may be induced to do the same.*

There are some places to which the priest is allowed to go when seeking alms, and some to which he is not; the former are called góchara and the latter agóchara. Among the places that are not allowed may be reckoned houses of ill-fame, for though no sin might be committed by the priest, either in act or thought, it would expose him to ridicule; houses of widows, or of women whose hus-

* Wisudhi Margga Sanné.

bands have gone to some distant place; places where there are grown-up women not given in marriage; or where there are catamites or hermaphrodites, as in such places obscene words may be heard; or where there are priestesses, lest the purity of both should be placed in danger: taverns, or places where there are persons in liquor; the palaces of kings; the mansions of noblemen; the dwellings of tirttakas or unbelievers; places where the people bear ill-will to the priests or the faithful, and would abuse or ill-treat them: all these places are to be avoided. Among the places that are allowed may be reckoned the dwellings of persons who have shown their charity by such acts as the digging of wells for the public benefit; or of persons who treat the priests with respect and invite them to pay frequent visits; or of persons who are sincere in the faith.

We also learn from the Milinda Prasna, that there are two modes of winyapti, or seeking alms. One is called k áya-winyapti, that which belongs to the body; and the other wáchi-winyapti, that which belongs to the speech. Of each of these modes of seeking alms there are two kinds; the one proper, or permitted; the other improper, or not permitted. Thus, when the priest approaches a house with the alms-bowl, he must remain as though unseen; he may not hem, nor may he make any other sign that he is present, and he is not allowed to approach too near the dwelling. If he falls into any of these practices it is a káya-winyapti that is forbidden; he transgresses the precept: and it is equally a transgression if he stretches out his neck like a peacock, or in any way bends his head that he may attract the attention of those who give alms; he is not allowed even to move the jaw, or lift up the finger, for the same purpose. The proper mode is for the priest to take the alms-bowl in a becoming manner; if anything is given, he remains to receive it; if not, he passes on. Budha has said, "The wise priest never asks for anything; he disdains to beg; it is a proper object for which he carries the alms-bowl; and this is his only mode of solicitation." When the priest asks for robes, seats, medicine, or any other of the sacerdotal requisites, it is a wáchi-winyapti that is forbidden; nor is he allowed to say of anything, that if he were to receive it, it would be a benefit to him; or to proclaim the benefit to be received from the giving of alms, that the people may be liberal to him. But when he is sick, he is permitted to ask for any medicine that he may require, without being guilty of any transgression.*

* Pátimokkhan. Wisudhi Margga Sanné. Milinda Prasna.

The fourth of the Thirteen Ordinances is called Sapadánachárikanga. The word apadána means the breaking, the not keeping or observing; and sapadána is the keeping, the observing. The name is given to this ordinance because it enjoins the passing in regular order or succession from house to house. By this ordinance the priest is forbidden to pass by any house when going with the bowl to receive alms, on account of its meanness or inferiority; but he may pass by the house if near it there be any danger, as from dogs. When he visits a village, street or house three successive days, without receiving anything, he is not required to go to the same place again; but if he receives only the least particle, it must be regularly visited. When he has gone out with the bowl, and not received anything, should he meet a person in the road who is carrying food intended for the priesthood, he may receive it; but if anything has previously been given him, this is forbidden. The priest who keeps the superior rule of the ordinance may receive food only from the house before which he stands, or from the hall where food is regularly given. It is said that no priest ever kept this precept like Maha Kásyapa. He who keeps the middle rule may remain only a short time before the house, and must then pass on. The inferior rule allows the priest to wait until the food is given, though there may be delay.

Though the priest is not required to go more than three times to the same house to receive alms when none are given, it is regarded as a merit, in certain cases, if he persevere. The priest Róhana went to the house of Sónuttara, the father of Nágaséna, for the space of six years and ten months with the alms-bowl, although in the whole of this period he did not receive so much as a spoonful of rice, nor any mark of respect. Abuse was all that was given him; until one day a girl peeped from behind the door, and said that it was early. On receiving this salutation he was greatly pleased. It so happened that on the same morning Sónuttara met him; and as he saw pleasure depicted in his countenance, he asked whether he had received anything at the house, and Róhana said that he had. Sónuttara was in great wrath that his orders should be disobeyed, as he had charged his household not to give anything to the priest; but when he enquired who it was that had dared to act thus, all the members of the family denied that they had done any such thing. The next day, when Róhana came with the alms-bowl, the offended master stood near the door of his house, and charged the priest with uttering an untruth; but he said that he had spoken correctly, as a kind word had been given him, and this was what he had received. Then Sónuttara concluded, that if a single word had given so much pleasure, a gift of food would produce much more. He therefore commanded that Róhana should have as much rice as he could eat, and that he should receive the same daily in future.* The patience of Róhana was, however, exceeded by that of Isidore, an Egyptian monk. When asking to be admitted into the house, he said to the abbot, "I am in your hands, as iron in the hands of the smith." The abbot ordered him to remain without the gate, and to prostrate himself at the feet of every one who passed by, begging prayers for his soul as for a leper. This command he obeyed, and remained in this humiliating position for the space of seven years. The first year he had a violent conflict; the second, tranquillity; and the third, pleasure.†

Though the priests are required to go from house to house, not omitting the meanest residence, if the inhabitants be willing to give alms, the spirit of this law is frequently evaded in Ceylon. The people of the lower castes usually live in houses that are contiguous to each other, so that the priest can avoid going near them without appearing to break the rule. In the village of Rillegalle, where I sometimes resided, the quarter inhabited by the washers was never visited by the priests; and an entire village at a little distance, inhabited by mat-weavers, was equally neglected.

The practice of mendicity as a religious observance is of very ancient origin; and its existence may be traced among nations that greatly differ in their general character. The rules to be observed by the Brahman mendicant are laid down with much precision. "Every day must a Brahman student receive his food by begging, with due care, from the houses of persons renowned for discharging their duties. If none of those houses can be found, let him go begging through the whole district round the village, keeping his organs in subjection, and remaining silent; but let him turn away from such as have committed any deadly sin. . . . Let the student persist constantly in such begging, but let him not eat the food of one person only; the subsistence of a student by begging is held equal to fasting in religious merit. . . . This duty of the wise is ordained for a Brahman only; but no such act is appointed for a warrior or a merchant."—Manu, Inst. ii. 183, 185, 188, 190. The

* Milinda Prasna. † Alban Butler, March 30.

sanyási is also enjoined (Inst. vi. 58) to refrain from receiving food after humble reverence, since by taking it in consequence of a humble salutation, though free, he becomes a sceptic. The householder (Inst. iv. 32) is to make gifts, as far as he has ability, to religious mendicants, though heterodox. The ἀγύρται were mendicant priests among the Greeks, who went about from place to place soliciting alms in behalf of the gods whom they adored. It is supposed that their origin was eastern. They were connected with the worship of Isis, Opis, and Arge. Their character was not good, and they were ready to inflict injuries on the enemies of those who paid them for that purpose.* The same priests among the Romans, bound by vows of temperance and abstinence, were supported on the charity of the public. They went their daily rounds to receive alms with the sistrum in their hands. But by their avidity much opposition was excited against their order. "Stipes aereas immo vero et argenteas, multis certatim offerentibus sinu recepere patulo; nec non et vini cadum et lactis et caseos avidis animis corradentes et in sacculos huic questui de industria preparatos furcientes, &c."—Apuleius, Metam. I. viii. It was proposed by Cicero to restrain their extravagance. "Stipem sustulimus nisi eam quam ad paucos dies propriam Idaeae Martis excepimus. Implet enim superstitione animos; exhaurit domos."—Cic. de Legib. L. ii. 9, 16.†

The mendicant orders among the Romanists came into notice in the thirteenth century; but the practice existed among the monks at a much earlier period. Jerome complains (Ep. 18) that men with hair like women, beards like the goat, a black cloak and bare feet, entered into the houses of nobles and deceived silly women, laden with sin. The friars differed from the monks only in being mendicants by profession. Even the ascetics who were not professedly mendicants were sometimes obliged to beg. The monks who founded Fountains' Abbey, about 1137, were at one time reduced to so much distress that the abbot went round the neighbourhood to ask alms, but without success, and they were reduced to feed on the leaves of trees, and on herbs gathered in the fields, boiled with a little salt.‡ According to some writers, there were three kinds of poverty among them; some had nothing, either of their own or in common; others had something in common, as

* Smith's Dictionary of Greek and Roman Antiquities.
† Middleton's Letter from Rome.
‡ Burton's Monasticon Eboracense.

books, clothes, food, &c., but nothing of their own; and others had a little of both kinds of property, but only necessaries, as food and clothes. It was requisite that the quester, whose office it was to collect the daily alms for the subsistence of the community, should be a man of great virtue and circumspection, as he was constantly exposed to temptations that to a monk must have been of the most formidable character. Such a one was the Capuchin, Felix of Cantalicio. It is said that Laurence Justinian, the first patriarch of Venice, when he went about the streets begging alms with a wallet upon his back, obtruded himself into the presence of the nobles, on purpose that he might meet with derision and contempt. Frequently did he stand before the door of his own house, and cry out, "An alms, for the sake of God!" but he would not enter in, nor ever took more than two loaves. The storehouse in which the provisions of the community were laid up for the year, having been burnt down, a certain brother lamented the loss, but he said cheerfully, "Why have ye embraced and vowed poverty? God has granted us this blessing that we may feel it." Francis called the begging of alms from door to door, "the table of the Lord." Many of the cities of Europe were divided or cantoned out into four parts, the first being assigned to the Dominicans, the second to the Franciscans, the third to the Carmelites, and the fourth to the Augustines. The towns of Norwich, Lynn, and Yarmouth, appear to have been quartered in a similar way; and in some instances the convents derived considerable revenue from the privilege of confessing, preaching, and begging in their respective districts. At the crosses in cities and other places sermons were delivered on Sundays and holydays, at which time money was collected from the audience.* There are also instances upon record in which the sole right of frequenting particular circuits was purchased by individuals, who appear to have been not at all diffident in trying to turn their privilege to the best account. Thus Chaucer speaks of his "merry Frere" in the following terms:—

"Ther n'as no man nowher so vertuous;
He was the beste begger in all his hous;
And gave a certaine ferme for the grant,
Non of his bretheren came in his haunt;
For though a widewe hadde but a shoo,
(So pleasant was his *In principio*)
Yet wold he have a ferthing or he went."

* Taylor's Index Monasticus.

The appearance of the mendicant orders was hailed with satisfaction, as it was supposed that it would be a means by which the corruptions of monachism might be avoided; but the rapacity of the members soon excited general disgust. Richard Fitz Ralph, archbishop of Armagh, objected to the pope and cardinals, relative to the mendicant orders, that "scarce could any great or mean man of the clergy or the laity eat his meat, but such kind of beggars would be at his elbow; not like other poor folks humbly craving alms at the gate or the door (as Francis did command and teach them in his testament) by begging, but without shame intruding themselves into courts or houses, and lodging there; where, without any inviting at all, they eat and drink what they do find among them, and, not with that content, carry away with them either wheat, or meal, or bread, or flesh, or cheese, although there were but two in the house, in a kind of an extorting manner, there being none that can deny them, unless he would cast away natural shame."* The corruption of these orders was fearlessly proclaimed by Wycliffe, who wrote "Of the Poverty of Christ," "Against Able Beggary," and "Of Idleness in Beggary;" and maintained: "sith open Begging is thus sharply damned in holy Writ, it is a foule Error to meyntene it, but that it is more error to seie that Christ was such a Beggar."† In the famous petition called "the Supplication of Beggars," presented to Henry VIII. complaining of the encroachments of the mendicant orders, their revenues are stated at £43,333 per annum, besides their temporal goods; and the supplicants add, that "four hundred years past these friars had not one penny of this money."‡ By the Stat. 22 Hen. VIII. c. 12, all proctors and pardoners (or itinerant vendors of indulgences) going about in any country, without sufficient authority, are to be treated as vagabonds.§

To many of the friars, the necessity of seeking their subsistence in this manner must have been equally repugnant. When Luther was in the convent of St. Augustine, he was prevented by the superiors from shutting himself up in his cell, that he might prosecute his studies, though offices the most menial had already been performed. They let him know that it was not by study, but by begging, that he was to benefit the cloister; and we have an insight into the kind of alms they most coveted, from their own

* Usher's Religion of the Ancient Irish, cap. vi.

† Giesler's Text-Book, § 123.

‡ Taylor's Index Monasticus.

§ Tyrwhitt's Notes to the Canterbury Tales, v. 710.

enumeration: "bread, corn, eggs, fish, meat and money." "Cum sacco per civitatem!" Away with your wallet through the town! cried the friars; and, laden with his bread-bag, he had to wander through all the streets of Erfurth, begging from house to house. On his return he had to shut himself up in his cell, or resume his taskwork. The Franciscans, by the rule of their order, were commanded to ask alms confidenter, which has been translated "sturdily." The graphic pen of Chaucer draws the following picture in the Sumpnoure's Tale. It is intended as the portrait of a preacher in Holdernesse.

"With scrippe, and tipped staf, ytucked hie,
In every hous he gan to pore and prie,
And begged mele and chese, or elles corn.
His felaw had a staf tipped with horn,
A pair of tables all of ivory,
And a pointel ypolished fetishly,
And wrote alway the names, as he stood,
Of alle folk that gave hem any good,
Askaunce that he wolde for hem preye,
'Yeve us a bushel whete, or malt reye,
A Goddes kichel, or a trippe of chese;
Or elles what you list, we may not chese,
A Goddes halfpenny, or a masse peny,
Or yeve us of your braun, if ye have any,
A dagon of your blanket, leve dame!
Our sustre dere! (lo, here I write your name)
Bacon or beef, or swiche thing as ye find.'
A sturdy harlot went hem, ay, behind,
That was hir hostes man, and bare a sakke,
And what men yave hem laid it on his bakke."

From these perversions of the original law of mendicancy, the priests of Budha are guarded by the rules laid down by their founder, which do not allow a single word to be spoken; and when the bowl is sufficiently filled, the priest is to return to his dwelling and eat the food he has received, of whatever kind it may be. They are sufficiently rapacious in other respects, and their love of litigation has brought discredit upon their order; but when carrying the alms-bowl I have never seen them otherwise than observant of the institute.

From some of the above quotations it would appear that the vessel carried by the mendicants for receiving the alms that were presented, was not always of the same description. The alms-bowl of the Budhist is a convenient article to carry, and answers all the purposes required by the priest, in countries where the green leaf, or the cocoa-nut shell, has not yet been superseded by articles of more complicated manufacture. There were some of the ancient ascetics in the east who went upon all fours, and ate their food like dogs. It is said, that when Diogenes saw a boy drink water out of the hollow of his hand, he took the cup from his wallet and threw it away, saying that the boy had exceeded him in frugality. The mendicant friars had a wallet or sack into which they put the provisions they received, and the Franciscans are represented as having their tunics full of pockets made for the same purpose. They sometimes took persons with them to collect money, as they were not allowed to receive it themselves; but this was contrary to an express rule, as the Franciscans are forbidden (cap. iv.) to receive it in any form whatever, either themselves or by a substitute, "vel per se, vel per interpositam personam." There was a complaint (Alvarus Pelagius, ii. 6) against the Franciscans, that some of the brethren wandered through countries and cities, soliciting and demanding pecuniary alms, frequently with great importunity, taking the servant backward, and filling their boxes and pockets with money; and that some received money, either with wax, or with wood, or with the cloak, and carried it about sewed up in their habits, tunics, or hoods.

In whatever country religious mendicancy is practised, the virtue of almsgiving will be raised to an undue elevation in the scale of merit. The ancient chronicles say that it was customary for the monarchs of Ceylon to give annually five times their own weight of treasure in alms. In an inscription at Pollonnaruwa, about A. D. 1200, is is said that the king gave annually five times his own weight, and that of his two principal queens and son and daughter, of treasure, in alms to "the priests and the Brahmans." In 1818, Kappitapola was executed at Kandy for rebellion against the British government. Early in the morning he was taken to the temple, and as he knelt in the sanctuary the chief priest recounted the principal meritorious actions of his life, such as the benefits he had conferred on the priesthood, the gifts he had given to the temples, and other similar acts. He then pronounced his last wish, which was, that in the next birth he might be born in the forest of Himála and finally obtain nirwána. The priest, in an impressive manner, declared that his merits were great, and concluded a benediction by saying, "As sure as a stone thrown up into the air returns to the earth, so certainly will you, in consideration of your merit, be present at the next appearance of a Budha, and receive your reward."

When about to die, the rebel turned to the Commissioner, an English gentleman, and saying, "I give you a share of the merit of my last religious offering," he unwound his upper cloth from his waist, and presented it to the temple, jocularly observing, that although it was ragged and foul, "the merit of the offering would not on that account be diminished, it being all he had to give." *

From its necessary connexion with the circumstances of the recluse, and its prominence in the system of Gótama, it will be requisite to enter upon the subject of almsgiving somewhat at length, although many of the statements we shall have to make are puerile in the extreme, and would not in themselves, apart from the light they throw upon the system, justify the expenditure of the time that has been required for their compilation. The evils arising from this feature of the system appear to increase as years roll on; and in consequence, the greater number of the following narratives are probably the invention of a period comparatively recent. They are principally taken from the works that are at present the most popular among the Budhists of Ceylon.

The faithful are required to give in alms of that which they have honestly earned by their own personal exertions; this offering is called dána, which means literally "a gift." There must be a willing mind respecting that which they offer, from the time that the intention of making the offering is formed to the time when it is presented, as well as after it has been made. There must be no regret for that which has been given, no wish to regain it. That which is thus given with a pure mind must be given to the Budhas, the Pasé-Budhas (who arise in the period in which there is no supreme Budha, and discover intuitively the way to nirwána, but are unable to teach it to others), the rahats, or the priests. It is requisite that the thing given, the intention of the giver, and the receiver of the gift, be all pure.

It is ever the rule of the Budhas to proclaim first the reward to be received for the giving of alms, and then to enforce the observance of the precepts; just as a child has some plaything given to it, whether it be a mimic plough, a bell, the sticks used in the game called kalli, a little bow and arrow, or a cart; but when he arrives at riper years he has to work, in order that he may gain for himself a livelihood. In the same way, the physician, when about to administer medicine, first mollifies the body of the patient by

* Marshall's Description and Conquest of Ceylon.

anointing it with oil for three or four days. The giving of alms softens the mind, and brings it into subjection, by which the ascetic is prepared for the exercise of the rites he is afterwards to practise.

Púјáwa is allied to dána, and is the offering of flowers, lights, and rice. These must be presented continually to the three gems. There are four divisions of almsgiving when practised in relation to the priests, called siwpasadána. They are:—1. Chíwara-dána, the gift of robes. 2. Ahára-dána, the gift of food. 3. Sayanásana-dána, the gift of a pallet on which to recline. 4. Gilánapratya-dána, the gift of medicine or sick diet.

There is also a dána called sánghika, which is divided into seven kinds. 1. The giving of robes, food, &c. to a supreme Budha, or his immediate disciples; this is the chief of the seven. 2. The giving of these things to the priests and priestesses, when assembled together, with a relic of Budha in their midst. 3. The giving of these things to the priests alone, under similar circumstances. 4. The giving of these things to the priestesses alone, under similar circumstances. 5. The giving of anything to the priests and priestesses, when permission has been previously asked. 6. The giving of anything to an individual priest, when permission has been previously asked from a sangha, or chapter of not less than four priests. 7. The giving of anything to a priestess, under similar circumstances. The reward that will be received for the offering of any of these gifts is like the atoms of the earth, it cannot be computed.

Of all the modes of acquiring merit, that of almsgiving is the principal; it is the chief of the virtues that are requisite for the attainment of the Budhaship; it is the first of the four great virtues, viz. almsgiving, affability, promoting the prosperity of others, and loving others as ourselves; it is superior to the observance of the precepts, the path that all the Budhas have trod, a lineage to which they have all belonged.

When the gift, the giver, and the receiver are all pure, the reward is proportionately great. When the giver possesses that which is good, but presents in alms that which is bad, it is called dána-dása; when he gives according to that which he has, whether it be good or bad, it is dána-sahaya; when he himself retains that which is bad but presents that which is good, it is dána-pati. The giver must have purity of intention. When he presents the gift he must think, May it be to me as a hidden treasure, that I may find again greatly increased, in a future birth. And he must think both before and after the gift is presented, that he gives to one who is possessed of merit. When any one gives that which has been procured by his own labour, he will have as his reward wealth, but no retinue or attendants. When he gives that which he has received from others, he will have attendants, but no wealth. When he gives both kinds he will have both rewards; but when he gives neither, he will have neither of the rewards. Kála-dána is the giving of alms to strangers, travellers, and sick persons, and in times of famine, and the giving of the first-fruits whether of the garden or the field. When alms are given without thought or affection, or by the hand of another, or when they are thrown to the receiver disdainfully, or given only after long intervals, or without any hope of reward, it is asat-purusha-dána; when the reverse, it is sat-purusha-dána. There is no reward for him who gives intoxicating liquors, or makes offerings to the tirttaka heretics, or gives to those who only dance and play and sing or exhibit indecencies, or make obscene paintings in some public place; but in some instances there may be a reward for those who give to musicians and singers, as when alms are given to those who beat the drum at religious festivals, or to the priest who chaunts the bana.

When alms are given to some, and not to others, it is like a partial shower; when they are given to all, it is like a universal rain; but when any one only thinks to give, and does not give, it is like the gathering of the clouds and the thunder when there is no rain.

He who gives alms in a proper manner will have continued joy; he will be admitted to the society of the wise; his fame will spread on all the six sides, and reach as high as the brahma-lóka; and after death he will be born in one of the déwa-lókas. The reward for the giving of alms is not merely a benefit that is to be received at some future period; it promotes length of days, personal beauty, agreeable sensations, strength, and knowledge; and if the giver be born as a man, he will have all these advantages in an eminent degree.

That which follows was declared by Gótama to Uggradéwaputra:—"There is no reward, either in this world or the next, that may not be received through almsgiving. By means of it the glories of Sekra, Mára, and Maha-Brahma (rulers of the celestial worlds), the Chakrawartti, the rahats, the Pasé-Budhas, and the supreme Budha are received."

When the five virtues of almsgiving are exercised, i. e. faith, observance of the precepts, the hearing of bana, liberality, and wisdom, the reward is appointed, whether it be in the brahma-lóka, déwa-lóka, or world of men, according to the wish formed by the giver; but when alms are presented without these virtues, no reward is specially appointed, as a piece of wood when thrown into the air falls to the ground on any of its sides, just as it happens.

There are some gifts that have a great reward from the giver, and none from the receiver; some that have the same from the receiver, and none from the giver; some that have a reward from both; and others that have a reward from neither. If the gift be presented with a pure mind, though the receiver be bad, it will be rewarded, as when Wessantara presented his children to the brahman Jújaka, who was a bad man. Sometimes the giver is bad, and the receiver good; but if both be bad the reward is small. A hunter once gave alms to one who did not observe the precepts, in order to benefit his brother who was a préta sprite, but he derived no benefit therefrom. The hunter then gave alms to one who did observe the precepts, and his brother was released from the préta-birth.

If a vessel be made clean, and water be given from it, even to a worm, the gift will receive a reward; how then can the full reward be told of those who give to men?

If any one gives food to dogs, crows, &c. with the intention of receiving merit, he will have long life, prosperity, beauty, power, and wisdom, in a hundred births. If any one gives food to a man who does not keep the precepts, with the same intention, he will have a similar reward in a thousand births; if he gives food to one who keeps the precepts, but is not acquainted with the dharmma, he will receive a similar reward in myriads of births; if to an upásaka, an asankya of births (the asankya being a number that requires 141 figures to express it); and yet more, in accumulative proportion, if to a sámanéra, an upasampadá, one who has entered the paths, a rahat, a Pasé-Budha, and a supreme Budha. In this proportion the reward accumulates:—according to the earth in a threshing-floor, in four miles, in sixteen miles, in the earth, in a sakwala.

In a former age Bódhisat was the son of a brahman, and was educated along with 100,000 princes from various parts of Jambudwípa. When their education was completed, all the princes invited him to go and live with them; but he chose to reside at Benares, where he became the king's próhita, or prime minister. Each of the princes went every year to see the king, and whenever they went they took rich presents for the minister. After some time, he gave away all these presents in alms to beggars; and the giving of the whole occupied seven years and seven months; he gave golden alms-bowls, couches, chariots, elephants, and many other treasures. But the giving of food, on one single occasion, to any one who has entered the first path that leads to nirwána, would produce greater merit to the giver than all the gifts of the próhita. The giving of alms to one in the second path produces greater merit by one hundred times than when given to one in the first path; and when given to one in the third, it produces greater merit by one hundred times than when given to one in the second; and when given to a rahat, produces greater merit by one hundred times than when given to one in the third path. When given to a Pasé-Budha, it produces greater merit by one hundred times than when given to a rahat. But when given to a supreme Budha it produces greater merit by sixteen times multiplied by itself sixteen times than when given to a Pasé-Budha. We will suppose that there are rows of thrones upon which the disciples of Budha are seated, extending from one end of Jambudwípa to the other, and that there are ten rows occupied by those who have entered the first path; five by those who have entered the second path; two and a-half by those who have entered the third path; one and a-half by rahats; and one by Pasé-Budhas. Now if all these were to receive an offering of alms, the merit of such an offering would be immensely great; but a single offering made to a supreme Budha would surpass even this in merit.

The narratives that illustrate the greatness of the reward to be received from the giving of alms are almost innumerable. They appear to vie with each other in the absurdity of their character; and therefore a small selection from them will be regarded as more than sufficient.

When the Bódhisat Suméda was in the forest of Himála, a rishi, or holy sage, came to him and offered him three flowers. By this act the sage was saved during the whole of 30,000 kalpas from being born in hell; he was always either a déwa or a man, and when born as man, he was always either of the royal or brahman caste. He was 500 times a déwa; 300 times Sekra; and in the time of Gótama, when he was a respectable brahman in Rajagaha, he entered the priesthood, and became a rahat.

A florist named Sumana, who resided in Rajagaha, and presented to a former Budha eight nosegays of jessamine flowers, received in the same birth elephants, horses, sons, daughters, females beautifully arrayed, and villages, eight of each; and eight of all kinds of ornaments, gems, and robes; was preserved from being born in hell during a hundred thousand kalpas, received blessings without number in the world of men; at last became the Pasé-Budha Sumana, and attained nirwána.

There was a poor weaver, who resided near the mansion of a charitable nobleman, and when beggars enquired the way to it, he was accustomed to point out the road with his finger. For this he was afterwards born as the déwa of a tree, and by the lifting up of his finger he could in a moment produce whatever he desired.

One day Budha and his priests went to a certain village to receive alms, but the people were unwilling to give them so much as a drop of water, until a female servant gave them a little from a vessel. As the water was poured out it did not become less, though she gave to all the priests. For this charitable act, she was afterwards born as a déwi.

There was a family in Rajagaha, all the members of which fell sick and died, except one woman, who escaped from the house through a hole made in the wall.* When at a little distance from the house she was approached by the priest Kásyapa, who was carrying the alms-bowl at the time, but as she had only a little dirty rice-gruel, she thought it was too mean to present as an offering. The priest however continued to remain near her, and as she thought it was out of kindness, she presented to him the gruel. For this she was born in the highest déwa-loka; but she had also acquired great merit in previous births.

There was a king of Ceylon, Síla Maha Tissa, who reigned in great splendour at Anurádhapura. In the earlier years of his reign, as he had heard that the most meritorious alms are such as are given from that which has been procured by personal labour, he

* There is a disease called ahiwátaka-róga, supposed to be caused by a pestilential blast, mixed with the breath of poisonous serpents, that comes upon a dwelling, when the flies first die; then the lizards and other reptiles; afterwards cats, dogs, goats, and cattle; and last of all human beings. There is no escape from it but by bursting through the wall; to depart through the door would be certain death.

went in disguise to the harvest field, where he worked as a common labourer; and when he received the walahana, the portion of rice that fell to his share as wages, he presented it to the priest Maha Suma. After this he worked three years in a sugar plantation, near the mountain Swarnnagiri, and gave the sugar that he received as wages to the priests. Thus he who had thousands of treasure and many thousands of attendants, worked with his own hands, that he might give the produce in alms.

In the time of Gótama Budha there was in the city of Sewet a rich man, who died, and the king of Kósala became the inheritor of his property. On going to worship Budha the king was late; and when the sage asked the reason, he replied, "There was a rich man in our city, who had plenty of good food, but he would eat only that which was common; when proper garments were brought to him he refused them, and made his clothes of pieces of rags; he went about in a shabby cart, covered by a leaf; he is now dead, and as he has no relative to be his heir, I have taken possession of his wealth, which has detained me beyond the usual hour." Budha then said, "If there be a pond infested with devils, the people are afraid to approach it; they do not bathe in it, nor do they drink the water; and as there is no benefit from it, it is allowed to dry up. In like manner, the wealth of the unwise man is of no benefit to himself, his parents, his wife, or his children. The rich man of whom you speak had no advantage from his wealth in this world, and he will have none in the next; he is now in the Rowra hell." The king enquired how it was that he had so much wealth, and no heart to enjoy it; when Budha informed him that in a former birth he resided in Benares, a most uncharitable man; but as he was one day going to the king's palace he met a Pasé-Budha seeking alms, upon which he commanded one of his attendants to take him to his house, and order some food to be given to him. His wife thought this was something new, and gave him food of the richest kind, which he received but did not eat, as he began to say bana. On the rich man's return he looked into the alms-bowl, and when he saw its contents, he thought, "If this had been given to my cattle or my slaves, it might have done me some good." "For ordering this food," said Gótama, "his reward was the wealth he has just left; but for afterwards regretting that food so good had been given, he was prevented from enjoying it." Thus it is necessary that what is given be given freely, with a spirit free from covetousness.

In Rajagaha there was a man whose employment it was to cut sugar-cane. One day, as he was walking along with a bundle of canes over his shoulder, he was followed by an upásaka, carrying a child, which cried for some of the cane. At first he refused to give it any; but afterwards threw for it a piece behind him. In the next birth he became a préta, and lived near a grove of sugar-cane; but when from hunger he went to take any of the canes that he might eat them, they bent down and struck him, so that he had no means of appeasing his hunger. It happened that Mugalan (one of the principal disciples of Gótama Budha) passed that way, to whom the préta made known what had occurred to him; when the priest informed him that it was in consequence of what he had done to a child in a former birth; but he recommended him to try and seize the canes, with his face turned away from them, in the same manner as he had thrown the cane to the child; which he did. The préta afterwards gave a cane to Mugalan as an offering, who presented part of it to Budha; and in the next birth the sprite became a déwa. Thus that which is given must be presented in a kind manner and with affection.

In a former age Gótama Bódhisat was a man of wealth, and as he was exceedingly charitable, he afterwards became Sekra. His descendants for four generations were also charitable, and went to the same déwa-lóka; but the fifth was a great miser. Sekra therefore called these déwas, and informing them that the merit of the family was now about to pass away, he directed them all to put on the appearance of brahmans, and go to the door of their former dwelling to ask alms. The first who went was ordered away; but he repeated a stanza, for which he received permission to remain. The same occurrence happened to them all. Then the rich man told his slave to give them rice in the husk, but they would not receive it; then unboiled rice, but they still refused it; and afterwards such rice, boiled, as is given to oxen; but when they attempted to eat it, it stuck in their throats, and they fell down as if dead. The master therefore told his slaves to take the rice away, and put in its stead such rice as he himself was accustomed to eat; after which he called together the citizens, and said that as he had given them good rice, it was no fault of his that they were choked. Then Sekra assumed the appearance of a déwa, and exposed his deception; but he also gave him good advice, telling him the merit of giving alms, by means of which he was induced to become charitable, and continued so until the day of his death, after which he was born a déwa. Thus, such food must be given as is commonly used, when alms are presented, and not that which is of an inferior kind.

A great feast was to be given to Piyumatura Budha and his priests, in a former age, by the citizens of Benares. The scribes went round from house to house, to know how many priests each householder would feed. Some gave their names for ten, and some for four hundred, according to their ability; but there was a poor labourer who could only put his name down to feed one; and he resolved that he would work a whole day, and devote whatever he received in wages to procure food for the priest. On arriving at home he informed his wife of the promise he had made, and she determined to assist him. The next day they both worked hard, and received good wages, with which they purchased the articles that were requisite for the feast. The merit of the couple being observed by Sekra, he went in disguise as a cook to the house, and requested employment. They told him their intention and circumstances; but he agreed to assist them without wages, if they were unable to pay him. When all was ready, the man went to the scribe to enquire what priest he was to have; but the scribe told him that, as he was so poor a man, he had paid no more attention to the matter. The labourer, on hearing this was sorely disappointed, and began to weep; when the bystanders, who had been attracted to the place by his expressions of sorrow, recommended him to go and inform Piyumatura. Accordingly he went at once to the wihára, and Budha, who was at that moment coming out of his residence, put the alms-bowl in his hand, though kings and nobles were waiting to receive it, who offered him untold treasures if he would give it up; but he still retained it. Budha went to his house, and partook of the food that had been prepared, which filled the whole city with its fragrance. As a reward for his charitable act, Sekra filled the labourer's house with jewels; he was afterwards ennobled by the king, and, when he died, was born in a déwa-lóka.

In the time of Dípankara Budha, Gótama Bódhisat was a rich man in Benares, who gave alms in such abundance that the whole of Jambudwípa was as if "all the ploughs had been hung up:" all persons ceased from labour. When Sekra saw this he became alarmed, (thinking that the merit of the rich man would be so great as to entitle him to receive the office he himself then held as ruler of a celestial world) and destroyed all his remaining substance, except a sickle, a cord, and a yoke. With these Bódhisat went to cut grass, resolving to give half his earnings to the poor; but when he saw so many in destitute circumstances he gave away the whole, and his wife and he had nothing to eat for the space of six days. At last he fainted away, when in the act of cutting grass. At this moment Sekra appeared to him, and offered to return him all his substance if he would cease to give alms; but he refused to make a promise to this effect. However, as Sekra now found out that he did not do this to obtain his throne in Tawutisá, he became propitious to him, and gave him an immensity of wealth.

There was a certain noble who did not keep the precepts, but he one day presented a mango to a priestess. When he died, he was next born, by night a déwa with a thousand beautiful attendants, and by day a préta; by night his body was like a flower of the garden, but by day like fire; by night he had the usual number of fingers, but by day he had two claws. Thus he was alternately punished for his crimes, and rewarded for the giving of the mango.

When Gótama, in the seventh year after he became Budha, went to the Tawutisá déwa-lóka, Ankura and Indaka were the first of the déwas who went to hear bana. Even before the arrival of Sekra, Maha Brahma, Mahéswara, and the other principal déwas, they approached the teacher of the three worlds. Indaka took his station on the right hand, and Ankura on the left; but as the déwas successively arrived, Ankura gradually receded to a greater distance, until he was twelve yojanas from Budha, whilst Indaka remained at his original station. Before Budha commenced the saying of bana to the assembled déwas, he declared to them how it was that this difference had been caused. "In a former birth," said the sage, "Ankura presented an offering twelve yojanas in extent, and gave alms continually during 10,000 years; but he gave always to the unworthy, as there were none in existence at that period who possessed merit. On the other hand, Indaka gave only a single spoonful of rice to the priest Anurudha. It is on account of the difference in the merit of those who received their respective gifts, that Indaka remains at my right hand, whilst Ankura retires to a distance." In like manner, when the husbandman scatters his seed in bad ground, though it be ever so much in quantity, the produce is small; whilst he who scatters his seed in good ground, though the quantity be small, gains an abundant harvest.

In this manner we might proceed, heaping together in palling profusion similar instances of the fertility of man's imagination, when that which concerns his subsistence is the object of regard. The noble principle implanted in the heart by God of sympathy, charity, or love, has in all ages been seized upon by men, who are either to be charged with selfishness, or with extreme ignorance of the teachings of the word of inspiration. How mournful the feeling that enters the spirit at the reading of such passages as the following, from the page of Chrysostom! "The fire," says he, speaking of the lamps carried by the virgins mentioned in the parable, "is virginity, and the oil is alms-giving. And in like manner as the flame, unless supplied with a stream of oil, disappears, so virginity, unless it have alms-giving, is extinguished. . . . Hast thou a penny, purchase heaven. . . . Heaven is on sale, and in the market, and yet ye mind it not! Give a crust, and take back paradise; give the least, and receive the greatest; give the perishable, and receive the imperishable; give the corruptible, and receive the incorruptible. . . . Alms are the redemption of the soul. . . . Almsgiving, which is able to break the chain of thy sins. . . . Almsgiving, the queen of virtues, and the readiest of all ways of getting into heaven, and the best advocate there." * St. Eligius, or Eloi, in the seventh century, exhorts the people to make oblations to the church, that when our Lord comes to judgment they may be able to say, "Da, Domine, quia dedimus." † Again, in a similar strain, Edgar says of this virtue, "Oh, excellent almsgiving! Oh, worthy reward of the soul! Oh, salutary remedy of our sins!" It was usual to recommend this mode of obtaining liberation from guilt. Nor were arguments wanting to set forth the propriety of this course.

> "For many a man so hard is of herte,
> He may not wepe although him sore smerte:
> Therefore in stede of weping and praieres,
> Men mote give silver to the poure freres."
>
> *Chaucer's Prologue*, v. 229.

By the exercise of charity the sick were taught to expect cures. The rich, as well as the poor, were accustomed to put a written schedule of their sins under the cloth which covered the altar of a

* Taylor's Ancient Christianity.
† Mosheim's Ecclesiastical History.

favourite saint, accompanied by a donation; and a day or two afterwards, when they re-examined the schedule, the virtues of the saint had converted it into a blank.*

Here we must pause. If these statements be true; if this be the appointment of God, how are we to reconcile with it the declarations of Scripture, that represent the redemption of man as requiring for its accomplishment the richest ransom that the whole universe can provide? Either these ancient teachers were mistaken, or Jesus of Nazareth died in vain. But, as Christ is "the wisdom of God," "in whom are hid all the treasures of wisdom and knowledge," all his acts must be invested with an infinite propriety and fitness; and it must have behoved him to suffer. Therefore, if man would seek to enter heaven, it must be by the method that He has appointed. Our hope of immortality cannot be fixed upon saintly absolution purchased by an obolus; the merits in which we are to trust are those of Him, "in whom we have redemption through his blood, the forgiveness of sins, according to the riches of his grace; wherein he hath abounded toward us in all wisdom and prudence." Apart from this trust, and the charity welling up from the purity of principle it instils, I may bestow all my goods to feed the poor, and give my body to be burned, but it will profit me nothing. Yet, how full of all that is beautiful are the arrangements of God! We need not look out for some rahat or Budha upon whom to bestow our alms, lest we fail of receiving an adequate reward. In the day when the eternal crowns shall be distributed to the victors of the cross, "the King shall answer and say unto them, Verily I say unto you, inasmuch as ye have done it unto one of the least of these my brethren, ye have done it unto me." How affecting the example that is presented for our imitation! "Ye know the grace of our Lord Jesus Christ, that, though he was rich, yet for your sakes he became poor, that ye through his poverty might be rich." "Walk in love, as Christ also hath loved us, and hath given himself for us." How exact, how discriminating, how powerfully impressive, are the words of the law! "As ye have opportunity, do good unto all men." "To do good and to communicate forget not, for with such sacrifices God is well pleased." Where little is given, little is required; where much is given, much is required. "Not grudgingly, or of necessity, for God loveth a cheerful giver."

* Fosbroke's British Monachism.

IX. THE DIET.

In taking upon himself the ten obligations, the priest of Budha resolves, according to the fifth, to refrain from the use of intoxicating drinks, as it is said that they lead to indifference towards religion. But the use of animal food is not absolutely forbidden; and in the whole economy of the institute there is a general indifference upon this question, which is in powerful contrast to the requirements of other orders of ascetics. This may have arisen from the fact that Gótama Budha died from eating pork; a circumstance too well known to be set aside by the more rigid of his disciples, who might otherwise have been ready to insist upon a dietetic discipline more extensive in its prohibitions. But although in certain cases, as in times of sickness, animal food is allowed, there are many regulations intended to guard against the abuse of this privilege.

We shall generally find that, when any of our natural desires are debarred the indulgence that they seek, the other appetites, that are not under the same restraint, will exert their liberty with the greater freedom. Hence it is to be supposed that the founder of an ascetic institute will here meet with one of his greatest perplexities. And his task is the more difficult, as eating and drinking cannot, like a luxury or a mere vanity, be entirely forbidden. The laws of the priesthood, as they appear in the Pátimokkhan, are numerous and comprehensive; but there is no rule relative to diet the breach of which is attended with permanent exclusion, suspension, or penance. The people of Ceylon not unfrequently express their displeasure against the priests, on the ground that they urge them to bring meat curries as offerings, whilst vegetable preparations are received with disdain. They appear to have degenerated since the time of Robert Knox, who says, "The people reckon it one of the chief points of godness to abstain from eating any flesh at all, because they would not have any hand, or anything to do, in killing any living thing; they reckon herbs and plants more genial food."

According to the Pátimokkhan, no priest is allowed to partake of food after the sun has passed the meridian. When ghee, butter, oil, honey, sugar, or other articles included in what is regarded as sick diet are received, they may not be kept in store by the priest more than seven days; unless in case of sickness, he may not receive food more than one day at a place where provisions are prepared for a number of persons; unless upon authorised occasions, he may not partake of food provided expressly for a number of priests; he may not, unless upon authorised occasions, eat his ordinary meal before going by invitation to any place to receive an offering of food; when, at any place, more than two or three bowls full of rice or other grain are presented to him, he may not accept them, unless he share them with the other priests; when a meal is given at any house, he may not, after receiving it, partake of food given by another person; no priest shall tempt another priest, who has already partaken of a meal given by invitation, to eat more, unless it be of food reserved from the same occasion; the priest may not partake of food reserved from the previous day; unless when sick, he may not solicit such luxuries as ghee, butter, oil, honey, sugar, fish and flesh, milk or curds; he may not with his own hand give food to a naked or wandering ascetic; when going with the alms-bowl, he may not enter a house; when invited, along with other priests, to partake of food at any place, he may not go before or after the appointed time, unless he inform the other priests; when any one offers to provide the proper diet for a priest in case he should be sick, he may not avail himself of it after the lapse of four months from the time it is given; he may not receive food from the alms-bowl of a priestess; unless when sick, he may not go to the house of one of the faithful (out of the ordinary course) to receive refreshments, without an invitation; and the priest who resides in a dangerous place, and has food brought to him, must warn those who bring it of their danger.

The food given in alms to the priest is to be received by him meditatively; it is not to be received carelessly, so that in the act of being poured into the alms-bowl some may fall over the sides; the liquor and the solid food are to be received together, without being separated; and the alms-bowl is not to be piled up above the mouth. The food is also to be eaten meditatively, with care, so that it is not scattered about; without picking and choosing, the particles that come first to hand being first to be eaten; the liquor and the solid food are to be eaten together, not beginning in the centre, and heaping the food up, nor covering the liquor with rice. The priest, unless when sick, may not ask for rice or curry to eat; he may not look with envy into the bowl of another; nor eat mouthfuls larger than a pigeon's egg, but in small round balls; he may not fill the mouth, nor put the hand into the mouth when taking food; nor talk when his mouth is full; nor allow particles to drop from his mouth; nor swallow his food without being properly masticated; and one mouthful must be swallowed before another is taken. He may not shake his hand to free it from the particles that may be attached to it, nor may the food be scattered about, nor the tongue put out, nor the lips smacked, nor the food sucked up with a noise. He may not lick his hands, nor the bowl, nor his lips, when he eats. A vessel of water may not be taken up when the hand is soiled from eating, and the rincing of the bowl is not to be carelessly thrown away. No priest can partake of food unless he be seated.

It will be remarked, that the rules relative to the manner of eating are here laid down with the utmost precision. We can imagine that, at the commencement of Budhism, as men of all grades were admitted to the priesthood, many rudenesses would be exhibited that would be extremely offensive in the sight of the prince whose doctrines they had embraced; and that it could only be by a series of regulations stooping down to the commonest acts they would be prevented from bringing the priestly character into contempt. It was therefore necessary to make laws, not only as to the quantity and character of the food, but also as to the manner in which it was to be eaten. From this we have an insight into the manners of the times, in reference to a class of society to which the ancient historian seldom directed his attention, owing to whose neglect in this particular we are ignorant of the manners of the mass, even when the conduct of monarchs and nobles is recorded with a fulness that is offensive.

The hours in which it is forbidden to eat food are called wikála. The appointed hours are from sunrise to the end of the fifteenth hour, i. e. until the sun has passed the meridian. The food that is eaten in any other part of the day or night is called wikála-bhójana; and by the sixth of the ten obligations the priest professes that he will reject this untimely or unseasonable food.*

The priests are commanded by Budha to be contented with as much as is requisite to appease their hunger, when they take the alms-bowl from house to house, and not to loiter on the ground; as those who eat more than a sufficient quantity will be led to take life and steal, and commit the five deadly sins, whilst those who are temperate will be enabled readily to keep the precepts, and practise

* Sadharmmaratnakáré.

all the ordinances that are prescribed. There were a certain number of parrots in the Himalayan forest that went from tree to tree, feeding upon the fruits they found; but there was one parrot that always remained upon the same tree, and when it died, it fed upon the bark. This was seen by Sekra, who as a reward for the moderation of the parrot, caused the tree to live again, and to put forth leaves and fruit. This example is worthy of being imitated by the priests.*

At one time Seriyut and Mugalan (the two principal priests of Gótama Budha) went into a forest for the benefit of solitude; but Mugalan fell sick. When Seriyut asked him if he had ever been attacked in the same way before, he said that he had when young; and when he further asked by what means he had been cured, he said that his mother had made him a confection of certain ingredients. This was overheard by a déwa that resided in a neighbouring tree, who went and informed the persons of a house where Seriyut was accustomed to go to receive alms. The ingredients required for the confection were therefore put into his bowl, and he took them to the sick priest. When Mugalan looked with his divine eyes to see by what means this had been brought about, he saw that it was through what he himself had said. But as it was given through what he had said, and to receive it would have been contrary to the precept, he threw the whole away; in that instant, however, the pain left him, and never returned again, though he lived afterwards forty-five years.

There was a priest in Chíwara Gumba who, when suffering from hunger, would not eat the fruit that had fallen from a tree, because it had not been given him by the owner; rather than break the precept by eating it, he suffered life to become nearly extinct, and was found in this condition by an upásaka, who took him upon his back, and while thus carried he attained rahatship.

On one occasion, when Gótama and his priests were in Weranja, a famine prevailed so extensively that the priests were not able to procure any food from the people when going from house to house with the alms-bowl; and they were compelled to live on some hard barley-cakes used as provender for horses.† The priest Mugalan requested permission to exert his supernatural power in order to obtain food, but the exercise was forbidden by Budha.

* Milinda Prasna.

† Gogerly's Essay on Budhism, Journ. Ceylon Royal As. Soc. i. 79.

The priest is not to eat as a pastime, nor for pleasure; nor to make the body strong, like the public wrestlers; nor to render it beautiful, like the dancers. As a man with a falling house props it up, as a man with a broken waggon puts in a piece of wood; so may the priest eat to preserve his body and prevent untimely death. As hunger is the most powerful of all the appetites, he may eat to ward it off. As a man and woman, when crossing a vast desert with a child, if their food fails them, eat the flesh of their own child in their anxiety to escape from the desert, with similar disgust must the priest eat his food, that he may escape from the evils of existence.*

It is said in the Wisudhi Margga Sanné, that there are ten modes of defilement (pratikúla sangignyá) produced by food, as seen under the following circumstances. 1. In going to the place where it is to be received. 2. Its reception. 3. The act of eating. 4. The ingredients with which it combines. 5. Its place of deposit. 6. Before it is digested. 7. After it is digested. 8. The fruit it produces. 9. Its discharge or emission. 10. The pollution from its touch.

1. In the journey that the priest must undertake to procure food, he will have to pass along roads that are difficult, dangerous, and dirty; he will be exposed to wind and cold; and he will see many disagreeable objects, filth of all kinds. 2. As he waits in different places to receive food, insects will come from dirty places and settle on his robe, and in his bowl; some persons will tell him to go away, whilst others will take no notice of him whatever, or look at him as if he were a thief, or perhaps abuse him; and in passing from place to place he will have to encounter foul smells and tread on many kinds of refuse. 3. In eating the food there will be many things to cause shame; the tongue must do the work of the hand, and before the food is swallowed it must be made of the consistence of the vomit thrown up by a dog. 4. When the food has passed into the stomach it becomes foul and corrupt. Even in the bodies of the Chakrawarttis and Budhas there are bile, phlegm, and blood. If the bile be too abundant, the food that has been eaten will become like mee oil; if the phlegm be too abundant, it will become like the juice of the keliya or nágabála fruit; and if the blood be too abundant, it will become like red dye. 5. The place to which the food descends is not a vessel of gold; in a child ten years of

* Wisudhi Margga Sanné.

age it is like a privy that has been used as many years without being cleaned, increasing in loathsomeness with the age of the individual. 6. When a shower in the hot season falls upon a village inhabited by low people, it runs into the cess at the extremity of the place, abounding with all kinds of filth; and when the sun arises froth and bubbles are formed upon the surface of this compost. In like manner, when food is taken into the body, in a little time it is mixed with all kinds of impure secretions, and the jataragni, or digestive fire, working upon the mass, causes it to appear with a surface like that of the compost. 7. When the food is digested, it does not become gold or gems, but is changed into excrement and urine. 8. The food passes away from the body by the nine apertures, but principally by the intestinal passage; and a part of it is ejected by the pores of the skin. 10. When the food is eaten it soils the fingers, teeth, and tongue; and even by continual washing it is not possible to take away the defilement and smell.

These are the ten modes by which the defilement arising from food is exhibited; and they are steadily to be meditated on by the priest, that the desire of food may be taken away. By this means, though nirwána should not be obtained, it will secure an inheritance in one of the celestial worlds.

The third of the Thirteen Ordinances is called Pindapátikanga, from pinda, pieces or morsels, and páta, falling, from the falling of the particles of food into the bowl of the priest. He who keeps this ordinance cannot receive food which has been given under any of the following circumstances:—for the sake of an assemblage of priests; that which has been given at an appointed time, or by invitation; that which is given to a certain number of priests, by sending them a tally, or some instrument upon which the number of the priests that are invited is marked: food given on a certain number of days in each half-moon; on the days called póya; on the day after the full-moon póya: food prepared for priests who are strangers, after their arrival; for priests who are going on a journey; for sick priests; for those priests who minister to their sick companions: food given statedly to a temple; regularly and constantly given; or given by the people of any village on certain appointed days. Thus there are fourteen different descriptions of food that are not to be received by the priest who keeps this ordinance. When food has been prepared for the assembly, it may be received by the priest without breaking the law if he has not been told for what purpose it was originally intended; or he may receive it from any place where food is given to an assembly regularly and without interruption, under certain circumstances.

When the priest who keeps the superior ordinance goes with the bowl to receive food, he may receive it from the house either immediately before or behind him, or from the halls where food is constantly given; but should any one say, "Do not carry the bowl to-day; I will take what is necessary to the place where you dwell," he may not receive the food that in this way is offered. He who keeps the middle ordinance may in this way receive food that is not more than sufficient for one day; but if the person offers to bring it the next day, it must be refused. The inferior ordinance allows the food to be thus received on three successive days, but not longer.

The second of the Twelve Sacred Observances of the Chinese is also called pin'd'apâtika, according to which the priest is to procure his food by taking the bowl, in order that he may extinguish all desire. He may not accept the invitation of any one. He must seek the nourishment that is necessary for the support of his material body and the accomplishment of his moral duties. He must make no difference with the food he receives, whether it be good or bad, nor feel any resentment in cases where he meets with a refusal, but keep his mind at all times in perfect tranquillity.*

The fifth of the Thirteen Ordinances is called Ekásanikanga, from eka, one, and ásana, a seat. He who keeps this ordinance may not eat food in two or three different places; he is to remain on one seat until he has finished his repast. When in the refectory he must look out for a proper seat, so that if a superior priest were to come in, he may not have to rise, in order to give place to him. Chúlábaya, learned in the sacred books, spake thus:—It is not proper to rise until the repast be finished; if the priest has sat down, but not begun to eat, he may rise; but if he has begun to eat, he may not rise, and if it should be required of him to rise, he may not sit down again to eat.

The priest who keeps the superior ordinance cannot receive more food than that which he has when he first sits down, though it be ever so little in quantity; but he may receive oil or honey, or anything that is allowed as sick diet, when he is not in health. He

* Remusat's Relation des Royaumes Bouddhiques, p. 60.

who keeps the middle ordinance may receive anything that is given to him previous to the end of his repast. He who keeps the inferior ordinance may receive more food, even though his repast be done, if he has not risen from his seat. He who eats again after he has risen from his seat breaks this ordinance.

The fourth of the Twelve Sacred Observances of the Chinese is called eka pânika, and is said to mean the rejection of a multiplicity of repasts, and the adopting of the custom of having one only.*

The sixth of the Thirteen Ordinances is called Pattapindikanga, from patta, the alms-bowl, and pinda, morsels. He who keeps this ordinance must eat from one vessel only. If he have at the same time liquid food and solid, he may eat first the one and then the other, but he may not put them in two separate vessels. If flesh has been put to the liquid, it must still be eaten without thinking of its disagreeable qualities, even though loathing should be caused; yet if vomiting follow, on the next occasion on which it is received, it may be separated from the other food. If any one receive sugar or honey, or anything else that is good to be taken with the liquid, they may be taken together. Though the priest eats from one vessel only, he may not take more than a proper quantity; all that he eats must first be put in the alms-bowl, even though it were something he might take in his fingers, as pepper-pods; what others might put on a leaf, must not by him be so put.

The priest who keeps the superior ordinance may throw away the refuse of sugar-cane, when he has sucked the juice, but all other things that are in the bowl he must eat; he may not break flesh, cakes, or any other substance, either with his teeth, hands, or an instrument, in order to divide it. He who keeps the middle ordinance may break his food with one hand, whilst holding the bowl with the other. He who keeps the inferior ordinance may break anything that is put into the bowl, in any way whatever. Any of the three who eats from a second vessel breaks this ordinance.

The seventh of the Thirteen Ordinances is called Khalupach'há-bhattikanga, from khalu, forbidden; pach'há, after; and bhatta, period of time: khalu is also a bird, that when eating any fruit, if it lets it fall, eats no more that day. The priest who keeps this ordinance cannot eat any more after he has met with that which is

* Remusat's Relation des Royaumes Bouddhiques.

akapa, i.e. if he has, for any reason, to refuse that which is brought to him when he is eating; or if he be presented with that which is improper to be eaten, from its loathsomeness or otherwise.

He who keeps the superior ordinance may only eat that which is in his mouth, and nothing more, although even the first handful of food that he takes is akapa. He who keeps the middle ordinance may eat that which is akapa but nothing more. He who keeps the inferior ordinance may eat as long as he remains on one seat.

The fifth of the Twelve Sacred Observances of the Chinese is called in Sanskrit khaloupas'waddhaktinka, and is said to enjoin that the food obtained by the mendicant is to be divided into three portions; one to be given to any person whom he sees to be suffering from hunger, and a second to be carried to some quiet place in the forest, and placed upon a stone for the birds and beasts. If he does not meet with any one who is in want, he is not to eat the whole of the food that he has received, but two-thirds only. By this means his body will be lighter and more active, and his digestion quicker and less laboured. He will be able readily to enter upon the practice of all good works. When any one eats too greedily, the intestines and belly become gross, and respiration is impeded. Nothing is more hurtful to the development of reason.*

It is said in the Wisudhi Margga Sanné that the priest who keeps the Thirteen Ordinances is to avoid the usual food of men, as ghee, honey, and sugar; and live on such things as galls and the urine of goats.

By many of the Budhists it is considered to be an act of great merit to make a vow never to partake of food without giving a portion to the priests. On one occasion, the monarch Duttagámini thus meditated :—In my childhood, my father and mother administered an oath to me, that I should never make a meal without sharing it with the priesthood. Have I, or have I not, ever partaken of a meal without sharing it with the priesthood? While thus pondering, he recollected that he had eaten a round chilly, or pepper-pod, at his morning meal, in a moment of abstraction, without reserving any part of it for the priesthood. He therefore decided that it was requisite for him to perform penance on that account, and he afterwards built a dágoba and wihára to expiate the crime.†

The subject of diet has not only engaged the anxious attention of

* Remusat's Relation des Royaumes Bouddhiques.
† Turnour's Mahawanso, cap. xxvi.

the founders of monastic institutions, but has also been regarded by legislators and moralists who have been under no such influence as the superstitions of the ascetic. It would be seen at once that the use of food, either to an excessive degree, or when prepared in a luxurious manner, unfitted men for the right performance of religious exercises, and that intoxicating liquors taken to excess had a moral effect still more to be reprehended. Hence the enforcement of various prohibitions relative to the quality and quantity of food; in some instances, however, applying only to particular classes of individuals, or to certain seasons. The brahman student is to beware of eating anything between morning and evening.* According to the Institutes of Manu (v. 51, 52, 53), "he who makes the flesh of an animal his food, is a principal in its slaughter; not a mortal exists more sinful than he who, without an oblation to the manes or gods, desires to enlarge his own flesh with the flesh of another creature: the man who performs annually for a hundred years, an aswamédha, or sacrifice of a horse, and the man who abstains from flesh-meat, enjoy for their virtue an equal reward." The only fast required of the Jews was on the great day of atonement. On one occasion Daniel mourned "full three weeks," and during this period "ate no pleasant bread," nor did flesh or wine come into his mouth.—Dan. x. 2. The Hebrew priests were not allowed to drink wine or strong drink when they went into the tabernacle of the congregation, Lev. x. 9; but it was supposed that they did not break this command if they drank no more than a log, or an egg-shell and a-half. By the regulations of the Orphic brotherhood the use of animal food was forbidden. The Essenes were permitted to partake of only a single plate of one kind of food; and as they took an oath at the time of their initiation, not to partake of any food that was not cooked by one of their own number, those who for any fault were excommunicated from their society were reduced to extreme distress, and sometimes perished from hunger. The rule prescribed by Manes may be sufficient to represent the practices of the early heretics. He insisted upon an entire abstinence from flesh, eggs, milk, fish, wine, and all intoxicating drinks; and his disciples were to support their shrivelled and emaciated bodies with bread, herbs, pulse, and melons. The followers of Saturninus, or the Syrian Gnostics, refused to partake of animal food, in order that they might avoid all contact with the evil prin-

* Manu, Inst. ii. 56.

ciple, which they supposed to be matter; and they taught that all those souls who purpose to return to God after death must abstain from wine, flesh, and wedlock, and from all that tends to sensual gratification. Both Pythagoras and Empedokles prohibited the eating of animal food, from the supposition that there is a κοινωνια between gods, animals, and men.

The rule of entire abstinence from flesh, though generally insisted upon, was not of universal obligation among the ancient monks. The Carthusians are not allowed to eat flesh, even in the most dangerous sickness. They fast eight months in the year, and in Lent, Advent, and all Fridays, reject all white meats, as eggs, milk, butter, and cheese. On Sundays and holidays they eat together in a common refectory, but on other days they dine alone in their cells, their food being carried to them by a lay brother, who puts it into each cell at a little window, without speaking a word. They are not permitted to eat in any other place but the convent, nor to drink anything but water. According to the rule of Benedict, the monks were allowed as their daily portion (Reg. 33, 40) twelve, or eighteen, ounces of bread, a hemina of wine, and two dishes of vegetables. The flesh of quadrupeds was strictly prohibited, except to the feeble and the sick. When the Lombards, in 580, destroyed the abbey in which Benedict had resided on Mount Cassino, the abbot escaped to Rome, taking with him the weight of the bread and the measure of the wine which were the daily allowance of each monk. No monk is allowed to eat out of the monastery, unless he is at such a distance that he cannot return the same day. The Cistertians never eat flesh except in times of dangerous sickness; unless upon extraordinary occasions, they abstain also from eggs, butter, milk, and cheese, but they can make use of these articles of diet when they have been given in alms. From the Septuagesima until Easter flesh is banished even from the infirmaries. They all take their food together in the refectory.

"In preieres and penaunces
Putten hem manye,
Al for the love of oure Lord
Lyveden ful streyte,
In hope to have after
Hevene rich blisse;
As aneres and heremites
That holden hem in hire selles,
And coveiten noght in contree
To carien aboute,
For no likerous liflode
Hire likame to plese."—*Piers Ploughman*, v. 49.

We have seen that the use of wine was not universally forbidden; but by the early canons the ascetics were prohibited from entering a public house. In the Anglo-Saxon church the priest was enjoined "to keep aloof from all parties assembled for the purpose of singing and carousing, and above all to preserve himself from drunkenness, the besetting sin of his countrymen." By the council of Cloveshoe, all inhabitants of monasteries are forbidden to drink to excess themselves, or to encourage such excess in others; they are to exclude from their entertainment coarse unseemly amusements, and never to allow their cells to become the resort of gleemen, harpers, and buffoons. Yet Alcuin accuses them of being addicted to "secret junketings, and furtive compotations." * In 1521, in the abbey of Whalley, containing about twenty monks, there was expended for red wine, the sum of £33 15*s.* 8*d.*; and for white or sweet wine, £9, which at the rate at which wine was then sold would give about eight pipes per annum.† The monks of Sallay brewed annually 255 quarters of malted oats and 104 of barley, and as the whole establishment consisted of about seventy persons, each individual would consume about 300 gallons annually; but a large allowance must be made for hospitality.‡

Many of the earlier ascetics took only one meal daily, which was generally after sunset; some fasted three or four days without any nourishment whatever; and even when partaking of food they lived only on wild herbs and roots, or on pulse steeped in cold water, and never touched anything that had passed the fire. The water that they drank was sometimes kept until it was offensive. From the time of his conversion, Pachomius never ate a full meal. Paul, the Thebaean, had half a loaf brought him every day, by a raven, except upon one occasion when he was visited by Anthony, and the provident bird brought a whole one. According to Athanasius, the food of Anthony was bread and salt, and his drink water; whilst feeding upon this diet, he neither became fatter nor thinner; and his meals were taken in private, as he was ashamed that he was obliged to eat. An account of the daily food of Hilarion has been preserved. From his twenty-first to his twenty-seventh year, he ate at first lentiles in half-a-pint of cold water, and afterwards

* Lingard's Anglo-Saxon Church.
† Whitaker's History of Whalley.
‡ Whitaker's History of the Deanery of Craven.

bread, salt, and water; from his twenty-seventh to his thirtieth year, wild herbs and undressed roots; from his thirty-first to his thirty-fifth year, six ounces of barley bread and parboiled cabbage without oil. But finding that he was becoming near-sighted, and his skin scurfy he added a little oil. From sixty-four till eighty he abstained altogether from bread, and substituted five ounces of a compound of flour and chopped cabbage.* Palladius contented himself with four or five ounces of bread daily, and one small vessel of oil in a year. Simeon Stylites took only one meal in the week, which was on the Sabbath. In Lent, he fasted so long that I must give the account in the words of my authority, lest I be accused of exaggeration. "At the foot of Mount Thelanissa," says Alban Butler, "he came to the resolution of passing the whole forty days of Lent in total abstinence, after the example of Christ, without either eating or drinking. Bassus, a holy priest, and abbot of 200 monks, who was his director, and to whom he had communicated his design, had left with him ten loaves and water, that he might eat if he found it necessary. At the expiration of the forty days he came to visit him, and found the loaves and water untouched, but Simeon stretched out on the ground, almost without any signs of life. Taking a sponge, he moistened his lips with water, then gave him the blessed eucharist. Simeon, having recovered a little, rose up, and chewed and swallowed by degrees a few lettuce leaves and other herbs. This was his method of keeping Lent during the remainder of his life." Catherine, of Sienna, accustomed herself to so rigorous an abstinence, that the eucharist was nearly the whole nourishment she took; and once she fasted, with the exception of what she took in the eucharist, from Ash Wednesday to Ascension Day. The food that Basil took was so small in quantity, that he appeared to live without it, and to have put on beforehand the life angelic. Paul, of Mount Latrus, for some weeks had no other subsistence than green acorns, which caused him at first to vomit, even to blood. A countryman sometimes brought him a little coarse food, but he principally lived upon what grew wild upon the mountain. When he wanted water, a constant spring was produced near his dwelling. In the midst of these privations, the ascetics preserved their equanimity, even upon the most trying occasions. Once, when Ephraim, of Edessa, had fasted several days, the brother who was bringing him a mess of pottage made

* Encyclopædia Metropolitana, art. Hermit; Hospinianus, De Monachis.

with a few herbs, let the pot fall, and broke it. The saint seeing him in confusion, said cheerfully, "As our supper will not come to us, let us go to it;" then sitting down he picked up his meal from the ground. When Arsenius, who had been a courtier, presented himself for admission before the monks of Scete, he was allowed to stand whilst the monks took their repast, and no notice was taken of him; but John the Dwarf, took a piece of bread and threw it down on the ground before him, upon which Arsenius fell down, and in that posture cheerfully ate the bread. Germanus began every meal by putting a few ashes in his mouth, and the bread he ate was from barley he had himself threshed and ground. Francis generally put ashes or water upon what he ate, even when it was only a little coarse bread.* Piers Ploughman says, v. 4086:—

"Ac ancres and heremites
That eten noght but at nones,
And na-moore er the morwe,
Myn almesse shul thei have,
And of catel to kepe hem with,
That han cloistres and chirches."

These legends are many of them incredible, and nearly all of them absurd. The only meats from which the Christian is to abstain are those offered to idols, and blood, and things strangled. —Acts xv. 29. We may eat "whatsoever is sold in the shambles;" and it is regarded by St. Paul as the sign of "a departing from the faith," a giving heed to "seducing spirits and doctrines of devils," when men command us "to abstain from meats, which God hath created to be received with thanksgiving of them which believe and know the truth: for every creature of God is good, and nothing to be refused, if it be received with thanksgiving."—1 Tim. iv. 3. The law of the Lord inculcates the relinquishment of certain kinds of food for an especial reason, and men make the law universal; they forget the reason, and make a merit of the act. The word of God enjoins temperance, and man demands total abstinence. These are perversions that may in some instances produce a temporary good, but they are in danger of inflicting a permanent evil upon the church by setting another law above the revealed will of God, or by carrying out one branch of that will to an undue extent, putting a part in place of the whole, and thus infringing God's prerogative as

* Alban Butler, passim: Professor Emerson, Andover, in the Bibliotheca Sacra.

the supreme legislator. The religion of Christ is one of cheerfulness and holy joy; the primitive believers "did eat their meat with gladness of heart;" and though there is a good moral in the words of Herbert, we must not allow the principle to rob us of our privilege "to rejoice evermore:"—

> "Take thy meat; think it dust: then eat a bit,
> And say with all, Earth to earth I commit."

X. SLEEP.

Whilst yet in innocence, Adam slept; and calm indeed must have been the midnight hour of Paradise. The repose of all animate creation would be profound; the beast as still in its slumber as the herbage upon which it reclined, or the flower that grew in beauty by the side of its lair. But the ancient ascetics regarded sleep as a part of animality they were to throw off to as great an extent as possible. With some it would be difficult to accomplish this design, as those persons who have few cares to perplex their minds are possessed of powers of sleep to which we whose lot has been cast in this restless generation must ever be utter strangers. The better informed among them would perhaps sometimes remember that Adam was neither deprived of wedlock, nor food, nor speech, nor sleep; and as they in their solitude were debarred from the former of these privileges, they would be tempted the more to indulge in the fourth, and to say to themselves, "a little more sleep and a little more slumber," when the rule of their order or their personal vow would call upon them with its stern voice to arouse themselves and pray; yet it is a hard task to resist sleep in some frames of the body, and the morning twilight would often see them nodding their heads like the bulrush when bowed down by the wind, at a time when they ought to have been erect as the trunk of the tree, blasted by the lightning and now decayed, into which they had crept at sunset.

In eastern climes the nights are so beautiful, and the bare ground so comfortable a place of rest, that in the Indian systems of asceticism we meet with little account of the modes of penance that are connected with sleep. It is an ordinance of the Dina Chariyáwa that the novice is to arise before daylight. There are sixty hours in the day, according to the mode of reckoning in India, thirty of which belong to the night, which is divided into three watches of ten hours each. It is said that Gótama Budha slept during one-third of the third watch, or three hours and one-third. In the first watch he preached or engaged in religious conversation; in the second watch he answered questions put to him by the déwas; and in the first division of the third watch he slept, in the second exercised meditation, and in the third looked abroad in the world with his divine eyes to see what being or beings it would be proper to catch in the net of truth during the day.*

The last of the Thirteen Ordinances is called Nésajjikanga, which is the same as nisajja, ni being a particle of emphasis, and sajjika the act of sitting. He who keeps this ordinance may not lie down to sleep, and during the whole of one watch of the night he must walk about. He may not recline at full length, but may walk, or stand, or sit. The priest who keeps the superior ordinance may not lean on any place, or make his robe into a seat, or take hold of a piece of cloth fastened to a tree. He who keeps the middle ordinance is allowed to make use of any of these assistances. He who keeps the inferior ordinance may make seats (in particular ways that are mentioned). None of the three are permitted to lie down.

The last of the Twelve Sacred Ordinances of the Chinese is called naïchadika. It prohibits the mendicant from lying down. A seated position is that which comports best with his design. His digestion and respiration are easily carried on, and he can bend his mind to that which is wise. Indolence leaves itself open to be attacked by vice, that seizes its advantage. The mendicant ought therefore to take his repose sitting, and his body ought not to touch the earth.†

This mode of penance has probably been carried to a greater extent by the Brahmans than by any other order of ascetics. And in their case it is not an incredible tale upon which we have to depend; they are presented before our eyes in vast numbers, with bodies and members so dry and withered, that they cannot have been brought to such a state without the practice of the most painful austerities. But it is the recluse alone who is called upon to endure these hardships. According to the sage Aurva, the householder, "after eating his evening meal, and, having washed his feet, is to go to rest. His bed is to be entire, and made of wood; it is

* Amáwatura. † Remusat's Relation.

not to be scanty, nor cracked, nor uneven, nor dirty, nor infested by insects, nor without a bedding; and he is to sleep with his head either to the east or to the south; any other position is unhealthy." *

There was an order of monks called ἀκοιμητοι, insomnes, the sleepless; and by other monks the same austerities were observed. One was called Rectus, from standing erect until his legs refused to hold him up any longer. Chrysostom persisted in remaining in a standing posture so long, that with this and other exercises he ruined his health. Anthony was accustomed to remain whole nights without sleep. Paul, the hermit, never lay down to sleep, but only leaned his head against a stone or tree. John, of Old Castile, only slept two or three hours in the night. Peter of Alcantara, knelt a great part of the night, sometimes leaning on his heels for a little rest; but he slept sitting, leaning his head against a wall. Pallodius neither stretched out his legs nor lay down to sleep; the night through he sat erect at his work of platting ropes, and sleeping only in a doze at his meals; an angel might be persuaded to sleep, but not he. Macarius continued abroad during twenty days and twenty nights, in order to conquer his propensity to sleep, until he was in danger of going mad; he remained erect during the forty days of Lent, neither bending the knee, nor sitting, nor lying down. The Ethiopian Moses persisted six years in standing erect the night through, never closing his eyes. Daniel, the Stylite, supported himself against the balustrade of his pillar, until, by continually standing, his legs and feet became swollen and full of ulcers. On one occasion, in the winter, he was found so stiff with cold, that his disciples had to soak some sponges in warm water, and rub him therewith, before he could be revived. Nor has our own country been without saints of the same order. Cuthbert was accustomed to spend whole nights in prayer; and to resist sleep he walked about the island in which he lived—Landisfarne. One night he was seen to go down to the sea-shore, where he went into the water until it reached his arm-pits, and continued there until the break of day, singing the praises of God. It is not said whether his position was affected by the tide.

By the rule of Basil, sleep was not to be continued after midnight, the rest of the night being devoted to prayer. Alexander, in 402, instituted the order of Akoemites, which differed from that

* Wilson's Vishnu Purána, 309.

of Basil only in this rule, that each monastery was divided into different choirs, which, succeeding each other, continued the offices of the church day and night without interruption. Among the Cistercians, the monks, who slept in their habits upon straw, rose at midnight, and spent the rest of the night in singing the offices.*

XI. THE TONSURE.

The prophet of Israel made use of a very significant figure to describe the calamities that were about to overtake his countrymen for their sins, when he said that, instead of "well-set hair" there should be baldness. The right arrangement of the hair tells of comfort and ease, and betokens a sense of the proprieties of social existence; whilst, if left in disorder, it tells with a voice equally truthful of carelessness or calamity. It is a great addition to the grace or dignity of the human form; and whether we see it in flowing ringlets upon the necks of children, or in the modest tresses of the matron as she walks in comeliness, or in the scanty locks upon the head of the aged, white as the falling snow, the appearance that it presents is in unison with the circumstances of the individual, and therefore beautiful. We cannot wonder, then, that the hair has been an especial object of dislike to the gloomy founders of all monastic institutions; and that they have been unsparing in their demand that it should either be entirely removed, or deprived of all its grace.

But in some instances there have been other motives for its removal. It has been supposed that it would promote the cleanliness of the person, or that, as it is a mere earthly excrescence, the body is more pure, and partakes more of divinity, when free from its presence. It is said that the Hebrew priests shaved off all their hair when inaugurated, and that when on duty they cut it every fortnight. They were not allowed, in cases of mourning, to make baldness upon their head, nor to shave off the corner of the beard—Lev. xxi. 5. The passage, "Uncover not your heads," Lev. x. 6, is by many of the Jews translated, "Let not the hair of your head grow," as was sometimes the custom of mourners. They supposed that this law, except in the case of the high priest, was only binding

* Hospinian, Giesler, and Alban Butler, passim.

during the period of their ministration. It is remarkable that, in the only rite approaching to asceticism in use among the Israelites, the Nazarite was required to allow his hair to grow long. The Egyptian priests every third day shaved every part of their bodies, to prevent vermin or any other species of impurity from adhering to their persons when engaged in their sacred duties. Hence Plutarch, in his exhortation to the priestess of Isis, says, "As the long robe and the mantle do not make a philosopher, neither does the linen garb and shaven head constitute a priest of Isis." The learned Origen was once shaved by his persecutors, when in Alexandria, and taken to the temple of Serapis, that he might be induced to join in an act of idolatry as a priest.

Among other nations the hair has been cut off for different reasons:—as a sacrifice; at marriage; after escape from imminent danger; after a campaign; on the day of consecration; and as a token of mourning. Sappho (epigram ii.) says of Timas,

> "Her loved companions pay the rites of woe,
> All, all, alas! the living can bestow;
> From their fair heads the graceful locks they shear,
> Place on her tomb, and drop the tender tear."
>
> *Fawkes's Sappho.*

The hair of Achilles was dedicated to the river-god, Spercheius. In honour of the Hyperborean virgins (Herod. iii. 34) who died at Delos, the Delian youths of both sexes celebrated certain rites, in which they cut off their hair. This was done by virgins previous to their marriage, who wound their hair round a spindle, and by the young men, who wound it round a certain herb, and placed it upon the strangers' tomb. The Spartan ephors, on entering upon office, issued a kind of edict, in which it was ordered "to shave the beard, μυσταξ, and obey the laws," the former being a metaphorical expression for subjection and obedience. At Sparta the beard was considered as a mark of freedom, as well as at Byzantium and Rhodes, where shaving was prohibited by ancient laws.* The slaves were shaved as a mark of servitude. The hair of the vestal virgins was cut off, probably at the time of their consecration.

Among the Scandinavians it was a mark of infamy to cut off the hair. The Dutch, when in possession of Ceylon, adopted this custom as a mode of punishment, which was continued by the English;

* C. O. Müller's History of the Dorians.

but when it was found that on this account the native soldiers refused to have their hair cut, it was no longer adopted.

From some of the above customs originated the tonsure, that designated the clerical or monastic state among Christians. In the early church, male penitents were required to cut off their hair and shave their beards, in token of contrition; and females had to appear with their hair in disorder. But the old ecclesiastical rules expressly enjoined the clergy (Constit. Apost. lib. i. c. 3) to wear their hair and beards long.* It is said by Alban Butler (Oct. 12) that the tonsure was introduced in the fourth or fifth century, after the persecutions had ceased. The first locks were sometimes cut off by the king or some other great personage. In the eighth century there were three varieties of tonsure: the Greek, in which the entire top of the head was shaven; the Roman, in a circular form, in imitation of the crown of thorns; and that of St. Paul, or the oriental, from the forehead to the crown. It is supposed that the custom among the British monks was to have the hair cut in the fore part of the head, in a semicircle, from ear to ear.† To say that a man was shaven, was equivalent to saying that he had become a priest or monk. When Wilfrid was admitted among the clergy, by receiving the tonsure, but not any holy order, Bede says simply, "Attonsus est," which Alfred translated, "He was shorn to priest." ‡ Hilarion was accustomed to cut his hair once yearly, a little before Easter. It was the custom in the community of Aicard, a French saint, for every monk to shave his crown on the Saturday. The founder having once been hindred on the Saturday from performing the usual operation, began to shave himself very early on the Sunday morning; but he was touched with remorse, and is said to have seen in a vision a devil picking up every hair he had cut off at this forbidden hour, to produce against him at the judgment seat of God. The aunt of Eustochium, whose history is related by Jerome (De Virgin. et ep. 22, 26, 27), having caused her hair to be gracefully curled, after the fashion of the times, a terrible angel appeared to her the following night, threatening her severely for having attempted to instil vanity into one who was consecrated as the spouse of Christ. The Capuchins wear their beards, not shaved close, but long and not clipped. Francis wore a beard, but it was very short, and his followers, who had long

* Riddle's Ecclesiastical Antiquities. † Burton's Monasticon.
‡ Lingard's Anglo-Saxon Church.

beards, were commanded to shave them.* The Templars, among other peculiarities of their institute, were commanded to wear their beards long. It is said of Chaucer's Monk, that

> "His hed was balled, and shone as any glas."

The Institutes of Manu contain the following regulations on the subject of the hair. "By the tonsure of the child's head, with a lock of hair left on it . . . are the seminal and uterine taints of the three classes wholly removed. . . . By the command of the Veda, the ceremony of the tonsure should be legally performed by the first three classes in the first or third year after birth.† . . . The ceremony of késanta, or cutting off the hair, is ordained for a priest in the sixteenth year after conception; for a soldier, in the twenty-second; for a merchant, two years later than that. . . . Sudras, engaged in religious duties, must perform each month the ceremony of shaving their heads. . . . Ignominious tonsure is ordained, instead of capital punishment, for an adulterer of the priestly class, where the punishment of other classes may extend to loss of life." ‡ The god Siva is represented as having matted hair; and the jatala ascetics among the Brahmans, wear their hair clotted together in inextricable involutions.

Among the Budhists, the priest, from the commencement of his noviciate, is shaved; and he is provided with a razor, as one of the eight articles he is allowed to possess, in order that his tonsure may be regularly performed. The law is, that the hair is not to be permitted to grow to a greater length than two inches; but it is the usual custom to shave once every fortnight. The priests shave each other, but it is not forbidden to have the operation performed by a laic. Among the Brahmans no one is allowed (Manu, Inst. iv. 9) to cut his own hair or nails. Until the year 1266, the monks of St. Augustine's, Canterbury, were accustomed to shave one another in the cloister; but frequent injuries ensuing through their awkwardness in that office, secular persons were hired. In some instances the camerarius provided razors and towels for the monks, and they were shaved by the infirmarius. In the Sempringham

* Alban Butler, passim.

† Times and seasons, and the phases of the moon, are closely observed in the Fylde, Lancashire, when the first operation of cutting the infant's nails and hair is to be performed, which for a whole year are carefully guarded from the scissors.

‡ Inst. ii. 27, 35, 65; v. 140; viii. 379.

rule the canons were shaved seventeen times per annum; but one of the Inquirenda of Henry's visitors was, "Whether ye bee wyckely shaven?" Shaving the beard began about the year 1200, lest the eucharist should be defiled by it.*

The priests of Budha never put a covering upon the head in Ceylon, though this custom appears not to be followed in other countries where the same religion is professed. They walk out uncovered, with the bald crown exposed to the fiercest beam of a tropical sun, but without appearing to feel any ill effect in consequence. It is said by Herodotus (iii. 12), that after a battle between the Persians and Egyptians, it was found that the skulls of the Egyptians were so hard, that a stone would scarcely break them; whilst those of the Persians were so soft, that they might be broken or pierced through with the greatest ease. The former were accustomed from their infancy to have their heads shaved, and go uncovered; whilst the latter always wore some form of head-dress. Hence it would appear that the skull, from exposure, becomes crass and callous.

In the metaphysical drama, called Prabodha-chandra-udaya, a Budhist is addressed thus:—"Aha! sinner that thou art, vilest of heretics, with thy shaven crown, drest like the lowest outcastes—uncombed one—away with thee!"†

There are fifteen evils connected with the growth of the hair, such as that it must be ornamented, anointed, washed, perfumed, purified, unloosed, tied, combed, curled, unknotted, and freed from vermin; and when it begins to fall off, there is regret. But the freedom from care and trouble is not the only advantage to be gained by cutting off the hair.‡ When the hair of the priest, or his nails, are suffered to grow long, his robe is dirty and full of holes, the perspiration is allowed to remain upon his body, and his various requisites are covered with filth, his mind will partake of the same uncleanness. When the lamp, or the oil, or the wick, are not free from dirt, the light that is given is not clear; in like manner, when the mind is unclean, the truths necessary to be known cannot be discovered, and the rites of asceticism cannot be properly exercised. But when the body is clean, the mind partakes of the same purity; and as the lamp, oil, and wick, when free from dirt, give a clear light, so the mind that is pure can discern the truths, and exercise the rites in a proper manner.§

* Fosbroke's British Monachism. † Wilson's Hindu Theatre.
‡ Milinda Prasna. § Wisudhi Margga Sanné.

XII. THE HABIT.

The use of dress is one of the consequences of sin; and though at its first adoption it was intended only as "the veil of shame," it has since been made the instrument of much evil, by ministering to pride and passion. Hence the wish of nearly all ascetics to prevent this evil, either by returning to the simplicity of man in innocence, or by making the garment of scanty dimensions, or by adopting a dress of mean appearance, coarse, rough and ragged.

The precepts given in the Pátimokkhan relative to the dress of the priest of Budha are numerous. He is permitted to have three robes,* called respectively sanghátiya, uttarasanggaya, and antarawásakaya, and is not allowed to retain an extra robe more than ten days; the whole three are always to be in his possession, unless danger be apprehended, in which case he may leave one robe in the village, but not more than six days, unless specially permitted. When cloth is received for a new robe it must be made up without delay; and when it is insufficient for the making of a robe, it may not be kept longer than a month, even when waiting for so much as is required to complete it; unless when the robe has been stolen or accidentally destroyed, another robe is not to be solicited from any one; when given under these circumstances, he is only to receive two; no priest shall persuade any one to collect money to purchase for him a robe; no robe that the giver has previously been requested to present may be received: the priest may not take money from the messenger of a king or other great person for the purchase of a robe, but the money may be given to some one else; and when the priest wants a robe he may go thrice to that person, and remind him that a robe is required, and if not then given, he may thrice try to obtain it by standing in silence; but if still refused, he may not make any further effort to procure it, except that he may inform the person who sent the money of the circumstance. A priest may not seek the extra robe allowed during the rainy months before the last month of the hot season, nor have it made up before the last half-month. When a priest has given a robe to another, he may not afterwards try to regain it, or have it

* The word robe may appear to be a misnomer as applied to the dress of a Budhist mendicant; but it had not always the dignity that is now attached to it, as our forefathers called the dress of a slave, roba garcionis.

taken away; he may not ask for cotton thread, and then give it to a weaver to be made into cloth for a robe; when he knows that the weaver is making cloth for a robe, he may not go to him and give instructions as to the manner in which he is to make it, promising him a present. The time for making the offering of a robe being at the end of the rainy season, when wass has been performed, the priest may not receive a robe more than ten days prior to that period. When the priest obtains a new robe it must be disfigured, by marks of mud or otherwise, before he puts it on; he may not give his robe to another, without the regular form of investiture. When a robe has been given in the regular form, he is not to make a complaint that it has been given with partiality. No cloth shall be used as a covering for a sore that is more than two spans in breadth and four in length. The priest may not wear in the rainy season a robe larger than six spans in length and two and a half in breadth; and he is never to wear a robe as large or larger than the robe of Budha, which was nine spans long and six broad (in each case the span of Budha being intended). The under robe is to be so worn that no part of the body from the navel to the knee be exposed, and with the upper robe the body is to be covered from the shoulders to the heels.

When the priest has forfeited a robe, on account of having kept it beyond the prescribed period, he is to deliver it up to a chapter. Approaching the assembly, and baring one of his shoulders, he worships the feet of the senior priests; then, kneeling down or sitting on his heels, he raises his clasped hands to his forehead, and says that the robe has been forfeited, being an extra one, and kept longer than ten days. The robe is delivered to the chapter, and another priest is appointed to receive it.*

In the missive sent by the sangha rája of Burma to the priests of Ceylon, that hierarch dwells at length upon the necessity of great attention being paid "to the proper adjustment of the robes," and quotes the following rules from the Sékhiyáwa:—"The precept ought to be observed that I should wear the upper robe so as to envelope the body. . . . The precept ought to be observed that I should enter the village or house, well covered with my robes." From the work called Khandakawatta, which is said to contain precepts taken from the Maha Waga and Chula Waga the following rule is taken:—"When the time is announced for the perform-

* Gogerly's Translation of the Pátimokkhan.

ance of any sacred duty, every priest should enter the village in a quiet orderly manner, putting on the robe so as to conceal the three mandala, or the parts of the body from the navel to the ankles, and envelope the body, tying the waist-band, covering the body with the upper robe doubled, and tying the knot, taking in the hand the alms-bowl, after having properly washed it." And again, the rája proceeds, "Some persons erroneously think, that to tie a band or sash round the upper robe, to prevent it from flying off, is not contrary to the Winaya; but to show that this is a mistake, I quote the following passage from the Chula Waga:—"Priests, do not wear a girdle, not even a string, round the small of the back: the priest who wears it is guilty of an offence requiring confession and absolution."

The physician Jíwaka having given two magnificent robes to Gótama Budha; the sage reflected that if the priests were allowed to receive robes of this description, they would be in danger from thieves; and he therefore intimated this danger to his attendant, Ananda, who cut them into thirty pieces, and then sewed them together in five divisions, so that the robe resembled the patches in a rice-field divided by embankments. On seeing this contrivance, Budha made a law that his priests should only have three robes at one time, and that they should always be composed of thirty pieces of cloth.*

When Gótama Bódhisat was the ascetic Sumédha, in the time of Dípankara Budha, he reflected that there are nine objections to the garment of the laic. 1. It is too magnificent. 2. It must be received from some one, as it does not appear by itself, and cannot be found in the forest. 3. It soon becomes soiled. 4. It is soon worn away, or is otherwise destroyed. 5. It cannot be procured at any moment, just when it is required. 6. It is a thing of value. 7. It may be stolen. 8. It enervates the body of the wearer. 9. It gives rise to evil desire. He also reflected that there are twelve advantages from wearing the garment of the ascetic (wák-chíwara, a covering made of bark, or of some other vegetable substance). 1. It is plain. 2. There is no necessity to apply to any one, in order to procure it. 3. It can be made by the ascetic's own hand. 4. It does not soon become soiled. 5. Thieves will not notice it. 6. It can easily be procured in any place. 7. It becomes the wearer. 8. It does not give rise to evil desire. 9. It does not

* Pujáwaliya.

cause covetousness. 10. It is readily put on. 11. It requires no trouble to procure it. 12. When evil desire has been destroyed, it does not cause its reproduction.*

The robe is to be put on by the priest as if it were a bandage to cover a sore, or a cloth to cover a skeleton; and he must carry the alms-bowl as if it were a vessel of medicine. There are some priests who put on the robe as young men, or even as lewd women, put on their garments, to attract attention; but this is contrary to the precepts. It may be put on to keep off the snow, as by extreme cold disease is produced, and the mind is prevented from exercising continued thought. Its principal advantage, however, is to cover the shame of the priest; other benefits are occasional, but this is without intermission.

When invited to receive the offering of a robe, the priest may not say that he does not desire it, that a few rags from the grave-yard will be sufficient for him, in order that he may receive the greater respect. By this means the people might be led to think that they will gain merit by giving to so holy a man, and thus be induced to bring him many offerings; and the priest who at first appeared so disinterested, will be led to ask for more and more, thus bringing discredit upon the truth.†

The king of Kósala one day presented to each of his 500 wives a splendid robe; but they made an offering of them to Ananda, when he came to the palace to say bana. The next day, as the king saw them in their former garments, he enquired what they had done with the robes; when they said that they had presented them to Ananda. The king, in anger, asked if the priest wanted to sell them, and went immediately to the wihára to enquire into the matter; but he spoke only to Ananda, and not to Budha, asking if Budha had not said that no priest was to have more than three robes. Ananda replied, "Yes, as his own property; but he is to receive whatever is presented, in order that the giver may thereby obtain merit. On a certain occasion the priest Wanawásatissa received a thousand bowls of rice-milk, which he gave to as many priests; and at another time he received a thousand mantles, which he disposed of in a similar manner. In the same way I received the 500 Kasi robes from the queens, and gave them to as many priests whose robes were old." The king enquired what the priests did with their old robes, and Ananda said, that "after stitching

* Pújáwaliya. † Wisudhi Margga Sanné.

them they took them for loose wrappers." The king: "What becomes of the former wrappers?" Ananda: "They cut away the old pieces, and taking the good pieces that are left, they make them into inner robes." The king: "What becomes of the inner robes that have been cast off?" Ananda: "They spread them upon the ground, that they may sleep upon them at night." The king: "What becomes of the cloths upon which they slept previously?" Ananda: "The priests spread them in the places where they dwell, to walk upon." The king: "What is done with the cloths upon which they formerly walked?" Ananda: "They make them into the rugs upon which they wipe their feet." The king: "What becomes of the former rugs?" Ananda: "They use them in preparing the clay of which their dwellings are built." The king's anger was appeased by these answers; and to show his satisfaction he presented to Ananda 500 other robes of similar value, greatly praising the institutions of Budha.*

The first of the Thirteen Ordinances is called Pansukúlikanga. The word pansu means earth, and may here be used in reference to the cloth about which the ordinance is instituted, which must be taken from the earth or ground; or it may be used as meaning anything mean or low. The word kúla means a heap, collection, or bank; it is also used for disgrace. The garment of the priest is called pansukúla; the priest observing this ordinance is called pansukúlika, and the observance itself pansukúlikanga. The priest who keeps this ordinance must resolve, "I will not receive the garment given by a householder; I will receive it only in accordance with the precept." This precept forbids the receiving of any cloth for the making of a garment that has not been found under one or other of the following circumstances:—The cloth that has been thrown into a burial-ground, or thrown away in the bazaar, or thrown out of a window with the intention of acquiring merit; the cloth used for the purification of a woman in childbirth; the cloth that a demon priest has tied round his head on the performance of some ceremony, and thrown away when going to bathe; the cloth thrown away by a person after bathing; the cloth thrown away by persons who have carried a corpse to the place of sepulture; the cloth eaten by cattle, or white ants, or rats; the cloth that has been partially burnt, and thrown away in consequence; the cloth that is torn at the end; the piece of cloth that is only a

* Pújáwaliya.

shred or remnant; the cloth that has been put up like a flag by persons who have sailed away in a vessel, which may be taken after they are out of sight; the flag tied in a battle-field after the fight is done; the cloth put on an ant-hill with an offering to a demon; the cloth that has belonged to a priest, or that has been used at the anointing of a king, or that has belonged to a priest who is a rishi; the cloth left in a road by mistake, after it has been seen that no one claims it; the cloth carried away by the wind; the cloth given by the déwas, like the one given to Anurudha; and the cloth cast on shore by the waves. Pieces of cloth that are found in any of these twenty-three ways may be taken by the priest for the making of his garment, and no other. There are three ways in which this ordinance, as well as the other dhutangas, may be kept; the superior, the middle, and the inferior. The superior allows the cloth to be taken only from the place of sepulture. The middle ordinance allows the priest to take the garment that has been put for him by another priest, in any place. The inferior ordinance allows him to take a garment that has been put at his feet by another priest. The priest who receives a robe from a householder breaks this ordinance; but he may receive it with the intention of giving it to another priest, without any fault. Even the things allowed are not in all cases to be taken. When the mother of the noble Tissa was confined, the cloth used at her purification, worth a hundred pieces of gold, was thrown into the street of Anurádhapura, called Jála-wéli, under the supposition that it would be taken by some priest observing this ordinance; but though it was seen by the priests, they did not take it, on account of its value.

As Gotáma Budha, when he proclaimed that Kásyapa was to be his successor, said, "Kásyapa, thou shalt wear my pansukúla robe," we may learn that the garment of the great sage was of this mean description. We may also infer from this expression that the reception of the habit of any public teacher was intended to convey the idea that the individual who received it had succeeded to the office of the person by whom it was previously worn. It may have been on this account that Elisha "took up the mantle of Elijah, that fell from him," at his glorious removal to the company of the ever happy.—2 Kings ii. 13.

The seventh of the Twelve Sacred Observances of the Chinese is said to teach that the mendicant ought not to wish for any kind of ornament; he is not to look for sumptuous habits, but to take those which are torn and tattered, and have been rejected by others. These he washes and cleans, and makes them into patched garments, solely to protect him from the cold and cover his nakedness. New garments and beautiful habits give rise to the desire of renewed existence, and agitate the mind; they also attract thieves.*

The second of the Thirteen Ordinances is called Téchiwarakanga, from té, three, and chíwara, a robe. The three robes are the one underneath, the one outside, and the sangala that covers all (answering to the peribolaem, which the Gangram canons observe was used by the ascetics). The priest who observes this ordinance cannot possess more than three robes at one time; if he possesses a fourth, the ordinance is broken. When cloth for the robes is received it may be put by for future use, if there be no tailor, or no thread, or no needle, until they can be met with; but it must be made up at the first opportunity that presents itself. If an old robe be cast away merely that a new one may be received, though the ordinance is not broken thereby, its spirit is disregarded. The priest who keeps the superior ordinance may put on one robe whilst the two others are dyed, if he lives near a village; but if he lives in the forest, he must dye all the three at the same time, and remain in the interval without clothing; yet, should any one approach, he must take one of the robes from the dye and put it on. The middle ordinance allows a robe to be put on during the process of dying, but the robe for this purpose must be one that was previously in the dye, and no other can be taken. The inferior ordinance allows the robe of another priest, or any common cloth, to be put on, whilst his own are in the dye; but it may not be retained when the process is done: he may nevertheless possess a piece of cloth like a sheet without breaking the precept. In addition to the three robes, the priest may not possess any other garment; but he may have a dat-kada, for the purpose of cleaning the teeth, if it be not more than a span broad and three cubits long.

The eighth of the Twelve Sacred Observances of the Chinese is called traitchîvarika, which signifies that the mendicant is to content himself with the kia cha of nine, seven, or five pieces. He has few desires, and is easily satisfied. He wishes neither for too much nor too little clothing. He is equally distant from those who are habited in white, and have a number of habits, and the heretics who are entirely naked; both the one and the other excess is

* Remusat's Relation des Royaumes Bouddhiques.

avoided: the three habits are a just medium. As for the rest, the word kia cha signifies, of different colours, on account of the pieces that form the habit of the first, second, and third order.

The three robes are said by Klaproth to be called in Chinese—1. Seng kia li (sanghât'i), meaning "réuni" or "doublé." 2. Yü to lo seng (outtarasanghât'i) meaning "habit de dessus." 3. An tho hoeï (antaravâsaka) meaning "habit de dessous." The first is used when visiting the palaces of kings and other public places; the second, when conducting worship or preaching; and the third, when in the interior of the dwelling.*

In Burma the priests observe only one part of the law. They tear the cloth into a great number of pieces, but take care that it shall be of the finest quality.†

The month succeeding the three months of the rainy season, in which wass is performed, is called in Ceylon chíwara-mása, or the robe-month. At this time the people purchase one or more pieces of cloth, according to their circumstances, which they present to the priests. The cloth for this purpose is called katina. It cannot be received except by a chapter, which must be constituted of at least five priests. When the cloth is offered, the priests hold a conversation among each other, and enquire, "Which of us stands in need of a robe?" The priest who is most in need of a garment ought now to make known his want; but this rule is not attended to, as the priest who has read the sacred books, or expounded them, during the performance of wass, whether the most destitute or not, usually receives the robe. The priest respectfully asks the rest of the chapter to partake of the merits produced by the offering. The assembled priests, assisted by the lay devotees, make the cloth into a robe, and dye it yellow; the whole of which process must be concluded in sixty hours, or a natural day.

On some occasions the robe is manufactured throughout, from the raw material, in the same space of time. The hall where the bana is read is seen filled with women, sitting upon the ground; some bring in the cotton from the tree, or free it from the pod, whilst others prepare it for the spinners, who make it into yarn; it is then handed over to the weavers, who sit outside with their simple looms, and make it into cloth. In the evening of the same day the cloth is received by the priests, who stitch it into a robe,

* Remusat's Relation des Royaumes Bouddhiques, xiii. 10.
† Sangermano's Burmese Empire, 89.

and dye it the prescribed colour. This custom is more practised in the maritime provinces than in the interior of the island. It is not an ordinance of Budha. The Egyptian priests had a garment woven in one day when they observed the festival in memory of the return of Rampsinitus from the infernal regions.—Herod ii. 123. The magic standard of the ancient Danes was also woven and embroidered by royal hands in one noon-tide.

The regulations made by Gótama upon the subject of dress, were probably in part intended to set aside the custom that appears to have prevailed throughout India in the age in which he lived, for the ascetics to be entirely destitute of clothing. When Alexander arrived at Taxila, he met with the gymnosophists, and was surprised at their extraordinary patience in the endurance of pain. It is related by Plutarch that when Onesicritus was sent to desire some of them to come and see the monarch, Calamus commanded him to strip, and hear what he said naked, otherwise he would not speak to him, though he were even a divine being. Some of the ancient ascetics of the west were contented with a costume equally primitive. When Zosimus had been in the Arabian desert about twenty days, he one day saw a strange figure, like a human being, with short white hair, but extremely sunburnt. Thinking it was some holy anchoret, he ran after the figure, when a voice said to him, "Abbot Zosimus, I am a woman; throw me your mantle." After covering herself, the woman, who proved to be Mary, of Egypt, said that she had lived in the desert forty-seven years, and in that period had not seen a single human being. There were other saints who had no other covering but their own hair; as was said of one of these worthies, "nuditatem suam divino munere vesticbat."

It is expressly stated by Gótama that one purpose of the robe is to preserve the priest's body from the attacks of musquitoes. Hence, in Budhistical works we meet with no such narratives as that which is related of Macarius. This great anchoret having one day killed a gnat that had bitten him in his cell, as a penance he hastened to the marshes, that abounded with flies that could penetrate the thick skin of the wild boar, and there remained six months, until his body was so much disfigured with sores and swellings that he could only be recognised by his voice. Bernard acted a wiser part: when his monastery was troubled by swarms of flies, he excommunicated them, and they all died. When Gótama retired to the shade of the midella tree, at the time he received the supreme Budhaship, there was a storm of wind and rain; but a snake-god, Muchalinda, came and entwined himself seven times round the body of the sage, extending his large hood over his head, and saying, "Let not Bagawa be affected by cold, or heat, or flies, or gnats, or wind, or sunbeams, or insects." Gótama accepted his protection, until the storm had passed away. In the native paintings that represent the sage in this position, his general appearance greatly resembles that of a monk ensconced in his hood.

It was customary, at an early period, for those Christians who assumed an ascetic course of life, to put on the pallium of the ancient philosophers. The monks of Egypt, according to Cassian, wore a mean habit, merely enough to cover their nakedness, with short sleeves. Libanius (Haeres. xlvi. c. 1) calls them "black-coat monks." The dress of Anthony was hair-cloth within and sheepskin without, which he never changed; but no one saw him naked until his death. He bequeathed one sheepskin to Athanasius, with an old blanket; another to Serapion; and his hair-cloth to his attendant. Hilarion never changed his sackcloth until it was worn out, and never washed it, saying that it is idle to look for neatness in a hair-shirt. The covering of Paul, the hermit, was made of the leaves of the palm-tree. John, of Alexandria, had a valuable blanket sent to him, but he used it only for one night, and the next day sold it and gave the price to the poor. When others were given to him, he acted in the same manner. Basil had only one tunic and one coat. Bruno had only one coarse habit. When Aphraates was once offered a garment, he said that he had only one, which he had worn sixteen years, and he was not willing to have two at the same time, or to exchange an old and faithful servant for a new one. The dress of Germanus was the same in winter as summer, and was never changed until it was worn to pieces. Thomas, when made archbishop of Valentia, kept for some years the habit he had worn in the monastery, which he continued to mend with his own hand. On the day when Francis renounced the world, he stripped himself of his clothes, in the fervour of his zeal; and when the cloak of a country labourer working for the bishop of Assize was brought, he cheerfully put it on, making upon it a cross with chalk or mortar. Afterwards he contented himself with one poor coat, which he girt about with a cord; and this habit, which was the dress of the poor shepherds and peasants, he gave to his followers, with a short cloak over the shoulders, and a hood to cover the head. When his rough garment became too soft, he sewed it with packthread. When he found that his vicar-general had put on a habit of finer material than the other friars, and adopted other novelties, he deposed him from office. Peter, of Alcantara, never wore any other garment but a habit of thick coarse sackcloth, with a short cloak. When the weather was very cold he left the door and window of his cell open, and took off his mantle, that when he again put it on and closed his door, his body might be refreshed with the warmth. The habit of Colette was of the coarsest description and made of more than a hundred patches sewed together. Turgesius, abbot of Kirkstall, in Yorkshire, was always clad in hair-cloth, frequently repeating to himself, "They who are clad in soft raiment are in kings' houses."

The various orders of monks were known by their dress, as each had some difference either in the shape or colour of the garment. Their most common appellation was frequently from the colour of their dress, as the Black and White Friars, and the Pied Friars, or Fratres de Pica, who were so called from their outer garment, which was black and white, like a magpie. The dresses of the monks were sometimes costly. In 1478, the sum of £5 was paid for the habit of the abbot of Whalley, and £39 for the habits of the monks, who were about twenty in number. Master William de Stowe, sacrist of Evesham, acquired four copes, one of cloth of gold, very fine, another of red velvet with pearls, a third of red satin of the best kind, and a fourth also of red satin with flowers of gold; he also procured three albs, one of which had a representation of the Deity in gold work, with the heads of the apostles also in gold.

The Egyptian priests, as well as the Pythagoreans and Essenes, wore white garments; and were confined to one particular mode of dress. The garb of the earlier Christian ascetics was also white. The monks with whom Chrysostom associated had garments made of the rough hair of goats or camels, or of old skins. The followers of Gregory Nazianzen had only one cloak, made of sackcloth. The monks of Pachomius wore on their shoulders a white goatskin, called a melotes; their tunic was of white linen, without sleeves, with a cowl of the same material. According to the rule of Benedict, the abbot was to appoint the dress of the fraternity, and each brother was to have two tunics, cowls, and scapularies, the best being worn when they went abroad. When travelling they wore breeches, but at other times their gown was to suffice. Their founder was indifferent to the colour, form, or quality of their dress, but recommended that it should be adapted to the climate, and similar to that of the labouring poor; when requisite it was to be mended with sacks and scraps. The Cistercensians exchanged the black habit of the Benedictines for a white one. The Janitareans wore a white habit, with a red and blue cross upon the breast. Peter, the venerable, says of the Carthusians, that their dress was meaner and poorer than that of other monks, and so short, scanty, and rough, that the very sight was frightful. The Dominicans wear a white robe with a white hood, over which, when they go out, they put a black cloak with a black hood. Ignatius appointed no other habit than the one used by the clergy in his time, that his disciples might be able the more readily to converse with persons of all ranks.*

Notwithstanding the example set by the more rigid of these ascetics, and the stringency of the monastic rules, there were many of the order who disregarded the institute, and even reverted to dishonourable means to procure costly habits. Piers Ploughman says,—

> "I found there freres,
> All the four orders,
> Preaching the people,
> For profit of hemselve.
> Glosed the gospel,
> As hem good liked;
> For covetise of copes
> Construed it as they would.
> Many of these master freres
> Now clothen hem at liking;
> For hir money and her merchandize
> Marchen togeders."

The love of dress was an ancient evil among our countrymen, and even the inmates of our monastic establishments partook of the same principle. At the beginning of the ninth century, Alcuin, in his letters to the rulers of the Anglo-Saxon monasteries, implored them "to prefer the virtues of their profession to the display of the hoods of silk, of bands round the waist, of rings on the finger, and

* Hospin. De Monachis. Alban Butler, passim. Giesler's Text-Book. Glimpses of the Dark Ages. Whitaker's History of Whalley. Tindal's History of Evesham.

of fillets round the feet."* As might be expected the principal difficulty was presented among the women. When Ethelwold, bishop of Winchester, saw at court the abbess Edith, daughter of king Edgar, in a splendid dress, he was so shocked that he said to her, "Daughter, the spouse whom you have chosen delights not in external pomp. It is the heart which he demands." "True, father," replied the abbess, "and my heart I have given to him. While he possesses it, he will not be offended with external pomp."† To those who have been accustomed to regard the earlier ages of the church as the most pure, and its recluses as the holiest of mankind, appeals like the following, from the pen of the martyr bishop of Carthage, must come with startling effect. "What do ornaments mean, what means decking of the hair, except to one who either has, or who is seeking, a husband? . . . . Peter dehorts *married* women from an excessive ornamenting of their persons, who might plead, in excuse of their fault, the will and taste of their husbands; but what excuse can *virgins* find for a like regard to dress, who are liable to no such interference? . . . Thou, if thou goest abroad, sumptuously arrayed, alluring the eyes of youth, drawing after thee the sighs of admirers, fomenting lawless passions, and kindling the sparks of desire, and even, if not destroying thyself, destroying others, and presenting to their bosoms a poisoned dagger, canst not excuse thyself on the pretence of preserving a mind pure and modest. Thy pretext is shamed by thy criminal attire, and thy immodest decorations, nor shouldest thou be reckoned amongst the maids of Christ, who so livest as if willing to captivate, and to be loved by, another." ‡ The monks had many maxims that were intended to teach them a better lesson. The following lines are from Old Rhymes of the Monastic Life, published by Fabricius, and quoted by Fosbroke, in his British Monachism:—

"Habens vestitum et victum,
Ut fert apostoli dictum,
Nihil quæras amplius,
De colore ne causeris,
Si fit vilis tunc læteris,
Et ficeris sobrius.
Cave ne fis curiosus,
In vestitu, nec gulosus
In diversis epulis."

* Lingard's Anglo-Saxon Church. † Ibid.
‡ Taylor's Ancient Christianity.

In some Budhistical countries there has been a similar departure from propriety; but in lands where the fashions of dress change not, and each class or caste has its appropriate costume, the temptations to this evil are less powerful in their influence. The garment now worn by the priests in Ceylon is entirely of a yellow colour, but there is a considerable difference in the shade, the dress of some appearing as if it were made of cloth that had been dyed by being steeped in the mud, whilst that worn by others is of silk, bright and glossy. A priest who frequently visited me had a silken vest that was presented to him by the king of Siam; and of this distinction, though an old man, he was not a little proud. The priests do not change their dress when proceeding to the performance of any ceremony, the usual robe being retained on all occasions. After the late rebellion in Ceylon, a priest who was sentenced to death for participation in the crime, having been shot in his robes, the governor of the island was greatly blamed, in the House of Commons and by the press, for allowing the execution to take place in this manner; but I think, unjustly; unless the priest expressed a wish to adopt another dress, and was forbidden by the authorities. No one had the right to deprive him of his robes, until he was degraded from office by the superior priests; and it would probably have been regarded by him as an additional insult if an attempt had been made to take them away at the time of his execution. The robes of the Burman priests are sometimes of woollen cloth, of European manufacture. The Tibetan priests wear silken vests, adorned with images, and have a lettered border of sacred texts woven into the scarf.

The adoption of one particular mode of dress by the ascetics was attended by a pernicious consequence, as it was supposed that merit might be gained by putting it on, though it covered a heart full of all corruption. According to a tradition of the Carmelites, Simon Stock, the prior general, 1251, received the scapulary from the Virgin. "The Virgin appeared to me," Stock is made to say, "with a great retinue, and holding up the habit of the order, exclaimed, This shall be a privilege to thee and to the whole body of the Carmelites; whosoever shall die in it will be preserved from the eternal flame." It was said by some of the Franciscans that their sainted founder went down once a year to purgatory, and set free the souls of all whose bodies were buried in the habit of his order.*

* Giesler's Text Book.

We have many proofs that among the ancients the use of ornaments, garlands, perfumes, and unguents was carried to an extravagant excess. In taking upon himself the ten obligations, the priest says, according to the seventh, "I will observe the precept that forbids the adorning of the body with flowers or garlands, and the use of perfumes and unguents." In the Institutes of Manu (ii. 178) there is a similar command; "let the brahmachári, or student in theology, abstain from chaplets of flowers." But this law is not always binding, as we read again (Inst. iii. 3); "the student having received from his natural or spiritual father the sacred gift of the Véda, let him sit, before his nuptials, on an elegant bed, decked with a garland of flowers." The use of garlands was denied by Solon to any of the Athenians who were proved to be cowards. Empedokles, when saying that he was honoured by all, adds that he was "covered with garlands." The oil with which Venus anointed the body of Hector was perfumed with roses. In Capua there was one great street called the Seplasia, which consisted entirely of shops in which ointments and perfumes were sold. Horace (Sat. I. v. 36) ridicules the pomposity of a municipal officer in the small town of Fundi, who had a shovel of red-hot charcoal carried before him in public, for the purpose of burning on it frankincense and other odours. "The preparation of perfumes among the Israelites required great skill, and therefore formed a particular profession. The rokechim of Exod. xxx. 25, 35; Neh. iii. 8; Eccles. x. 1, called apothecary in the authorised version, was no other than a maker of perfumes. So strong were the better kinds of ointments, and so perfectly were the different component substances amalgamated, that they have been known to retain their scent several hundred years. One of the alabaster vases in the museum at Alnwick castle, contains some of the ancient Egyptian ointment, between two and three thousand years old, and yet its odour remains."* That the number of ornaments then in use was excessive we may learn from Isa. iii. 18—23. In the full dress of an eastern prince there were sixty-two different ornaments, the names of which are on record. And in restricting the priests to three robes of a prescribed kind, Gótama may have had in view the evils connected with a multiplicity of dresses. The Talmud enumerates eighteen several garments that belonged to the clothing of the Jews.

Kitto's Cyclopedia, art. Perfume.

The ascetics had less authority for their peculiarities with respect to clothing than for some other of their customs, as even the angels, whom they loved so much to imitate, are represented as being clothed, when they visit our lower world, and as having "shining garments." In the Scriptures there is the same golden mean observed upon the subject of dress, that distinguishes the sacred record from all other writings. The garments of men and women are not to be of the same kind, Deut. xxii. 5; and extravagance in dress is censured; but no restrictions are enforced that would be oppressive to the wearer, or make him an object of ridicule to the world. "I will," says the apostle Paul, "that women adorn themselves in modest apparel, with shamefacedness and sobriety, not with braided hair, or gold, or pearls, or costly array; but (which becometh women professing godliness) with good works."—1 Tim. ii. 9. With which agreeth the admonition of the apostle Peter:—"Whose adorning, let it not be that outward adorning of plaiting the hair, and of wearing of gold, or of putting on of apparel; but let it be the hidden man of the heart, in that which is not corruptible, even the ornament of a meek and quiet spirit, which is in the sight of God of great price."—1 Peter iii. 4.

XIII. THE RESIDENCE.

Neither in the ten obligations binding upon the priest of Budha, nor in the precepts of the Pátimokkhan, is a residence in the forest insisted upon as a necessary privation. Gótama Budha, and the priests by whom he was usually accompanied, resided in wiháras. Nevertheless, the importance of a complete abandonment of all the conveniences of social life is frequently inculcated in the sacred books; and he is regarded as the sincerest recluse who resides in the wilderness, far away from the roof of a house, or even the umbrageous canopy of a tree. The usual name by which the laic is designated is that of grahapati, meaning literally the ruler or chief of a house; but the word house is here to be regarded as referring rather to the family than to the place of residence. Among the Singhalese the word wihára is now more generally used of the place where worship is conducted; whilst the dwelling of the priest is called a pansala, from pan, leaves, and sala, a dwelling, or a place to which any one is accustomed to resort, from a root which signifies to go.

In the age of Gótama, the practice of asceticism appears to have prevailed throughout India in its most rigorous form, and to a great extent. But by the institutions of Budha, the infliction of self-torture is discountenanced; and though some of the ordinances cannot be observed without much painful suffering, the primary idea in their appointment appears to have been that of privation and not of penance. Yet it was foreseen, or experience had already taught, that the enthusiasm of vast masses of celibates, frequently in solitude, but occasionally congregated for some common purpose, was too powerful an impulse to be brought under any ordinary mode of control; and therefore, whilst the calmer spirits were allowed the advantage of a contemplative life, away from the temptations of ordinary existence, the fervour of individuals was directed into such a course, that it might be allowed the utmost extravagance of exercise, amidst the solitude of the wilderness, without producing any pernicious consequence beyond the personal limit of the ascetic.

The apparent contradiction between the command given to the people to build wiháras, and the advice given to the priests to dwell in solitude, did not escape the notice of Milinda. The reply of Nágaséna, when enquiry was made as to the reason of this anomaly, was to the following effect:—"The beast of the forest has no settled dwelling; he eats his food here or there, and lies down to sleep in whatever place he may happen to be; and the faithful priest must in these respects be like him. But still, from the building of wiháras there are two advantages. 1. It is an act that has been praised by all the Budhas, and they who perform it will be released from sorrow and attain nirwána. 2. When wiháras are built the priestesses have an opportunity of seeing the priests (and receiving instruction). Thus there is a reward for those who build dwellings for the priests; but the faithful priest will not prefer such a place for his residence."

In a former age the ascetic Sumédha reflected that there are eight objections to residing in a house:—1. It causes much trouble in its erection. 2. It requires continual repair. 3. Some more exalted personage may require it. 4. The persons living in it may be numerous. 5. It causes the body to become tender. 6. It affords opportunity for the commission of evil deeds. 7. It causes the covetous thought, This is mine. 8. It harbours lice, bugs, and other vermin. He then reflected that there are ten advantages to be derived from residing under a tree:—1. Such a place can be found with ease. 2. It can be found in any locality. 3. When seeing the decay of the leaves, the priest is reminded of other impermanences. 4. It does not cause any covetous thought. 5. It does not afford any opportunity for evil deeds. 6. It is not received from another. 7. It is the residence of déwas. 8. It requires no fence around it. 9. It promotes health. 10. As the ascetic can meet with it anywhere, it is not necessary for him to think that he will have to return to the place he previously occupied.*

When the priest resides in a fixed habitation, there are many things that require his attention; there are also many conveniences, such as access to good water; and all these things have a tendency to gain his affections, and induce the love of that which is connected with existence. But there are some priests to whom these things are not a snare, and who can use them without harm. There were two persons respectably connected who took the obligations of the priesthood at the wihára of Thúpáráma, near Anurádhapura. One of them afterwards went to the forest of Pachinákandarája, where he resided five years. As he found it beneficial thus to live in solitude, he resolved to go and inform his friend of the advantage he had received, that he might be induced to enter upon the same course. When the day dawned, after his arrival at the wihára, he thought thus:—"The people who assist the priests will now send them cakes and rice-gruel, and whatever else they require;" but nothing of this kind took place. He then thought that as the people did not bring any food, the priests would go with the bowl to the city to receive alms. At the proper hour he accompanied his friend to the city, and, though the food they received was trifling, they went to the appointed place and ate it. He now supposed that in a little time the people would be cooking their own rice, and that then the priests would be plentifully supplied. But the portion they received was small; and they said that this was the quantity usually presented. The two priests afterwards set out to go to the forest; but when they reached a potters' village in the way, it was found that the stranger had left at the wihára his walking-stick, his cruse for holding oil, and the bag in which he put his sandals; but on mentioning this to the resident priest he

* Pújáwaliya.

learnt that his friend had no earthly possession whatever, as even the seat and bed that he used belonged to the chapter. The priest from the forest then said that it would be of no benefit to such a person to go to the solitude to which he had been invited, as all places were alike to him; whilst at Thúpeáráma he had many privileges: he was near the relics of the Budhas; he could hear the reading of the bana at the Lóhaprásáda; there were many dágobas; he could see many priests; it was as though a supreme Budha were alive. He therefore recommended his friend to remain where he was, and he returned to the forest alone.

It is recommended that when slésmáwa, phlegm, or móha, ignorance, is in excess, the priest should reside in the open forest; when pita, bile, or dwésa, anger, at the foot of a tree; when wáta, wind, or rága, evil desire, in an empty house.*

It is directed in the Pátimokkhan, that the residence of the priest, if it be built for himself alone, shall be twelve spans, according to the span of Budha in length, and seven in breadth, inside. The site must be chosen in a place that is free from vermin, snakes, wild beasts, &c., that the life of the priest, or of those who resort to him, may not be in danger, and that the destruction of animal life may not be caused by its erection. There must be a path around it wide enough for the passage of a cart. Before possession is taken a chapter of priests must see that it is not larger than the prescribed limits. Whether the residence is intended for one priest or for many, this rule must be enforced. When the dwelling is erected the priest may direct materials to be brought two or three times from grounds not under immediate cultivation, that the parts requiring stability may be rendered firm; but this number of times is not to be exceeded.

In the time of Gótama Budha, a priest who resided at Isigilla, near Rajagaha, having had his hut thrice broken down by the inhabitants, and being a potter, prepared a house entirely of earth. Collecting grass, wood, and other combustibles, he burnt it thoroughly, so that it became of a beautiful red colour, appeared like a golden beetle, and was sonorous as a bell. But when Budha saw it, he reprimanded him severely for having burnt the clay, without any feeling of compassion for the sentient beings he had destroyed during the operation, and commanded that it should be broken down.†

* Wisudhi Margga Sanné.

† Gogerly's Essay on Budhism; Journ. Ceylon Branch Royal As. Soc. i.

The eighth of the Thirteen Ordinances is called Aranyakanga. The word áranya means a forest. The priest who keeps this ordinance cannot reside near a village, but must remain in the forest. If there be a boundary to the village, or a wall, he must remain as far from it as a strong man can throw a stone; and if there be no boundary, he must reckon from the place where the women of the last house are accustomed to throw the water when they have washed their vessels. If there be only a single waggon or a solitary house, it must be regarded as a village; whether there be a boundary or not, if there be people, or if people are intending to come, it is the same as a village. All places not coming under this description may be considered as the forest. It is said in the Abhidharmma, that the forest begins at the distance of the length of 500 bows from the village. If a superior priest be sick, and that which is necessary for him cannot be obtained in the forest, he may be taken to a village; but the priest who accompanies him must leave before sunrise the next morning; though his superior should even be dangerously ill, he cannot remain in the village to assist him. The priest who keeps the superior ordinance must always remain in the forest. He who keeps the middle ordinance may remain in a village during the rainy season, in which wass is performed. He who keeps the inferior ordinance may remain in a village during the four months of the hot season, as well as during the four months of the rains. Whoever enters a village to hear bana, and for this purpose alone, does not violate the rule; but he must go away before sunrise, and may not remain when the bana is concluded. Budha declared that the priest who resides in a forest had his respect. The recluse of the forest does not meet with those things that suggest what is improper to enter into the mind; he becomes free from fear, though living in solitude; the love of existence passes away, through his being continually exposed to wild beasts and other dangers. When at a distance from men, there is the true privilege of solitude, an advantage that even Sekra does not receive. To him who lives thus, the second ordinance will be as a shield, and the rest of the ordinances as so many weapons; the forest will be as an arena of battle, and, as if in a chariot, he will proceed to conquer Mára, or evil desire.

The first of the Twelve Sacred Observances of the Chinese is called a lan jo (âranyaka), according to which the mendicant ought always to dwell in a "lieu de repos, lieu tranquille." It is the means of avoiding the troubles of the mind, of removing the dust of desire, of destroying the causes of revolt, and of obtaining transcendental wisdom.*

The ninth of the Thirteen Ordinances is called Rukhamúlikanga, from rukha, a tree, and mula a root. The priest who keeps this ordinance must avoid all tiled houses, and live at the root of a tree (the root being defined to be the space within which the leaves fall on a calm day, or on which the shadow of the tree falls at noon); but trees of the following kinds are prohibited: a tree at the limit of a country; a tree in which any déwa resides who receives offerings from the people; a tree whence gum is taken, or edible fruits are gathered; a tree in which there are owls, or a hollow tree; and a tree in the midst of the ground belonging to a wihára. The priest who keeps the superior ordinance may not live in a place that is pleasant or agreeable. From the spot in which he resides he must put away the leaves with his foot. He who keeps the middle ordinance may live in a place prepared by others. He who keeps the inferior ordinance may call a novice to prepare a place for him, by sprinkling sand, and putting a fence round, as if it were a house. The priest must leave the tree, if ever there should be a festival near it. None of the three can live in a house without breaking the ordinance; and it is also broken if the priest goes to any place where there is a concourse of people. When he sees the leaves falling he is to think of the impermanency of all things. This ordinance was much commended by Gótama Budha. It was at the root of a tree that he received his birth, became Budha, preached his first sermon, and died.

The tenth of the Twelve Sacred Observances of the Chinese is called vrikchamoûlika. The mendicant who has not attained to wisdom amidst the tombs ought to meditate under a tree, and there to search out reason, as did Budha, who accomplished under a tree the principal circumstances of his life.†

The tenth of the Thirteen Ordinances is called Abbhókásikanga, from abbhi, open, void, and okása, space. The priest who keeps this ordinance may not live in a place where there are people, or at the root of a tree; but in an open space. He may enter the wihára to hear bana; and he may go to hear bana, or to say bana to another, if called for that purpose; as may the priest who observes the preceding ordinance. He may enter the refectory, or

* Remusat's Relation. † Ibid.

the place where water is warmed for the priests to bathe, when going to hear or say bana; he may also go inside to place a seat for a superior priest, if there be not one previously; when going along the road, if he sees an aged priest carrying the alms-bowl, or any other requisite, he may carry it for him to relieve him, or even for a young priest, if he be weak; when it rains he may go for shelter to any place in the middle of the road, but he may not leave the road for that purpose, nor is he allowed to run; but when carrying the requisites of another he may go quickly, and may seek a place of shelter, even though it be not in the middle of the road; yet he may not remain when the rain is over. The same rules apply to the priest who observes the preceding ordinance. The priest who keeps the superior ordinance cannot live near a tree, or a rock, or a house; but in an open space he may put up his robe as a screen. He who keeps the middle ordinance may remain under an overhanging rock. He who keeps the inferior ordinance may live in a cave into which the rain percolates, a threshing-floor when the people are gone, a shed made with leaves or with talipot, or a lodge made for the purpose of watching the rice-fields. Any of the three who lives in a place where there are people, or at the root of a tree, and not in an open space, breaks this ordinance.

The eleventh of the Twelve Sacred Observances of the Chinese is called âbhyavakâshika. The mendicant, remaining under a tree, and partly covered by its shade, minds not the cold. It is true that the rain and humidity reach him, that the dung of birds defiles him, and that he is liable to be wounded by venomous beasts; but he is at liberty to exercise meditation. Remaining upon the ground his spirit is refreshed; the shining of the moon seems to purify his mind; and he can more readily become entranced.*

The eleventh of the Thirteen Ordinances is called Sosánikanga, from sosána, a cemetery, or place where the dead have been deposited, or where dead bodies have been burnt. The priest who keeps this ordinance must always reside in a cemetery, and it must not be near a village. Until twelve years have passed over from the time a body is burnt, the place may be regarded as a sosána. The priest may not make a place like a court of ambulation, nor frame a hut; he may not sit in a chair or recline on a couch; and he is forbidden to provide water, as if it were a priest's regular dwelling. This is a very difficult ordinance, and must be observed

* Remusat's Relation.

with much sorrowful determination. When walking, he must turn his eye in part towards the cemetery; and when he enters it, it must not be by the principal road, but by an unfrequented bye-path. When walking in the day-time, if he sees a tree or an ant-hill, he must mark what it is, and he will then not be afraid of what he may see at night. He may not cast stones at the devils he may see or hear. He may not remain away from the place a single night: he must always be there at midnight, but at dawn may leave it; he must not eat any kind of food that is agreeable to the devils or that is made with sesamum, mée, flour, flesh, or sugar (lest evil should befall him from the wish of the devils to possess these things for their own benefit); he must look out for the bones left by dogs and other animals. He may not enter any house, as he lives in the midst of the smoke arising from the funeral pile and of the stench proceeding from dead bodies. The priest who keeps the superior ordinance is always to remain in some place where there is the burning of bodies, the stench of corruption, and weeping for the loss of friends. He who keeps the middle ordinance may remain in the place where there is any one of these three. He who keeps the inferior ordinance may remain in any place where a body has been deposited within the space of twelve years. The priest who remains away from the sosána a single night breaks this ordinance.

The ninth of the Twelve Sacred Observances of the Chinese is called s'màs'ànïka. To dwell among the tombs brings to the mind of the mendicant just ideas relative to the three things that are the first gate of the law of Foe, "l'instabilité, la douleur, et le vide." He here sees the spectacle of death and of funerals. The putridity and corruption, the impurities of every kind, the funeral piles, the birds of prey, generate within him thoughts relative to the impermanency of all things and hasten the progress of that which is good.*

The residences of the priests in Ceylon are usually mean erections, being built of wattle, filled up with mud, whilst the roof is covered with straw, or the platted leaves of the cocoa-nut tree. Their residences in Burma appear to be of the same description, but those in Siam are much superior, having richly-carved entrances, and ornamented roofs. None of the fervour of the original institution is now manifested among the Singhalese. About the year

* Remusat's Relation.

1835 there was a priest near Negombo who professed never to reside in a house, and to subsist entirely upon fruits. From the singularity of his appearance, and the mystery of his life, he was an object of great terror to children. Though regarded by some persons as sincere, his conduct was generally condemned, and he was thought to be of weak intellect.

This mode of asceticism is of too striking a character not to have had many imitators in the west. Mary, of Egypt, resided in the desert beyond the Jordan forty-seven years. During the first four years of the penance of Hilarion he had no other shelter from the inclemencies of the weather than a little hovel, made of reeds and rushes woven together. He afterwards built a little cell, still to be seen in the time of Jerome, which was only a little longer than his body, four feet broad, and five feet in height. Martinianus lived many years upon a rock surrounded by water, in the open air. James, of Nisibis, chose the highest mountains for his abode, retiring to a cave in the winter, and the rest of the year living in the woods, in the open air. Martin, of Tours, had a cell built of wood, his monks having generally cells of a similar description, whilst some resided in various holes dug in the sides of the rocks. In the sixth century it was customary in some places for a monk, celebrated for his virtues, to be chosen, who was afterwards to lead the life of a recluse, walled up in a cell, and spending his whole time in fasting, praying, and weeping. Marcian shut himself up in a small enclosure, out of which he never went, his cell being so low and narrow, that he could neither stand nor lie in it without bending his body. But the most singular residence was that of Simeon Stylites, who passed thirty years of his life upon the top of a column, which was gradually raised from nine to sixty feet in height.

Even in our own inclement country, the zeal of these ancient ascetics has been emulated. Simon Stock, a youth of Kent, in the twelfth year of his age, retired to the forest, and resided in the hollow of a large oak tree. When the anchorets of England retired from the world, the ceremony of seclusion was generally presided over by the bishop. Their cells, twelve feet square, had three apertures, one for receiving the housel, another for food, and the third for lights. The door was generally walled up, and the anchoret was not permitted to come out, "but by consent and benediction of the bishop, in case of great necessity."

XIV. OBEDIENCE.

The yoke of the recluse must in many instances be exceedingly painful of endurance. Far away is he from all the amenities of the world, though formed by the hand of God to seek their enjoyment; he is often alone, and has much leisure, by which the melancholy circumstances of his situation are almost continually presented to his mind; the silence and solitude that are around him people themselves with shapes that appear to him with mockery and gibe, until his own spirit seems to add its powers to the number of his persecutors; and in the place where he expected to find peace there is only disappointment and vexation. Yet if he be a coenobite also, there are occasional opportunities of intercourse with other men, all of whom are enduring the same piercing of the soul by that which is more cruel than the serpent's tooth; and if permitted the exhibition of the slightest symptom of dissatisfaction, or to communicate to each other their individual woes, the heaviest bar and the strongest wall would be insufficient to retain them within the bounds by which they are circumscribed. The gloomy abstractedness, the sunken eye, channelled brow, hollow cheek, pallid countenance, and attenuated frame, with which the painter delights to present to us the monk, are the faithful semblances of a sad reality; and these emaciations are too frequently the result of painful exercises of discipline imposed by an imperious master, and not from vigils and penances self-imposed, that the body may be subdued, and the whole man be soul. The code of discipline to which he is subject is therefore most severe and stringent in all that relates to intercourse with members of the same fraternity: to his superior, he must be in every respect submissive; to his equal, reserved; and to his inferior, distant. The necessity of implicit obedience is therefore insisted upon in all monkish canons. It is one of the eight things requisite to monastic perfection, and is called "the cardinal virtue of monks." In the monasteries founded by David, the patron of Wales, the candidates for admission had to wait ten days at the door, during which time they were tried with harsh words and repeated refusals, in order that they might learn to die to themselves; and they were afterwards required to discover their most secret thoughts and temptations to the abbot. In the Regula Benedicti, cap. 5, it is said, "Primus humilitatis gradus est obedientia sine mora;" and in the first chapter it is said that the rule and life of the Franciscans is this, "to obey the holy gospel of our Lord Jesus Christ, living in obedience, without property, and in chastity." But to see this principle in perfection we must examine the institutes of the Jesuits. The most perfect obedience and self-denial were the two first lessons that Ignatius inculcated upon his novices. They were told at the door, as they entered, that they must leave behind them all self-will and private judgment. In his letter to the Portuguese Jesuits, On the Virtue of Obedience, he says that this alone brings forth and nourishes all other virtues. He calls it the peculiar virtue and distinguishing characteristic of his society, in which, if any member suffer himself to be outdone by those of other orders in fasting or watching, he must yield to none in obedience. He adds that true obedience must reach the understanding as well as the will, and never suffer a person even secretly, to complain of, or censure, the precept of a superior; nor is it a less fault to break the laws of obedience in watching than in sleeping, in labouring than in doing nothing. No particular bodily austerities are prescribed by the rules of the society; but there are two practices that are to be most rigorously observed. The first is called the rule of Manifestation, by which every member is required to discover even his inclinations to his superior; the second is, that every member renounces his right to his own reputation with his superior, giving leave to every brother immediately to inform his superior of his faults, without first observing the law of private correction, which in common cases is acknowledged to be right.*

The profound respect that was paid by the inmates of the monastery to their abbot may be learnt from the following extract of a MS. in the British Museum relative to the abbey of Evesham. "The newly-elected abbot, if he were consecrated out of the monastery, shall, when he returns, be received by us in a festive procession. After his instalment by the prior, he is everywhere to be received with particular reverence. We must be reverently obedient to him in all things lawful: and as he passes along, either through the cloister, through any of the offices, or any where except in the dormitory, all shall stand up and bow to him while passing. . . . . No one shall walk abreast with him, except to mass. Wherever he shall sit, no one shall presume to sit down by him, unless he command him so to do. If bidden to sit down by him, that person shall bow to him in a devout manner, and thus humbly take his seat. . . . .

* Hospin. De Monachis. Alban Butler, July 31.

Whoever shall give anything into his hand, or receive anything from him, shall kiss his hand. Wherever he shall be present, there should be observed the strictest order and discipline. When he shall reprehend any monk who has behaved or spoken amiss, whether it be within the cloister or not, that monk shall afterwards entreat his pardon in a humble manner, as if in the chapter-house, and shall stand before him till ordered to sit down; and as long as he sees him to be angry, so long shall he entreat for pardon, till his wrath be appeased." *

The Essenes paid so great a respect to each other, that if ten of them were sitting together, no one would speak if it were contrary to the wishes of the nine; and if a senior among them were only touched by a junior, he had to wash himself from the pollution, as he would have had to do if touched by a stranger. The results to which the law of obedience led were of a varied character. The director of John, the Dwarf, bade him, as his first lesson, plant a dry walking-stick in the ground, which he was to water every day until it brought forth fruit. The novice was obedient, though he had to fetch the water a considerable distance; but in the third year the stick actually took root, put forth leaves and buds, and produced fruit, which John gathered and gave to his brethren, telling them that it was the fruit of obedience. When Lanfranc, afterwards archbishop of Canterbury, was once reading a Latin sentence he was stopped and told by his superior to pronounce the e in docere short. Though he knew that he was right, he made the alteration as commanded, saying that it was a greater sin to disobey the abbot, who commanded him in Christ's name, than to adopt a wrong quantity. A similar story is told of the still more celebrated Thomas Aquinas. It was part of the Benedictine rule, that when two monks met, the junior was to ask benediction from the senior; and when he passed by the junior was to rise and give him his seat, nor to sit down till he bade him. When the abbot entered the chapter, all descended one step and bowed to him, standing on the same step until he sat down. When he went out with benediction, the monks met him on their knees, and gave the kiss of charity, to his hand first, and afterwards to his mouth, if he offered it. When the monks delivered anything to him they kneeled, kissing his hand if he was seated. No brother was allowed (cap. 37) among

* Tindal's History of Evesham.

the Benedictines to cross the threshold of the monastery without the permission of his superior.

It is probable that in this part of the institute the ascetic would meet with his heaviest cross. By the constitution of our species, as social beings, we are necessitated on many occasions to give up our own will; and whenever new associations are formed, whether as a family, a club, an order, a sect, a city, or a country, there are additional barriers to the exercise of the individual will. But in all these instances there is an interchange of assistance, a reciprocity of kindly offices, and an acknowledged advantage, that causes the momentary sacrifice on our part to be recompensed in a thousand modes, that are more than an equivalent for the loss we have had to sustain; so that the home in which the family is congregated, or the country by which the exercise of our national institutions is bounded, are magic words that have often been the most powerful impulse in the rallying cry that has led men on to victory or death. But there is in man a natural propensity to usurp a greater authority than that which is properly conceded to him, on account of the position in which he is accidentally placed as a ruler. In this respect we are true children of the father-fiend, who is made to say that he had rather reign in hell than serve in heaven. It is a base lie that he utters, as he would readily give up his sovereignty to be the lowest of the seraphs that ministers before the throne; but it is one so consonant with our own corrupt imaginations that we give it credence, until maturer thought has convinced us that it is an empty boast. In the monastic institutes this passion has been carried out to its utmost limit. The recluse was taught that all within, as well as all without, is to be abandoned; that not only the *mine* but the *me* was to be sacrificed at the ascetic altar. The superior aimed at exercising an influence like that of the steam-engine of some extensive manufactory in modern times, which throughout the vast edifice over which it rules is the motive power by which every thread is thrown and every wheel revolves. There was a restriction upon all the senses of the monk, that there might be no outward irregularity; and if the mind wandered, however innocently, from the prescribed course, the weakness was to be confessed to the superior and absolution sought. In the Pátimokkhan the misdemeanours that require confession and absolution form the more numerous class.

When viewed in connexion with this severity of discipline, some of the names given to the monks and nuns, as brother, and abbot;

sister, and abbess; appear to be singularly inappropriate, as the tender associations to which they allude ought to have no place in the breast of the recluse, if the principle of asceticism be right. He is not allowed to love any being whatever upon earth; the order or the institute, a thing of the imagination, is to engross the place of every relationship; and it sometimes usurps the place of God. The titles given to the superior priests of Budha are more consistent with their circumstances, being equivalent rather to prior or archimandrite. Jerome did not approve of the word abbas, as he thought that its use was contrary to the command, to "call no man father upon earth."

Among the Budhists, so strict a rigidity of social discipline is not required, as the priests are enjoined to take the alms-bowl from house to house, in order to procure food. This itself is an employment, enough to engage the attention without producing fatigue, whilst it affords them the opportunity of exercise; and by bringing them into contact with much that is beautiful in the world without, is equally beneficial to the body and the mind. We have therefore no reason to suppose that in the pansal there is exercised the cruelty of the western inquisitor, who too frequently wrings tears and blood from the reluctant inmate of his dark prison-house before his spirit is subdued or his heart broken. Nevertheless, there is the recognition of the same principle; every mark of respect is to be paid to the superior priest, and the causing of a division among the priesthood is one of the sins from the penal consequences of which there is no possible release by means of anything that can be done in the present state of existence.

The following precepts are contained in the Pátimokkhan: The priest is forbidden to bring a groundless charge against another priest, in order to have him excluded from the community; he is not to take hold of some trifling matter, and found a charge thereon; with all solemnity he is charged not to sow dissensions, or to endeavour to perpetuate existing divisions, among the priesthood; no one is to aid and abet a priest who is causing divisions; the priest is not to refuse admonition; when spoken to on account of any evil conduct, he is not to say that the priests are captious and partial; he is not to use contemptuous speech, nor to slander the priests; unless with permission, he is not to declare to others the crimes of the priests; he is not to go to the place previously occupied by another priest, in order to annoy him, and cause him to leave; he is not from anger, to expel another priest, or cause him to be expelled; he is not to act unkindly, or do anything that would discompose another priest; he is not to hide, or cause to be hid, even in sport, the articles belonging to another priest; he is not to bring forward again a cause that has been once decided; he is implicitly to obey the precepts called Sahadammikan (laws binding on all the priests); he is not to be angry with another priest and strike him or push against him; he is not to suggest doubts against another priest, in order to annoy him, nor is he to listen when other priests are in debate or at strife; and he is not to consent to any ecclesiastical procedure, and then complain of the investigation.

The law declaring that the priest shall not take hold of any trifling matter and found a charge thereon was enacted by Gótama Budha under the following circumstances. A certain priest wishing to ruin another priest, named Dabbo, was unable to accomplish his object without resorting to an equivocation, as the conduct of Dabbo was blameless. Walking one day with his fellow-priests, and seeing a flock of goats, he said that he would give to one of the he-goats the name of Dabbo, and to a she-goat the name of Mettiya (a priestess who had been previously excluded), in order that he might be enabled to declare that he had seen Dabbo and Mettiya guilty of improper conduct. An investigation took place, but the equivocation was detected; and this law was enacted in consequence.*

It is forbidden to the inferior priests to be in the company of the superior, or those who are more aged, without paying them proper respect. They are not to jostle them, nor to go in front of them when seated; nor are they to sit on a higher seat, or to talk when near them, or when talking with them to use action with their hands and feet; they are not to walk near them with their sandals on, or to walk about in some part of the same court at a higher elevation, or to walk at the same place at the same time. They are not to go before them or press upon them, when carrying the alms-bowl. They are not to be harsh with the novices. And they are not to take upon themselves matters with which they have no right to interfere, such as to put firewood in the place where water is warmed for bathing, or to shut the door of the bath, without permission.†

The crime called sangha-bhéda, or the causing of a division

* Gogerly's Translation of the Pátimokkhan; Ceylon Friend, Dec. 1839.
† Wisudhi Margga Sanné.

among the priesthood, is one of the five deadly sins, for which the delinquent must suffer during a whole kalpa in hell. It cannot be committed by a laic or a novice; it can only be done by one who has received upasampadá ordination.* The five deadly sins have been already enumerated, p. 37.

Some of these regulations will remind the reader of the forms observed on board our men of war. The strictness of the discipline that is enforced is the salient point at which the monk and the soldier meet; and though the warrior and the recluse form an antithesis, in this as in many other instances extremes have been made to meet from some partial resemblance, and in the year 1119, a military order was founded in Jerusalem combining the monastic life with the tumult of the camp and the strife of the battle.

XV. THE EXERCISE OF DISCIPLINE.

The code of ecclesiastical law called Pátimokkhan, is to be recited bi-monthly in a chapter of not fewer than four priests. But the ascetic brotherhood appear ever to dislike being reminded of their duty, as this rule is not attended to in Ceylon, and an abbot of Wardon, in his letter of resignation, assigns the following as one of the reasons why he could no longer hold the office. "They be in nombre xv brethern, and excepte iij of them, non understande ne knowe ther rule nor the statutes of ther religione." Yet according to the Regulations of Benedict all the monks who are able, are to learn the rules of the order memoriter.

Before the Pátimokkhan is read, the place of assembly must be swept, low cushions prepared for the priests to sit upon, and water placed for them to drink. There are twenty-one persons who may not be present, as laics, eunuchs, &c. Between each priest a space is to be left of two cubits and a-half. The chapter is not legally constituted if all the priests are under ecclesiastical censure for the same crime. In that case it will be necessary that they be absolved by some one who is not guilty; but if they be guilty of different faults they can absolve each other, after confession, and then proceed to business. When one section of the rule is read, the enquiry is made three times if all that are present have observed

* Milinda Prasna.

the precept; and if no answer is given, it is supposed to be in the affirmative; but if any one has broken the precept, and does not confess it, he is regarded as being guilty of a wilful lie. When a priest has been guilty of any of the thirteen crimes that involve suspension and penance, and shall conceal the fact, upon its discovery he is placed under restraint as many days as he has concealed it, then for six nights he is subject to a kind of penance, and after this period he may be restored to his office by a chapter, at which twenty priests must be present. No priest is allowed to question the utility of reading the Pátimokkhan, in the manner prescribed, and if any priest is convicted of manifesting impatience relative to the reading of this code, he is to confess his crime and receive absolution. The matters brought before the chapter are to be deliberately investigated, and the sentence is to be determined by the majority. The modes of punishment that are appointed are of the mildest description, including reprimand, forfeiture, penance, suspension, and exclusion. The principal exercises of penance appear to be, sweeping the court-yard of the wihára, and sprinkling sand under the bó-tree or near the dágobas. In one legend it is stated that some ascetics, who were required as penance to go to the Ganges and take up a portion of sand which they were to bring to a certain place, had by this means, in the course of time, made a mound of sand that was many miles in extent. It was the custom of Pachomius to carry sand from one place to another, in the night season, when he wished to overcome his drowsiness.

It is said in the Wisudhi Margga Sanné, that when a priest falls into an error, or commits a fault, that is comparatively of little moment, he is to seek forgiveness from a superior priest; and if all who reside in the same wihára are inferior to himself, he is to go to some other wihára for the purpose. Until absolution is thus received, the evils arising from the fault continue to exist.

In Burma, when a priest is detected in the violation of the law of continence, the inhabitants of the place where he lives expel him from his monastery, sometimes driving him away with stones. The government then strips him of his habit, and inflicts upon him a public punishment. The grand master, under the predecessor of Badonsachen, having been convicted of this crime, he was deprived of all his dignities, and narrowly escaped decapitation, to which punishment he was condemned by the emperor. Whenever a priest has been guilty of a violation of the rules of his order, he is required to go immediately to his superior, and kneeling down before him, confess his crime. There are some sins, of which confession must be made, not merely before the priest, but before all who are assembled in the chapter. A penance is then imposed upon the delinquent, which consists of prayers (or, more probably, of stanzas from the bana), to be recited for a certain number of days, according to the time he has suffered to elapse without confession; and these prayers must be said in the night. A promise must also be given to refrain from such faults in future, and pardon asked of all the priests for the scandal given, with a humble request to be again admitted into the order. But these regulations are at present much neglected, as the priests content themselves with an indefinite mode of confession, something resembling the Confiteor of the Romanists.*

Among the Benedictines, when an offence was committed, there was, first, private admonition, then public reproof, separation from the society of the brethren, corporal punishment, expulsion; the delinquent was permitted to return thrice, but after the fourth relapse he was ejected for ever. The discipline of some of the orders was extremely severe. According to the rule imposed by an Irish saint, Columban, the monk who did not say Amen at grace, before and after meals, was to have six lashes; he who talked in the refectory was also to have six lashes; and he who coughed at the beginning of a psalm was to be treated in a similar manner, as well as he who touched the chalice with his teeth, or smiled during the time of divine service. They who spoke roughly and frowardly were to receive fifty lashes, as well as they who were disrespectful to the superior. For small faults the chastisement was six lashes; for greater, especially in things relating to the mass, sometimes 200 lashes were given, but never more than twenty-five at one time. When a monk had finished his task of work, if he did not ask for more, penance was enjoined. Among the punishments were prolonged fasts, silence, separation from the table, and humilations.†

The clergy were anciently punished by suspension; by being mulcted of a portion of their salary; by being forbidden to exercise some of the duties of their office; by degradation, as from the rank of priest to that of deacon; and by non-admission to the sacrament of the Lord's Supper, unless they approached the table as laymen. The inferior clergy were liable to imprisonment and stripes. In

* Sangermano's Burmese Empire. † Alban Butler, Nov. 21.

large cities there were houses of correction, decanica, attached to the churches. In extreme cases excommunication was resorted to, after which there was no possibility of restoration to the clerical dignity.*

The authority of the popes of Rome was never displayed in such appalling magnificence as when they laid the nations under an interdict. It was then that the prophecy was fulfilled, which spake of him "who opposeth and exalteth himself above all that is called God, or that is worshipped; so that he as God sitteth in the temple of God, shewing himself that he is God."—2 Thess. ii. 4. As the ancient kings are represented as being moved from beneath to meet the monarch of Babylon on his entrance into sheol, so we can imagine the princes of all times, from those who had merely executed justice to those who had waded through seas of gore, going forth to do homage to these "vicegerents of the Almighty," when their "pomp was brought down to the grave," for having so far surpassed all other potentates, in the strength of the spell they dared to mutter, the terribleness of the fears they aroused, and the varied character of the miseries they inflicted upon men. It was not merely that all religious offices were suspensed, that the churches were closed against the laity, the altar against the performance of marriage, and the churchyard against the burial of the dead; in addition, the clergy were placed in deadly opposition to the laity, and the laity to the clergy. The consequences of this antagonism were sometimes tremendous, as when John cast into prison Geoffry, archdeacon of Norwich (for having abdicated the functions of his office as a judge of the exchequer when he heard that his king was excommunicated), and caused him to be wrapped in a sheet of lead shaped like an ecclesiastical mantle, leaving him, without food, to perish under the weight of the metal by which he was oppressed. At the period of the same interdict the ecclesiastics, generally, were exposed to ill-treatment and murder from all ranks. They had suspended the privileges of the church to punish the people, and the people suspended the privileges of the state to punish them.

It was the peculiar privilege of the commandries of the Knights Hospitalars to be permitted to receive persons under sentence of excommunication. By a rule of their order persons who had been denounced might take refuge in their churches, where lights were directed to be kept continually burning. The Hospitalars might

* Riddle's Christian Antiquities.

visit interdicted persons when sick to administer consolation, and inter them when dead with the rites of the church in the cemeteries belonging to their own order; if they passed through an interdicted place, they, and they alone, could perform mass in the churches; and if even a whole city or province were excommunicated the people could still resort to the commandries for the offices of religion. There were certain monasteries, as that at Bury, that had also the privilege, as a peculiar mark of pontifical favour, of exemption from the general effects of the interdict. "With the doors shut, without ringing of bell, and with a low voice," the services were at such times to be performed.*

It appears from the Tibetan works on Budhism that the priests of Gótama were accustomed to put under ban, or interdict, any person or family, in the following mode. In a public assembly, after the facts had been investigated, an alms-bowl was turned with its mouth downwards, it being declared by this act that from that time no one was to hold communication with the individual against whom the fault had been proved. According to the text, no one was to enter his house, or to sit down there, or to take alms from him, or to give him religious instruction. After a reconciliation had taken place, the ban was taken off by the alms-bowl being placed in its usual position. This act was as significant as the bell, book, and candle; but much less repulsive in its aspect and associations.

XVI. MISCELLANEOUS REGULATIONS.

The priests in Ceylon are seldom seen with anything in the hand, unless it be the alms-bowl, or the fan which, like a hand-screen, is carried to prevent the eyes from beholding vanity. They are usually followed by an attendant, called the abittayá. When the priest receives the offering of a fleece of wool, he is forbidden by the Pátimokkhan to carry it a greater distance than three yojanas.

The priest is forbidden to dig the ground, or to cause it to be dug; he is not to cut trees or grass; he is not to sprinkle water in which there are insects upon grass or clay, or cause it to be sprinkled; he is not to go to view an army, unless there be a sufficient reason, in which case he may remain with the army two or three

* Taylor's Index Monasticus.

nights, but not longer, and in this period he may not go to the place of combat, or to the muster of troops, or to see any sight connected with the army. The priest may not, when in health, kindle a fire to warm himself, or cause one to be kindled, unless it be the mere lighting of a lamp, or some similar act.*

The disgusting filthiness exhibited by some of the ancient monks is seldom presented among the priests of Budha. Cleanliness of the person is inculcated; but the priest is not allowed to bathe more frequently than once a fortnight, unless it be in six weeks of the summer and the first month of the rainy season, or when sick, or engaged in work or travelling, or when there is rain accompanied by wind. The priests of Egypt, according to Herodotus (ii. 37), washed themselves in cold water twice every day and twice every night. Among the Benedictines, the monks in health, and especially the young, were commanded (Reg. cap. 36) to be sparing in the use of the bath; but it might be used by the sick as often as was necessary. The more rigorous climate in which the greater part of the ascetics of Christendom resided, would cause the more ancient institute to be greatly modified, in order that it might become adapted to its novel circumstances. The monks in the fens of Lincolnshire, as well as those that have had to live amidst the everlasting snows of the Alps, would have perished, if not allowed the warmth of a fire. Hence the calefactory was a necessary apartment in all the monasteries of the north; and would no doubt be a favourite place of resort to those of the fraternity who were the tenderest, the merriest, or the most indolent.

The priest is to use a tooth-cleaner regularly in the morning. It is generally made of some fibrous substance. The Brahmans have a similar observance. "A brahman rising from sleep is enjoined, under penalty of losing the benefit of all rites performed by him, to rub his teeth with a proper withe." †

In the sacred writings there are frequent allusions to customs connected with the strangers who visited the wiháras, from which we may infer that they received all necessary attention and assistance; but in every instance that I remember, the reference is to priests alone, and it does not appear that laymen are permitted, when travelling, to take up their abode within the precincts of any place occupied by the sramanas of Budha. There was therefore no edifice attached to the wihára, like the xenodochium, in which any

* Pátimokkhan. † Colebrooke's Miscellaneous Essays, i. 124.

traveller might receive temporary relief, and in which a certain number of the poor were relieved by a daily alms. The monks were indebted to this institution for a great part of their popularity; but though in the olden time it was a useful and almost necessary establishment, it was liable to be much abused, and its proceedings would often bring sorrow to the minds of the more conscientious brethren.

The priest may not enter the village, or sit down in it loudly laughing, but speaking in a low tone, with a steady gait; not swinging the arms about, or turning the head, or with his arms placed on his hips, or with his head covered. He may not sit on his heels in the village, or sit lolling. And he is not to perform the offices of nature standing, nor upon any growing vegetable substance, nor in water.*

There are some precepts contained in the Pátimokkhan that cannot be understood unless the circumstances that gave rise to them are known; such as, that "if any priest shall place a bed or stool with unfastened legs upon the upper terrace of a residence, and sit or lie down upon it, it is páchittiyan, a fault requiring absolution and confession." This law was enacted on account of a priest who lay down upon a bed with a loose leg in this position, and the leg falling down materially injured a priest who was below.

In taking upon himself the seventh of the ten obligations, the priest declares, "I will observe the precept that forbids attendance upon dancing, singing, music, and masks." The Brahmans were placed under a similar restraint. "Let the student in theology abstain from . . . dancing, and from vocal and instrumental music. . . . The Brahman must not gain wealth by music or dancing, or by any art that pleases the sense. . . . Let him neither dance nor sing, nor play upon musical instruments, except in religious rites. . . . Brahmans who profess dancing and singing, let the judge exhort and examine as if they were Sudras."—Manu, Inst. ii. 178; iv. 15, 212; viii. 102. That the drama was much cultivated in India at an early period, we may learn from Wilson's Hindu Theatre and other sources. But these exhibitions have ever been condemned by the more thoughtful among mankind. Diogenes said that the Olympic games were only great wonders to a set of fools. It was decreed by the council of Constantinople, held A. D. 681, that no monk should be allowed to witness theatrical exhibitions.

* Pátimokkhan.

By taking the ninth of the ten obligations the priest declares that he will forego the use of high or honourable seats, or couches. The ancients appear to have been most extravagant in the costliness of their beds and couches. The prophet Amos (vi. 4) pronounces woe upon those who "lie upon beds of ivory, and stretch themselves upon their couches . . . that chant to the sound of the viol and invent to themselves instruments of music." Among the offerings made to the temple at Delphi by Croesus were a great number of couches decorated with gold and silver. We are informed by Chrysostom that the beds of the principal Antiochians were of ivory, inlaid with silver and gold. Clemens of Alexandria, in his Paedagogue, book ii. cap. 9, condemns the use of beds of carved ivory, with silver feet, in imitation of animals or reptiles, and upon which are coverlets embroidered with gold. He says that silver sofas, and beds of choice woods ornamented with tortoise-shell and gold, with coverlets of purple, are to be abandoned; and asks if we shall rest the worse because our beds are not of ivory, or our coverlets tinted with Tyrian dyes.

The priest is not allowed to take even so little as a blade of grass, when it is not given; and if he takes a sandal, or anything of the same value, or above that value, he ceases to be a son of Sákya, as the withered branch that is severed from the tree ceases to put forth the tender bud or to bear fruit.

He is not allowed knowingly to deprive any animal, though it be even so insignificant as an ant, of life; and if he deprives any human being of life, even though it be by the causing of abortion, he ceases to be a son of Sákya, as the mountain that has been severed in two cannot again be united.*

In the time of Gótama there was a priest who was under the influence of passion; and as he was unable to maintain his purity he thought it would be better to die than to continue under this restraint. He therefore threw himself from a precipice near the rock Gijakúta; but it happened that as he came down he fell upon a man who had come to the forest to cut bamboos, whom he killed, though he did not succeed in taking his own life. From having taken the life of another he supposed that he had become párájiká, or excluded from the priesthood; but when he informed Budha of what had taken place, the sage declared that it was not so, as he had killed the man unintentionally; his intention being to take his

* Kammawáchan.

own life. Budha, however, made a law forbidding the priests to commit suicide.* Several stories are related in the Tibetan Dul-vá, of suicide or poisoning among the priests, or of causing themselves to be slain or deprived of life, out of grief or despair, upon hearing of the various kinds of miseries or calamities of life. Budha, in consequence, prohibited any one from discoursing on these miseries in such a manner as thereby to cause desperation.† A similar story is related of Hegesias, whose gloomy descriptions of human misery were so overpowering, that they drove many persons to commit suicide, in consequence of which he received the surname of Peisithanatos.

In the city of Wésáli there was a priest, who one day, on going with the alms-bowl, sat down upon a chair that was covered with a cloth, by which he killed a child that was underneath. About the same time there was a priest who received food mixed with poison into his alms-bowl, which he gave to another priest, not knowing that it was poisoned, and the priest died. Both of these priests went to Budha, and in much sorrow informed him of what had taken place. The sage declared, after hearing their story, that the priest who gave the poisoned food, though it caused the death of another priest, was innocent, because he had done it unwittingly; but that the priest who sat upon the chair, though it only caused the death of a child, was excluded from the priesthood, as he had not taken the proper precaution to look under the cloth, and had sat down without being invited by the householder.‡

It is said by Budha, in the Brahma Jála Sútra, that there are some sages who attend places of amusement, where there are recitations, masques, and dancing, and combats are exhibited between men, animals, or birds; they also play at various games of chance, and practice all kinds of buffoonery; and they love jesting and sports that are childish or vain. They prognosticate the nature of future events, and pretend to tell whether they will be prosperous or adverse from the voices of animals and birds, as well as from the marks upon their bodies, from meteors, the appearance of fire in any particular direction, earthquakes, dreams, and the manner in which cloth is eaten by rats or insects. They pretend to foretell the fate of princes and empires; they deal in spells, invocations, elixirs, and panaceas; they teach the sciences, and write deeds and contracts; they practise certain ceremonies with fire fed by a par-

* Milinda Prasna. † Csoma Körösi. ‡ Milinda Prasna.

ticular kind of spoon, and from the manner in which it burns they predict the future. But all these practices are disreputable, and are to be avoided by the faithful priest.*

No priest is allowed to make false pretensions to the possession of rahatship; and if any priest acts contrary to this precept, he ceases to be a son of Sákya; as the palm-tree cannot continue to grow when deprived of the branches that form its head.†

There are thirty-two subjects upon which the priests are forbidden to converse:—about kings, as to their array; robbers, the royal guard, armies, narrations that cause fear, wars, harangues, food, drink, garments, vehicles, couches, garlands, perfumes, music, villages, as to the pleasantness of their situation or otherwise; towns, cities, provinces, relatives, women, intoxicating liquors, streets, khumbandas (imaginary beings of a most disgusting appearance), deceased relatives, wealth, the origin of the earth, the origin of the sea, the sayings of the sceptics, mental error, sensual enjoyments, and their own imaginations.‡

There are sixty-three charitas, influences, or states of the mind, of which the principal are rága, dwésa, and móha. 1. Rága, complacency, pride, or evil desire. 2. Dwésa, anger, of which hatred is a component part. 3. Móha, unwiseness, ignorance of the truth. The manifestation of these principles is diversified, as seen in the conduct of different priests, according to, 1. The position of the body. 2. The work that is performed. 3. The manner of eating. 4. The objects that are seen. 5. The natural disposition or general conduct.

1. The position of the body. The priest who is under the influence of the first principle, when he walks puts his foot down gently; both his feet are put down and lifted up in an uniform manner, and they are gracefully bent when moved. The priest under the influence of the second seems to plough the ground with his feet, or to dig it; he walks hurriedly, and lifts his foot with violence. The priest under the influence of the third has no uniformity in his gait; he puts his foot down as if he were doubtful or afraid, and walks as if he were fatigued. This is declared by Budha in the Mágandhiya Sútra. In like manner, when the first priest sits down or reclines, it is done gently; his feet and hands are put in the proper place, and he rises in a quiet manner. The second sits down quickly, and rises as if in displeasure. The third throws

* Wisudhi Margga Sanné. † Kammawáchan. ‡ Pújáwaliya.

himself down in any way, puts his hand and feet in any posture that suits his convenience for the moment, and when he rises it is as if with reluctance.

2. The work that is performed. The first priest, when he prepares to sweep any place, takes hold of the broom in a proper manner, neither too firmly nor too loosely, and sweeps evenly. The second seizes the broom with violence, sends the dust or sand here and there, and sweeps without any uniformity. The third holds the broom loosely, throws the dirt away carelessly, and does not sweep clean. It is the same with all other things. The first does them in the best manner, the second with a bang, and the third negligently. The first, as another instance, puts on his robe in such a manner that it appears round and full; the second wraps it closely round his body; and the third puts it on loosely.

3. The food that is eaten. The first priest likes food of a delicious flavour; he makes the rice into neat round balls, and throws it into his mouth gently. The second likes sour things, or those that are highly seasoned; he fills his mouth and eats in haste. The third has no partiality for any particular kind of food; he lets it fall whilst he is eating, and throws it into his mouth without care.

4. The objects that are seen. The first priest, when he sees any common thing looks at it as if it was something wonderful; if it is only good in a trifling degree, his attention is arrested; he looks over any faults that there may be, and is loth to leave that which pleases him. The second, when he sees anything that is not pleasing, turns away from it at once. If there be only a trifling fault he is angry; he does not acknowledge the good that there may be, and he turns away as if it was unworthy of his regard. The third looks at all things without manifesting any emotion; if anything is depreciated he commends it, or if it is praised he commends it too.

5. The general conduct. The first priest does not see his own faults; he boasts to others of things he does not possess; he is deceptive, proud, and covetous; he likes his bowl, robe, and person to appear to the best advantage. The second cannot endure the faults of another; he seeks to destroy the good name of other priests, envies their prosperity, and goes about to injure their possessions. The third goes on without diligence or care; his mind

is in doubt; he is never settled; he is unwise, without discrimination, and does not perceive error.

When the priest who is under the influence of the first principle enters upon the exercise of the ordinances, it will be an advantage to him to reside in some place that has a dirty floor and clay walls, or under the shelter of a rock, or in a hut made with straw, or in some place that is covered with dust, defiled by birds, broken down, very high or very low, and altogether uncomfortable; there should be no good water near it; the road to it should be infested by wild beasts, and in bad order; such furniture will be good for him as is covered with cobwebs and of a disagreeable appearance; his robe should be torn at the end, threadbare, like a net, rough, heavy, and therefore difficult to keep out of the dirt; his alms-bowl should be of dirty clay, or pierced with nails, or of heavy iron, disgusting as a skull; he should go to seek alms where there is a bad road, a great distance to go, the houses are far asunder, and the people difficult to find; where the food will be given him by a low slave, and be made in a filthy manner, of inferior rice, with bad whey, toddy, or rotten fruit; nor is it well for him to lie down, but to stand or walk about; and his kasina-mandala (a magical circle that will afterwards be explained) should be made in some disagreeable form. By this means his pride or evil desire will be subdued.

The priest under the influence of dwésa should reside in a place that, on the contrary, is clean, pleasant, and beautiful, and where there are plenty of people; his robe should be made of the cloth of China, Sóchára, Kósala, or Kasi, or of fine cotton, or of goat's hair, light and graceful; his bowl should be round as the bubble; the village that he visits should neither be too near nor too distant; nor is it good for him to sit or to lie down, but to stand or walk, and his kasina-mandala should be made in some agreeable form. By this means his anger or hatred will be subdued.

The priest under the influence of móha should reside in an open place, not surrounded by trees; he should be where there are plenty of people; it is good for him to walk, and his kasina-mandala should be the size of the brazen dish called teti; not smaller. By this means his ignorance will be subdued.

There are three other states:—1. Sardháwa, confidence. 2. Bódhi, wisdom. 3. Witarka, reasoning. The priest who is under the influence of the first principle may be known by his being always cheerful; he delights in hearing bana; he does not associate with the worldling; he does not hide his own faults; and he seeks the assistance of the three gems. The priest under the influence of the second is kind and tractable; he eats his food slowly, and is thoughtful; he avoids much sleep, and does not procrastinate; and he reflects on such subjects as impermanency and death. The priest under the influence of the third talks much; he delights in being where there are many people; his mind is never settled; at night he thinks he will do this or that; indeed he is always thinking; but he does not try to do in the day what he had resolved upon at night, and his thoughts continually pass from one subject to another. Such a priest should reside in a place where the doors are thrown open; it is a disadvantage when there are people near him, or gardens, tanks, or green hills. It is therefore better for him to live in some such place as a cave, or in the midst of trees; his thoughts must be restrained, or he will continually reason; and his kasina-mandala must be small.*

In an inscription, cut about the year 262 in the rock near the temple of Mihintala, in Ceylon, the following passages occur:—"The resident priests at this wihára shall make it a constant practice to rise at the dawn, meditate on the four preservative principles, perform the ablution, and then, having attired themselves with the robe, in the manner prescribed in the Sékhiyá, they shall resort to the Æt wihára, and having there performed the religious offices, afterwards partake of rice-gruel and rice, and shall duly administer to the priests who could not attend on account of sickness, such things, at their respective cells, as the physicians had prescribed. . . . To the expounders of the Abhidharmma pitaka shall be assigned twelve cells; to those who preach from the Sútra pitaka seven cells; and to such of the resident priests as read the Winaya pitaka, five cells, with food and raiment. . . . All the lands that belong to this wihára shall, with the products thereof, be enjoyed by the priesthood in common, and shall not be subdivided and possessed separately. . . . When orders are issued to the dependants or retainers, or when any of them are to be dismissed, it shall be with the concurrence of the whole community of priests, and not by the will of an individual. . . . Those who have services and offices allotted to them shall attend duly at their respective places, excepting those who may have gone on wihára service to a distance; those who have to attend at the place where rice is issued, and at the place

* Wisudhi Margga Sanné.

where rice and gruel are prepared in the morning, will not be allowed to be absent. . . . If the servants attached to the places where offerings are made embezzle or squander the offerings made thereat, laborious work shall be imposed upon them. . . . Those who have only assumed the yellow robe, but engage in traffic inconsistently therewith, and destroy life (by such occupations as the chase) shall not be permitted to dwell around the mount. . . . Throughout the domains of this wihára, neither palm-trees, nor mee-trees, nor any other fruit-bearing trees, shall be felled, even with the consent of the tenants. . . . If a fault be committed by any of the cultivators, the adequate fine shall be assessed according to usage, and, in lieu thereof, the delinquents shall be directed to work at the lake, in making an excavation not exceeding sixteen cubits in circumference and one cubit in depth. If he refuse so to labour, the assessed fine shall be levied." *

Not long previous to his death, Gótama Budha, in the city of Rajagaha, propounded unto Ananda various precepts, in sections of seven, which were declared to be imperishable. The first series was to the following effect:—The priests were enjoined to meet frequently (for the performance of religious ordinances), and to assemble in great numbers; to rise from these meetings simultaneously, and simultaneously and unanimously discharge their sacerdotal duties; to abstain from establishing that which has not been prescribed, from abrogating that which has been established, and to accept the precepts as they are laid down, and inculcate and maintain them; to support, reverence, respect, and obey the elders of the priesthood, of great experience, venerable by their ordination, fathers of the community, and chiefs of the sacerdotal body, and to learn from them that which ought to be acquired; to overcome the desires that cause the wish for regeneration in another mode of existence; to delight to dwell in the wilderness, and to keep their minds embued with pious aspirations. It is declared that, as long as these precepts are observed, the designs of the priests must prosper, and cannot fail.

The priests were enjoined in the second series to abstain from excessive indulgence in allowable gratifications; to abstain from unprofitable gossip; to abstain from an indolent existence; to avoid the omission of meeting together in chapters; to shun the society of evil-doers; to abstain from becoming the friends of the unwise; and never to relinquish the pursuit of the rahatship.

* The Ceylon Almanac, 1834.

In the Analysis of the Tibetan Kah-gyur, by Csoma Körösi, there are allusions to many of the observances of the priesthood, among which the following may be enumerated :—The observances are of a very comprehensive description, extending not only to moral and ceremonial duties, but to modes of personal deportment, and the different articles of food or attire. The precepts are interspersed with legendary accounts, explaining the occasion on which Sákya thought it necessary to communicate the instructions given. The order in which converts are received into the order of the priesthood, either by Sákya or his disciples, is particularized; two presidents are appointed, and five classes of teachers ordained; the questions to be propounded are given, and the description of persons inadmissible from bodily imperfections or disease explained; a variety of rules on the subject of admission is laid down; the behaviour of the person after admission is regulated; the cases in which he should require the permission of his principal specified, and various moral obligations prescribed, particularly resignation and forbearance, when maltreated or reviled. No person is to be admitted except in full conclave, nor any one allowed to reside among the priests without ordination. Confession and expiation should be observed every new and full moon, in a public place and congregation, the ceremony being fully detailed. There are a number of precepts of a whimsical character, such as that a priest shall not wear wooden shoes, nor lay hold of a cow's tail in assisting himself to cross a river. There is a treatise on the subject of dress, particularly on the fitness of leather or hides for the shoes of the priests, and on the drugs and medicaments the priests are allowed to use or carry about. The priests are permitted to eat treacle, to cook for themselves in time of famine, to cook in ten kinds of places, to eat meat under certain restrictions, and to accept gifts from the laity. They are to wear not more than three pieces of cloth, of a red colour, to wear cotton garments when bathing, to be clean in their dress and in their bedding, and never to go naked. Refractory or disputatious brethren are first to be admonished in the public congregation (of the priests), and if impenitent to be expelled from the community.*

* Abstract of the Contents of the Dul-vá, or first Portion of the Káh-gyur, from the Analysis of Mr. Alexander Csoma de Körös. By H. H. Wilson, Sec. A. S. Journal of the Asiatic Society of Bengal, No. 1, Jan. 1832.

XVII. THE ORDER OF NUNS.

In the commencement of Budhism there was an order of female recluses. The names they receive are generally equivalent to those that are given to the males, with a feminine termination; but the name of priestess is applied to them less properly than that of priest to the men. In their case, as well as in that of the other sex, it is not an intact virginity that is lauded, but the future abandonment of sexual intercourse.

The first female admitted to profession was Maha Prajápati, the foster-mother of Gótama Budha. The wife of the sage, Yasódhara, and several other of his principal female relatives, abandoned the world at a subsequent period. It was stated upon the admission of the queen-mother that there were eight ordinances to which the priestesses would be required to attend. "Women are hasty," said Gótama;* "they are given to quarrel, they exercise hatred, and are full of evil. If I exalt them to the principal places in this institution, they will become more wilful than before; they will despise my priests; but unto them who act thus there can be no benefit from profession; they cannot attain the paths (that lead to nirwána). There must therefore be eight ordinances of restraint, that they may be kept in, as the waters of the lake are kept in by the embankment. 1. The female recluse, though she be a hundred years old, when she sees a sámanéra novice, though he be only eight years old and just received, shall be obliged to rise from her seat when she perceives him in the distance; go towards him, and offer him worship. 2. The female recluses shall not be permitted to go to any place at their pleasure. When they go to receive instruction, they must retire at the conclusion of the service, and not remain in any place beyond their appointed limit. 3. Upon the day of every alternate póya festival they must go to the priest and request to be instructed. 4. At the end of the performance of wass they must join with the priests to conclude the ceremony. 5. Any female who wishes to perform the act of meditation called wap may be allowed to retire for the purpose during the period of two póyas, or fifteen days, but not for a longer time. 6. When any female recluse wishes to become upasampadá, and receive the superior profession, she must previously exercise herself in all things that

* Pújáwaliya.

are appointed, for the space of two years, and at the end of this period must receive the privilege in a chapter composed of the professed of both sexes. 7. The female recluse is not to speak to the priest in terms of disparagement or abuse. 8. She must not be allowed to teach the priest, but must herself listen to the instruction he gives, and obey his commands. These eight ordinances are enjoined upon all the female recluses who would receive profession in this institute, and are to be observed continually until the day of their death." The better sex is not treated with much respect by Budhist writers. One sentence will be sufficient to show this:—Mátu gámo námo pápo.* "That which is named woman is sin;" i. e. she is not vicious, but vice. Upon another occasion Gótama said, "Any woman whatever, if she have a proper opportunity, and can do it in secret, and be enticed thereto, will do that which is wrong, however ugly the paramour may be; nay, should he be even without hands and without feet." But in order to show that this declaration is not true, the king of Ságal, in one of his conversations with Nágaséna, repeated the instance of a woman, Amará, who, though a thousand times solicited by a man whose appearance was like that of a king, in a place where there was no second person to see what was done, resisted his entreaties, and kept herself pure. Nágaséna replied, that the declaration of Budha was made when relating the crime committed in a former age by the queen Kinnará, who secretly stole away from the palace when the king slept, and committed sin with a man whose hands and feet had been cut off, and who was ugly as a préta sprite. "And think you," said the priest, "that if Amará had met with a proper opportunity she would not have done the same? This opportunity was not presented; she was afraid of others, and of the sorrow she must have endured in the world to come; she knew the severity of the punishment she would have to receive for such a sin; she was unwilling to do anything against the husband whom she loved; she respected that which is good and pure; she abhorred that which is mean; she was a faithful and virtuous wife; and all these things (with many others of a similar kind) took from her the opportunity of doing wrong. She might have been seen by men; if not seen by men, she might have been seen by the préta sprites, or by the priests who have divine eyes, or by the prétas that know the

* Gogerly's Essay on Transmigration and Identity. Ceylon Friend, Oct. 1838.

thoughts of others; or, if unseen by any of these, she could not have hid herself from her own sin and its consequences; and it was by these causes she was prevented from doing wrong." This was a curious mode of confirming the declaration of Budha; but it unfolds before us the Budhistical motives for resisting sin.

In the works I have read there are few allusions to the female recluses, and it is probable that this part of the system, from being found to be connected with so many evils, was gradually discontinued. The priestesses carried the alms-bowl from door to door, in the same manner as the priests, and are represented as being present at the meetings of the sangha, or chapter. They could only be admitted to the order by a chapter composed entirely of females. The convents were in some instances contiguous to the residences of the priests; but the intercourse between members of the two orders was guarded by many restrictions. To violate a priestess involves expulsion from the priesthood, without the possibility of restoration.

Clemens Alexandrinus, in his account of the eastern ascetics, notices the virgins called Σεμναι. In one of the caves of Ajunta there is painted a female worshipper of Budha, in the act of teaching, surrounded by a group of smaller figures who are attentively listening, one of whom is supposed to be a Brahman. There are at present no female recluses in Ceylon. It is said by Robert Knox that, at the period of his captivity, the ladies of Kandy were accustomed to beg for Budha. "The greatest ladies of all," he says, "do not go themselves, but send their maids, dressed up finely, in their stead. These women, taking the image along with them, carry it upon the palms of their hands, covered with a piece of white cloth; and so go to men's houses, and will say, We come a begging of your charity for the Budha, towards his sacrifice. And the people are very liberal; they give only of three (four?) things to him; either oil for his lamp, or rice for his sacrifice, or money, or cotton yarn for his use." Occasionally, in more recent times, a female has been known to shave her head and put on a white garment; but these instances are rare.

The priestesses or nuns, in Burma, are called Thilashen: they are far less numerous than the priests. The greater part of them are old women; but there are also some that are young, who, however, forsake the sisterhood as soon as they can procure husbands. The Burman nuns shave the head, and wear a garment of a particular form, generally of a white colour. They live in humble dwellings, close to the monasteries, and make a vow to remain chaste so long as they continue in the order; but they may quit it whenever they please. Any breach of their vow is punished by their secular chief. The profession of a nun is not much respected by the people, and in general may be looked upon as only a more respectable mode of begging. They openly ask for alms in the public markets, contrary to the custom of the priests, who only "expect charity." There are a few recluses of a more respectable class, commonly widows, who have funds of their own, or are supported by their relatives.* The nuns in Siam are less numerous than in Burma.

The nuns in Arrakan are said to be equally common with the priests: they either reside in convents, or live separately in some house constructed near a temple, superintending the offerings, and leading a life of religious abstinence. The greater part have remained in continence from their youth; others have retired from the world at a more advanced age, and in some instances after marriage; but only when that marriage has not been productive of children. Their dress is similar to that of the priests, and their discipline in every other respect alike. The may-thee-laying are an inferior order, wearing white dresses, and having their heads shaven. They live in convents of their own, and their discipline is less severe than that imposed upon the priests, as their knowledge of the doctrines of the faith is less extensive.†

In China the nuns are said, by Bishop Smith, to be generally women of coarse manners and unprepossessing appearance. Their dress is very like that of the priests, their heads being entirely shaven, and their principal garment consisting of a loose flowing robe. An abbess whom he saw wore a black silk cap over her crown, in the centre of which was a hole, through which her bare head was perceptible.‡

Frequent mention is made by travellers of the worship of the Queen of Heaven by the Budhists of China. It appears that her name is Tien-how, and that she is equally venerated by Confucians and Budhists. According to the legend she was a native of the province of Fokien, in early life distinguished for her devotion and

* Crawford's Embassy to the Court of Ava.
† Foley's Tour through Rambree. Journ. As. Soc. Jan. 1835.
‡ Smith's China.

celibacy.* It was in the thirteenth century, under the Soong dynasty, that she became deified; and though her worship is not inconsistent with the principles of Budhism, she was of course unknown to its earlier teachers.

The eight ordinances of restraint enforced by Gótama, as above, are enumerated by Remusat as being known to the Chinese, with slight variations.† There are also eight sins and eight acts that are mentioned by him as demonstrating, when committed, that the female recluse has abandoned the precepts of Budha, and deserves to be shunned by all. The acts are, to hold the hands of a man with an evil intention, to touch his dress, to be with him in a retired place, to sit with him, to converse with him, to walk with him, to lean upon him, and to give him a meeting.

Among the followers of Pythagoras there was an order of females, the charge of which was given to his daughter. The Druids admitted females into their sacred order, and initiated them into the mysteries of their religion. The priestesses of the Saxon Frigga, who were usually king's daughters, devoted themselves to perpetual virginity. At an early period of the church, virginity began to be unduly exalted, and in nearly all places there were females who, though not recluses, were regarded as possessing a virtue more excellent than that which fell to the portion of the other members of the Christian polity. At first admired, they were then looked upon as being super-human, and at last as being super-angelic, inasmuch as they continued in this state from choice, and were enabled to retain their purity by the reception of special grace, whilst the angels were chaste from the necessity of their original constitution. When in the church they were separated from the rest of the worshippers by a partition, probably similar to the lattice-work screen that is now used to separate the women from the men in the eastern churches and the synagogues of the Jews; and sentences of Scripture were painted upon the walls for their instruction. But they resided with their relations at home, convents being then unknown; and, from the cautions that were given to them by the fathers, we may infer that they were not always willing "to see the stir of the great Babel," without sometimes "feeling the crowd." We have evidence that their situation, as well as that of other females, received the anxious attention of the rulers of the church, from the number of works upon this subject still extant, that were written

* Davis's Chinese. † Remusat's Relation.

at the period preceding the disruption of the Roman empire, when the last generations of a mighty nation revelled in the undisturbed enjoyment of the luxuries transmitted from their more energetic ancestors, and the votaries of pleasure were hurried on towards the goal of eternity amidst scenes of revelry that, in the rapidity of their succession, the seductiveness of their character, and the magnificence of their preparation, will probably have no parallel so long as the world shall endure. By Tertullian were written: De Cultu Foeminarum; Ad Uxorem; De Virginibus Velandis. By Cyprian: De Disciplina et Habitu Virginum. By Ambrose: De Virginibus; De Virginis Institutione; De Hortatione ad Virginitatem; and, doubtful, De Virginis Forma Vivendi; De Virginis Lapsu. By Chrysostom: Quod Regulares Foeminae Viris cohabitare non debent; In Eos qui Sorores adoptivas habent; De Virginitate; Ad Viduam juniorem. By Gregory Nyssen: De Virginitate vera et incorrupta.* And these works were in addition to many allusions to the same subjects in their letters, homilies, and other writings. The "canonical virgins" and "virgins of the church," are recognized by Tertullian and Cyprian; and in the fourth century monastic establishments for females were introduced. They were also called ascetriae, monastriae, castimoniales, sanctimoniales, and nonnae. The inmates were not obliged to remain for life in this seclusion, and in certain cases were permitted to retract their vows; but they could not return to the world without exposing themselves to great scandal. It was said of them (Hieron. Ep. 97) "ut aut nubant, si se non possunt continere; aut contineant, si nolunt nubere." Monks or nuns might profess their obedience to a particular monastic rule in the hands of an abbot or abbess; but the consecration of a virgin was reserved expressly for the bishop. We learn from Ambrose (De Virg. Inst.) that when a virgin was professed she presented herself before the altar, when the bishop preached to her, and gave her the veil which distinguished her from other virgins; but her hair was not cut off as in the case of monks. In many instances the nunnery afforded a secure retreat to the unprotected female from the violence of the monsters in human shape who then almost every where abounded.

In some instances, monks and nuns resided in the same convent. It is said in Tanner's Notitia Monastica that, after the Conquest, it was usual for the great abbies to build nunneries upon some of their

* Cave's Lives of the Fathers.

manors, which should be priories to them, and subject to their visitation. In some instances the nunneries belonged to a different order from the house to which they were subject; as at Shouldham, where the canons observed the rule of Augustine, whilst the nuns were under that of Benedict. Lingard says that, during the first two centuries after the conversion of our ancestors, nearly all nunneries were built upon the principle of those attached to Fontevrault, which contained both monks and nuns under the government of an abbess, the men being subject to the women. The abbey of St. Hilda, at Whitby, was of this kind. In one part was a sisterhood of nuns, and in another a confraternity of monks, both of whom obeyed the authority of the abbess. "There were two monasteries at Wimborne," says Ralph of Fulda, who wrote the life of St. Lioba, "formerly erected by the kings of the country, surrounded with strong and lofty walls, and endowed with competent revenues. Of those, one was designed for clerks, the other for females; but neither (for such was the law of their foundation) was ever entered by any individual of the other sex. No woman could obtain permission to come into the monastery of the men; nor could the men come into the convent of the women, with the exception of the priests who entered to celebrate mass, and withdrew the moment the service was over."* The princess Bridget, of Sweden, built a monastery in which she placed sixty nuns, and, in a separate enclosure, thirteen priests, four deacons, and eight lay-brothers. The men were subject to the prioress in temporals; but in spirituals the women were under the jurisdiction of the friars, as the order was instituted principally for the women, and the men were only admitted to render them spiritual assistance. The convents were separated by an enclosure; but so near, that both classes made use of the same church, in which the nuns kept choir above in a doxal, and the men underneath, without their being able to see each other. Sion House, near London, was the only monastery of this order in England.†

In Italy there are orders, as of the Collatines, or Oblates, the members of which reside in a monastery, but make no vows except a promise of obedience. They can go abroad, inherit property, and the restrictions under which they are placed are few. Some abbies of this description are said to be filled by ladies of rank.

* Lingard's Anglo-Saxon Church.

† Alban Butler. Oct. 8.

XVIII. THE SACRED BOOKS.

The Budhas, the sacred books, and the priesthood, are regarded as the three most precious gems. They are all associated in the threefold formulary repeated by the Budhist when he names, as an act of worship, the triad to which he looks as the object of his confidence and his refuge. There is thus among the Budhists the same reverence paid to the number three, that we witness in nearly all ancient systems, as in the Brahma, Vishnu, and Siva of the Brahmans; the Amoun-ra, Amoun-neu, and Sevek-ra of the Egyptians; and the Jupiter, Neptune, and Pluto of the Greeks and Romans.

The importance of the possession of a written code, regarded as having been given by inspiration, may be seen in the fact that no system of religion has yet become extinct that has presented a record of this description. However absurd the document may be in itself, or however unintelligible the style in which it is written, it has appeared as the palladium of the system it contains. Hence the missionaries to the east have a difficulty to contend with that was not presented to the early messengers of the cross in any of the countries where they principally laboured. But from the same cause the priests of India are encumbered by weapons that may be wrested from their hands, and used to their own destruction. When it is clearly proved to them that their venerated records contain absurdities and contradictions, they must of necessity conclude that their origin cannot have been divine; and the foundation of the systems being once shaken, the whole mass must speedily fall, leaving only the unsightly ruin, as a monument of man's folly, when he endeavours to form a religion from the feculence of his own corrupt heart, or the fancies of his own perverted imagination. And there is another thought that must not be forgotten. Whenever the Scriptures have been translated into any language, from that time there have always been individuals speaking that language who have believed in the truths they contain, so long as the dialect has continued in use as a vernacular medium of intercourse.

In our notice of the sacred books of the Budhists we propose to consider:—1. Their names and divisions. 2. The history of their transmission. 3. The honours they receive and the benefits they confer in return.

I. *Names and Divisions.*—The second of the three great treasures is called Dhammo, or in Singhalese, Dharmma. This word has various meanings, but is here to be understood in the sense of truth. It is not unfrequently translated "the law," but this interpretation gives an idea contrary to the entire genius of Budhism. The Dharmma is therefore emphatically, the truth. In common conversation this venerated compilation is called the Bana; the books in which it is written are called bana-pot; and the erection in which it is preached or explained is called the bana-maduwa. The word bana means literally the word; from the root bana, or wana, to sound. In the names that have been given by different religionists to their sacred books there is a considerable similarity of meaning, which is generally marked by simplicity. Thus, we have the Scriptures, or the writings; the law, torah, from the root torah, instruction; the Talmud, from the root lamad, to learn; the Gemara, from a root of similar meaning, gamar, to learn; the Mishna, from the root shamah, to repeat; the Koran, from the root karaa, to read; the Zand Avasta, from zand, the Persian language, and avasta, word; and the Veda, from vida, to know. The different portions of the Dharmma, when collected together, were divided into two principal classes, called Suttáni and Abhidhammáni. These two classes are again divided into three collections, called respectively in Singhalese:—1. Winaya, or discipline. 2. Sútra, or discourses. 3. Abhidharmma, or pre-eminent truths. The three collections, as already intimated (page 1), are called in Pali, Pitakattayan, from pitakan, a chest or basket, and táyo, three; or in Singhalese, Tunpitaka. A Glossary and a Commentary on the whole of the Pitakas were written by Budhagósha, about the year A. D. 420. They are called in Pali, Atthakathá, or in Singhalese, Atuwáwa. The Rev. D. J. Gogerly has in his possession a copy of the whole of the sacred text, "and the principal of the ancient comments, which, however, form but a small portion of the comments that may exist." As this gentleman resided in 1835, and some subsequent years, at Dondra, near which place the most learned of the priests in the maritime provinces in Ceylon are found, he had admirable facilities for securing a correct copy of the Pitakas. Mr. Turnour states that the Pali version of the three Pitakas consists of about 4,500 leaves, which would constitute seven or eight volumes of the ordinary size, though the various sections are bound up in different forms for the convenience of reference.

1. The Winaya Pitaka contains the regulations of the priesthood.

It is said to be the life of the religion of Budha, as where discipline is at an end, religion is at an end. It is divided into five books:—1. Párájiká. 2. Páchiti. 3. Maha Waggo, or Maha Waga. 4. Chúla Waggo, or Chula Waga. 5. Pariwárá Pátá. "The Párájiká and Páchiti contain the criminal code; the Maha Waggo and Chúla Waggo the ecclesiastical and civil code; and the Pariwárá Pátá is a recapitulation and elucidation of the preceding books, in a kind of catechetical form."

This Pitaka contains 169 banawaras, which appear to resemble the sidarim into which the books of the Old Testament were divided by the Jews, being the portion read in the synagogue upon one Sabbath day. The first sixty-four banawaras constitute the Bhikkhuni-wibhango; the next eighty, the Maha Waggo; and the last twenty-five, the Pariwárá Pátá. As each banawara contains 250 stanzas, called gáthás or granthas, composed of four pádas, or thirty-two syllables, in this Pitaka there must be 42,250 stanzas. The Commentary on it, called Samantapásadiká, contains 27,000 stanzas. Thus, in the whole of the Winaya Pitaka, including the text and the comment, there are 69,250 stanzas.

The Párájiká occupies 191 leaves; the Páchiti 154; the Maha Waggo 199; the Chula Waggo 196; and the Pariwárá Pátá 146; each page containing about nine lines, and averaging 1 foot 9 inches in length.

2. The Sútra Pitaka contains seven sections. It is said in the commentary called Sumangala Wilásiní, as translated by Turnour, that the Suttan is so called "from its precise definition of right; from its exquisite tenor, from its collective excellence, as well as from its overflowing richness; from its protecting (the good), and from its dividing as with a line (or thread)." For each of these epithets various reasons are given. It is said to overflow, "because it is like unto the milk streaming from the cow." It is like a line, "because as the line (suttan) is a mark of definition to carpenters, so is this suttan a rule of conduct to the wise." In the same way that flowers strung together upon a thread, or line, are neither scattered nor lost, "so are the precepts which are contained herein united by this (suttan) line." The seven sections, called sangis, are as follows:—1. The Díghanikáyo, or Dik-sangi, written upon 292 leaves, with eight lines on each page, and 1 foot 10 inches long. It contains three warggas, Sílaskhanda, Maha, and Páti, and has 64 banawaras, or 16,000 stanzas, including 34 sútras of greater

length (dígha, long) than the rest, the first being the Brahmajála-sutra. 2. The Majjhima-nikáyo, or Medum-sangi, written upon 432 leaves, with eight and nine lines on each page, and 1 foot 11 inches long. It contains three pannásas, Múla, Majjhima, and Upari, and has 15 warggas, including 80 banawaras, 152 sútras, of moderate (majjhima, middle) length, and 21,250 stanzas. 3. The Sanyutta-nikáyo, or Sanyut-sangi, written upon 351 leaves, with eight and nine lines on each page, and 2 feet 2 inches long, It contains five warggas, Sata, Nidhána, Skhanda, Saláyatana, and Maha. It has 100 banawaras, 7,762 sútras, classed (sanyutta) under different heads, and 25,000 stanzas. 4. The Anguttara-nikáyo, or Angótra-sangi, written upon 654 leaves, with eight or nine lines on each page, and 1 foot 10 inches long. It has six nipátas, Tíka, Chatuska, Panchaka, Chasattaka, Atthanawaka, and Dasa-ékádasa; and it has also 120 banawaras, 9,557 sútras, in different classes (anga, members), and 44,250 stanzas. 5. The Khudaka-nikáyo, or Khudugot-sangi, contains 15 books, some of which are in the form of sermons, and has 44,250 stanzas:—(1.) The Khudapátan, written upon four leaves, with eight lines on each page, and 2 feet 4 inches long. (2.) The Dhammápadan, or Dam-piyáwa, the Paths of Religion, written upon 15 leaves, with nine lines on each page, and 1 foot 8 inches long. It contains 423 gáthás, which appear to have been spoken on various occasions, and afterwards collected into one volume. Several of the chapters have been translated by Mr. Gogerly, and appear in the Friend, vol. iv. 1840. The Singhalese paraphrase of the Paths, is regarded by the people as one of their most excellent works, as it treats upon moral subjects, delivered for the most part in aphorisms, the mode of instruction that is most popular among all nations that have few books at their command, and have to trust in a great degree to memory for their stores of knowledge. A collection might be made from the precepts of this work, that in the purity of its ethics could scarcely be equalled from any other heathen author. (3.) The Udánan, written upon 48 leaves, with nine lines on each page, and 3 feet long. It contains compilations from other parts of Budha's discourses. (4.) The Itti-attakan, written upon 31 leaves, with eight lines on each page, and 1 foot 9 inches long. (5.) The Suttá-nipátan, written upon 40 leaves, with nine lines on each page, and 2 feet long. (6.) The Wimána-watthu, written upon 158 leaves, with seven and eight lines on each page, and 1 foot 9 inches long. (7.) The Péta-watthu, written upon 142 leaves, with eight and nine lines on each page, and 1 foot 8 inches long. (8.) The Théra-gáthá, written upon 43 leaves, with nine lines on each page, and 2 feet 4 inches long, contains instructions to the priests. (9.) The Therí-gáthá, written upon 110 leaves, with eight lines on each page, and 1 foot 7 inches long, contains instructions to the priestesses. (10.) The Játakan, containing an account of 550 births of the Bódhisat who afterwards became Gótama Budha. The text and commentary are blended into one narrative, in which form it is written upon 900 leaves. (11.) The Niddéso (of the size of which I have not met with any account). (12.) The Pathisambhidan, or Pratisambhidáwa, written upon 220 leaves, with eight lines on each page, and 1 foot 11 inches long. (13.) The Apadánan, written upon 196 leaves, with ten lines on each page, and 2 feet long. (14.) The Budha-wanso, written upon 37 leaves, with eight lines on each page, and 2 feet long. (15.) The Chariyá-pitako, written upon 10 leaves, with eight lines on each page, and 3 feet long.

It is said in the Sadharmmálankáré that the whole of the five sangis contain 142,250 stanzas; but this does not agree with the separate numbers as stated in the same work. The commentary contains 254,250 stanzas. Hence the whole of the Sutra-pitaka, including both the text and commentary, contains 396,500 stanzas.

3. The Abhidharmma-pitaka was addressed by Budha to the déwas and brahmas. "The books are not in the form of sermons, but specify terms and doctrines with them, with definitions and explanations." It contains seven sections. 1. The Dhammasangani, written upon 72 leaves. 2. The Wibhanga, written upon 130 leaves. 3. The Kathá-watthu, written upon 151 leaves. 4. The Puggalan, or Pudgala-pragnyapti, written upon 28 leaves. 5. The Dhátu, written upon 31 leaves. 6. The Yámakan written upon 131 leaves. 7. The Patthanan, written upon 170 leaves. The whole of these leaves are 2 feet 4 inches long, and average about nine lines on each page.

The text contains 96,250 stanzas, and in the commentaries Arthasáliníya, Sammówinódana, and Sattaka, there are 30,000; so that in the whole of the Abhidharmma-pitaka, including both the text and commentary, there are 126,250 stanzas.*

* For the names of the books, their divisions and their size, I am indebted to Turnour, and for the character of their contents to Gogerly, see Turnour's Mahawanso; Turnour's Examination of the Pali Budhistical Annals, Journal Bengal As. Soc. July 1837; Gogerly's Essay on Budhism, Journal Ceylon Branch Royal As. Soc. vol. I. part i. The other parts of the information contained in this section are taken from the Singhalese Sadharmmálankáré,

From the above statements it will be seen that whilst the commentary on the Winaya and Abhidharmma Pitakas is smaller, that on the Sutra Pitaka is much larger, than the text.

The Atthakathá, Atuwáwas, or commentaries, as well as the text of the Pitakas, were defined and authenticated at a convocation (to the history of which we shall presently refer), and repeated at a second and third, without any alteration, except that an account of the previous convocations was added. When Mahindo, son of the monarch Asóka, introduced the religion of Budha into Ceylon, he carried thither in his memory the whole of the commentaries, and translated them into Singhalese. By Budhagósha, about A.D. 420, they were again translated from Singhalese into Pali; and it is this version alone that is now in existence, the original Pali version and the translation into Singhalese having alike perished. These commentaries are therefore more recent than the text; and from the slight opportunities I have had of ascertaining their contents, I should infer that they abound much more with details of miraculous interposition than the Pitakas that they profess to explain. It is said in the Mahawanso, cap. xxxvii, that "all the théros and ácháriyos (preceptors) held this compilation in the same estimation as the original text." Not long ago, this was also acknowledged by the priesthood of Ceylon; but when the manifest errors with which it abounds were brought to their notice, they retreated from this position, and now assert that it is only the express words of Budha that they receive as undoubted truth. There is a stanza to this effect, that the words of the priesthood are good; those of the rahats are better; but those of the all-knowing are the best of all. We learn from Colebrooke, that "it is a received and well-grounded opinion of the learned in India, that no book is altogether safe from changes and interpolations until it has been commented; but when once a gloss has been published, no fabrication could afterwards succeed; because the perpetual commentary notices every passage, and in general explains every word."*

1. All the discourses of Budha are said† to be one, as to sangwara, observance, and they are also one as to rasa, design. From the moment that Gótama obtained the state of a supreme Budha to the time of his dissolution, i. e. during an interval of forty-five years, in all that he uttered, to whatever order of intelligence, he

* Miscellaneous Essays, i. 90.

† Sadharmmálankárè, &c.

had only one design, which was, to assist sentient beings in the reception of nirwána. 2. The discourses of Budha were two-fold, as to the classes called Dharmma and Winaya. 3. They were three-fold, as to their division into root, centre, and summit; and as to first, middle, and last; and also as to the pitakas, Winaya, Sútra, and Abhidharmma. 4. They were five-fold, as to the nikáyas, Dik, Madyama, Sanyut, Angóttara, and Kudugot. 5. They were nine-fold, as to the angas, Suttan, Geyyan, Weyyákaran, Gáthá, Udánan, Itiwuttakan, Játakan, Abbhúta-dhammo, and the Wédattan.* The Suttan includes the sútras; the Geyyan includes the sútras that are partly in prose and partly in metrical stanza; the Weyyákaran includes the whole of the Abhidharmma, the prose sútras, and the words of Budha that are not included in any of the other angas; the Udánan includes the 82 sútras delivered by Budha in the form of stanzas expressive of joy or satisfaction; the Itiwuttakan includes the 110 sútras commencing with this formula, It was thus said by Bhagawat; the Játakan includes the 550 births of Gótama Bódhisat; the Abbhúta-dhammo includes the sútras that detail supernatural events, and begin with the word "priest!" and the Wédattan includes the sútras that by their utterance conferred the wisdom (of the paths) upon those who listened. 6. The discourses of Budha are divided into 84,000, as to the separate addresses. This division includes all that was spoken by Budha. "I received from Budha," said Ananda, "82,000 khandas, and from the priests 2,000; these are the 84,000 khandas maintained by me." 7. They are divided into 275,250, as to the stanzas of the original text, and into 361,550, as to the stanzas of the commentary. All the discourses, including both those of Budha and those of the commentator, are divided into 2,547 banawaras, containing 737,000 stanzas, and 29,368,000 separate letters. 8. They are asankya as to the matters upon which they treat.

* The Nepaulese have a similar division, with the addition of three names that are not found in this arrangement. "The Bauddha scriptures are of twelve kinds, known by the following twelve names: 1. Sútra. 2. Geya. 3. Vyákarana. 4. Gátha. 5. Udan. 6. Nidan. 7. Ityukta. 8. Jataka. 9. Vaipulya. 10. Adbhuta Dharma. 11. Avadán. 12. Upadésa." The Upadésa appears to be an unauthorised addition, from a Brahmanical source, as it is said to treat of "the esoteric doctrines equivalent to tantra, the rites and ceremonies being almost identical with those of the Hindoo tantras, but the chief objects of worship, different, though many of the inferior ones are the same."—Hodgson's Illustrations.

II. *History and Transmission.*—The system propounded by Gótama Budha was not committed to writing either by himself or his immediate disciples. It is asserted that his discourses were preserved in the memory of his followers during the space of 450 years, and that after the elapse of this period they were reduced to writing in the island of Ceylon. The documents themselves are an evidence that some considerable period must have passed over between the death of Budha and the compilation of the Pitakas in their present form. They contain the record of numerous events that can never possibly have happened; and it would require a length of time to elapse before simple facts could be distorted into fictions so palpably absurd, in those cases in which the account is founded in truth; and a period equally long would be required before the legends they contain could be invented, or when invented become generally received; as they abound in the grave recital of miraculous events and supernatural interferences, that any inhabitant of the earth would have known to be false, if published near the life-time of Budha. Four hundred years would be a sufficient period to allow of these perversions; and as the Pali language, the dialect in which the Pitakas are composed, has long ceased to be spoken, we may conclude that it could not have been at a much later era the sacred books were written.

For the establishment of the text of the Pitakas, it is said that three several convocations were held. The first was at Rajagaha, at that time the capital of Magadha, in the eighth year of Ajásat, sixty-one days after the death of Budha, or B.C. 543. The whole of the text of the Pitakas was then rehearsed, every syllable being repeated with the utmost precision, and an authentic version established, though not committed to writing. As the whole of the persons who composed this assembly were rahats, and had therefore attained to a state in which it was not possible for them to err on any matter connected with religion, all that they declared was the truth; every doctrine was correctly delivered, and in the repetition of the words of Budha, and of the other interlocutors, the ipsissima verba were faithfully declared. The rahats did not possess inspiration, if we consider this power to mean a supernatural assistance imparted ab extra; but they had within themselves the possession of a power by which all objective truth could be presented to their intellectual vision. They therefore partook of what in other systems would be regarded as divinity. The second convocation was held at Wésáli, at that time the capital of Kálásóka, in the tenth year of his reign, one hundred years after the death of Budha, or B.C. 443, in consequence of the prevalence of certain usages among the priesthood that were contrary to the teachings of Budha. The text of the Pitakas was again rehearsed, without any variation whatever from the version established by the former convocation. The third convocation was held at Pátaliputra, near the modern Patna, in the seventeenth year of Asóka, 235 years after the death of Budha, or B.C. 308. The Pitakas were again rehearsed, without either retrenchment or addition.* The history of the first of these convocations is thus recorded in the Singhalese Sadharmmálankáré.†

Whilst Gótama was yet in existence, he appointed Maha Kásyapa to be the chief or president of his disciples; and to him he committed the care of his religion when he should have attained nirwána.‡ Accordingly, after the demise of Budha it was arranged that a convocation should be held, to be attended by 500 of the most eminent of the rahats, with Maha Kásyapa at their head. On the twenty-first day after the death of the great sage, the priests who had been present at the burning of his body, went away to their separate places of abode; and the sacred edifices that were out of repair were put in proper order.§ By degrees the 500 rahats arrived at Rajagaha (the place that had been appointed for their assembly), after passing through the intermediate villages and

* In the Tibetan division of the Káh-gyur the second convocation is omitted; the third convocation is placed in the 110th year after the death of Gótama; and the last revision of the Pitakas is said to have taken place only 500, instead of nearly 1000, years after his death. But it is possible that this reference may be to some revision unknown in Ceylon, and not to that of Budhagósha. Journ. Bengal As. Soc. July, 1837.

† An account of these convocations, translated from the Pali commentary on the Pitakas, by the Hon. G. Turnour, appears in the Journal of the Bengal Asiatic Society for July and September, 1837.

‡ On a certain occasion Shákya sent the half of his sitting couch, or pillow, to Mahakashyapa, one of his principal disciples, to sit on with him, by which act he tacitly appointed him his successor as an hierarch after his death. Csoma Körösi. But in the Pali commentary it is said that Gótama appointed Kásyapa as his successor, by investing him with his own robe.

§ It is stated in the commentary that the priests were afraid lest the tirttakas should say, "The pupils of Gótama kept up their wiháras whilst their teacher was alive; on his death they have abandoned them." The priests are also said to have set themselves to the reparation of the sacred edifices that they might prevent their enemies from reproaching them by saying, "The enormous wealth bestowed by the great (in founding the structures) is lost." But if there be any truth at all in the matter, it is probable that the priests hastened home to secure their temples, and thus prevent them from being appropriated by other teachers or religionists.

towns. One of their first acts was to request a suitable place for the holding of the convocation from the monarch of that city, Ajásat, now in the eighth year of his reign, who appointed for this purpose the cave Saptapárnni, near the rock Wébhara. This cave was painted in a beautiful manner, representations of various kinds of flowers and creepers appearing upon its sides, whilst many parts were inlaid with gold, silver, and gems. The floor was sprinkled with perfumes, and curtains of many colours were hung around. There were 500 seats covered with cloth for the priests; and in the centre, looking towards the east, a throne for the person who recited the bana, with an ivory fan placed near it. Around the cave were seven circles of guards of different kinds, some of whom were giants, and others were mounted upon horses or elephants. When the whole had been prepared, Ajásat informed the priests, who, as soon as they learnt that the cave was ready, went to the place and took possession of the seats that had been appointed for them. There were 499 rahats, with Maha Kásyapa as their chief. It was observed that one seat was empty, and on enquiry it was found that it belonged to Ananda. Then Ananda, who only at this moment attained rahatship, to show the reality of its reception, arose up out of the ground in their midst, and took his appointed seat, the one that had hitherto been vacant. Upon this Maha Kásyapa, who by this token perceived that he had become a rahat, said that if Budha had been alive he would have said Sádhu on account of so great a wonder, and that it was therefore proper for them to do the same: so the whole assembly three times pronounced, Sádhu.

As the convocation was now complete, Maha Kásyapa said, "Which shall we repeat first, the Winaya, or the Abhidharmma?" The priests replied, "The Winaya is the life of Budhism; if this is properly defined, our religion will continue to exist; therefore let us first define the Winaya Pitaka." The president enquired, "Whom shall we appoint as the principal person to repeat and define this Pitaka?" "When Budha was alive," said the priests, "he declared that Upáli was most perfectly acquainted with the Winaya, and that no one had a clearer understanding of the divine words than he; therefore let it be Upáli." Accordingly, Upáli having received permission, rose from his seat, did obeisance to the assembly, and ascended the throne in the midst of the hall, when he took the ivory fan into his hand, and remained with his face towards the east. Maha Kásyapa then enquired,* "What is the first section of the Winaya? When was it spoken? On whose behalf? On account of what transgression?" "The first section," said Upáli, "was spoken by Budha in Wésali, on account of Sudinna, who had transgressed the precept of chastity." In the same way the investigation was carried on respecting all the other sections of the Winaya; and the cause, the person, the fault, the rule or ordinance established in consequence, and the additional rule, were declared.† The enquiry was in all cases made by Maha Kásyapa, and answered by Upáli, who repeated all things to the convocation in a full and perfect manner, so that not a single letter, or the least particle, of the Winaya Pitaka, was lost. When the whole was concluded, Upáli again did obeisance to the assembly, and retired to his own seat.

As the Winaya was thus completed, Maha Kásyapa enquired who was to rehearse the Sútra Pitaka; and the assembly replied that it must be Ananda, as his competency for the task had been proclaimed by Budha. When permission had been given, Ananda ascended the throne, and declared in order the place where, on whose account, and for what cause, the various sútras were delivered. The first sútra is the Brahmajála; it was delivered in the garden of Ambalattika, between Rajagaha and Nálanda, on account of Brahmadatta, a mánawaka, and Suppriya, a paribrájika, who had a dispute with each other relative to the merits of Gótama. At the commencement of Ananda's discourse, the déwas who were present began to say to each other, "The most excellent Ananda is of the Sákya race; he is a relative of Gótama; Gótama, when he was alive, proclaimed his pre-eminence; and it may be that he also has become a supreme Budha." But as Ananda perceived the thoughts of the déwas, he made known to them his real position; and when they heard him say of the sútras he repeated that they were spoken by Gótama in Jetawanna, or in some other locality, as the case might be, and that he only declared what he himself had heard, they knew from this that he was not a supreme Budha, as they had at first supposed. Nevertheless, when the whole had been rehearsed, the priests and déwas did him great honour.

* The Purânas are invariably written in the form of a dialogue, in which some person relates its contents, in answer to the enquiries of another.

† The subjects are thus enumerated by Turnour: the origin, the party concerned, the exhortation made, the sequel or application of the exhortation, and the result as to the conviction or the acquittal.

The Dik-sangi was delivered in charge to Ananda, that by him it might be preserved; the Medum-sangi, to a disciple of Seriyut; the Sanyut-sangi, to Maha Kásypa and his disciples; and the Angótra-sangi, to Anurudha and his disciples.

The Abhidharmma was recited by Maha Kásyapa, all the rest of the assembled rahats repeating simultaneously the words that he spoke.

In the establishment of this important matter, the canon of the sacred code, seven months were occupied; after which the convocation was dissolved. As five hundred priests were present, it is called the Pancha Sataka Sangha, or the Convocation of the Five Hundred.*

The interest connected with the second convocation being chiefly historical in its character, I omit the account of its proceedings; but as the reign of Asóka, in which the third convocation was held, is regarded by the Budhists as the proudest era in their annals, and the monarch himself was a religious devotee of considerable eminence, we are not permitted to treat the great council held under his auspices in the same summary manner. The native historians have described his reign in colours of the most exaggerated brilliance; but this is in consistence with their general manner: they cover their sky with rainbows, or stud it with suns instead of stars.

In the 219th year after the demise of Gótama Budha, Piyadása, son of Bindusára, and grandson of Chandragutta,† became the sole

* It is also called Patima Sanghiti, or the First Convocation, and Thériká, because it was held exclusively by théro priests.

† "This," it is said by Professor Wilson, in his valuable Notes to the Vishnu Purána, "is the most important name in all the lists, as it can scarcely be doubted that he is the Sandrocottus, or as Athenaeus writes more correctly, the Sandrocoptus, of the Greeks. The relative positions of Chandragupta, Vidmisára or Bimbisára, and Ajtasatru, serve to confirm the identification. Sákya was cotemporary with both the latter, dying in the eighth year of Ajátasatru's reign. The Mahawanso says he reigned twenty-four years afterwards; but the Váyu makes his whole reign but twenty-five years, which would place the close of it B. C. 526. The rest of the Saisunága dynasty, according to the Váyu and Matsya, reigned 143 or 140 years; bringing their close to B. C. 383. Another century being deducted for the duration of the Nandas, would place the accession of Chandragupta B. C. 283. Chandragupta was the cotemporary of Seleucus Nicator, who began his reign B. C. 310, and concluded a treaty with him B. C. 305. Although therefore the date may not be made out quite correctly from the Pauránik premises, yet the error cannot be more than twenty or thirty years. The result is much nearer the truth than that furnished by Buddhist authorities. According to the Mahawanso 100 years had elapsed from the death of Buddha to the tenth year of Kálásoko. He reigned other ten years, and his sons forty-four, making a total of 154 years between the death of Sákya and the accession of Chandragupta, which is consequently placed B. C. 389, or about seventy years

monarch of Jambudwípa. Previous to this, whilst he reigned in Udéni he had a son, Mahindo, and a daughter, Sanghamittá, both of them extremely beautiful; and as he daily increased in wealth and majesty, and was successful in all his engagements, he was called, in consequence, Asóka (literally, the sorrowless). Riches, pleasures, and honours, he possessed in the greatest abundance; but at this period he practised many cruelties, and his name was in consequence again changed to Chandásoka (the word chanda meaning wrathful, passionate). The déwas brought him daily from the Anótatta lake* sixteen vessels of water; also various kinds of medicines, supplies of beetle creepers to make splinters for cleaning the teeth, the richest mangos and other fruits, garments of five colours from the magical (kalpa) tree near the Chaddanta lake, napkins upon which to wipe the fingers, and the cloth called Utra, resembling the jasmine. He had also fragrant substances wherewith to anoint the body, and collyrium from the nága-lóka. Parrots brought daily 9000 yalas of the rice that grows spontaneously upon the borders of the Chaddanta lake, and it was freed from the husk by mice, that in the process broke not a single grain; bees brought honey, which they prepared and left, without taking any for themselves; bears worked in the forges with sledge-hammers; tigers guarded his cattle, and, until the herds were secured for the night, went not to seek their prey; birds of sweet song perched near the palace, and delighted the king with their music; and pea-fowl danced in his presence, exhibiting their splendid plumage.

too early. According to the Buddhist authorities, Chan-ta-kutta or Chandragupta commenced his reign 396 B. C. Burmese Table; Prinsep's Useful Tables. Mr. Turnour, in his Introduction, giving to Kálásoko eighteen years subsequent to the century after Budha, places Chandragupta's accession B. C. 381, which, he observes, is sixty years too soon; dating, however, the accession of Chandragupta from 323 B. C. or immediately upon Alexander's death, a period too early by eight or ten years at least. The discrepancy of dates, Mr. Turnour is disposed to think, proceeds from some intentional perversion of the Buddhistical chronology. Introd. p. L. The commentator on our text says that Chandragupta was the son of Nanda by a wife named Murá, whence he and his descendants were called Mauryas. Col. Tod considers Maurya a corruption of Mori, the name of a Rajput tribe. The Tiká on the Mahawanso builds a story on the fancied resemblance of the word to Mayúra S. Mori, Pr. a peacock. There being abundance of pea-fowl in the place where the Sákya tribe built a town, they called it Mori, and their princes were thence called Mauryas. Turnour, Introduction to the Mahawanso, p. xxxix. Chandragupta reigned, according to the Váyu Purána, twenty-four years; according to the Mahawanso, thirty-four; to the Dipawanso, twenty-four."—Wilson's Vishnu Purána, p. 468.

* It was not unusual for kings to have their water brought from a great distance. Cyrus drank no water but that of the Choaspes, of which he carried with him a supply in vessels drawn by mules.—Herod. l. 141.

Like his father and grandfather, Asóka gave alms daily to 60,000 tirttakas in his palace. One day he observed from an upper story that in eating their food they made a great noise, and were exceedingly rude. He therefore commanded his nobles to assemble in his presence the different priests, of whatever kind, to which each individual noble was accustomed to give alms. In compliance with this command pandangas, paribrájikas, nigandas, ajíwakas, and other tirttakas were collected together. Proper seats had been provided; but when the king gave permission for them to sit down, some sat on high seats, some on low, and others on seats of a middle elevation; whilst others again sat on the mats that were spread on the ground; the whole without any order. After they had partaken of the food they were dismissed. The next day they were again assembled for a similar purpose; but the king observed that they who had sat on high seats the day before were now on low seats, and that they who had sat on low seats were now on high seats, and that they stared about without any appearance of propriety in their behaviour. From this the king knew that they were all alike ignorant of what was right. Not many days afterwards he saw the sámanéra Nigródha, and was struck by the decorum of his manner. This Nigródha had been the elder brother of the king in a previous birth, as will appear from the following narrative.

There were three brothers, who were honey merchants. The elder brother was accustomed to collect the honey in the country; the second took it to the city of Benares; and the younger brother resided in the city to dispose of it by sale. It happened that a Pasé-Budha, who resided in the cave Nandamúlaka, was sick; and another Pasé-Budha, who perceived that he might be cured by honey, went to Benares in order to procure some, and alighted in the street, where he was seen by a poor woman going to fetch water, who asked him what it was that he wanted; and when he said that he was seeking honey, she pointed in the direction where the younger brother resided, and said that it might be procured there. When receiving the honey, the alms-bowl of the Budha overflowed, and some of it was spilt upon the ground, which greatly pleased the brother, and he thought thus:—"By virtue of this deed may I become king of Jambudwípa, and as the honey is spilt upon the earth, may my power extend a yojana above the earth into the air, and a yojana below into the ground. When the Budha had received the honey, the woman brought a cloth (the only one she possessed, and it had been washed for the purpose), which she put round the bowl, and asked what was the wish that had been expressed by the merchant. When she had heard it, she also wished that, by virtue of what she had done towards the procuring of the honey, she might become his queen. The other brothers, on going home, asked what had become of the honey; and when they were told, they were angry with their younger relative; one wishing that the Budha had been at the other side of the sea, and the other calling him an outcaste; but when they were expostulated with, they became reconciled, and wished that they might partake in the merit. The younger brother became Asóka; the brother who wished that the Budha were at the other side of the sea became Déwánanpiyatissa, king of Ceylon, and the other brother, who called him an outcaste, was born in an outcaste village, at the foot of a banian tree, whence he was called Nigródha.

This Nigródha was the son of Sumaná, queen of Sumana, who, when she heard that her lord had fallen in battle, fled from the city to an adjacent village inhabited by herdsmen, being at the time pregnant. The déwa of a nigródha (banian) tree, seeing her situation, invited her to take up her abode near his residence; and further assisted her by causing a dwelling to appear, which he presented for her use, and then vanished away. It was here that Nigródha was born. The chief of the herdsmen waited on her like a servant, and provided for her all that she required. When the prince was seven years of age, the priest Maha Waruna, who had perceived his merit, requested permission from his mother the queen to admit him into the priesthood, who consented; and whilst he was undergoing the initiatory process of having his hair cut off, he became a rahat. On the morning of a certain day, after he had rendered service to the superior priests, he resolved upon visiting his mother, and on his way thither he entered the city by the southern gate, and had to cross the city that he might reach the northern gate; but he did not look about him beyond the distance of a yoke, and passed along in a manner that gave great delight to all who saw him. It happened that as he approached the palace he was seen by the king, who, after he had observed him some time, thus reflected:—"When any one is in fear, he looks hither and thither as he passes along; but this child, to whom play would be natural, remains with his eyes fixed, and carries his limbs in the most graceful manner; the faith of this child, whatever it be, is certainly that which was taught by the Most Excellent." It was by means of the merit he had attained in a previous age that his attention was now attracted to the sámanéra. The king commanded him to be called; but, when approaching the royal presence, his manner was not changed, neither did his eyes wander. The king said that, if there was any seat proper for him to occupy, he was requested to sit down. Nigródha looked round, and when he saw that no superior priest was present, he gave his alms-bowl into the hands of the king, and seated himself upon the throne. On seeing this, the king thought, "He will this very day become the chief of the palace;" and he then gave him the food that had been prepared for himself, of which he took as much as he required. Asóka, greatly delighted, asked him if he were acquainted with the doctrines of Budha; and when the sámanéra replied, that as he had only lately been admitted to the priesthood, he was not able to declare them to any great extent,* the king requested him to make known to them a little of what he knew. The priest reflected:—"This is a cruel king; he takes life; he delays to acquire merit; it will be right to say something that will be applicable to his circumstances." He therefore began to deliver the discourse called appamáda-waggo (the word appamáda meaning non-dilatoriness; haste, diligence); but when he had spoken two lines of the first stanza, the king said that he would not trouble him to repeat further, as his doubts were now solved, and he received the true faith. The next day Nigródha visited the palace in company with thirty-two other priests, and after they had said bana, the king repeated the threefold protective formulary, received the five precepts, and had the faith of a novice. On the following day he was invited to bring double the number of priests; and the day after a similar invitation was given. Thus, the number invited was doubled every successive day, until those who attended were 60,000, all of whom received as much food as they required. The king erected the Asókáráma monastery, and presented it to the priesthood. Nigródha, when twenty years of age, received the upasampadá ordination, and afterwards became president of the sangha.

From this period the king was called Dharmmásóka. Every day he gave in alms five lacs of treasure, for the support of the faith. Not reckoning what was received from the eighty-four thousand

* This declaration is inconsistent with the wisdom usually ascribed to the rahat.

cities of the kingdom, the fifty-six treasure cities, the ninety-nine maritime cities, and the ninety-six kelas and one lac of towns, and saying nothing of the smaller places, he received daily from the tolls taken in the metropolis five lacs; viz., one lac at each of the principal gates, and one lac at the hall in the centre of the city. The lac received at the central hall was expended in providing requisites for the priests of the Asókáráma monastery alone, after four pools had been made into baths for the priests at a vast expense. Of the four lacs received at the gates, one was expended in providing flowers, oil, rice, and similar offerings, to be presented in the name of Budha; another in providing requisites for the priests who said bana; and a third for the rest of the priesthood. The remaining lac was presented to Nigródha, who received every day, at three several times, morning, noon, and night, upon festive elephants, in grand procession, robes, perfumes, food, and 500 vases of flowers. By this means vast numbers of the priests throughout Jambudwípa were clothed, and received sustenance.

In the fourth year of the reign of Asóka, the sub-king Tissa, and Aggibrahmana, the king's son-in-law, with a lac of other persons, embraced the priesthood and became rahats. In the same year, as he was one day presenting gifts to the 60,000 priests in the wihára of Asókáráma, he enquired of them how many discourses Gótama had delivered; and when he was told by Moggaliputta-tissa that the number was 84,000, he resolved upon building a monastery in 84,000 of the cities of Jambudwípa.* For this purpose he gave in one day ninety-six kelas of treasure. The king then asked who had made the greatest offering that had ever yet been presented to Budha, and Moggaliputta-tissa replied that the monarch himself was the principal donor, as no one had offered gifts so rich as he, even in the lifetime of the sage. The king, on hearing this, enquired if he might consider himself as a partaker in the faith, or as admitted into the grand privileges of Budhism; but he was informed that he was not. Then said he, "if one who has presented so many gifts, and exercised so much faith, is not a partaker in these privileges, who is?" The priests made known to him, as they saw the advantages the faith would thereby receive, that if

* In 1823, an inscription in Pali referring to one of the 84,000 shrines, that had been erected upon the same spot, was found at Budha Gaya; and in several other parts of India, monuments bearing this monarch's name are still in existence.

any one were to cause his son or daughter to enter the priesthood, he would be considered as a true religionist. The king looked in the face of the prince Mahindo, at that time about twenty years of age, and asked him if he were willing to enter the priesthood. The prince, who had earnestly desired it from the time that his uncle Tissa had embraced the sacred possession, replied, "Sire, I am willing." The princess Sanghamittá was also near, about eighteen years of age, and the king looking towards her said, "Mother, can you also take the vows?" and as she had wished to do so from the time Aggibrahmana, her husband, had separated from her for the same purpose, she replied, "It is good, sire; I will become a priestess." When this was concluded, the king, with much satisfaction, enquired if he were now regarded as one of the faithful, and the answer he received was in the affirmative. Moggaliputta-tissa became the president (upajjháyo) and Maha Déwa the reader, on the admission of the prince to the priesthood, as a sámanéra; and when he received the upasampadá ordination, at which time he became a rahat, Majjhanti was the president. On the admission of the princess to the sacred profession, the rahat Ayupáli was the president, and Dharmmapálini the reader; and she also became a rahat on the day that she received the upasampadá ordination. It was in the sixth year of the king's reign that these two illustrious personages embraced the priesthood. The prince acquired the understanding of the three Pitakas, with the various ordinances, in three years, and became the principal disciple of his preceptor.

When the tirttakas saw the prosperity attendant upon the religion of Budha, they sought admission into the priesthood; but they continued the practice of many things that were contrary to the Winaya. When these abuses came to the knowledge of Dharmmásoka, he commanded Moggaliputta-tissa to expel from the priesthood 60,000 tirttakas who had transgressed the ordinances, and from 60,000 faithful priests to choose a thousand for the holding of a convocation of which he was to be the president. These commands were obeyed, and the convocation assembled in the monastery of Asókáráma. The recitation of the sacred code occupied nine months; after which the priests were dismissed to their respective residences. This was the third great convocation. It was held in the 17th year of the reign of Dharmmásoka, and in the 235th year after the dissolution of Budha.

This account is taken by the Singhalese translator from the Commentary on the Pitakas, written by Budhagósha, and must have been compiled upwards of 700 years after the third convocation. The narrative has received many additions that we must reject as inconsistent with the truth; and though many of these fictions are too absurd to deserve serious contradiction, it is of some importance to notice, that the accuracy of the dates given to these assemblies has been called in question by the late Mr. Turnour, in his "Examination of the Pali Budhistical Annals," inserted in the Journal of the Bengal Asiatic Society, Sept. 1837. Mr. Turnour, though he saw no reason to doubt "the correctness of the Budhistical era, founded on the death of Sákya, or B. C. 543," distrusts the date given to the second and third convocations. It is said in the original authorities that no fewer than eight of the leading members who officiated at the second convocation had seen Budha. As the earliest age at which they could be admitted as novices was seven years, they must have been at least 107 years old. Moreover, it is said that Sabbakámi, who presided in the same convocation, had lived in the possession of the upasampadá ordination 120 years; and he must therefore have been at this period 140 years old, as this rite cannot be received under the age of twenty. Yet, the third convocation, only 135 years later, was presided over by Moggaliputta-tissa, at that time seventy-two years of age, who is represented as being the sixth remove in regular succession from the death of Gótama. It may be said that these are not absolute impossibilities; but there is another argument against their correctness, founded on data of an entirely different description. The third convocation is said to have been held in the seventeenth year of the reign of Asóka, or B. C. 308. But it was in the year B. C. 326 that Alexander invaded India, at which time Sandracottus reigned at Pátaliputra; and if Sandracottus is the same as Chandagutta, there must be a discrepancy between the European and Budhistical chronologies of about sixty-five years. It would therefore seem, that the date of the last convocation has been falsified, in order that the introduction of Budhism into Ceylon* might be invested with the greater lustre, from being effected by the son of so illustrious a monarch as the supreme ruler of India, and one who had rendered so much assistance to the religion of Gótama upon the continent.

The adjustments of these dates is, however, of minor importance, compared with the question of the credit due to the history of the

* See the chapter entitled, The Modern Priesthood.

convocations as a statement of facts. It is possible that the convocations took place, and for the purposes specified; but it is not credible that the entire text of the Pitakas could be retained in the memory for the space of six generations, allowing that the statement relative to the number of the hierarchs is correct. Yet it would be unfair not to notice, that from our own personal experience we can form no idea of the retentiveness of the memory under other circumstances. Herodotus was astonished at the powers of memory exhibited by the Egyptian priests. The Druids are said by Caesar to have been able to repeat a great number of verses by heart, no fewer than twenty years being sometimes expended on the acquirement, as it was accounted unlawful to commit their statutes to writing. It is supposed that the poems of Homer and Hesiod were preserved in the memories of the rhapsodists, by whom they were recited, for the space of 500 years; and in the middle ages the poems recited by the minstrels were of considerable length. The rythm of the verse would aid the memory; and as a great part of the Pitakas is in metrical stanza, the priests would have a similar assistance. They would have another advantage in the great number of repetitions, not only of epithets and comparisons, but also of historical details and doctrinal formulas, that are constantly presented. But with every artificial aid it was possible to possess, it is utterly incredible that the whole text of the Pitakas could be retained in the memory of any one man, however extraordinary might be his power of mental retentiveness.

The idea of the preservation of revealed truth by tradition was already familiar to the Budhists, from the manner in which it was supposed that the Vedas were originally transmitted. The original Veda is believed by the Hindus to have been revealed by Brahma,* and to have been preserved by tradition, until it was arranged in its present order by a sage, who thence obtained the surname of Vyása, or Vádavyása, that is, compiler of the Vedas. The sacred books were divided into four parts, which are severally entitled Rich (from the verb rich, to laud, as properly signifying any prayer or hymn, in which a deity is praised); Yajush (from the verb yaj, to worship or adore); Sáman (from the root shó, convertible into só and sá, and signifying to destroy, as denoting something which

* The Budhists say that the three Vedas were propounded originally by Maha Brahma, at which time they were perfect truth; but they have since been corrupted by the Brahmans, and now contain many errors.

destroys sin); and Atharvana. Each of these parts bears the common denomination of the Veda. The Atharvana is commonly admitted as a fourth Veda, but is regarded as of less authority than the others; and it is supposed by Wilkins and Sir W. Jones to be of more modern origin. There are also divers mythological poems, entitled Itihása and Purános, which are reckoned as a fifth Veda. Vyása taught the several Vedas to as many disciples: viz., the Rich to Paila, to Yajush, to Vaisampáyana, and the Saman to Jaimini; also the Atharvana to Sumantu, and the Itihása and Puránas to Súta.*

Different parts of the Pitakas may have been remembered by different persons; and the portions remembered by each being collected together, the text may have been compiled therefrom according to its present arrangement. This, indeed, appears to have been the method in which the Koran was in part compiled. Whenever Mahomet revealed a new portion of matter, it was taken down by a scribe, and copied by his followers, who also learnt it by heart. At the warrior's death, these writings were all in confusion; and as Abu Bekr reflected that already many were slain in the wars who were acquainted with different passages that had been revealed, he ordered that the whole should be collected, both those that had been written and those that were retained in the memory, lest any portion should be lost; and from these he compiled the Koran under its present form.† As the contents of the Koran are confessedly thrown into great confusion, it is probable that this tradition is founded upon truth; and though the text of the Pitakas is presented under a greater regularity of arrangement, we may conclude that its origin was after a similar method. The nucleus of the sacred books was probably formed at an early period, after which successive additions were made, until some council or convocation invested with the proper authority established the canon, and prevented the innovations that would otherwise have been attempted. When the style in which the Pitakas are written has been more carefully examined, differences may be noted from which the relative antiquity of the several parts may be ascertained; as the differences of style between the books of the Septuagint are decisive evidence that they were not simultaneously translated, in the manner maintained by the ancient Jews.

Thus we see that the transmission of the text to the period of the

* Colebrooke's Miscellaneous Essays, i. 10. † Sale's Koran.

third convocation, in the mode set forth in the work itself, was not possible; even allowing that in the first convocation a canon professing to be authoritative was established. But this is not the only difficulty. It is further stated that the text was preserved in the same way from the time of Asóka to that of Wattagamani, who reigned in Ceylon from B. C. 104 to B. C. 76. It was then, according to the Mahawanso, cap. xxx, first committed to writing. "The profoundly wise priests had theretofore orally perpetuated the text of the Pitakattayan and the Atthakathá. At this period these priests, foreseeing the perdition of the people (from the perversions of the true doctrines) assembled; and in order that religion might endure for ages, recorded the same in books." The traditions of the Burmans are in accordance with these statements. They say that "the communications of Gótama, made at first to his immediate disciples, were by them retained in memory during five centuries or more; and were afterwards agreed upon in several successive general councils, and finally reduced to writing on palm-leaves in the island of Ceylon, in the 94th year before Christ."* The three Pitakas are therefore not a record that has come down to us from the age of Gótama. They were written in the 94th year B. C.; and though it is said by the Budhists that they were orally preserved, in a manner the most perfect, from the death of Budha to that period, the statement is not worthy of credit, as it would be impossible under ordinary circumstances, and we deny that men with powers like those attributed to the rahats ever existed.

In the enumeration of the sacred books of the Budhists by Csoma Körösi, no mention is made of their oral transmission, nor of their being reduced to writing in Ceylon. "The great compilation of the Tibetan sacred books, in 100 volumes, is styled Ká-gyur, or vulgarly, Kan-gyur, i.e. Translation of Commandment,† on account of their being translated from the Sanscrit, or from the ancient Indian language, by which may be understood the Pracrita, or dialect of Magadha, the principal seat of the Budhist faith in India at the period. These books contain the doctrine of Shákya, a Budha, who is supposed by the generality of Tibetan authors to have lived

* Crawford's Embassy to Ava.

† A copy of this collection, in 100 volumes, was made at the expense of the Bengal Asiatic Society, under the direction of Csoma Körösi, which cost 13,000 francs. This magnificent work was presented by that Society to the Asiatic Society of Paris, and afterwards placed in the Cabinet of Manuscripts belonging to the Royal Library, that it might be carefully preserved and at the same time rendered accessible to all oriental students.

about 1000 years before the beginning of the Christian era. They were compiled at three different times, in three different places, in ancient India. First, immediately after the death of Shákya; afterwards in the time of Ashoka, a celebrated king, whose residence was at Pataliputra, 110 years after the decease of Shákya. And, lastly, in the time of Kaniska, a king in the north of India, upwards of 400 years from Shákya, when his followers had separated themselves into eighteen sects, under four principal divisions, of which the names both Sanscrit and Tibetan are recorded. The first compilers were three individuals of Shákya's principal disciples. Upáli compiled the Vinaya Sutram; Anandah, the Sútrantah; and Kashyapa, the Prajnyá-páramitá. These several works were imported into Tibet, and translated there between the seventh and thirteenth centuries of our era, but mostly in the ninth. . . . The Ká-gyur collection comprises the seven following great divisions, which are in fact distinct works. 1. Vinaya, or Discipline, in thirteen volumes. 2. Prajnyá-páramitá, or Transcendental Wisdom, in twenty-one volumes. 3. Buddha-vata-sanga, or Buddha Community, in six volumes. 4. Ratnakúta, or Gems heaped up, in six volumes. 5. Sútranta, or Aphorisms, or Tracts, in thirty volumes. 6. Nirvána, or Deliverance from Pain, in two volumes. 7. Tantra, or Mystical Doctrine, Charms, in twenty-two volumes: forming altogether exactly 100 volumes. The whole Ká-gyur collection is very frequently alluded to under the name, in Sanscrit, Tripitakah, the three Vessels or Repositories, comprehending under this appellation, 1st, the Dulvá, or Vinaya; 2nd, the Do, or Sútra; 3rd, the Sher-ch'hin, or Abhidharmah." * From this extract, in which I have omitted the Tibetan names, it will be seen that the sacred books of Tibet must in a great measure be the same as those of Ceylon; but from another extract from the same author, it will appear that the account of their origin is widely different. It is translated from the Index or Introduction to the 100 volumes of the Ká-gyur, and is there taken from the fourth Commentary on the Kála Chakra Tantra. "After Tathagata, the most accomplished Budha, the Bhagaván, had been delivered from pain (or sorrow, i.e. had died) here in Aryadésha, the compilers *writing* in three books, the three vehicles (or works on three-fold principles) they expressed all the three true repositories of Sutra, of Tathagata, in his language. The Prajnyá-páramitá and the Mantras in Sanscrit;

* Analysis of the Dulvá, by Alex. Csoma Körösi, Asiatic Researches, vol. xx.

the several sorts of Tantras in several languages, Sanscrit, Pracrit, Apabransha, in that of the mountaineers, and all sorts of melechchas. The compilers thus collected all the doctrines taught by the all-knowing. Accordingly all the three Vehicles (yánam) in Tibet were written in the Tibetan language; in China, in Chinese; in Great China, in Great Chinese; in the Parsika country, in the Parsik language. On the north of the Sita (Jaxartes) river, in the language of the Champaka country, the Ape or Monkey country, and of the Gold land." * The traditions of the Nepaulese upon the same subject differ in a degree equally great from those of Ceylon. "The most important work of the speculative kind now extant in Nepaul is the Raksha Bhagavati, consisting of no less than 125,000 slocas. Its arrangement at least, and *reduction to writing*, are attributed (as are those of all the other Bauddha scriptures) to Sakya Sinha. Whatever the Buddhas have said (sugutai desita) is an object of worship with the Bauddhas. Sakya having collected these words of the Buddhas, and secured them in a written form, they are now worshipped under the names of Sutra and Dharma." † These statements are so much at variance with each other, that no conclusion can be come to as to the age in which the Pitakas were compiled, until further researches have been made; and as the subject has been purposely mystified by the Budhists, it is probable that it never will be established upon a basis so firm as to leave no room for doubt.

Until an analysis of the Pitakas has been published, and its more important portions have been translated at length, no compendium of Budhism can be formed containing an authoritative and perfect exhibition of its doctrines. This task is not beyond the capacity of one individual; but it would require for its right accomplishment an early attention to languages, a familiar acquaintance with the literature of metaphysics, indomitable perseverance, the opportunity of reference to the more learned of the native priests, and a more lengthened period of residence in an eastern clime than is usually the lot of the severe student. The core of the system appears to lie in a very narrow compass, and as we have frequently had to notice, its repetitions are endless. "I had contemplated the idea,"

* Journal Bengal As. Soc. March, 1838.

† Hodgson's Illustrations. But at a subsequent period the same author says, "Sakya, like other Indian sages, taught orally, and it is doubtful if he himself reduced his doctrines to a written code, though the great scriptures of the sect are generally attributed to him."

Mr. Turnour writes, "at one period, of attempting the analysis of the entire Pitakattayan, aided in the undertaking by the able assistance afforded to me by the Budhist priests, who are my constant coadjutors in my Pali researches; but I soon found that, independently of my undertaking a task for the efficient performance of which I did not possess sufficient leisure, no analysis would successfully develop the contents of that work, unless accompanied by annotations and explanations of a magnitude utterly inadmissible in any periodical." *

In size, the Pitakas surpass all western compositions, but are exceeded by the sacred books of the Brahmans. The four Vedas, when collected, form eleven huge folio volumes. The Purânas, which constitute but part of the first of the Up-angas, extend to about 2,000,000 of lines. The Râmâyana rolls on to 100,000 lines; whilst the Mahabharat quadruples even that sum. The poems of Homer extend to 30,000, and the Æneid of Virgil to nearly 10,000 lines. The old epic poem called Danaïs or Danaïdes, mentioned in the Tabular Raica, but now lost, contained 5,500 verses. The Æthiopis of Arktinus contained 9,100 verses. Diogenes Laertius asserts that Aristotle wrote forty-four myriads of lines; and yet that Epicurus wrote more than Aristotle, and Chrysippus more than Epicurus. Josephus mentions that his own Antiquities contain 60,000 lines. The German Percival, a romance of the middle ages, has nearly 25,000, and the German Tristan more than 23,000 verses. The Paradise Lost of Milton has about 10,000 lines. The Koran has about 6,000 verses, 77,639 words, and 323,015 letters. The Hebrew Old Testament, according to the Masorites, contains 815,140 letters. The English Old Testament has 592,439 words, and 2,728,800 letters; the English New Testament, 181,253 words, and 838,380 letters; or in the entire English Bible, 773,692 words, and 3,567,180 letters. But according to the computation of Turnour, the text alone of the Pitakas contains 4,500 leaves, each page being about 2 feet long, and containing nine lines. Thus $4{,}500 \times 2 \times 9 = 81{,}000$ lines. These lines are written without any space between the words, and we may therefore conclude that in one line there are at least as many as ten lines of any ordinary poetical measure. Therefore $81{,}000 \times 10 = 810{,}000$. Again, the commentary extends to a greater length than the Pit-

* Journal Bengal As. Soc. July, 1837.

akas, so that there must be nearly 2,000,000 lines in the whole of the sacred books.

It was at one time supposed by many orientalists that the sacred books of the Budhists were originally written in Sanskrit, and afterwards translated into the different languages in which they now appear. This idea arose, in part, from the fact that numerous Budhistical works are found in this language in Nepaul; but Mr. Hodgson, who was long of this opinion, which he defended with much research and his usual energy of expression, now states "that the honours of Ceylonese literature and of the Pali language are no longer disputable." The Budhistical works in Sanskrit discovered by that gentleman are now found to be copiously interspersed with passages in various Pracrits, Pali among the rest, pretty much in the manner of the Hindu drama, wherein this mixture of less finished dialects with the Sanskrit is of common occurrence.* It was announced that "the original books of Budha" were at Jesselmere, and they were called "the Sybelline volumes which none dare even handle;" but at a later period, when Major Dixon, in compliance with the wish of the Bengal Asiatic Society, made enquiry as to the supposed existence of this extensive Budhist library, he could only hear of one single work relating to the religion of Gótama.†

The Pali was the vernacular language of Magadha in the time of Gótama Budha. The decyphering of the alphabet, by the late J. Prinsep, in which the ancient inscriptions scattered throughout India are written, as well as the legends upon ancient coins, has led to the establishment of the fact that "the wonder-working Pali" held universal sway during the prevalence of the Budhist faith in India, and that even in Bactria and Persia this language, or something very closely resembling it, prevailed. According to M. Bopp, the relation between these two idioms is nearer than that which subsists between most of the distinct branches of the Indo-European system, and it may be compared to the degree of affinity which the Latin bears to the Greek, or the old Norse to the Maeso-Gothic.‡ The high state of cultivation to which the Pali language was carried, and the great attention that has been paid to it in Ceylon, may be inferred from the fact, that a list of works in the possession of the Singhalese that I formed during my residence in

* Hodgson's Illustrations, 1841. † Journal Bengal As. Soc. March, 1837.
‡ Prichard's Physical History of Mankind, iv. 22.

that island, includes thirty-five works on Pali grammar, some of them being of considerable extent. The oldest of the grammars referred to in these works is by Kachcháyano, but the original is not now extant in Ceylon. It contains the well-known stanza:—"There is a language which is the root (of all languages); men and brahmas at the commencement of the kalpa, who never before heard or uttered a human accent, and even the supreme Budhas, spoke it; it is Mágadhi." The Singhalese suppose that it is also the language of the déwa and brahma lókas. They have a legend as to its antiquity similar in character to the story related of Psammitichus, when two new-born infants were shut up in a solitary cottage, attended by a shepherd who was not to speak to them, that by the language they first made use of to express their wants, the primitive language might be known.

III. *The Honours received by the Sacred Books, and the Benefits they confer.*—The Dharmma being regarded as the second of the three greatest treasures in the possession of either men or déwas, the honours that it receives are commensurate with the estimation in which it is held. It is literally worshipped, and benefits are expected to be received in consequence of this adoration, as much as if it were an intelligent being. The books are usually wrapped in cloth, and when their names are mentioned an honourific is added, equivalent to reverend or illustrious. Upon some occasions they are placed upon a kind of rude altar, near the road-side, as I have seen the images of saints in Roman Catholic countries, that those who pass by may put money upon it in order to obtain merit. The same custom is mentioned by Knox as being frequent during the time of his captivity. The Nava Dharma and other works are regularly worshipped in Nepaul. The Hindus pay a similar respect to their shastras, anointing them with perfumes, adorning them with garlands, and offering to them worship.

The praises of the bana are a favourite subject with the native authors. Whenever an opportunity is presented they launch out into a strain of commendation, heaping epithet upon epithet with untiring zeal; and in some works the same phrases are many times repeated, with an exactness that is very distasteful to the western reader. A few extracts from this prolific source are here inserted.

The discourses of Budha are as a divine charm to cure the poison of evil desire; a divine medicine to heal the disease of anger; a lamp in the midst of the darkness of ignorance; a fire, like that which burns at the end of a kalpa, to destroy the evils of repeated existence; a meridian sun to dry up the mud of covetousness; a great rain to quench the flame of sensuality; a thicket to block up the road that leads to the narakas; a ship in which to sail to the opposite shore of the ocean of existence; a collyrium for taking away the eye-film of heresy; a moon to bring out the night-blowing lotus of merit; a succession of trees bearing immortal fruit, placed here and there, by which the traveller may be enabled to cross the desert of existence; a ladder by which to ascend to the déwa-lókas; a straight highway by which to pass to the incomparable wisdom; a door of entrance to the eternal city of nirwána; a talismanic tree to give whatever is requested; a flavour more exquisite than any other in the three worlds; a treasury of the best things it is possible to obtain; and a power by which may be appeased the sorrow of every sentient being.

The dharmma is perfect; having nothing redundant, and nothing wanting. But it requires attention, that the benefits it offers may be received. Though the teacher may attain great happiness, and enter nirwána, it does not follow that the disciple will necessarily possess the same privileges; he may be like one who binds the crown upon the head of another. Therefore each one for himself must exercise meditation, and observe the ordinances, that he may attain wisdom.

For the right understanding of the discourses of Budha, a knowledge of the following subjects is required:—the five khandas, the six áyatanas, the four dhátus, the four satyas or great truths, and the paticha-samuppáda, or circle of existence. These five subjects are called bhúmi, or the ground. Síla-wisudhi, the right observance of the precepts, and chitta-wisudhi, purity of mind, are called múla or root, as being the root set in the previous ground. Drishti-wisudhi, purity of knowledge, kankhá-witarana-wisudhi, the entire removal of doubt, maggámagga-gnyána-dassana-wisudhi, the knowledge of what belongs to the paths (leading to nirwána) and what does not, patipadá-gnyána-dassana-wisudhi, the knowledge of what is necessary to be done in order to attain felicity, and gnyána-dassana-wisudhi, are called serira, the stem or trunk. Thus the five principles called bhúmi will be as the ground, and the five subjects as the root, from which will be produced the serira as the tree, by the exercise of meditation; and from that will be produced the attainment of the paths. The four paths, the fruition of the paths, nirwána, and the bana, are the ten dharmmas—dasa dharmma.

On a certain occasion the priest Kálábudharakshita, who resided in the cave called Rajagiri, near Anurádhapura, repeated the Kála-karáma-sútra, at the foot of a timbiri tree. Whilst thus engaged, he began to perspire; but the sun appeared in one quarter, and the moon in another, and caused a breeze to arise that he might thereby be cooled. At the same time, like a beautiful woman opening her mouth so that her teeth may just be perceived, all the buds of the trees in the forest began to unfold themselves partially; all the bees began to murmur an offering of praise; all the pea-fowl, doves, and other birds remained in silence, lest they should disturb the sound of the bana, and they listened attentively for the commencement of the recitation, thinking every moment that it would begin; even the apes and other animals all remained in anxious expectation. When the priest began to speak, his voice rose from the midst of the assembly like thunder from a rain-cloud; from rainbow lips his tongue moved, like the play of the lightning; and the words came from his rain-cloud mouth, falling upon the hearts of those who listened, like a shower of divine instruction, filling as many tanks and pools. At that time Sardhá-tissa was king of Anurádhapura, who, having heard that the priest Kálábudharakshita was about to say bana, took with him seven of his faithful attendants, and went to the timbiri tree, where he remained during the whole of the night watches without being perceived. When the day dawned, and the darkness had passed away, like evil desire from the hearts of the worshippers, the priest imparted the five obligations to the assemblage. The king then came from his concealment, commended the skill of the priest, and took the obligations. On being asked at what time he had come, he said that he arrived during the recitation of the first stanza, and had remained there ever since. The priest replied, that his majesty was of a delicate frame, and that it must have fatigued him to remain so long; but he graciously made answer, "If you were the speaker, I could remain to hear bana during the whole of either of our lives. I have heard every word, and I would rather inherit only so much of this realm of Lanká as could be covered by the point of a goad, than have missed the privilege of hearing it." The king then lauded the priest; and the priest, the people, and the déwas praised the king. After this Sardhá-tissa informed the priest that he had never previously heard bana of the same description, and asked him how he had learnt so many particulars respecting the virtues of Budha, and if more could be declared upon the same subject. Kálábudharakshita replied, that it was from the three pitakas, the discourses on the 550 births, the 299 kathá-wastus, and the 17,575 sútras, he had learnt these things. "What!" said the king, "is there more bana, in addition to that which you have repeated to us?" The reply of the priest was this: "What I have declared bears the same proportion to all the sayings of Budha that a single grain does to the harvest of a thousand fields; or a drop of water, the size of a mustard seed, to the whole body of the ocean; or the portion of earth taken up by a small bird, to the entire mass of the earth; or the atom that an ant takes into its mouth, to the carcase of an elephant; or the rain that merely covers a splinter of wood, to the flood that would overflow the four continents; or the portion of sky covered by the wing of a bird when flying, to the whole expanse of the heavens. That which I have declared is little; that which I have not declared is immeasurable." The king was so much delighted with what he had heard, that he said, if he had been a universal emperor he would have given the four great continents to those who say bana; if he had been king of Jambudwípa, he would have given the whole of that portion of the world; if he had been king of the déwas, he would have given the déwa-lokas; but that as he was only king of Lanká, this small realm was all that he could give; yet this he freely offered. The priest said in answer, "We accept what you have given, that you may enjoy the merit of the gift; but we return it to you again, as we have no need of two kingdoms; that of the dharmma is sufficient for us. Respect the three gems, regard the precepts, reign righteously, and be blessed both in this world and the next." The king, after worshipping the priest, returned to his palace in the city.

The advantages to be received from listening to the bana are represented by the native authors as being immensely great; and there is scarcely any benefit presented to the mind of the Budhist that may not be derived from the exercise. This is in conformity with the sentiments generally entertained in the east, as the Brahmans also assert of their puránas, that "it is an act of the greatest merit, extinguishing all sin, for the people to read these books or hear them read." In the earliest ages of Budhism, when the bana was in the vernacular language of the people, we may suppose that great effects were produced by its recitation, and by the discourses that were delivered in explaining its doctrines and duties; but its rehearsal has now degenerated into an unmeaning form, leading the people to found their hopes of blessedness upon an act that cannot in any way be beneficial. A few additional extracts may form a suitable conclusion to our account of the Sacred Books.

The Brahmans say that the destruction of evil desire may be effected by the reading of the Bharata or Rámayana; but this is not possible. It is only by listening to the bana of Budha that this effect can be produced.

There are two principal modes of dána, or almsgiving. 1. Dharmma-dána, providing for the recitation of the bana, or the giving of religious instruction. 2. Amisa-dána, presenting robes, alms-bowls, and other requisites of the priesthood; and giving cattle, garments, and ornaments, to supply the necessities of the poor. Of these two modes, the former is the most meritorious.

The déwas in Tawutisá being on one occasion assembled together, propounded to each other four questions:—1. What is the principal dána? 2. What is the principal taste or enjoyment? 3. What is the principal desire? 4. What is the principal evil? The déwas of 10,000 sakwalas considered these questions continually for the space of twelve years, but were unable to come to any conclusion. They therefore went to the four guardian deities, called waram; but neither could they determine the questions. Upon which they referred the matter to Sekra, who said that they had better go at once to Budha; and when they went, he accompanied them. After hearing these questions, Gótama replied, "1. Of all modes of dána, dharmma-dána is the chief. 2. Of all enjoyments, that of the dharmma is the most exquisite. 3. Of all desires, that of the dharmma is the most excellent. 4. Of all evils, the repetition of existence is the greatest." Budha said further, "Were any one to give the three robes to Budha, the Pasé-Budhas, or the rahats, though the material of their fabric were as soft and smooth as the tender bud of the plantain, the hearing or reading of one single stanza of the bana would bring him a greater reward; indeed its reward would be more than sixteen times greater."

Were any one to fill the bowl of Budha with the choicest food, or to present oil, sugar, honey, or other medicaments in the greatest abundance, or to build thousands of wiháras splendid as those of Anurádhapura, or to present an offering to Budha like that of

Anépidu, the hearing or reading of one single stanza of the bana would be more meritorious than all. He who listens not to the bana is unable to procure merit. Even Seriyut, whose wisdom was vast as the rain that falls during a whole kalpa, could not attain nirwána without hearing the bana of Budha; it was from hearing a stanza repeated by Assaji that he was enabled to enter the paths.

The dharmma brings to those who listen to it with affection, though it be only for a little time, all the happiness of the déwa-lókas, the joy of the brahma-lókas, received during myriads of years; the greatness of the chakrawartti, and the other advantages of the world of men; the pleasures that are to be obtained in the worlds of the nágas, suparnnas, and other beings; and the wisdom of the supreme Budhas.

There was a virgin in Kapilawastu, of the Sákya race, who heard bana, and had great merit. As she was a woman she could not become Sekra, or Maha Brahma, or a chakrawartti; but when she died she became a déwa, changing her sex, and received a glory like that of the ruler of Tawutisá.

There was a certain déwa, who was aware that in eight days he must die, and be re-born in a place of torment; but as he perceived that Budha, and he alone, had the power to help him, he went and heard bana, by which he was enabled to enter the paths.

It may be asked why all who heard Budha had not the power to become rahats, and the reply is this:—"When the king partakes of food, he gives a portion to the princes who are near him, and they receive as much as their hands will hold. In like manner, when the Budhas say bana, it can only be effectual to those who listen, in proportion to their capacity for receiving its advantages, though in itself it is always good."

In the time of Kásyapa Budha there were two priests who lived in a cave, and were accustomed to repeat aloud the Abhidharmma Pitaka. In the same cave there were 500 white bats, that were filled with joy when they heard the bana of the priests, by which they acquired merit, so that they afterwards became déwas, and in the time of Gótama were born in the world of men. They were the 500 priests who kept wass at Sakaspura, with Seriyut, when Budha visited him from the déwa-lóka. Now if these bats, merely from hearing the sound of the words of the Abhidharmma, without understanding them, received so great a reward, it is evident that the reward of those who both hear and understand them must be something beyond computation.

The dharmma softens the hearts of even such obdurate beings as Angulimála, Suchiróma, Khararóma, Bakabbrahma, Sachaka, and Déwadatta. It establishes friendship between beings that have naturally the greatest antipathy to each other, as between the asurs and the déwas, the nágas and the garundas, snakes and frogs, elephants and lions, tigers and deer, crows and owls, and cats and rats. It is as a witness to tell the beings in the world of men, that they who are under the power of demerit will be born in a place of misery, by this means saving them from this awful state; even as Asóka, the king, was saved from his inveterate scepticism, and led to attend to the precepts. It shines upon the darkness of the world, as the rays of the sun, when this luminary has ascended the Yugandhara rocks, shine upon the lotus flowers of the lake, causing them to expand, and bringing out their beauty.

XIX. MODES OF WORSHIP, CEREMONIES, AND FESTIVALS.

The Budhists of the present age are image-worshippers; but it is not known at what period they adopted this custom, nor indeed at what period it was introduced into India. The first notice of idolatry is in connexion with the history of Abraham, whose father "served other gods," and there is an ancient tradition, that he was a maker of idols. All the nations with which the patriarchs had intercourse appear to have been image-worshippers. But if we may trust the most ancient uninspired writers, both eastern and western, this practice was of more recent establishment among other nations. Among the Greeks, the first objects of worship were nothing more than a pillar, a log of wood, or a shapeless stone. The original image of the Ephesian Artemis, as seen upon coins, was little more than a head with a shapeless trunk. When statues were introduced, they were of the rudest form; and it would have been regarded as sacrilege to make any innovation upon the ancient model. The profession of idol-carvers being hereditary would seem to indicate that they had originally belonged to some other race. According to Eusebius, the Greeks were not worshippers of images until the time of Cecrops, and Lucian tells us that even the ancient Egyptians had no statues in their temples. In the Homeric poems there is only one allusion to a statue as a work of art. The substitution of images for the more ancient objects of worship was supposed to have been brought about by Egyptian settlers.* Numa forbade the Romans to set up an image; so that for the space of 170 years from the founding of the city, "they made no image, nor statue, nor so much as a picture."—Clemens. Alex. Strom. lib. 1. The British Druids had no images among them; as it was contrary to the principles of the Celtic religion to represent any gods by the human figure.†

It is said by Professor Wilson that the religion of the Vedas was not idolatry, their real doctrine being the unity of the Deity in whom all things are comprehended. The prevailing character of their ritual is the worship of the personified elements. Image-worship is alluded to by Manu, but with an intimation that the Brahmas who subsist by ministering in temples are an inferior class.‡ With this agrees the testimony of Dr. Stevenson. "It is manifest," he says, "from every page of the Sâma and Rig Vedas, that Agni was adored under the element of fire, that Mitra had no emblem but the sun which shines in the firmament, and that Vayú's presence was only known by hearing his voice resound through the sacrificial hall. The genius of the pestle and mortar is indeed addressed as well as the genius of the mortars; but no image in any human or bestial form appears ever to have been made, except when the genius of the oblation was addressed; the barley-meal of which it was composed being formed into something like the shape of a human head. But with this doubtful exception, no image was introduced into the Jyotishtoma, Somayága, or other sacred brahmanical rites authorised by the Vedas. Polytheistical the worship undoubtedly is, but not idolatrous in the proper and distinctive sense of that term." §

The Budhists of Ceylon have a legend that in the lifetime of Gótama Budha an image of the founder of their religion was made by order of the king of Kósala, and the Chinese have a similar story; but it is rejected by the more intelligent of the priests, who regard it as an invention to attract worshippers to the temples. The images of Budha are called Pilamas, which means literally a counterpart or

* See Histories of Greece, by Thirlwall and Grote.

† Smith's Religion of Ancient Britain.

‡ Wilson's Vishnu Purana, Preface.

§ Journal Royal As. Soc. vol. viii.

likeness, and though they are not coeval with Budhism, they must have come into use at an early period. In the inscription at Mihintala, A. D. 246, mention is made of the great house of the pilama. Fa Hian, A. D. 400, saw many of these images in his travels. At Tho li, in northern India, he saw a statue of wood, 80 feet high, of the future Budha, Maitrí, the likeness of whom had been brought from the fourth heaven by a rahat. At Sewet he saw the statue of sandal-wood made by the king of Kósala, which was said to be the model of all the statues afterwards erected. At Anurádhapura he saw an image of blue jasper, 23 feet 6 inches high, set with precious stones, and sparkling with inexpressible splendour. In its right hand was a pearl of great value. At Amarapura there is an image of Budha, 20 cubits high, said to have been made during the life-time of the sage.

The wiháras in which the images are deposited are generally, in Ceylon, permanent erections, the walls being plastered, and the roof covered with tiles, even when the dwellings of the priests are mean and temporary. Near the entrance are frequently seen figures in relievo, who are called the guardian deities of the temple. Surrounding the sanctum there is usually a narrow room, in which are images and paintings; but in many instances it is dark, the gloom into which the worshipper passes at once, when entering during the day, being well calculated to strike his mind with awe; and when he enters at night the glare of the lamps tends to produce an effect equally powerful. Opposite the door of entrance there is another door, protected by a screen; and when this is withdrawn an image of Budha is seen, occupying nearly the whole of the apartment, with a table or altar before it, upon which flowers are placed, causing a sense of suffocation to be felt when the door is first opened. Like the temples of the Greeks, the walls are covered with paintings; the style at present adopted in Ceylon greatly resembling, in its general appearance, that which is presented in the tombs and temples of Egypt. The story most commonly illustrates some passage in the life of Budha, or in the births he received as Bódhisat. The wiháras are not unfrequently built upon rocks, or in other romantic situations. The court around is planted with the trees that bear the flowers most usually offered. Some of the most celebrated wiháras are caves, in part natural, with excavations carried further into the rock.

The images of Budha are sometimes recumbent, at other times

upright, or in a sitting posture, either in the act of contemplation, or with the hand uplifted, in the act of giving instruction. At Cotta, near Colombo, there is a recumbent image 42 feet in length.* Upon the altar, in addition to the flowers, there are frequently smaller images, either of marble or metal, the former being brought from Burma and the latter from Siam. In the shape of the images, each nation appears to have adopted its own idea of beauty, those of Ceylon resembling a well-proportioned native of the island, whilst those of China present an appearance of obesity that would be regarded as anything but divine by a Hindu. The images made in Siam are of a more attenuated figure, and comport better with our idea of the ascetic. According to Hodgson, there are in Nepaul images of Budha with three heads and six or ten arms. Bishop Smith gives a lively description of the idol-manufactories in China. In one of the narrow streets of Amoy he entered an idol-shop, where idols of every pattern and quality were procurable, the prices varying from several dollars each to the low sum of six cash, equal to about one farthing. The licensed permission of the mandarins to pursue the vocation of idol-maker was visibly depicted on a sign-board in the shop. On another board was a notice that precious Budhas were there manufactured or repaired. A large number of idols, of every shape, and in every stage of manufacture, were lying around. Another idol-manufactory had the sign suspended over the door, "The golden Budha shop." These shops were to be seen at every quarter of a mile, and presented groups of images, some black with age and sent thither for regilding, and others gaudily painted and fresh from the hand of the artist. Some had stern visages; some wore the expression of pleasure; and all looked exceedingly grotesque.†

In the court-yard of nearly all the wiháras in Ceylon, there is a small déwála, in which the brahmanical deities are worshipped. The persons who officiate in them are called kapuwas. They marry, and are not distinguished by any particular costume. The incantations they use are in Sanskrit; but they do not understand the meaning of the words, and repeat them merely from memory. Europeans are not allowed to enter the déwálas, and it is difficult to ascertain the exact nature of the rites therein performed. In the sanctum are the armlets or foot-rings of Pattiné,‡ or the weapons

* Selkirk's Recollections of Ceylon. † Smith's China.

‡ Alfred required Guthrum and the other Danish chiefs to swear on the holy ring, or bracelet, consecrated to Odin, an oath which more than any other they were fearful to violate.

of the other deities, with a painted screen before them; but there are no images, or none that are permanently placed; in some of the ceremonies temporary images are made of rice, or of some other material equally perishable. In some instances, as at Lankátilaka, near Kandy, the wihára and déwála are under one roof.

The cave-temple at Dambulla is one of the most perfect wiháras now existing in Ceylon, and as it is also one of the most interesting spots in the island, the following description of it will not be regarded as out of place. It is from the pen of Forbes, to whom the island is greatly indebted for the manner in which he has illustrated its early history and present antiquities.

"The rock of Dambulla appears to be about 400 feet in height. On the north side it is bare and black. To the south its huge overhanging mass (about 150 feet from the summit) by some art and much labour, has been formed into wiháras. The ascent to them is over a bare shelving rock, except where the steep path leads through a patch of jungle, and the entrance to the platform in front of them is through a miserable gateway.

"The wihára called Maha Dewiyo (supposed to have been built by the assistance of Vishnu) is narrow, and requires to be lighted by torches. It contains a gigantic figure of Budha recumbent, the statue, as well as the bed and pillow on which it reclines, being formed from the solid rock. The figure is well executed, and is 47 feet in length. At its feet stands an attendant, and opposite to the face a statue of Vishnu. This long, narrow, and dark temple, the position and placid aspect of Budha, together with the stillness of the place, tend to impress the beholder with the idea that he is in the chamber of death. The priest asserts that the position and figures are exact, both in resemblance and size; that such wás Budha, and such were those who witnessed the last moments of his mortality. To favour this illusion, the priest takes care to place the few lights in the best position, and to keep the face shaded.

"The front of the Maha Rája, and indeed of all the temples, is formed by a wall under the beetling rock; and these sacred caverns are partly natural and partly excavated. The Maha Rája wihára is 172 feet in length, 75 in breadth, and 21 feet high at the wall; but the height gradually decreases to the opposite side. The bad effect of this angular shape is in part done away by a judicious distribution of the figures and their curtains. In this temple there are upwards of fifty figures of Budha, most of them larger than life; also a statue of each of the déwas, Sáman, Vishnu, Nátha, and the déwi Pattiné, and of two kings, Walagam Báhu and Kirti Nissanga. Walagam Báhu was the founder of this temple, B. C. 86. Kirtti Nissanga, after he had repaired the dilapidations occasioned by the Malabar invaders, A. D. 1195, caused all the statues to be gilded; and so ornamented the place that it obtained the name of Rangiri, or the Golden Rock. There is a very handsome dágoba, the spire of which touches the roof at its highest part; and in a small square compartment, railed in, and sunk about two feet below the level of the floor, a vessel is placed to receive the water which constantly drops from a fissure in the rock, and is exclusively kept for sacred purposes. The whole of the interior, whether rock, wall, or statue, is painted with brilliant colours, but yellow much predominates. In one place the artist has attempted to depict part of the early history of the island, beginning with the voyage of Wijaya, which is represented by a ship with only the lower masts, and without sails; and alongside are fishes as large as the vessel. In representing the building of the great dágobas at Anurádhapura, the proportions are not better preserved; and these artificial mountains appear to be little larger than the persons employed in finishing them. . . . .The ornamental paintings, where proportion was not of paramount consequence, are very neat; and all the colours appear to be permanent and bright, although some have not been renewed for upwards of fifty years.

"The Pass Pilama and two Alut Wiháras are formed on the same plan, but are inferior in size and ornament to the Maha Rája. In one of them is a statue of king Kirtti Srí, the last benefactor of Dambulla, and a zealous supporter of Budhism. On the rock platform, which extends in front of all the temples, a bó-tree and several cocoa-nut trees, have been reared, and have attained a great size, despite their bare situation, equally exposed to tempests, and to the scorching heat and long droughts to which Dambulla is liable. Near the Maha Dewiyo wihára, neatly cut in the rock, is a long Singhalese inscription of considerable antiquity, and on other parts of the rock are several inscriptions.* The summit of the rock commands a delightful view. . . . It was once surmounted by three

* These inscriptions are in the character deciphered by the late James Prinsep, a name that ought never to be mentioned by the orientalist without some expression of respect for his varied accomplishments, and of regret for his loss.

dágobas, which have been crumbled down and been washed away. About fifty feet from the summit there is a pond in the rock, which the priests assert is never without water." *

The author of this description possessed great facilities for giving an accurate account of the places here mentioned, as he was many years the agent of Government for the district in which they are situated, a respectable artist, and well-acquainted with the Singhalese language. I visited Dambulla in 1829; and again in 1838, with my wife and infant, who were returning from Trincomale, after being shipwrecked on the eastern coast of the island. Upon my last visit I noticed a considerable difference in the brilliancy of the colours. When upon the summit of the rock, alone, I was surrounded by a tribe of white monkeys. By their antics and incessant chattering they appeared anxious to impart to me some matter of grave import; but as it is probable that none of them were ever Englishmen in former states of existence, nor I a monkey, we could hold no communication with each other, and our interview led to no practical result.

It is said that there were sixty-four sacred caves near the city of Anurádhapura, in the days of its Budhistical eminence. In several narratives connected with the history of Gótama Budha cave-temples are spoken of in such a manner as to induce the belief that they were then of common occurrence. The places that he visited are frequently said to be gal-lénas. In some instances there appear to have been monoliths, with conical roofs. Mugalan resided in a place of this description when beset by a band of robbers at the instigation of some rival tirttakas. The keyhole of the door was the only aperture it contained. The spots in which Budha and his disciples had resided would probably be first adopted as places of worship, when it became the custom to adore their relics.

In the ancient legends the wiháras in which Gótama resided are represented as being extremely splendid; indeed they are to be equalled only by the talismanic structures of the Arabian genii. One near the city of Sewet, the capital of Kósala, erected by the merchant Anépidu, is said to have cost 180 millions of golden masurans. From the remains yet in existence upon the continent of India, we are warranted in concluding that at an early period the temples in which the Budhists worshipped, and their priests resided, were of elaborate execution, and some of them extensive. A

* The Ceylon Almanac, 1834.

paper was read before the Royal Asiatic Society, Dec. 5, 1843, entitled, "On the Rock-cut Temples of India, by James Fergusson, Esq." This paper is inserted in the Journal of the Society, No. xv. and was reprinted, with some additions, in illustration of a work he published, containing views of the Ajunta and other rock-cut temples, in one volume folio. Nearly all the temples of this description in India were visited by Mr. Fergusson. The whole are classed under the following heads:—First, wihára, or monastery caves; the first subdivision of this class consisting of natural caverns or caves slightly improved by art; the second, of a verandah opening behind into cells for the abode of the priests, but without sanctuaries or images; in the third this arrangement being extended by the enlargement of the hall, with a recess, in which is generally a statue of Budha, thus making it both an abode for the priests and a place of worship. By far the greatest number of Budhist excavations belong to this last division. The most splendid are those at Ajunta, though one at Ellora is also fine; and there are also some good specimens at Salsette, and perhaps at Junir. The second class consists of chaitya (dágoba) caves, one or more of which is attached to every set of caves in the west of India, though none exist in the eastern side. The plan and arrangement of all these caves are exactly the same. Mr. Fergusson believes that the Karli cave, which is the most perfect, is also the oldest in India. The caves that do not come under these two classes are brahmanical.

As it was stated that the paintings in these caves were rapidly going to destruction, the Court of Directors of the East India Company issued orders that means should be adopted for their preservation. In consequence, the Government of Madras has employed an officer of their establishment, Capt. R. Gill, to clear out the caves of Ajunta, to furnish full details of their construction, and make copies of the paintings. Fourteen paintings have already been transmitted from this interesting spot, and are now in the library at the India House. They are thus artistically described in the Athenæum, Feb. 3, 1849:—"The paintings, considered as the production of so early a period, may be regarded as objects of very high import in pictorial art. In many of them certain striking coincidences with Siennese and Pisan art, under the influence of Byzantine taste, are to be remarked. There are the same diagrammatic manifestations of the human form and the human countenance; similar conventions of action and of feature; a like constraint in the choice of action and the delineation of form, in consequence of a like deficiency in knowledge of the human subject; and a like earnestness of intention and predominance of dramatic display. That these pictures were executed at distinct times and by various hands there is internal evidence. While however they offer such proofs of the progress of art, there is in some of them one quality too singular not to be remarked on. There is a compliance with the principles of perspective in architectural details in the very pictures in which these same principles are violated in the relative scales of the parts in the assemblage of human forms. The sense of light and shade, or the art of making figures obvious and clear at a distance, is found in these coinciding with the early Italian art before alluded to. The sense of colour is little more advanced in them than in Egyptian art, as made known to us through the medium of Rosellini, or than in most other aboriginal conditions of art. Assigning the date of these pictures to the period suggested by the author of the preceding memoir (a very learned authority on such subjects) it is at least remarkable that evidence of perspective should be found so very much earlier than the date of any existing specimens known in Southern Europe. The earliest examples of the application of perspective principles in Italian art date somewhere about the middle of the fourteenth century."

The temples of Burma are said by Crawford to be inferior to those of Siam, where the sacred edifices have the doors, windows, and roofs of richly carved wood. Whilst the Siamese temples are spacious buildings, much ornamented in the interior, the majority of the modern temples in Burma are mere masses of brick and mortar. But for every temple in Siam there are twenty in Burma; none but the rich and powerful building temples amongst the Siamese, whilst among the Burmans it is a common mode of obtaining merit, even with the inferior classes, who thus exhibit their respect for religion, rather than in endowing monasteries.*

No wihára has recently been erected in Ceylon of durable material or imposing appearance. The enthusiasm of the masses in favour of the religion of their ancestors has passed away, and individuals are too poor to be able to lavish large sums upon the priests.

Attached to one of the wiháras in Kandy, near the burial-place of the kings, there is an area which was regarded as a sanctuary under

* Crawford's Embassy to the Court of Ava.

the native government. The right of sanctuary agrees well with monastic pretension and principle. Matthew of Westminster says of the sanctuary at Hexham, "Now, if a malefactor, flying for refuge to that church, was taken or apprehended within the four crosses, the partye that tooke or laid holde of hym there, did forfeit two hundredh; if he tooke hym withyn the towne, then hee forfetted four hundredh; if withyn the walles of the churche, then six hundredh; if withyn the churche, 1200; if withyn the doores of the quire, then 1800 besides penance; but if hee presoomed to take hym oute of the stoone chair near the altare, called fridstol, or from the holie relics behinde the altare, the offence was not redeemable with anie somme." These places were frequently complained of as a great grievance. Stow says in his Chronicle, "Unthrifts riot and run in debt upon the boldness of these places; yea, and rich men run thither with poor men's goods; there they build, there they spend, and bid their creditors go whistle them; men's wives run thither with their husband's plate, and say they dare not abide with their husbands for beating; thieves bring thither their stolen goods, and live thereon; there devise they new robberies, nightly they steal out, they rob and reave, and kill, and come in again, as though these places gave them not only a safeguard for the evil they have done, but a licence to do more." The vestal virgins were permitted to demand the release of any criminal they might meet accidentally in the street. The priests of Budha in Burma had until recently so much authority, that they even withdrew condemned criminals from the hand of justice. Capital punishment was a rare occurrence in the kingdom; for no sooner did the priests hear that a criminal was being led to execution, than they issued from their convents in great numbers, with heavy sticks concealed under their habits, with which they furiously attacked the ministers of justice, put them to flight, and led away the culprit to their temple. Here his head was shaved, the yellow robe was put upon him, and by these ceremonies he was absolved from his crime, and his person rendered inviolable; but they do not now venture upon these bold measures, unless they are sure of the protection of the mandarins.*

The limits of the wihára, as well as of the places in which bana is publicly read, are to be defined by a chapter. The form to be used appears in the Kammawáchan. It is not a consecration, but

* Sangermano's Burmese Empire.

simply an appointment of boundaries; an act of this kind being necessary in relation to all places where regulars are permitted to congregate. The consecration of churches began in the fourth century, and appears to have been connected with the jus asyli which was then claimed. It is a fitting rite when properly conducted; but when the spot thus consecrated is regarded as a place in which the whole of the ministerial duty may be performed, or as conferring upon the word preached, or the supplication presented, a power which it does not possess in other places, a consequence is produced that is in opposition to the extent of privilege conferred upon the church by Christ. The whole world, to its utmost limit, has been consecrated by the shedding of the Redeemer's blood; and, as if in reference to the coming down of the glory that overpowered the priests at the dedication of the tabernacle, it is expressly stated, that "all the earth shall be filled with the glory of the Lord."

A glowing description is given in the Mahawanso of the consecration of a site at Anurádhapura, by Dewananpiyatisso, who began to reign B. C. 307. When the monarch was about to define the limits of a garden that he intended to devote to the priesthood, he approached the priests worthy of veneration, and bowed down to them; and then proceeding with them to the upper ferry of the river, he made his progress, ploughing the ground with a golden plough. The superb state elephants Mahápadumo and Kunjaro having been harnessed to the golden plough, Dewananpiyatisso, accompanied by the priests and attended by his army, himself holding the shaft, defined the line of boundary. Surrounded by vases exquisitely painted, which were carried in procession, and by gorgeous flags, tinkling with the bells attached to them; sprinkled with red sandal dust, guarded by gold and silver staves, the concourse decorated with mirrors of glittering glass and with garlands, and with baskets borne down by the weight of flowers; triumphal arches made of plantain trees, and females holding up umbrellas and other decorations; excited by the symphony of every description of music; encompassed by the martial might of his empire; overwhelmed by the shouts of gratitude and festivity which welcomed him from the four quarters of the earth;—this lord of the land made his progress, ploughing amidst enthusiastic acclamations, hundreds of waving handkerchiefs, and the exaltation produced by the presenting of superb offerings. Having perambulated the precincts of the wihára, as well as the city, and again reached the river, he completed the demarkation of the consecrated ground.*

It is to be supposed that an atheistical system will pay little regard to acts of worship. The people, on entering the wihára, prostrate themselves before the image of Budha, or bend the body, with the palms of the hands touching each other and the thumbs touching the forehead. They then repeat the three-fold formulary of protection, called tun-sarana, stating that they take refuge in Budha, in the Dharmma, and in the Sangha; or they take upon themselves a certain number of the ten obligations, the words being first chanted in Pali by a priest, or in his absence by a novice. Some flowers and a little rice are placed upon the altar, and a few coppers are thrown into a large vessel placed to receive them; but no form of supplication is used; and the worshipper goes through the process with feelings kindred to those with which he would irrigate his field, or cast his seed-corn into the ground, knowing that in due time, as a natural consequence, he will reap the reward of his toil. When special offerings are presented, or a particular wihára visited, or a ceremony attended that is out of the common course, it is usually with the expectation of receiving some specific boon, which may be relative either to this world or the next.

The assistance derived from the three gems, Budha, the Truth, and the Associated Priesthood is called sarana, protection. The invocation of the triad is noticed by a Mahometan traveller in Tibet, who calls its constituents God, his prophet, and his word. By Remusat it is translated "Boudha, la loï et le clergé." A king of China, of the dynasty of Siang, once sent a present of all kinds of perfumes to a prince of Korea; but the prince did not know for what purpose they were intended, until informed by a priest of Budha recently come to the country, who told him that they were to be burnt, and that if whilst they were burning any wish was formed, the triad to whom the perfume was grateful would cause the wish to be accomplished. The king's daughter was at this time sick. The priest was therefore commanded to burn the perfumes in the proper manner, that her disease might be removed; and as the ceremony had its desired effect, he was amply rewarded.† There are minor, perhaps essential, differences in the Budhism of different countries; but the worship of the triad appears to be universal.

The protection derived from the three gems is said to destroy

* Turnour's Mahawanso, cap. xv. † Remusat's Relation, p. 43.

the fear of reproduction, or successive existence, and to take away the fear of the mind, the pain to which the body is subject, and the misery of the four hells. The protection of Budha may be obtained by listening to the bana or keeping the precepts; and by its aid the evil consequences of demerit are overcome. The protection of the dharmma is like a steed to one who is travelling a distant journey. The protection of the sangha is ensured by a small gift in alms or offerings. By reflecting on the three gems, scepticism, doubt, and reasoning will be driven away, and the mind become clear and calm. There is no other way of overcoming the evil consequences arising from the sequence of existence but by trust in Budha.

When the king is worshipped, on account of his greatness; or the teacher, on account of his learning, the benefit is small: but if any one worships the three gems, he will receive their protection. When any one is worshipped on account of relationship, or from fear, or from respect, there may be no wrong committed; but by the worship of the three gems the benefit of the paths will be gained, and relief from all sorrow. The protection of Budha is denied to any one who goes near a dágoba, or other sacred place, and does not worship; or to any one who, when in sight of a sacred place, or an image of Budha, covers his shoulder with his garment, holds an umbrella over his head, rides in any vehicle, bathes, or goes aside for any private purpose. The protection of the dharmma cannot be received by any one who refuses to hear bana when called for the purpose, or who listens to it in an irreverent manner, or who does not keep its precepts, or who does not affectionately proclaim its excellencies to others. The protection of the sangha cannot be received by any one who sits near a priest without permission, or who says bana without being appointed, or opposes a priest in argument, or remains in the presence of a priest with his shoulders covered, or holding an umbrella, or remains seated in any vehicle when riding near him. An offence done to one single priest is done to the whole association; and he who transgresses in any one of these ways is guilty of disrespect to the tun-sarana, and can derive therefrom no assistance.

There was an upásaka in the time of Anomadassa Budha, who was unable to become a priest, as his parents were blind, and he had to support them. But he received the tun-sarana from a certain priest, by means of which he enjoyed eight blessings during many myriads of years; never, in the whole of this period, being born in hell, but always in the world of men, or a déwa lóka.

In a former age, six hundred merchants set out by sea for a distant country, intending there to trade; but during the voyage a storm came on, and they were in great danger. As one of the merchants remained fearless and calm, though the others were greatly agitated, they enquired whence his tranquillity proceeded; and he informed them that previous to embarking he had received the sarana from a priest. He then, at their request, imparted to them the same sarana, and they repeated after him the formulary of protection in sections of a hundred. As the first hundred repeated it, they were up to their ancles in water; the second hundred, on repeating it, were up to the knee; and the third hundred, nearly over head. The ship was lost, but the merchants were all born in a déwa-lóka; and through this repetition of the sarana received many blessings in future ages.

A youth, after completing his education, was taking a large sum of money to pay his teacher for the instruction he had received; but as Budha foresaw that he would be waylaid by a robber, and murdered, he seated himself by a tree near which the youth would have to pass, and when he came up stopped him, and taught him the tun-sarana. A little time afterwards the youth was killed, but as he was meditating at the time on the sarana, he was born in a déwa-lóka.

The king of Ságal, on one occasion said to Nágaséna, "You declare that although a man live in sin a hundred years, taking life and committing other crimes, if he thinks of Budha once when at the point of death, he will be born in a déwa-lóka; this I cannot believe. You say again that if a man only once takes life, and does not think of Budha, he will be born in hell; this also I cannot believe." Nágaséna replied, "How so? If we put ever so small a pebble in the water it will sink; but a hundred yálas of stones may be put into a boat, and floated across the river without difficulty; and it is the same with those who acquire merit."

These legends, with the exception of the last, are selected from a work that is very popular in some parts of Ceylon, the name of which I was not able to ascertain. They bear testimony to the fact that the repetition of the tun-sarana is regarded as an opus operatum that will be a sure defence against every calamity; but it leads to the same evil consequences that are presented by all people among whom similar formularies are in common use.

Although it is supposed that image-worship received no sanction from Gótama, it is generally allowed that the worship of the bó-tree under which he attained the Budhaship was of very ancient origin. Near this tree the city of Budha Gaya was afterwards erected, which, from the vast extent of its ruins, must at one time have had a numerous population; but it appears to have fallen as rapidly as it arose. When visited by Fa Hian, in the fifth century, it was completely deserted. A bó-tree flourishes at present at the same place, which is regarded by the Budhists as the very tree under which Gótama sat; but it is thought by European travellers to be not more than a hundred years old. In 1833, it was visited by two envoys from the king of Burma, who were accompanied by Captain G. Burney; and a translation of the report they presented on their return, made by Colonel H. Burney, appears in the Asiatic Researches, vol. xx. In the court-yard of nearly every wihára in Ceylon there is a bó-tree, which is said to be taken from the tree at Anurádhapura, brought over to the island in the beginning of the fourth century B.C. as will afterwards be more particularly noticed.

The authority to worship the bó-tree is derived from the following occurrence. At the time when the usual residence of Gótama was near the city of Sewet, the people brought flowers and perfumes to present to him as offerings; but as he was absent, they threw them down near the wall, and went away. When Anépidu and the other upásikas saw what had occurred, they were grieved, and wished that some permanent object of worship were appointed, at which they might present their offerings during the absence of the sage. As the same disappointment occurred several times, they made known their wishes to Ananda, who informed Budha on his return. In consequence of this intimation, Budha said to Ananda, "The objects that are proper to receive worship are of three kinds, serírika, uddésika, and paribhógika. In the last division is the tree at the foot of which I became Budha. Therefore send to obtain a branch of that tree, and set it in the court of this wihára. He who worships it will receive the same reward as if he worshipped me in person." When a place had been prepared by the king for its reception, Mugalan went through the air to the spot in the forest where the bó-tree stood, and brought away a fruit that had begun to germinate, which he delivered to Ananda, from whom it passed to the king, and from the king to Anépidu, who received it in a golden vessel. No sooner was it placed in the spot it was intended to occupy in the court, than it at once began to grow;* and as the people looked on in wonder it became a tree, large as a tree of the forest, being 50 cubits high, with five branches extending in the five directions, each 50 cubits in length. The people presented to it many costly offerings, and built a wall around it of the seven gems. As it had been procured by means of Ananda, it was called by his name. Budha was requested to honor it by sitting at its foot as he had sat at the foot of the tree in the forest of Uruwela; but he said that when he had sat at the foot of the tree in the forest he became Budha, and that it was not meet he should sit in the same manner near any other tree.†

The vastness of the ruins near Budha Gaya is also an evidence that the original bó-tree must have been visited by great numbers of pilgrims, and have been regarded with peculiar veneration. It is said that not long after the death of Gótama a number of priests went to worship this tree, among whom was one who in passing through a village was accosted by a woman as he sat in the hall of reflection; and when she learnt whither he was bound, and the advantages to be gained by making an offering to this sacred object, she listened with much pleasure, but regretted that as she was poor, working in the house of another for hire, and had not so much as a measure of rice for the next day, it was not in her power to make any offering besides the cloth she wore; and this cloth, after washing it, she presented to the priest, requesting him to offer it in her name to the bó-tree, that she might receive the merit resulting therefrom. The priest acceded to her request, and offered the cloth as a banner. At midnight the woman died, but was born in a déwa-lóka, where she lived in the greatest splendour, arrayed in the most beautiful garments. The day after the priest visited the tree he retired to the forest, and fell asleep; when a female appeared to him, with many attendants, singing sweetly and playing the most enchanting music. The priest asked her who she was, and she said, "Do you not know me? I am the female in whose name you presented the cloth. Yesterday I was mean and filthy, but to-

* Two days after Athens was burnt by the Persians, the olive placed by Minerva in the citadel was observed to have grown a cubit, according to Herodotus, or two cubits, according to Pausanias.

† Pansiya-panas-játaka-pota.

day I am clean and beautiful; and this I have gained through the merit of the offering at the bó-tree."

The Singhalese suppose that it is not now possible to visit this tree, on account of the savage nature of the country in which it flourishes. A certain queen is said to have found access to the spot, but she went to it through the air on a magical horse. It is thought by the Budhists generally that it is exactly in the centre of the earth. The Greeks had a similar superstition relative to Delphi, which they called umbilicus terrae. They said that two birds were sent by Jupiter, one from the east and the other from the west, in order to ascertain the true centre of the earth, which met at Delphi. When at Jerusalem, in 1833, I saw the Greek pilgrims presenting lights to a marble pillar in their own part of the Church of the Sepulchre, under the supposition that it stands in the centre of the world. Sir John Mandevil notices the same custom as being in existence 500 years ago. "And ther nygh wher our Lord was crucyfied is this writen. . . . . in Latyn, Hic Deus noster Rex ante secula, operatus est salutem in medio terre; that is to seye, This God owre Kyng, before the worldes, hath wrought hele in mydds of the erthe." The Chinese also regard their country as the centre of a system, and call it choong-kuo, or the central nation.

The similarity has been remarked between the bó-tree and the aspen of Syria, with regard to the constant quivering of their leaves.* The Budhists say that out of respect to their great sage, the leaves of the bó-tree "have always an apparent motion, whether there be any wind stirring or not;" and the Syrians "aver that the wood of the cross of our Saviour was made of aspen, and that the leaves of the aspen have trembled ever since in commemoration of that event." Near Belligam, a village on the southern coast of Ceylon, is the figure of a king, cut in the side of the rock, called Kushta Rája, or the Leprous King. It is not known who he was, but the tradition is, that he was struck with leprosy for having one day passed under a bó-tree without paying it the proper honours.

It is usual to plant a bó-tree upon the mound under which the ashes of the Kandian chiefs and priests have been deposited. Robert Knox tells us that it is considered an act of merit to plant one of these trees, as it is supposed that in a little time afterwards the planter

* Bennett's Ceylon and its Capabilities.

will be taken to heaven; but he says that "the oldest men only that are nearest death in the course of nature do plant them, and none else, the younger sort desiring to live a little longer in this world before they go to the other." The same writer informs us of a ceremony that I do not remember to have met with during my residence in the island. "Under the tree, at some convenient distance, about ten or twelve feet at the outmost edge of the platform they usually build booths or tents; some are made slight, only with leaves, for the present use; but others are built substantial, with hewn timber and clay walls, which stand many years. These buildings are divided into small tenements for each particular family. The whole town joins, and each man builds his own apartment, so that the building goes quite round, like a circle; only one gap is left, which is to pass through the bó-tree, and this gap is built over with a kind of portal. The use of these buildings is for the entertainment of the women, who take great delight to come and see these ceremonies, clad in their richest and best apparel. They employ themselves in seeing the dancers, and the jugglers do their tricks, who afterwards by their importunity get money from them, or a ring off their fingers, or some such matter. Here also they spend their time in eating betle, and in talking with their consorts, and showing their fine clothes. These solemnities are always in the night; the booths all set round with lamps; nor are they ended in one night, but last three or four, until the full moon, which always puts a period to them."*

As the bó-tree (ficus religiosa) is dedicated to Gótama Budha, so the banian (ficus Indica) was dedicated to his predecessor, and other Budhas had also their appropriate tree. The next Budha, Maitrí, will háve the ná, iron-wood tree.

In the inscription upon the lát of Feroz Sháh, near Delhi (with which the inscriptions at Allahabad, Mattiah, and Radhia substantially agree) no mention is made of any kind of worship besides that which is paid to the bó-tree. These pillars were erected by Asóka, who flourished in the 218th year of the Budhist era. These ancient records make it the more probable that image-worship is of more recent introduction. "It is tolerably certain," says Mr. Fergusson, "that the adoration of images, and particularly of that of the founder of the religion, was the introduction of a later and

* Knox's Account of his Captivity in Ceylon.

more corrupt era, and unknown to the immediate followers of the deified."

Few species of idolatry have been more common than arborolatry. It has been said that, among the Greeks and Romans, nearly every deity had some particular tree; and that nearly every tree was dedicated to some particular god. It was under the oak that the Druids performed their most sacred rites, and the principal tree of the grove was consecrated with ceremonies of a description peculiarly solemn. The ancient inhabitants of Canaan appear to have been greatly attached to the sacred groves in which they were accustomed to worship; and the Israelites were especially commanded to destroy them. Perhaps the solemn gloom they produced would have overpowered the minds of the Hebrews, and have led them to admire and venerate, and then partake in the idolatry; or they might be used for abominations that the people of God were to flee from as from the pestilence. Yet these gardens and groves were a snare to them, and drew them away from the service of the sanctuary.

> "When I had brought them into the land
> Which I swore that I would give unto them,
> Then they saw every high hill and every thick tree;
> And there they slew their victims;
> And there they presented the provocation of their offerings;
> And there they placed their sweet savour;
> And there they poured out their libations."—Ezek. xx. 28.

> "On the tops of the mountains they sacrifice,
> And on the hills they burn incense;
> Under the oak and the poplar,
> And the ilex, because her shade is pleasant."—Hos. iv. 13.

It was declared by Gótama Budha to Ananda, in the legend inserted above, that the objects proper to be worshipped are of three kinds :—1. Serírika. 2. Uddésika. 3. Paribhógika. The first class includes the relics of his body, which were collected after his cremation. The second includes those things that have been erected on his account, or for his sake, which, the commentators say, means the images of his person. And the third includes the articles he possessed, such as his girdle, his alms-bowl, the robe he put on when he bathed, the vessel from which he drank water, and his seat or throne. There is another threefold division of the same objects. 1. Paribhógika. 2. Dhátu. 3. Dharmma. The second includes the same things as the first division of the preceding series; and the third refers to the doctrines that Budha taught, the bana, or the sacred books. All these are called chaityas, on account of the satisfaction or pleasure they produce in the mind of those by whom they are properly regarded.

In nearly every place where there are evidences of Budhistical worship, the dágoba is to be seen; in some instances rising to an elevation that has only one parallel among the works of man. The name is derived from dá, dátu, or dhátu, an osseous relic, and geba, or garbha, the womb. The word tope is not unfrequently used in the same sense, from thúpa, a relic. "A tope," says Professor Wilson, "is, or has been, a circular building of stone, or brick faced with stone or stucco, erected on a platform, which has been built upon either a natural or artificial elevation. It is distinguished, according to Mr. Masson, from a tumulus, by having a distinct cylindrical body interposed between a circular basement and a hemispherical cupula. This is, no doubt, the case at Sarnath, and in most of the topes of Afghanistan. In the great tope of Manikyala, however, the perpendicular part between the basement and dome scarcely constituted a perceptible division. At Bhilsa, Amaravati, and still more in Ceylon, time, vegetation, and decay have effaced these distinctions, and the tope occurs as a mound rising conically from an irregularly circular base. Steps usually lead up to the basement of the building or the platform on which it stands. It seems not unlikely that the cupola was crowned by a spire. Such embellishments usually terminate temples in Buddhist countries, to which these topes are considered analogous, as well as the dahgopas, which present other analogies. They are also found upon what may be considered miniature representations of the topes which have been discovered within them; and the Ceylon topes have evidently been thus terminated. Traces of spires are visible on the summits of the great mounds of Abhayagiri and Jaitawana. The dimensions of the topes vary considerably. Many of those in Afghanistan are small, and the largest are not of great size: the circumference of few of them at the base exceeds 150 feet, and their elevation apparently does not often reach 60 feet. . . . Many of the topes have yielded no return to the labour expended upon opening them; others have been rich in relics. It is a curious circumstance, noticed by Mr. Masson, that where these substances which appear to be the remains of a funeral pile, as ashes and animal exuviæ, most abound, the relics of antiquity are least abundant. The most conspicuous objects are, in general, vessels of stone or metal; they are of various shapes and sizes; some of them have been fabricated on a lathe. They commonly contain a silver box or casket, and within that, or sometimes by itself, a casket of gold. This is sometimes curiously wrought. One found by Mr. Masson at Deh Bimaran is chased with a double series of four figures, representing Gautama in the act of preaching; a mendicant is on his right, a lay-follower on his left, and behind the latter a female disciple; they stand under arched niches resting on pillars, and between the arches is a bird; a row of rubies is set round the upper and lower edge of the vessel, and the bottom is also chased with the leaves of the lotus: the vase had no cover. Within these vessels, or sometimes in the cell in which they are placed, are found small pearls, gold buttons, gold ornaments and rings, beads, pieces of white and coloured glass and crystal, pieces of clay or stone with impressions of figures, bits of bone, and teeth of animals of the ass and goat species, pieces of cloth, and folds of the Tuz or Bhurj leaf, or rather the bark of a kind of birch on which the Hindus formerly wrote; and these pieces bear sometimes characters which may be termed Bactrian; but they are in too fragile and decayed a state to admit of being unfolded or read. Similar characters are also found superficially scratched upon the stone, or dotted upon the metal vessels. In one instance they were found traced upon the stone with ink. Within some of the vessels was also found a liquid, which upon exposure rapidly evaporated, leaving a brown sediment, which was analysed by Mr. Prinsep, and offered some traces of animal and vegetable matters." *

The dágoba of Sarnath, near Benares, is a solid mass of masonry, from forty to fifty feet in diameter, originally shaped like a beehive, the upper part having crumbled down. It is cased externally with large blocks of stone, well fitted and polished, and has a broad belt of ornamental carving near the base, which represents a wreath.

The Shwadagon pagoda at Rangoon stands on the summit of an eminence, and is 338 feet high. In shape it is said to resemble an inverted speaking trumpet, and it is surmounted by a tee of brass, richly gilded, forty-five feet high. Its circumference at the base is 1355 feet. It is the most ancient monument in the country, more than 2500 years having elapsed since its foundation was laid. It is

* Wilson's Ariana Antiqua.

said that underneath it are relics of the four last Budhas; viz. the staff of Kakusanda, the water-dipper of Kónágama, the bathing garment of Kasyapa, and eight hairs from the head of Gótama.*

The height of the Budhistical monument at Manikyala, in the Punjab, from the summit of the artificial mound upon which it is situated, to the summit of the structure itself, is said by Elphinstone to be about 70 feet, and the circumference is 150 paces. According to the same author, "some broad steps, now mostly ruined, lead to the base of the pile round the base to a moulding on which are pilasters about four feet high and six feet asunder; these have plain capitals, with parallel lines and beadings. The whole of this may be seven or eight feet high, from the uppermost step to the top of the cornice. The building then retires, leaving a ledge of a foot or two broad, from which rises a perpendicular wall about six feet high; about a foot above the ledge is a fillet, formed by stones projecting a very little way from the wall, and at the top of the wall is a more projecting cornice." Above this complex basement, which may be taken to be from sixteen to twenty feet high, rises a dome approaching in shape to a hemisphere, but truncated and flat near the summit. The greater part of the outside is cased with stones about three feet and a-half long, cut smooth, and so placed that the ends only are exposed. In 1830, General Ventura, in the service of Runjit Sing, sank a perpendicular shaft in the centre of the platform on the summit, and at various depths found repositories, one below another, at intervals of several feet. These contained coins of gold, silver, and copper, boxes and vessels of iron, brass, copper, and gold. The copper coins were considered to be some of those struck by the Indo-Scythian kings, Kadphises or Kanerkes, who are thought to have reigned about the latter part of the first and the commencement of the second century. There are fifteen other dágobas in the same neighbourhood, one of which was opened by Court, another officer in the service of Runjit Sing, and was found to contain a coin of Julius Caesar, one of Mark Antony, and none of a much later date.†

The Nepaulese have a work entitled Dwavinsati Avadán, which contains an account of the fruits of building, worshipping, and circumambulating the dágoba. At the base of the structure are placed images of the Dhyani Budhas.

* Asiatic Researches, vol. xvi.
† Thornton's Gazetteer, art. Manikyala.

The principal dágobas in Ceylon are at Anurádhapura; and though time has divested them of a part of their original majesty, they are yet most imposing in their appearance. The Abhayagiri was originally 405 feet high, being only about fifty feet less than the highest of the pyramids of Egypt, or the dome of St. Peter's, at Rome, and fifty feet higher than St. Paul's, at London. Its elevation is not now more than 230 feet. The wall around the platform upon which it is built extends to the distance of one mile and three-quarters. The Jaitáwanarâma, completed A.D. 310, was originally 315 high, but is now reduced to 269 feet. It has been calculated that the contents of this erection are 456,071 cubic yards, and that a brick wall twelve feet high, two feet broad, and ninety-seven miles long, might be built with the materials that yet remain. The Túpárâma exceeds the others in elegance and unity of design, and in the beauty of the minute sculptures upon its tall, slender, and graceful columns.* Around two of the dágobas are rows of pillars that appear to have supported a roof, and before the dilapidation of the city the portico to which they belonged must have afforded a grateful retreat from the sunbeam, that in this vast plain seems to come down with unusual power. All the mounds in this neighbourhood have been built of brick, and covered over with a preparation of lime, cocoa-nut water, and the juice of the paragaha. This composition is of so pure a white, and can be so highly polished, that when perfect the structures must have resembled a crystal dome or a half-melted iceberg.

In 1820, a dágoba was opened in the Raigam Korle, on the western coast of Ceylon, by C. E. Layard, Esq., at that time collector of Colombo. The interior contained a small square compartment of brick-work, mathematically correct in its bearings towards the cardinal points, and having in the centre, in a vertical line from the supposed position of the apex, a hollow vase of stone, with a cover of the same material. Within this receptacle was found a small piece of bone, and some thin pieces of plate-gold, which was probably used as the covering of a relic; a few old rings, three small pearls, crystal and cornelian beads, small specimens of the white gircon, ruby, sapphire, and glass; a small pyramid of cement, solid, a few clay images of the sacred nága; and two lamps, one of brass and the other of clay, and similar to those at present used in Ceylon.†

* Forbes's Eleven Years in Ceylon.
† Bennett's Ceylon and its Capabilities.

By the Chinese traveller, Fa Hian, mention is made of a sacred mound at Anurádhapura, 122 metres high, covering an imprint of Budha's foot. He saw another mound in Kandahar, which was 216 metres, or 708 feet high, and one at Khotan, in Tartary, 250 feet high. Remusat, in his Notes to the Foĕ Kouĕ Ki, enumerates eight principal topes that were in existence at the period of Fa Hian's travels. They were situated at the wihára of Jétáwana, one of the principal residences of Gótama; at Kapila-wastu, his birthplace; on the bank of the river Níranjara, near which he became a Budha; at Benares, Kanoudj, Rajagaha, and *Belle Ville*, (Kalyâna near Colombo ?) and at Kusinára, on the spot where he died.

In the most ancient times of which we have any authentic record, subsequent to the deluge, the erection of structures bearing a resemblance to the dágoba appears to have prevailed. Without mentioning the ruin at Babylon, supposed to be the remains of the tower of Babel, we may notice that there is a mound at Accad, Gen. x. 10, surmounted by a mass of brick-work, rising to the height of 125 feet above the sloping elevation upon which it stands. The ruin consist of layers of sun-burnt bricks, cemented together by lime or bitumen. Similar piles are found near many of the ancient Babylonian towns. The mound near the ruins of Nineveh, called by the natives Koyonjuk-tepe, is said to be a truncated pyramid, with regular steep sides and a flat top. It was measured by Rich with a cord, which gave 178 feet for the greatest height, and 1850 feet for the length of the summit. The tomb of Alyattes, father of Croesus, consisted of a large mound of earth, supported by a foundation of great stones. This monument still exists. Hamilton says, in his Researches in Asia, that it took him about ten minutes to ride round its base, which gives it a circumference of nearly a mile. Towards the north it consists of the natural rock. The upper part is composed of sand and gravel. On the top there is a circular stone ten feet in diameter, placed there as an ornament for the apex of the tumulus. It was considered, in the time of Herodotus, as being inferior only to the gigantic edifices of Egypt and Babylon.—Herod. i. 92, iii. 343. Alyattes was cotemporary with Gótama Budha. The mausoleum erected by Artemisia to perpetuate the memory of her husband must also have been a monument of great splendour. It is worthy of remark, that three

* Remusat's Relation, p. 179.

of the seven wonders of the world were sepulchral in their character.

The ancient edifices of Chi Chen, in Central America, bear a striking resemblance to the topes of India. The shape of one of the domes, its apparent size, the small tower on the summit, the trees growing on the sides, the appearance of masonry here aud there, the style of the ornaments, and the small doorway at the base, are so exactly similar to what I had seen at Anurádhapura, that when my eye first fell upon the engravings of these remarkable ruins, I supposed that they were presented in illustration of the dágobas of Ceylon.

No comparison can be formed between the Budhistical structures and the pyramids of the Nile, as to the effect they produce upon the beholder. The æsthetical character of the Egyptian edifices would be entirely changed if they had been exposed to the common influences of the atmosphere, and if, as is the case with nearly all the topes of India, trees were growing in rich profusion upon their sides and summits. In the neighbourhood in which I now reside there is the chimney of a cotton mill, circular, of considerable altitude, that gradually decreases in diameter from the bottom to the top. The foundation rests upon the ground, without any pedestal; and there are buildings at a little distance, leaving an open space around it like a court. This column gives me, when seen from its base, and especially in some particular shades of light, a more perfect idea of the interminable than any other object I ever saw, though I have visited the pyramids, and seen many of the most remarkable edifices in the world. From this circumstance I have sometimes been led to suppose that if the pyramids were seen through the openings, properly arranged, of a portico similar to those that were originally carried round some of the dágobas at Anurádhapura, the effect would be much more striking than when viewed from any position in which they can now be seen. The unbroken lines of the pyramid agree well with the severity that prevails throughout the architecture of Egypt; but any idea of the interminable is entirely foreign to the mind of the Budhist; it does not enter into any one of his associations; and in the sacred mounds by which he endeavours to present an objective manifestation of that which he regards as the most wonderful, the sight is relieved by the rounded form in which it appears, still telling of repetition and revolution, rather than of the limitless and infinite. The westerns, with their characteristic daringness, have taken the dome of India and poised it in the air; and as they have made it hollow, so that it can be seen from beneath, an additional effect is brought out that can never be produced by a solid construction. The Chinese, in their pagodas or towers, have retained the Budhistical type, but have adapted it to their own ideas of taste.

The circumambulation of the dágoba is frequently mentioned in the books as being practised by the ancient ascetics. Among the Nepaulese it is regarded as one of the most pious acts of Budhist devotion. According to Ward, the Brahmans regard the circumambulating of a temple as a work of merit, raising the person to a place in the heaven of the god or goddess whose temple he thus walks round.

Any mark of disrespect to the dágoba is regarded as being highly criminal, whilst a contrary course is equally deserving of reward. When Eláro, one of the Malabar sovereigns, who reigned in Ceylon B. C. 205, was one day riding in his chariot, the yoke-bar accidently struck one of these edifices, and displaced some of the stones. The priests in attendance reproached him for the act; but the monarch immediately descended to the ground, and prostrating himself in the street, said that they might take off his head with the wheel of his carriage. But the priests replied, "Great king! our divine teacher delights not in torture; repair the dágóba." For the purpose of replacing the fifteen stones that had been dislodged, Eláro bestowed 15,000 of the silver coins called kahapana. Two women who had worked for hire at the erection of the great dágoba by Dutugámini were for this meritorious act born in Tawutisá. The legend informs us that on a subsequent occasion they went to worship at the same place, when the radiance emanating from their persons was so great that it filled the whole of Ceylon.*

The Nepaulese repeat mental prayers during the circumambulation of the dágoba, and a small cylinder, fixed upon the upper end of a short staff or handle, is held in the right hand and kept in perpetual revolution.† Fa Hian mentions that the Samaneans of Kiĕtchha, a country that, according to Klaproth, has not been identified, used wheels, in the efficacy of which they had great confidence. These wheels are called in Tibetan, hGor-læ, in Mongol kurdou, and in Sanscrit chakra. In Tartary and the adjacent countries they are still much used; and are supposed by Remusat to represent

* Turnour's Mahawanso. † Hodgson's Illustrations.

the periodical revolutions of the universe; but it is more probable that they are intended to exhibit the sequence of sentient existence.

The reverence paid to the dágobas arises from the supposition that they contain relics. The miracles performed by the "holy bones" of the Budhas and their disciples vie in the absurdity of their character with the legends of the saints; and although the errors elaborated in the time of the later fathers, and during the middle ages, present many striking parallelisms to the practices of the Budhists, the resemblance is here the most perfect. In the fourth century, when Fa Hian commenced his travels, relic-worship appears to have been universal among his co-religionists. The bones of Gótama, the garments he wore, the utensils he used, and the ladder by which he visited heaven, were worshipped by numbers of devout pilgrims; and happy did the country consider itself that retained one of these precious remains. In order to procure them, splendid embassages were dispatched, armies were collected, and battles were fought. Nor were the remains of Gótama the only treasures of this kind that were then possessed. One city is said to have rejoiced in the possession of the entire bones of Kásyapa, a Budha who preceded Gótama; but the existence of relics so ancient is inconsistent with the system as received in Ceylon. The bones of Gótama were collected after his cremation;* and the manner of their dispersion and their subsequent history is still upon record. The most celebrated relic now in existence is the Daladá, or left canine tooth of the sage.

The natives of Ceylon believe that this relic is now in their possession. It is an object of worship to all Budhists, and by the Kandians is regarded as the palladium of the country, the sovereign power of the island being supposed to be attached to its possession. It is a piece of discoloured ivory, or bone, slightly curved, nearly two inches in length, and one in diameter at the base; and from thence to the other extremity, which is rounded and blunt, it considerably decreases in size. The sanctuary of this relic is a small chamber in the wihára attached to the palace of the former kings of Kandy, where it is enshrined in six cases, the largest of which, upwards of five feet in height, is formed of silver, on the model of a dágoba. The same shape is preserved in the five inner ones, two of them being inlaid with rubies and other precious stones. The outer case is ornamented with many gold ornaments and jewels

* Relation, cap. v. note 6. † T'húpa-wansa.

which have been offered to the relic; and at night, when the place is lighted up by lamps, its appearance is very brilliant, far surpassing that of the British regalia, as I saw them some years ago in the Tower of London. In a work called the Daladáwansa, composed about the year A.D. 310, in Elu, and translated into Pali verse by Dharmmarakkhita, in the reign of queen Líláwati, who was deposed A.D. 1200, it is said that Khéma, one of the disciples of Budha, procured the left canine tooth of Gótama when his relics were distributed, which he took to Dantapura, the capital of Kálinga. Here it remained 800 years, when the Brahmans informed Pándu, the lord paramount of India, who resided at Pátaliputra, that his vassal, Gúhasiwa worshipped a piece of bone. The monarch, enraged at this intelligence, sent an army to arrest the king of Kálinga, and secure the bone he worshipped. This commission was executed, but the general and all his army were converted to the faith of Budhism. Pándu commanded the relic to be thrown into a furnace of burning charcoal, but a lotus arose from the flame, and the tooth appeared on the surface of the flower. An attempt was then made to crush it upon an anvil, but it remained embedded in the iron, resisting all the means employed to take it therefrom, until Subaddha, a Budhist, succeeded in its extraction. It was next thrown into the common sewer; but in an instant this receptacle of filth became sweet as a celestial garden, and was mantled with flowers. Other wonders were performed, by which Pándu also became a convert to Budhism. The relic was returned to Dantapura; but an attempt being made by the princes of Sewet to take it away by force, it was brought to Ceylon, and deposited in the city of Anurádhapura. In the fourteenth century it was again taken to the continent, but was rescued by Prákrama Báhu IV. The Portuguese say that it was captured by Constantine de Braganza, in 1560, and destroyed; but the native authorities assert that it was concealed at this time at a village in Saffragam. In 1815, it came into the possession of the British government; and although surreptitiously taken away in the rebellion of 1818, it was subsequently found in the possession of a priest, and restored to its former sanctuary.* From this time the keys of the shrine in which it was deposited were kept in the custody of the British Agent for the Kandian Provinces, and at night a soldier belonging to the Ceylon Rifle Regiment mounted

* Forbes's Dangistra Daladá; Ceylon Almanac, 1835. Turnour's Account of the Tooth Relic of Ceylon; Journal, Bengal As. Soc. Oct. 1837.

guard in the temple, there being from time to time public exhibitions of the pretended tooth, under the sanction of the British authorities, by which the cause of heathenism was greatly strengthened and the minds of sincere Christians were much grieved; but in 1839 a pamphlet was published, entitled "The British Government and Idolatry," in which these untoward proceedings were exposed, and the relic has since been returned to the native chiefs and priests, by a decree from the Secretary of State for the Colonies.

The Budhists teach, that they who, according to their ability, offer to the dágobas seats, flowers, lamps, or similar articles, with acts of worship, made with an affectionate mind, and accompanied by meditation, will be rewarded in this world and the next, and by receiving nirwána. On one occasion Gótama said to Ananda, "Though neither flowers nor anything else should be offered, yet if any one only look with a pleasant mind at a dágoba or the court of the bó-tree, he will undoubtedly be born in a déwa-loka; it is unnecessary to say that he who sweeps these sacred places, or makes offerings to them, will have an equal reward; furthermore, should any one die on his way to make an offering to a dágoba, he also will receive the blessedness of the déwa-lokas." This was declared by Budha previous to his dissolution, as he lay in the garden, between the two sal trees.

The seat upon which Gótama was accustomed to sit when alive, came into the possession of a certain priest; and there was associated with him an upásaka, who built for it a dágoba, in which it was placed. Near the same place was a priest of Iswara, with whom they had frequent disputes as to the superiority of their respective objects of worship. As they could come to no decision they appealed to the king, who said that the victory should be awarded to the priest who on the seventh day from that time could exhibit the greatest miracle. On the day appointed great numbers were assembled to witness the contest; and in the presence of the multitude, the priest of Budha addressed the dágoba and said, "Budha has attained nirwána; the agra-sráwakas (Seriyut and Mugalan) have attained the same state; I have therefore no trust but in thee!" In an instant the venerated seat came from the midst of the dágoba, and remained suspended in the air. The victory was therefore declared to be on the side of Budha.

The dágobas, as erected in honour of the rahats, have some of them the power of working miracles, but not all. There are some rahats who previous to the reception of nirwána determined that such and such wonders shall take place at their chaityas. Sometimes the déwas, out of compassion to men, cause wonders to be performed at the chaityas of certain rahats. At other times the faithful, whether women or men, present flowers, or perfumes, or robes, to a chaitya and determine within themselves that certain wonders shall be there performed; and by the power of this determination, the wonders take place. But in other cases the chaityas are not endowed with these gifts.

When the Chakrawartti dies his relics are collected together and placed in a tope, and those persons who respect them and make offerings to them, will be rewarded; they will either become a chakrawartti in this world, or Sekra in the déwa-lóka.

Another form of relic-worship is seen in the respect paid to the impressions of Gótama's foot, called srí-páda. On the third visit of the sage to Ceylon, in the eighth year after he obtained the Budhaship, he left an impression of his foot on the summit of the mountain usually known by the name of Adam's Peak, 7,420 feet above the level of the sea, intended as "a seal, to declare that Lanká would be the inheritance of Budha."* In the same journey he left other impressions of a similar kind in different parts of India. The summit of the peak is annually visited by great numbers of pilgrims. The footstep is said, by Dr. Davy, to be a superficial hollow five feet three inches and three-quarters long, and between two feet seven inches and two feet five inches wide. The footstep of Budha is not the only one that has received worship. There is a lake called Kosah Nag, on the north side of Fuhti Panjal, one of the mountains bounding the valley of Kashmir, on the south. It is held in great veneration by the Hindus, who call it Vishnu Paudh, the foot of Vishnu, in consequence of a legend that the deity produced it by stamping the ground with his foot. It was said in the age of Sulpicius Severus that the footsteps supposed to have been made by our Lord at his ascension suffered no diminution in the sharpness of their outline, though they were daily the object of veneration to great numbers of people. When in Jerusalem, in 1833, I saw a chapel upon the mount of Olives, of an octagonal form, with small marble pillars, in the floor of which is a cavity said to be the print of one of our Lord's feet, left at the time he ascended from this place. The pilgrims take casts of it in

* Sadharmmaratnakáré.

wax. It has at present no resemblance to a foot, but may have lost the virtue it formerly possessed, and been worn away by the kisses of its deluded visitors. The other footstep was formerly shewn. It was an ancient belief that these marks could never be hid by a pavement or covered by a roof. There is a legend that when Augustine landed at Thanet, he left as perfect a mark in the rock as if it had been wax; "and the Romanists will cry shame on our hard hearts," says Fuller, "if our obstinate unbelief, more stubborn than stone, will not as pliably receive the impression of this miracle."

The soles of Budha's foot are represented as being divided into 108 compartments, like a pictorial alphabet, each of which contained a figure. The Budhists of different countries have pictures of the sacred footstep, and as each figure is minutely described in their books, the representations are generally uniform. One of the titles of the monarch of Siam is, "the pre-eminently merciful and munificent, the soles of whose feet resemble those of Budha."

I have said, in the first chapter, page 5, that "at their death the Budhas cease to exist; they do not continue to be Budhas, nor do they enter upon any other state of being." The inconsistency of worshipping an extinct being must be at once apparent; but there would be no incongruity in the act, if it could be proved that the grand principles of Budhism are correct. This subject has been argued at length between Nágaséna and Milinda. Not long after the monarch had embraced the faith of Budha, he said to the priest by whom his conversion had been effected, "The tirttaka unbelievers argue in this manner:—If Budha now receives the offerings of men, he has not attained nirwána, as in that state all cleaving to existing objects is destroyed; he is still connected with the world; he is yet existent (bháwayata-ætulatwa); he is in the world, and has the same attributes as other beings; therefore the assistance that he can render is imperfect, vain, and worthless. But if he has attained nirwána, he is not connected with the world; he is not existent; he cannot receive the offerings that are made to him; there is therefore no benefit from presenting them, as he has no life, no being, aprána. None but a rahat can answer this argument of the tirttakas; therefore be pleased, venerable priest, to set aside this difficulty." Nágásena replied, "Budha has attained nirwána, in which there is no cleaving to existence; he does not receive the offerings that are presented; at the foot of the bó-tree, when he became a supreme Budha, all evil desire was destroyed; he has now attained nirwána. Who is it that affirms that Budha now receives the offerings? Thus did Seriyut declare:—'Budha receives the offerings that are made by déwas and men, but without any earthly cleaving, or desire towards them. This is the general practice, the universal law, of the infinite Budhas who have appeared.'" On hearing this the king said, "The father magnifies the son, and the son the father; therefore this is not an argument that we can bring before the unbelievers; each one praises his own; be pleased, therefore, to bring forward some other argument that will convince the sceptics." Nágásena: "Budha has attained nirwána; he does not receive the offerings that are made to him by the people of the world; nevertheless, those who make offerings to the relics of the Budhas, or listen to their bana, will receive the three great favours, viz: the happiness of this world, of the déwa-lokas, and of nirwána. Thus when grass or fuel has been thrown into a fire that has been kindled, is there any desire to receive them on the part of the fire?" Milinda: "The fire has no mind, and therefore cannot receive them on account of desire." Nágaséna: "When that fire, that although it has no mind, receives the grass and fuel, is extinguished, is the world without fire?" Milinda: "No; any one who wishes to produce fire may do so by the friction of two pieces of wood." Nágaséna: "Therefore they who say that no benefit can be received from the making of offerings to Budha, utter that which has no foundation in truth. Whilst Budha was in the world, the glory that he possessed may be compared to a brilliant flame; now that he has attained nirwána, his passing away is like the extinguishing of that flame; but as the flame receives the grass or fuel that is thrown into it, though without any desire on its part, so, although Budha does not receive the offerings of the faithful, the reward of those offerings is certain. For as any man may procure a flame by the rubbing together of two pieces of wood, by the light of which he will be able to carry on whatever work he has in hand, so the faithful, by making offerings to Budha, and reflecting on the excellencies of the dharmma, will reap the reward for which these exercises are practised. There is another comparison to which you must listen. There is a high wind; it shakes the trees, and causes them to fall, and then dies away: after thus passing away, is it from desire that it again returns?" Milinda: "This cannot be, because it has got no mind." Nágaséna: "Does the wind that passes away make some sign to the wind that is to come?" Milinda: "No; any one may cause wind by means of a fan; when he is warm, he can cool himself in this way." Nágaséna: "Therefore the unbelievers that say there is no benefit from the making of offerings to Budha speak falsely. As the wind spreads itself in every direction, so is the virtue of Budha everywhere diffused; as the wind that has passed away is not again produced, so there is no reception of the offerings on the part of Budha. As men are subject to be annoyed by the heat, so are déwas and men afflicted by the threefold fire of evil-desire, enmity, and ignorance; and as men when thus annoyed cause a wind to refresh their persons by means of a fan or some other instrument, so are they assisted who seek the protection of Budha; and the threefold fire is extinguished, although Budha has attained nirwána, and does not receive the offerings that are presented. Another comparison may be given. A man strikes the drum, and causes a sound to be produced; the sound dies away; is it afterwards again produced?" Milinda: "No; the sound has passed away; but the same man can cause a repetition of the sound by again striking the drum." Nágaséna: "In like manner, though Budha has attained nirwána, the benefit to be received from the making of offerings and meditating on the bana, is still certain. This benefit is gained, though Budha does not receive the offerings. Budha foresaw the things that would happen in future times, and he said to Ananda, 'Ananda, when I am gone, you must not think that there is no Budha; the discourses I have delivered, and the precepts I have enjoined, must be my successors, or representatives, and be to you as Budha.' Therefore, the declaration of the tirttakas that there is now no benefit from the presenting of offerings to Budha is utterly false; though he does not receive them, the benefit to the giver is the same as if he did. Again, does the earth say, 'Let such and such trees grow upon my surface?'" Milinda: "No." Nágaséna: "Then how is it that flowers, and buds, and shrubs, and trees, and creepers passing from one to the other, are produced?" Milinda: "The earth, though itself unconscious, is the cause of their production." Nágaséna: "Even so, though Budha is now unconscious, he is nevertheless the source of benefit to those who seek his protection. That which is the opposite of evil desire, enmity, and ignorance, is thus like the root of merit set in the ground; the exercise of samádhi is like the trunk of the tree; the doctrines of the bana are like the hard wood in its heart; the four sangwara precepts are like the boughs and main branches; the five forms of knowledge called wimukti, that reveal the way in which emancipation is to be obtained, are like the colours and perfume of the flowers; and the fruition of the paths leading to nirwána is like the immortal fruit; and all this is brought about by Budha, though he has attained nirwána, and is unconscious. Again, in the intestines of camels, horses, asses, goats, cattle, and men, worms are bred; * does this take place with their consent and consciousness?" Milinda: "No." Nágaséna: "Again, there are ninety-eight diseases to which men are subject. Do these diseases come with their consent; or do they say, Let these diseases come?" Milinda: "No; they are produced in consequence of evil deeds that have been performed in previous births." Nágaséna: "If that which has been done in a former birth can cause these disorders of the body, and is not without the power of producing consequences; even so, though Budha has attained nirwána, and is unconscious, any service done for him may nevertheless receive a reward. Again, Did you never hear of the yaká Nandaka, who struck the head of Seriyut with his hand, and the earth clove, and he went down to hell? Was this cleaving of the earth brought about by the will and appointment of Seriyut?" Milinda: "No; this could not be; the world and all the beings that inhabit it might pass away; the sun and moon might fall to the earth, and Maha Méru be destroyed; but Seriyut could not will the endurance of sorrow by any being whatever; the rising of anger would at once be overcome by the virtue he possessed as a rahat; he could not be incensed even against his murderer. It was by the power of his own demerit that Nandaka was sent to hell." Nágaséna: "It was even so; but if this demerit, though unconscious, could cause the yaká to be taken to hell, so may merit, though also unconscious, cause those who possess it to be taken to a déwa-loka, and receive happiness. Thus, O king, when the tirttakas say, 'If Budha receives the offerings of men, he is yet in the world of sentient being; but if he has attained nirwána, he is unconscious, he cannot assist those who seek his protection; and there is therefore no benefit to be derived from the offerings that are made to him;' their argu-

* The presence of worms and other parasites in the bodies of animals was well known to Hippocrates, Galen, and the ancients generally. The skill of modern science has not yet discovered a cause for the existence of these entozoa that is considered as entirely satisfactory by professional men.

ment is of no value, it is vain and deceitful." In this way the venerable priest answered the questions of the great king; like the man who shakes the branches of the jambu tree fifty yojanas in height, and succeeds in procuring its immortal fruit.*

It appears wonderful that any being possessed of reason can receive these comparisons as conclusive argument; but they who know not the truth are led to believe "a lie," and no order of evidence is so well calculated "to hide pride from man," as the history of his religious practices and opinions. On passing forward to the hortatory usages of Budhism, we might expect to meet with something of more practical utility; but even here the beneficial effects that might otherwise be produced are nullified by the almost exclusive use of a dead language. The protestants of christendom are now almost the only religionists in the world who uniformly make use of the vernacular tongues in their public ministrations.

It was an ordinance of Budha, that the priests, who were then supposed to dwell most commonly in the wilderness, should reside during the three months of the rainy season in a fixed habitation. This season is called wass; and it is at this period that the priests read bana to the people. The place of reading, called the bana-maduwa, is usually a temporary erection, the roof having several breaks or compartments, gradually decreasing in size as they approach the top, in the form of a pagoda, or of a pyramid composed of successive platforms. There is one of these erections in the precinct of nearly all the wiháras; but they are frequently built in other places, as may be most agreeable to the wishes of the people by whom they are erected as an act of merit. In the centre of the interior area is an elevated platform, for the convenience of the priests; and the people sit around it, upon mats spread on the ground. No part of the rough material of the maduwa is seen, as the pillars and the roof are covered with white cloth, upon which mosses, flowers, and the tender leaf of the cocoa nut are worked up into various devices. Lamps and lanterns are suspended in great profusion and variety, the latter being formed of coloured paper, similar to those used by the Chinese at their festivals. It is accounted an act of merit for the people to hold lamps in their hands, or upon their heads, whilst the priests are reading. The impression produced by the scene presented in some localities is most striking, and forms the most magnificent sight ever seen by

* Milinda Prasna.

many of the worshippers. The females are arrayed in their gayest attire, their hair being combed back from the forehead and neatly done up in a knot, fastened with silver pins and small ornamental combs, in the arrangement of which they display considerable taste. The usual dress of the men is of white cotton, which the fullers have beaten upon stones and spread out in the air, until it presents a purity never seen in climes where the sun has less power. Flags and streamers, figured handkerchiefs and shawls, float from every convenient receptacle. At intervals, tomtoms are beat; the rude trumpet sends forth its screams; and the din of the music, the murmur of the people's voices, the firing of musketry and jinjalls, and the glare of the lamps, produce an effect that is not much in consonance with the place of instruction or an act of worship. Not unfrequently there are skeleton trees, covered over with silver tissue, various ornaments resembling gems being pendant from the branches. They are said to represent the magical kalpa-tree, that gives whatever is required from it; but there is this difference, that they receive rather than give, as their real intention is to receive offerings from those who come to worship. They have occasionally been covered with the leaves of tracts given at the festivals; hung there in derision, but presenting one of the best modes of publication that their distributors could desire. In some conspicuous place there is a large copper-pan, into which the alms of the people are thrown. The individual offerings are small, but when collected together they must form a respectable sum.

At a bana-reading held at Pantura, in 1839, nearly 100 priests were present. The pulpit was placed upon a pivot, so that it turned round continually. At night fireworks were exhibited. An individual who personated a messenger from the déwa-loka was dressed like a chief of the highest rank. On his entrance he was guarded by two persons who were dressed like kings, with crowns upon their heads and swords in their hands. Another attendant, in magnificent array, rode upon an elephant, and a third upon horseback. Fifty men, in the uniform of British soldiers, continually fired volleys in the air. On the pulpit, around which stood the priests chaunting verses in Pali, were hung the official swords of eight native chiefs, and a gold medal presented to a native by Sir Robert Brownrigg, when governor of the island.

The platform in the centre of the hall is sometimes occupied by several priests at the same time, one of whom reads a portion of the sacred books. The copies of the bana now used are beautifully written in large characters, upon the best talipot leaves that can be procured, with marks, to point out the conclusion of the sentences, made with some coloured composition. They are read in a kind of recitative, "in a manner between singing and reading," as it is said that the Scriptures were recited in the early church, which was also most probably the tone used by the rhapsodists and by the jongleurs of the middle ages. This method is admirably adapted to assist the reader or reciter, as, when the eye does not readily catch the word, or the memory reach it, the voice can continue to dwell, by a shake or quaver, upon the last syllable, without the unpleasant sensation that would be produced if the book was read in the usual tone of voice; as in this case there is no alternative, but either to repeat the former part of the sentence, or abruptly to stop. Upon some occasions one priest reads the original Pali, and another interprets what is read in the vernacular Singhalese; but this method is not very frequently adopted. It is the more usual course to read the Pali alone, so that the people understand not a word that is said; and were the advices of even the most excellent description in themselves, they would be delivered without profit to the people assembled. A great proportion of the attendants fall asleep, as they commonly remain during the whole night; whilst others are seen chewing their favourite betle. As might be supposed, there are evidences of unconcern in that which ought to be the principal object of the festival; but there is none of that rudeness which would be exhibited in a promiscuous assemblage of people in some countries that are much higher in the scale of civilization. Near the reading-hall there are booths and stalls, in which rice-cakes, fruits, and other provisions, and occasionally cloth and earthenware, are sold; and the blind and the lame are there, with their stringed instruments, sitting by the wayside to receive alms; so that the festival is regarded as an opportunity for amusement, as well as for acquiring merit, and answers the general purpose of a wake or fair. Whenever the name of Budha is repeated by the officiating priest, the people call out simultaneously, "sádhu!" the noise of which may be heard at a great distance; and the effect is no doubt pleasing to those who have not been taught that it is in vain for the unlearned to say Amen, when they know not the meaning of that which is spoken. The readings are most numerously attended upon the night of the full moon, when a light is thrown upon the landscape in Ceylon that seems to silver all things visible, from the tiny leaflet to the towering mountain, and a stillness sleeps in the air that seems too deep to be earthly; and were the voices of the multitude that now come forth at intervals other than from atheist lips, the spirit might drink in a rich profusion of the thoughts that come so pleasantly, we can scarcely tell whether the waking dream be a reality, or a vision of some brighter land.

Now and then an individual priest becomes popular, either from the sweetness of his voice, or the manner in which he explains the bana; but the eastern style of oratory is very different to that with which we are most familiar, as the emphasis, the intonation, and the whole manner of the speaker, so still and passionless, is contrary to the method we should regard as alone calculated to arrest the attention or be impressive of the truth. A speaker of this description has been well described by Dr. Judson. "I went," says this venerated missionary, "for the second time, to hear a popular Burman preacher. On our arrival we found a zayat, in the precincts of one of the most celebrated pagodas, lighted up, and the floor spread with mats. In the centre was a frame raised about eighteen inches from the ground, where the preacher, on his arrival, seated himself. He appeared to be about forty-five years old, of very pleasant countenance, and harmonious speech. He was once a priest, but is now a layman. The people, as they came in, seated themselves on the mats, the men on one side of the house, and the women on the other. It was an undistinguished day, and the congregation was very small, not more than one hundred. . . . When all things were properly adjusted, the preacher closed his eyes, and commenced the exercise, which consisted in repeating a portion from their sacred writings. His subject was the conversion of the two prime disciples of Gaudama, and their subsequent promotion and glory. His oratory I found to be different to all that we call oratory. At first he seems dull and monotonous; but presently his soft, mellifluent tones, win their way into the heart, and lull the soul into that state of calmness and serenity, which, to a Burman mind, somewhat resembles the boasted perfection of their saints of old. His discourse continued about half an hour; and at the close, the whole assembly burst out into a short prayer, after which all rose and retired. This man exhibited twice every evening, in different places. Indeed he is the only popular lay preacher in the place. As for the priests, they preach on special occasions only, when they are drawn from their seclusion and inactivity, by the solicitations of their adherents." *

There are other objects of attraction at the bana-maduwa, besides the reading of the sacred books. A labyrinth is made of withs, ornamented with the cocoa-nut leaf; and it is a source of amusement to thread its mazes, and find the way to the place of exit. The Budhists of Arakan have a similar custom. In some instances lines are drawn upon the ground, in an open space, and dancers are introduced. These lines are regarded as the limits of the territory belonging to different yakás and déwas; and the last is appropriated to Budha. One of the dancers advances towards the first limit, and when he is told to what yaká it belongs, he calls out the demon's name in defiance, uttering against him the most insulting language; and declaring that in spite of all the opposition that can be brought against him, he will cross the limit, and invade the territory of its infernal possessor. Then, passing the limit in triumph, he acts in the same manner towards all the other demons and divinities who have had divisions assigned to them, until at last he approaches the limit of Budha. Still he professes to be equally fearless, and shouts defiance against the woolly-headed priest who carries the alms-bowl from door to door like a common mendicant; but the moment he attempts to pass the limit he falls down as if dead; and as he is regarded as suffering the punishment of the blasphemy he has dared to utter, all who are present applaud the greatness of him whose prowess is thus proved to be superior to that of all other beings.

The bana is usually read upon the days called poho. This word signifies change, and the festivals are held on the poho-dina, or póya-dawas, the days on which there is a change of the moon. In each month there are four póya days:—1. Amáwaka, the day of the new moon. 2. Atawaka, the eighth day from the time of the new moon. 3. Pahaloswaka, the fifteenth day from the time of the new moon, or the day of the full moon. 4. Atawaka, the eighth day from the time of the full moon. The word waka means the thirtieth part of a lunar month. It is said by Professor Wilson, that "the days of the full and new moon are sacred with all sects of the Hindus;" but according to Manu the sacred books are not upon these days to be read. "The dark lunar day destroys the spiritual teacher; the fourteenth day destroys the learner; the eighth and

* Memoir of Mrs. Judson.

the day of the full moon destroy all remembrance of scripture; for which reason the Brahman must avoid reading on those lunar days."—Manu, iv. 114. The ancient Britons called their week,* as do their descendants at this day in the Principality, wyth-nos, "eight-nights," and their fortnight, pythew-nos, "fifteen-nights."

The people are informed that there will be great merit to the faithful laic who becomes an upásaka, from the keeping of the eight precepts upon póya days. These days must be kept with clean garments and with clean minds, or the merit will be inferior. The upásaka must remember on the preceding day that it is the póya day on the morrow, and must prepare the food that will be required, and resolve upon keeping the precepts. On the morning of the day on which the póya takes place he must eat his food, and then go to some priest or priestess, or to some upásaka acquainted with bana, or to some person who knows only the precepts ordained by Budha. When approaching such a person, he must do it with great reverence, and say, "It is my intention to keep the precepts." He must first repeat the threefold formulary of protection, then the five precepts, and afterwards the one relative to elevated seats, making in all eight. When there is no proper person from whom to receive them, he may repeat them by himself, without the assistance of another. When keeping póya it is not right to do any work that will injure another, or to incite any one to do the same thing. Upon these days it is not proper to trade, nor to calculate the profits of trade.† When in the house, the upásaka must eat his food in

* Smith's Religion of Ancient Britain.

† There were advantages connected with the observance of the Sabbath, at its primeval institution, that have not yet been fully brought out. Had this day been properly observed from the beginning, idolatry could never have existed; and not only would a seventh part of all toil have been prevented, but sentiments of kindness would have been diffused, that would also have prevented the existence of all the severer forms of social and political misery. Take away idolatry and its consequences from man's history, and substitute a knowledge of the existence of God; reduce the overt acts of human selfishness in the proportion that must necessarily have taken place if the Sabbath had always been rightly attended to, and what would now have been the position of the world! Here is a glorious theme for the exercise of the imagination; and I should rejoice to see it elaborated by some competent mind.

The sacred days of the heathen are much more strictly kept than is generally supposed. "The manner in which all public feriae (by the Romans) were kept bears great analogy to our Sunday. The people generally visited the temples of the gods, and offered up their prayers and sacrifices. The most serious and solemn seem to have been the feriae imperativae; but all the others were generally attended by rejoicings and feasting. All kinds of business, especially lawsuits, were suspended during the public feriae, as the same manner as the faithful priest, and afterwards return to the pansal to receive instruction, or he must in private reflect on the impermanency, sorrow, and unreality connected with all things.

they were considered to pollute the sacred season. The rex sacrorum and the flamines were not even allowed to behold any work being done during the feriae; hence, when they went out, they were preceded by their heralds, who enjoined the people to abstain from working, that the sanctity of the day might not be polluted by the priest's seeing persons at work. Those who neglected this admonition were not only liable to a fine, but, in case their disobedience was intentional, their crime was considered to be beyond the power of any atonement; whereas those who had unconsciously continued their work, might atone for their transgression by offering a pig. It seems that doubts as to what kinds of work might be done at public feriae were not unfrequent, and we possess some curious and interesting decisions, given by Roman pontiffs on this subject. One Umbro declared it to be no violation of the feriae, if a person did such work as had reference to the gods, or was connected with the offering of sacrifices: all work, he moreover declared, was allowed, which was necessary to supply the urgent wants of human life. The pontiff Scaevola, when asked what kind of work might be done on a dies feriatus, answered that any work might be done, if any suffering or injury should be the result of neglect or delay; e. g. if an ox should fall into a pit, the owner might employ workmen to lift it out; or if a house threatened to fall down, the inhabitants might take such measures as would prevent its falling, without polluting the feriae."—*Smith's Dictionary of Antiquities, art. Feriae, by Dr. Leonhard Schmitz.*

Our Saxon forefathers were equally mindful of the sanctity of the Christian Sabbath. "The church service was publicly performed (among the Anglo-Saxons) on every day in the year; but it was only on Sundays and festivals that it was performed with full solemnity. By the promulgation of Christianity, the Jewish religion with its rites had ceased to exist: the Sabbath had been succeeded by the Sunday, the day of rest by a day of worship, the seventh by the first day of the week; and we are told by the most ancient writers, that the preference was given to the first day, because it was on that day that God began to fashion the earth for the habitation of man, on the same day that the Saviour by his resurrection completed the great work of our redemption, and on the same that the new law was published to the world by the descent of the Holy Ghost on the apostles. This institution was of course introduced by the missionaries among the converts, who were taught that the Sunday was a day sacred to the service of God, and that to devote it to secular employments, incompatible with such service, was a profanation and sacrilege. Impressed with this opinion, the Anglo-Saxon legislature came to the aid of the church, and prohibited on the Sunday, not only all predial labour and every sort of handicraft, by which men of low and servile condition were accustomed to earn their livelihood; but also the field sports of hunting and hawking, the dissipation of travelling, the sale or purchase of merchandize, the prosecution of family feuds, the holding of courts of justice, and the execution of criminals. The transgressor under any of these heads was liable to the punishments prescribed in the doom-book. If a clerk was convicted of working on a Sunday, he was adjudged to pay a fine of one hundred and twenty shillings; if a free servant, acting of his own will, to the loss of liberty, or a fine of sixty shillings; if a bondman acting in the same manner, to be whipped, or to pay the price of his hide, which was ten shillings. In like manner, the lord who compelled others to labour paid a mulct of thirty shillings, and forfeited the services of his bondmen, who became free. One exception, however, was allowed in favour of those who could plead a reasonable excuse for travelling on that day. 'Sunday,' says the lawgiver, 'is very solemnly to be reverenced: therefore we command

The being who even for a single day keeps the eight precepts will have greater glory than a chakrawartti, a reward that cannot be told. But though this is declared, it gives no adequate idea of

that no man dare on that holy day to apply to any worldly work, unless for the preparing of his food; except it happen that he must of necessity journey. Then he may ride, or row, or journey by such convenience as may be suitable to his way; on the condition that he hear his mass, and neglect not his prayers.'

"From the exemption from labour thus granted to the working-classes, the Sunday itself was called a freolsday, or day of freedom, and the manner of keeping it, in conformity with the preceding regulations, the freolsung, or freedom of the Sunday. But the day was not then comprised within the same hours as it is now with us. Our ancestors, like the Hebrews, made the evening precede the morning, and reckoned the Sunday from sunset on Saturday to sunset on the following day. To these twenty-four hours the freolsung was at first confined; but at a later period, some time before the reign of Edgar, though probably no change had taken place in the ecclesiastical computation, the freedom of the Sunday was enlarged in favour of the working population, beginning at the hour of nine on Saturday, and lasting till the dawn of light on Monday morning.

"With respect to the religious duties of the Sunday, it was ordered by the Council of Cloveshoe, that the clergy should 'devote it to the worship of God exclusively; that all abbots and priests should remain the whole day at their minsters and churches, and celebrate the solemnity of the mass; that they should shun all external engagements, all company of seculars, and all travelling not of absolute necessity, and should employ themselves in teaching their dependants the rules of a holy life, and of religious conversation from the Holy Scriptures, and that they should frequently exhort the people to repair again and again to the church to hear the word of God, to receive instruction, and to be present at the mysterious service of the mass.'

"The duties expected from the laity may be collected from the following injunction:—'It is most right and proper that every Christian man, who has it in his power to do so, should come on Saturday to the church, and bring a light with him, and there hear the vesper song, and after midnight the uhtsong, and come with his offering in the morning to the solemn mass; and, when he is there, let there be no dispute, or quarrel, or discord; but let him, with peaceful mind, during the holy office, intercede with his prayers and his alms (his offering) both for himself, with his friends, and all the people of God. And after the holy service, let him return home, and regale himself with his friends, and neighbours, and strangers; but at the same time, be careful that they commit no excess either in eating or drinking.' It was in the 'holy and ghostly kirk,' (the parish church, not any private chapel) 'and at the high and solemn mass,' that they were summoned to attend, because there and at that time they would hear the 'commands of God's word' explained, and receive instruction in their respective duties. 'Wherefore,' it concludes, 'we command all men, whatever may be their rank, to attend at the high mass, with the exception only of the hallowed maidens, whose custom it is not to go out of their minsters: these should continue within the inclosures of their minsters, and there hear mass.'"—*Lingard's Anglo-Saxon Church.*

These extracts may be regarded as somewhat irrelevant; but the reverence with which I regard the Sabbath, the anxious desire I feel to see its privileges every where extended, and the fear I entertain lest the circumstances of the times should lead to a more general desecration of this holy day, must be my apology for their insertion. The longest note in the work will not have been appended in vain, if the example of the Roman or Saxon should lead any of my readers to pay greater respect to "the Sabbath of the Lord."

the reward that will be received by him who pays a proper regard to one single póya-day. This reward may be divided into sixteen parts, and one of these sixteen parts may be subdivided into sixteen parts again, and the same method of division may be carried on sixteen times; but the last sixteenth will be more than that which has been declared.

When persons are sick they send for a priest to read the bana, who is brought with much ceremony, and treated with great respect. The priest continues to recite the sacred word, until the invalid either recovers or dies. The tones in which it is chaunted produce a mournful impression, and by this means a spirit of thoughtfulness may be encouraged; but further than this there is no benefit, as the meaning of the words is not understood.

There is a ceremony called Pirit, or in Pali Páritta, which consists in reading certain portions of the bana. As it is thought by the Singhalese, that nearly all the afflictions that men suffer proceed from the malice of the demons called yakás, they have numerous ceremonies by which they suppose that their anger can be appeased, or their enmity rendered inoxious; but the only one that professes to be sanctioned by Gótama is the reading of the Pirit. I was present on one of these occasions, in 1828, at a village near Matura. The discourses constituting the Pirit have been translated by the Rev. D. J. Gogerly; * and from the description of the ceremony given by that gentleman, to which some of my own personal recollections are added, the following account is compiled.

About sunset numbers of persons arrived from different quarters, the greater proportion of whom were women, bringing with them cocoanut shells and oil, to be presented as offerings. As darkness came on, the shells were placed in niches in the wall of the court by which the wihára is surrounded; and by the aid of the oil and a little cotton they were soon converted into lamps. The wall around the bó-tree was similarly illuminated; and as many of the people had brought torches, composed of cotton and resinous substances, the whole of the sacred enclosure was in a blaze of light. The gay attire and merry countenances of the various groups that were seen in every direction gave evidence, that however solemn the professed object for which they were assembled together, it was regarded by all as a time of relaxation and festivity. Indeed the grand cause of the popularity of this and similar gatherings is, that they are the

* Ceylon Friend, April, 1839.

only occasion, marriage festivals excepted, upon which the young people can see and be seen, or upon which they can throw off the reserve and restraint it is their custom to observe in the ordinary routine of social intercourse.

The service continues during seven days, a preparatory ceremony being held on the evening of the first day. The edifice in which it is conducted is the same as that in which the bana is read upon other occasions. A relic of Budha, enclosed in a casket, is placed upon a platform erected for the purpose; and the presence of this relic is supposed to give the same efficacy to the proceedings as though the great sage were personally there. For the priests who are to officiate another platform is prepared; and at the conclusion of the preparatory service a sacred thread called the pirit núla is fastened round the interior of the building, the end of which, after being fastened to the reading platform, is placed near the relic. At such times as the whole of the priests who are present engage in chaunting in chorus, the cord is untwined, and each priest takes hold of it, thus making the communication complete between each of the officiating priests, the relic, and the interior walls of the building.

From the commencement of the service on the morning of the second day, until its conclusion on the evening of the seventh day, the reading platform is never to be vacated day or night. For this reason, when the two officiating priests are to be relieved by others, one continues sitting and reading whilst the other gives his seat to his successor, and the second priest does not effect his exchange until the new one has commenced reading. In the same way, from the morning of the second day till the morning of the seventh day, the reading is continued day and night, without intermission. Not fewer than twelve, and in general twenty-four, priests are in attendance, two of whom are constantly officiating. As they are relieved every two hours, each priest has to officiate two hours out of the twenty-four. In addition to this, all the priests engaged in the ceremony are collected three times in each day: viz. at sunrise, at midday, and at sunset, when they chaunt in chorus the three principal discourses of the Pirit, called respectively Mangala, Ratana, and Karaníya, with a short selection of verses from other sources. After this the reading is continued till the series of discourses has been read through, when they are begun again, no other than those in the first series being read until the sixth day, when a new series is commenced.

On the morning of the seventh day a grand procession is formed of armed and unarmed men, and a person is appointed to officiate as the déwadútayá, or messenger of the gods. This company, with a few of the priests, proceeds to some place where the gods are supposed to reside, inviting them to attend prior to the conclusion of the service, that they may partake in its benefits. Until the messenger and his associates return, the officiating priests remain seated, but the reading is suspended.

At the festival I attended the messenger was introduced with great state, and sulphur was burnt before him to make his appearance the more supernatural. One of the priests having proclaimed that the various orders of gods and demons were invited to be present, the messenger replied that he had been deputed by such and such deities, repeating their names, to say that they would attend. The threefold protective formulary, which forms part of the recitation, was spoken by all present, in grand chorus. In the midst of much that is superstitious in practice or utterly erronious in doctrine, there are some advices repeated of an excellent tendency; but the whole ceremony being conducted in a language that the people do not understand, no beneficial result can be produced by its performance.

The folly of the priests in confining their public ministrations to the simple reading of the bana, or to the offering of expositions that are equally unintelligible, has caused the class of persons called upásakas, in some districts, and especially in the neighbourhood of Matura, to go about from house to house, after the manner of the Scripture readers, reading works on religion that are written in the vernacular Singhalese, accompanied with familiar expositions. It is by this means that Budhism is in many places principally supported. It would appear that in Nepaul there has been a similar transfer of the duty of teaching from the priest to the laic, as the Vajra Acharayas, who are there the most active ministers, are married; and the extract from Mrs. Judson's Memoir, inserted above, would seem to intimate that in Burma also there is the manifestation of equal negligence on the part of the sramanas.

XX. MEDITATION.

As the priests of Budha who lived according to the rules of the original institute were much in solitude, it was necessary that regulations should be laid down for their guidance when in this position. Accordingly, the Pitakas, as well as their other works, abound with advices that are only applicable to the circumstances of the recluse. The general character of these instructions may be learnt from the following translations, taken principally from the Wisudhi Margga Sanné.

There are five principal modes of bháwaná, or meditation:— 1. Maitrí. 2. Mudita. 3. Karuná. 4. Upékshá. 5. Asubha.

No one can enter aright upon the exercise of meditation who has not previously kept the precepts. But if there be any one who is thus prepared, let him, at the close of the day, or at the dawn, seek a place where he will be free from interruption, and with the body in a suitable posture, let him meditate on the glory of the Budhas, the excellence of the bana, and the virtues of the priesthood.

1. *Maitrí-bháwaná.*—When the priest has arrived at a convenient spot, and placed himself in a proper position, let him exercise this wish: "May all the superior orders of being be happy; may they all be free from sorrow, disease, and evil desire; may all men, whether they be priests or laics, all the déwas, all who are suffering the pains of hell, be happy; may they be free from sorrow, disease, and evil desire." Then the same wish must be exercised relative to all sentient beings in the four cardinal points, all in the four half-points, all above and all below, taking each of these ten directions separately and in order; or if they cannot be taken separately, it will suffice if this wish be exercised: "May all beings be happy; may they all be free from sorrow, disease, and pain." This is maitríbháwaná, or the meditation of kindness. Maitrí is the same as snéha, affection, and, according to the grammarians, snéha is the opposite of kródha, hatred. Maitrí and kródha cannot exist together. It is not the affection of trishná, or mere passion; of this kind of snéha, móha or ignorance is the cause, which leads to evil desire. In the snéha of maitrí there is no evil desire; it is that which one friend feels for another.

In the exercise of this mode of bháwaná, the thoughts must not at first be fixed upon one whom the priest dislikes; nor on any particular friend; nor on any one that is indifferent to him, neither liked nor disliked; nor on any enemy (as by thinking of any person who is known, the mind will be more or less disturbed.) The thoughts must not at this time be fixed upon any individual in particular, nor on any one that is dead. There was a young priest who exercised maitrí-bháwaná upon his preceptor, but he did not arrive at nimitta (the interior illumination for the acquiring of which he entered upon the exercise.) He therefore went to another priest, and asked him how it was that he could not arrive at nimitta. The priest replied that he must first ascertain whether the person upon whom he meditated was alive or dead, as no nimitta could be received when maitrí-bháwaná was exercised for the dead.

The first meditation of the priest must be on himself; * "may I be free from sorrow, anger, and evil desire;" thus he must think. But by this exercise alone no one can arrive at samádhi, or perfect tranquillity of mind, even if practised a hundred years. He must therefore go on to desire that what he has wished to receive himself may be granted to all sentient beings; and that what he has wished to be warded from himself may be warded from all sentient beings. After this he may endeavour to exercise maitrí-bháwaná upon his enemies.

The man that is your enemy thinks of you in this way. If you are of a disagreeable person, sick or sorrowful, poor, mean, and friendless, he rejoices. He is again delighted if in the other world you are not in a place of happiness; and he does all he can to injure you. Enmity is like a shed in a place of sepulture, on fire at both ends, and in the middle filled with the dung of dogs and jackalls; such a place is utterly worthless; people do not approach it to take either fire or fuel. He who indulges in enmity cannot practise the precepts, and that which he wishes for others will recoil upon himself.

When the priest finds it difficult to exercise the meditation of kindness upon his enemy, he must think that when the words are bad, the actions are sometimes good; that when the words and actions are bad, the mind is sometimes good; and that when the mind and actions are bad, the words are sometimes good. Again, if his enemy have only a few things about him that are good, and many that are bad, he must think of the good alone, and forget the

* It is said in the Angótra-atuwáwa that the first exercise of the priest must be upon his enemy, then upon a person in misfortune, afterwards upon a friend, and lastly upon himself; but it is said in the Wisudhi-Margga-Sanné that this is contrary to the Pali text, and cannot therefore be correct.

bad entirely. But if he be all bad, and have nothing good, the priest must think of the misery he will have to endure in the other world, whilst suffering for many ages the pains of hell. By this means sympathy will be produced. When the three, the mind, the words, and the actions are all good, there can be no difficulty in the exercise. And when the priest is still unable to accomplish the exercise, he must think further of the consequences of enmity. If the principle be indulged in, it will prevent him from being born in a brahma-lóka, and from becoming Sekra or a chakrawartti; if he should be born among men he will have to live on offal thrown away from the houses of the rich; or he will be born in hell. He who indulges in enmity is like one who throws ashes to windward, which come back to the same place and cover him all over.*

Should this exercise prove ineffectual, the priest must reflect on what is said in the Anamatagra-sútra. All persons have had in previous births parents, children, brothers, sisters, and other near relatives. The priest must think that the person with whom he is at enmity may have been one of them, and may have toiled for his benefit in various ways. By this means his enmity will be overcome.

But if the enmity still continues, he must call to remembrance what are the rewards of affection. He who possesses it will gain respect; he will not have unpleasant dreams; nor be in any danger from fire, poison, or weapons; he will have a pleasant countenance, and will not lose possession of his senses when about to die; and if not a rahat, he will be born in a brahma-lóka.

And if all these reflections are insufficient, the priest must think, "What am I at enmity with? is it with the hair, or with the bones, or with what?" Thus his hatred will have nothing upon which to fasten; even as nothing can be placed upon the mustard-seed, or painted upon the air.

There is yet one more expedient. The priest must give something to the person with whom he is at enmity, or must receive something from him, if he is willing to give it; and in this manner, even should the enmity have existed from previous ages, it will be overcome. There was a priest in the Situlpaw wihára who was three times expelled, but he was unwilling to leave. After all he said to the principal priest, "My mother, an upásikáwa, gave me this alms-

* There is a common saying among English sailors that nothing ought to be thrown to windward but ashes and hot water.

bowl; the value of it is eight kahawanas; I obtained it in a proper manner; and I now present it to your reverence." The superior priest received it, and by this means his enmity was appeased. The giving of alms is a blessing to him who receives as well as to him who gives, but the receiver is inferior to the giver.

The priest who exercises maitrí-bháwaná must have equal affection for himself, his friend, the person who is indifferent to him, and his enemy. Were a man to come to the priest with whom the others associated, and say that he must have one of the four to offer in sacrifice, he must not ask for a moment who is to be given up; he must at once offer himself as the victim.

The exercise of maitrí-bháwaná is agreeable to the déwas, even as the attention of the child who ministers to his parents, and in all things assists them. It will ward off danger. Whilst a cow was giving suck to its calf, a hunter tried to pierce it with a javelin, but his efforts were in vain; he could not take its life. It was not by the power of samádhi, or any other attainment, that this took place; it was from the affection manifested towards its offspring at the moment; and in this way may be learnt the greatness of the meditation of kindness.

In the exercise of maitrí-bháwaná, if the priest sees any one that is in distress, he must wish that his misfortunes may be removed; but if he sees no one of this description, he may reflect that any person whatever whom he meets must suffer in consequence of his transgressions, and must then wish that his sufferings may be removed. As the man led out to execution is pitied by the people, who bring him food, liquor, and betle, and he appears like a man enjoying himself, though every step he takes brings him nearer to death; such, the priest must think, is the situation of all men; they now appear to be prosperous, but it is only for a moment; the day of misfortune will most certainly come.

2. *Karuná-bháwaná.*—In the practice of this mode of meditation the priest must exercise the wish, "May the poor be relieved from their indigence, and receive abundance." This is karuná-bháwaná, or the meditation of pity. Karuná is thus produced. When we see any object in distress, we feel kampáwíma, agitation, in the mind; and from this arises karuná, pity or compassion. It is said in the tíkáwa that when we see distress of any kind, we feel the wish to relieve it; and this feeling is karuná.

3. *Mudita-bháwaná.*—In the exercise of this mode of meditation

the priest must express the wish, "May the good fortune of the prosperous never pass away; may each one receive his own appointed reward." This is mudita-bháwaná, or the meditation of joy. The principal meaning of mudita is joy, but it is not the joy arising from earthly possessions. It feels indifferent to individuals, and refers to all sentient beings. It is allied to both maitrí and karuná.

As the husbandman first portions out a certain plot of ground, and then ploughs it, so the priest who exercises any of the above three modes of meditation may first direct his attention to a certain number of persons, then to the inhabitants of a street, and so on in order to the whole village, the kingdom, the sakwala, and the outer sakwalas.

4. *Asubha-bháwáná.*—The principal meaning of the word asubha is inauspicious, that which is the opposite of good fortune, or that which produces dissatisfaction, aversion, and disgust. In this exercise the priest must reflect that the body is composed of thirty-two impurities; that as the worm is bred in the dunghill, so it is conceived in the womb; that it is the receptacle of filth, like the privy; that disgusting secretions are continually proceeding from its nine apertures; and that, like the drain into which all kinds of refuse are thrown, it sends forth an offensive smell. This is asubha-bháwaná.

The body exists only for a moment; it is no sooner born than it is destroyed; it is like the flash of the lightning as it passes through the sky; like the foam; like a grain of salt thrown into water, or fire among dry straw, or a wave of the sea, or a flame trembling in the wind, or the dew upon the grass. He who exercises bháwaná must reflect upon these comparisons, and learn that thus impermanent is the body.

By a continued repetition of birth and death, the sentient being is subject to constant suffering; he is thus like a worm in the midst of a nest of ants; like a lizard in the hollow of a bamboo that is burning at both ends; like a living carcase bereft of hands and feet and thrown upon the sand; and like an infant that because it cannot be brought forth, is cut from the womb piecemeal. He who exercises this mode of bháwaná must think of these comparisons, and of others that are similar, and remember that their application is universal. These are the signs connected with dukha, sorrow, or suffering.

The body is unreal, even as the mirage that appears in the sunshine, or a painted picture, or a mere machine, or food seen in a dream, or lightning dancing in the sky, or the course of an arrow shot from a bow. He who exercises bháwaná must reflect on these comparisons, that in like manner the body is unreal. These are the signs called anata.

The three reflections on the impermanency, suffering, and unreality of the body are as the gates leading to the city of nirwána.

The ascetic who would practice asubha-bháwaná must apply to some one who is able to instruct him, who must take him to the cemetery, and point out to him the offensive parts of a dead body; but if he hears that there is a body in the forest, he must not go there, as he may be in danger from the wild beasts that are attracted to the same spot; nor must he go to any place that is very public, as in such a spot his mind would be distracted by the various scenes that he would witness, and he would meet with women. A man must not meditate on the body of a woman, nor a woman on the body of a man. When about to leave the wihára, he must inform the superior priest of his intention, as in the place where the body is deposited there will be noises from yakás and wild beasts, and he may become so much afraid as to be sick. The superior priest will see that his alms-bowl and other utensils are taken care of during his absence. There is another reason why he should give notice of this intention. The cemetery is a place resorted to by robbers, and when they are chased they might throw down their stolen articles near the place where the priest was meditating; and when the people come in pursuit and see the articles near him, they might accuse him of the theft; thus he might be exposed to much trouble. But if the superior priest could affirm that he went to meditate, he would be freed from suspicion at once. He must go to the place of meditation with joy; as a king goes to the hall where he is to be anointed, or a brahman to the yága sacrifice, or a poor man to the place where there is hidden treasure. He may take with him a staff to drive away dogs and wild beasts. In the exercise, he must turn his eyes and ears inward, and must not allow them to wander after anything that is without, save that he must remember the direction in which he came. In approaching the body he must not come from the leeward, or he may be overpowered by the smell, and his mind will become confused; but if there be in the other direction any rock, fence, water, or other hinderance, he may approach the body from the leeward, provided he cover his nostrils with the corner of his robe. In fixing his eyes on the body he must look athwart the course of the wind; he must not stand near the head or the feet, but opposite the abdomen; not too near, or he may be afraid, nor too far off, or the offensive properties will not rightly appear. He must meditate on the colour of the body: its sex, age, and different members, joints, and properties; that this is the head, this the abdomen, and that these are the feet; and he must pass in order to the different parts of the body, and number every joint, from the foot to the head. Thus, in relation to the hair of the head, the following reflections must be made:—"It is different to all other parts of the body, even to the hair that grows in other places; it is in every respect impure; when not regularly cleaned, it becomes offensive; and when thrown into the fire it sends forth a disagreeable smell." Fixing his eyes on the body, he must think a hundred and a thousand times on its offensiveness; that it is like a bag filled with wind, a mass of impurity; and that none of its excretions can be taken in the hand. And at times he must shut his eyes and think inwardly and intensely on the same subjects. All dead bodies are alike; the body of the king cannot be distinguished from that of the outcaste, nor the body of the outcaste from that of the king.

5. *Upékshá-bháwaná.*—In the exercise of this mode of bháwaná all sentient beings are regarded alike, one is not loved more than another nor hated more than another; towards all there is indifference. This exercise is superior to all the others, and is practised by the rahats. This is upékshá-bháwaná, or the meditation of equanimity.

The four modes of meditation, maitrí, karuná, mudita, and upékshá, are called Brahma-wihara-bháwaná, on account of their superiority. They are practised by Maha Brahma.

The difference in these four modes is thus illustrated. There is a mother who has four sons, all of whom she regards, but in a different manner. The first is a child, the second sick, the third a youth, and the fourth a grown-up man. The mother loves the first because he is the little one; she pities the second, and administers to him medicine; and she rejoices in the promise and circumstances of the third; but about the fourth she cares comparatively little, as he is able to provide for his own wants.

In these exercises of meditation, taken from the Sáleyya Sútra Sanné and the Wisudhi Margga Sanné, there are many sentiments that are worthy of praise; but the wishes of the recluse are of no real value, as they lead to no practical effort of humanity. They remind us of what has been said by St. James. "If a brother or sister be naked, and destitute of daily food; and one of you say unto them, depart in peace, be ye warmed and filled; notwithstanding ye give them not those things which are needful to the body, what doth it profit?" Yet the priests of Ceylon pride themselves upon the exercise of karuná-bháwaná, and suppose that it gives them a superiority of excellence to the messengers of the cross; but the Christian does what the Budhist only wishes to be done.

The loathsomeness of the body is a common topic of illustration among the sages of India. They present it under the most disgusting associations, in an imagery as varied as it is extensive. "The body," says Gótama, "is covered with skin, humid and filthy; from its nine apertures, the secretions are continually exuded; because its offensiveness cannot be taken away, it is like an incurable wound; the wise regard it as a lump of excrement; it sends forth continually a disagreeable odour; and at last it turns into a mass of putridity and corruption." * The sage had two sisters who were vain of their beauty; but he caused the image of a most beautiful maiden to appear to them, which excited their envy. Then he caused her in an instant to become wrinkled, her teeth to fall out and hair to become grey, on seeing which their vanity passed away. Upon another occasion, when a priest had formed a criminal passion for a woman, who soon afterwards died, Gótama caused the body to be kept until it became putrid. He then said to his followers:—"Man, when he is alive, can move himself and pass from one place to another; but when he is dead he is nothing but a motionless trunk. This body, which is composed of 360 bones, of 900 veins, and as many muscles, is full of intestines, phlegm, and mucus; from nine different apertures disgusting matter is discharged; a stinking perspiration exudes from all its pores, and yet there are people so foolish, as not merely to cherish their own bodies, but also to fall in love with those of other persons. This body, which even when alive is so disgusting, when it is dead becomes a carcass, which its own relations cannot look upon without horror. After two days it begins to smell, on the third it becomes green and black; worms come from it in every part; and, when in the grave,

* Milinda Prasna.

it is gnawed by the most despicable insects. Whoever considers these things will be convinced that in the body there is nothing but decay and misery; and therefore he will cast off all affection for it, and turn all his desires to nirwána, where these things do not exist." *

There are many advantages to be derived from meditating upon the attributes of the body. The merit of presenting an offering to a supreme Budha, it is said, is exceedingly great; but the merit of him who trusts in the whole of the three gems with a right mind is greater; and still greater is the merit of him who loves all sentient beings for so small a space as is occupied by the falling of the milk from the udder of a cow to the vessel placed to receive it. Superior to this, however, is the merit of him who keeps the five precepts; yet greater than all is the merit of him who for the space of a finger-snapping meditates on the three signs connected with existence, sorrow, impermanence, and unreality. In a former age there were fifty friends, who, having found the dead body of a woman, collected wood and made a funeral pile, upon which they burnt it. When they saw the blisters rising upon the body from the action of the fire, they reflected upon the position in which all must be placed, and then meditated upon the three gems. They were, in consequence, ever afterwards born either as déwas or men, never receiving any inferior existence; and in the time of Gótama they became rahats. The same Budha had a disciple called Chullapanta, who in a former age was a king. One day, when he had ascended his chariot, and the horse had run some distance, the whole body of the animal was covered with sweat, by the sprinkling of which his robe was soiled. The king, on seeing what had occurred, reflected that the impurity proceeding from the body stains even the most beautiful apparel; and through the merit of this reflection he was ever afterwards born in a superior state of existence.†

The moralist, when he would persuade mankind to thoughtfulness, has ever dwelt upon the ravages of disease, and the offensive accompaniments of death; but the life of the ascetic is in many instances a perpetual comment upon the declaration of God, "dying thou shalt die." When Socrates was about to drink the hemlock, he declared that to think about death is the chief office of the philosopher. The earlier recluses retired to the tombs, as did Anthony,

* Sangermano's Burmese Empire.
† Sáleyya Sútra Sanné.

who was left alone in the house of death, and when his friends had closed the door was afterwards seen only at intervals. At the consecration of a nun of St. Bridget four sisters brought her coffin, which, during mass, remained in the gate through which the nun was introduced, with earth sprinkled upon it. In the monasteries of this order there was a grave constantly open, at which the abbess and convent daily attended and performed divine service, that they might be reminded of the short and uncertain duration of human life. In the infirmary of some of the monastic establishments there was a stone upon which the dying monks were washed and received extreme unction; and upon this stone the brethren were directed to sit and meditate, as a kind of penance.

Yet these very associations have sometimes been made use of as incentives to merriment and revelry. At the entertainments given by the ancient Egyptians, just as the company was about to rise from the repast, a small coffin was carried round, containing a perfect representation of a dead body. This was shown to the guests in rotation, the bearer exclaiming, "Look at this figure; after death you will resemble it; drink then, and be happy."—Herod. ii. 78.

XXI. ASCETIC RITES AND SUPERNATURAL POWERS.

The Budhists believe that it is possible, by the performance of certain ceremonies, and the observance of a prescribed course of moral action, to arrive at the possession of supernatural powers. The subject is one of almost limitless extent; but our notice of it must be principally confined to the rite called Kasina, a description of which will be given at length; and we shall afterwards allude to other methods, by which it is supposed that a miraculous energy may be received. A few remarks upon the general question will be inserted at the end of the 22nd chapter.

There are ten descriptions of kasina:—1. Pathawi, earth. 2. Apo, water. 3. Téjo, fire. 4. Wáyo, wind. 5. Níla, blue. 6. Píta, golden. 7. Lóhita, blood-red. 8. Odáta, white. 9. Alóka, light. 10. Akása, space.

1. *Pathawi Kasina.*—The priest who exercises pathawi-kasina

must take earth, in the way appointed, and must exercise meditation, looking for the nimitta illumination, like the man who sees himself in a mirror. Though the word pathawi is used, which is a feminine noun, it must be regarded as of the neuter gender. The sign may be either a place made by himself for the occasion, or he may take the circular threshing-floor in a field, or any other place that, in a similar manner, has a limit; but it is forbidden to take for the purpose a place that has no limit. The kasina-mandala, or circle, must be of the size of a winnowing fan, or the brazen porringer called a teti, which, being small, the priest can easily fix his eye upon it, as it must be of such a kind that, whether the eye be shut or open, the circle may be present to the mind. The mind must be firm, pondering over the sign again and again. The priest must reflect on the benefit to be derived from the exercise, regarding it with joy, as if it were a great treasure; and he must not allow his mind to wander off after any other object whatever. Not thinking about anything else, he must resolve that, by this means, he will obtain relief from decay and death. Thus, being freed from evil desire, he will enter upon the first dhyána.

When any one has enjoyed the benefits to be derived from the teachings of the Budhas in a former birth, or attained to the state of a rishi, and thereby been enabled to enter upon the fourth and fifth dhyánas, it will not be necessary for him to make a circle of earth, as a ploughed field or a threshing-floor will serve the same purpose. Thus, when men pass through a desert with which they are not acquainted, and meet with water, they put something as a mark, that they may know the place again, and they are guided by this mark the next time they pass along the same road; but when they have become well acquainted with the spot, from frequently passing and repassing, they do not require any mark to guide them to the water, as they can find it without this assistance. So the priest who has been accustomed to perform kasina in former births, does not require the same sign as others to assist his meditations. It was by this means that the priest Mallaka, by looking at a ploughed field, was enabled to enter the fifth dhyána, then to attain widarsana,* and become a rahat. When the priest has not practised these things in a former birth, he must learn the course of discipline from a competent teacher, that he may know also the faults that are to be avoided in the exercise.

* For an explanation of the terms used in this chapter, consult the Index.

The kasina circle must not be blue, golden, blood-red, or white. The clay of which it is formed must not be of any of these colours (as they are the colours of other kasinas); it must be of a light red, aruna, the tint that the sky assumes at dawn, or the colour of the sand deposited by the Ganges. The frame upon which the circle is placed must not be erected too near a wihára, where there may be disturbance from the sámanéra novices. A place must be chosen for the purpose at the limit of the grounds attached to the wihára, under the shade of a tree, or of a projecting rock; or a temporary pansal may be made for the occasion. The frame, made of four sticks, may either be set up in such a way as to be removable to another place, or it may be fixed in the ground. Upon the top a piece of cloth, a skin, or a mat, must be extended, upon which the clay must be spread, free from grass, roots, pebbles, and sand; and it must be well tempered, and made very smooth. Gradually it must be kneaded and worked, until it is of the proper consistency; and it must be formed into a circle one span and four inches in diameter. If the frame be fixed in the ground, it must be small at the bottom, and broad at the top, like the flower of the lotus. If sufficient clay cannot be procured of the proper colours, the body of the circle may be formed of any other clay, with a layer of aruna clay spread over the surface. Whether the circle be moveable or fixed, it must be of the prescribed size. When it is said that it must be of the same size as a winnowing fan, or a brazen porringer, it is not a large one that is intended, but one of the common size. It is essential that there be a limit to the thing which is taken as a sign, and it is on this account that its dimensions are pointed out. The space exterior to the circle may be of a white colour. The juice of the sandal-wood tree will not give the colour that is required.

The priest must take water that falls from a rock, and therewith render the clay perfectly smooth and even, like the head of a drum; then, having bathed, he must sweep the place where the frame is erected, and place a seat, without any irregularities on its surface, one span and four inches high, at the distance of two cubits and one span from the frame. Remaining upon this seat, he must look at the circle, and exercise meditation. If the seat be further distant than the prescribed space, he will not be able to see the circle properly: and if nearer, its imperfections will be too apparent. If it be higher, he will have to bend his neck to see the circle; if lower, his knees will be pained. Thus seated, he must reflect on the evils resulting from the repetition of existence, and on the manner in which it is to be overcome; on the benefits received by those who practise the dhyánas and other modes of asceticism; and on the excellencies of the three gems; and he must resolve upon securing the same advantages. He must not keep his eyes open too long, lest he become confused. The circle must be seen, but not too clearly, or his object cannot be gained; still, it is necessary that it be seen with a certain degree of distinctness, or his aim will be equally frustrated. He must be like a man who watches an elephant: not too intent, nor too careless: or, like a man looking at himself in a mirror, who does not notice the form of the instrument, but regards his own appearance alone. The colour of the circle must be noticed, but not with too much pleasure or satisfaction. It is not enough to think that it is composed of earth. The priest must also remember that the earthly particles of his own body are composed of the same element. For this purpose he must think of the different names that are given to earth, such as pathawi, mahi, médini, bhúmi, wasudhá, and wasundará. Any of these names may be chosen, and, for a time, he may reflect on that exclusively; but as the epithet most commonly used is pathawi, upon this he must meditate with greater frequency and intensity. Until nimitta is received, sometimes with his eyes open, and at other times with them shut, he must continually regard the circle, though the exercise has to be repeated a hundred or a thousand times. When the circle appears to the mind as clearly with the eyes shut as with them open, the nimitta may be regarded as accomplished.

The exercise is not to be continued after the nimitta has been received, or it will again be lost. It is better, therefore, for the priest not to remain in the same place; because, if he does so, his eyes will wander towards the circle. Going from thence to his usual place of residence, he must there exercise meditation. That time may not be lost in the washing of his feet, he must put on shoes, which must be made of skin, that there may be no noise when he walks; and he will require a staff, that dangers may be warded off. If by any means the nimitta should be destroyed, he must again take his shoes and staff, and carry on the meditation as before, until it be recovered. By the power of nimitta the thoughts that prevent the exercise of dhyána will be restrained; scepticism will pass away, and purity will be received, by which the angas, or constituent parts of the dhyánas, will be accomplished. There are two kinds of nimitta, ugrána and pratibhága. In the former, the imperfections of the circle are seen; in the latter, they are not, as the circle assumes the appearance of a clear mirror, or of a conch shell of the purest white, or of the orb of the moon when entirely free from clouds, or of the bird koká when the sky is dark and lowering;* it is therefore a thousand times superior to the ugrána mimitta, and is without colour, shape, or outward appearance. The pratibhága nimitta is only received by those who practise the meditation by which samádhi is produced.

Of samádhi there are two kinds, upachári and arppana, which cause the destruction of those things that act as an enemy to the dhyánas. In upachári samádhi the mind is not rightly firm, not entirely at rest or calm; it is like a child that is unable to walk properly, and is continually falling; as the nimitta is sometimes received, and then lost again. But arppana samádhi is more powerful; it is like a man who rises from his seat, and walks steadily for the space of a whole day; as, when it is received, the mind continues in one even frame, undisturbed and unshaken. Though pratibhága nimitta may be received with upachári samádhi, its acquirement in this way is difficult; the priest must therefore endeavour to obtain arppana samádhi, and he must guard the nimitta that he receives with all care, as the treasurer of a chakrawartti guards the wealth that is under his charge. When the nimitta is not preserved, so many of the dhyánas as have been received will be lost; because nimitta is an assistance to the dhyánas. He who would receive arppana samádhi must be careful in seven matters. 1. His residence, which must be free from that which is disagreeable to him. Such a place was the wihára Chúlanáda, in Ceylon, in which 500 priests became rahats; but how many in Situlpaw and other places entered the paths, cannot be told. 2. The road he traverses when he goes with the alms-bowl in search of food, which must be within the distance of 750 bows. 3. Conversation: he must not speak about the thirty-two things that are forbidden to be noticed by the priest; nor must he say too much even upon subjects that

* I resided several years upon the sea-coast of Ceylon, and on the approach of the monsoon, when the whole heavens were black as Erebus, have often admired the appearance presented by the plumage of the sea-birds, which at that time assemble in great numbers; their wings appearing of a whiteness the most pure, when contrasted with the deep darkness of the surrounding sky.

are allowed. 4. Company: he must not converse with improper persons, even though it should be about things that are allowed as subjects of conversation. It is only with those that are seeking samádhi, or have attained it, that he must converse, as communication with others will be like the muddy water, that defiles the clean and pure. There were some inexperienced priests in the Kelapaw wihára, who lost the nimitta they had gained, by talking to improper persons. 5. Food: some priests like sweet food, and some sour. He who would receive samádhi must have that kind of food which is most agreeable to him. 6. The season: some prefer heat, and others cold; and in this case also, the time most agreeable to the individual must be chosen for the exercise. 7. The position of the body: that posture must be chosen which is most pleasant, whether it be walking, standing, sitting, or lying down; and in order that the priest may discover this, he must practise each of the positions during three days. By attending to all the matters herein set forth, arppana samádhi will be accomplished; but if it is not yet received the ten arppana kowsalya, or proprieties, must be more closely attended to, such as that the person and robe must be kept clean; for when the hair is long, and the body, robe, or alms-bowl dirty, the mind cannot be kept pure. In the same way, if the wick and the oil are not clean, the lamp will not burn brightly.

Samádhi is that which keeps the thoughts together, as the drop of water that causes the grains of sand to adhere together and form a ball. It is like the flame of a lamp that burns steadily. It prevents the perturbation of the different faculties of the mind.

Samádhi is the principal root of all the other virtues; all others are inferior to it, come after it, and bend towards it. In the conical roof of a dwelling, all the beams are inferior to the boss in the centre; they are all inclined towards it, and joined to it. Again, in an army composed of many different sections, all are inferior to the king by whom it is commanded; all are directed by him and acknowledge his superiority. In like manner, samádhi is the chief of the attainments possessed by him who seeks nirwána. It was declared by Budha, that he who possesses samádhi may readily acquire all other attainments.

2. *Apo Kasina.*—The practice of ápo-kasina agrees in most respects with that of pathawi-kasina, but there are a few differences, which will here be stated. When the priest has exercised this kasina in a former birth, he may take as the sign a tank, a pond, a

lake, or the sea. There was Chúlasíwa, who thinking it right that he should become an ascetic, took ship at the port of Máwatu, in Ceylon, and set sail for some country in Jambudwípa. On his way, the circle of the horizon became to him as a kasina-mandala, and he performed the exercise of ápo-kasina. The priest who has not practised this kasina in a former birth, must catch a portion of water in a cloth as it falls from the sky in rain, before it has reached the ground; it must be of one colour, the four colours blue, golden, blood-red, and white being avoided; or if rain cannot be procured, any other water that is free from agitation may be used instead. This water must be poured into an alms-bowl or some other vessel of a similar kind, and placed in some convenient part of the court of the wihára, or in a retired spot in some other locality; and the priest, sitting down near it in the manner prescribed, must begin to meditate. He must not think of the colour of the water, nor of its other properties; but must reflect that the perspiration and other watery particles in his own body are of the same nature as that upon which he looks. He must then think of and repeat, the various names that are given to water by the people of the world, such as ambu, udaka, wári, salila, and ápo. By this means he will arrive at ugrána nimitta, but as this nimitta is not free from disquietude, it must pass away, like the bubble upon the water. The pratibhága nimitta will then be attained, as the imperfection of the water, such as that it is liable to be raised into waves, will become apparent. After this the ascetic must proceed to the acquirement of the different dhyánas.

3. *Téjo Kasina.*—When any one wishes to perform téjo-kasina, fire must be used as the sign. If the exercise was performed in a former birth, he may take as the sign the flame of a lamp, or fire from the oven, or the fire that is accidentally kindled in the forest by the friction of two dry branches. In this way, Chittagutta made use of a lamp that was burning at a póya festival; and by meditating upon it he arrived at nimitta. But if this kasina was not performed in a former birth, the priest must take wood, dry and firm, that it may burn long, and cutting it into small pieces he must place it at the root of a tree, or in the court of the wihára, where it must be ignited. When all has been thus prepared, he must take a mat made of shreds of bamboo, or a skin, or a cloth, and making in it an aperture one span and four inches in diameter, he must place it before him, and then sit down, as in the practice of the other ka-

sinas. Looking through the aperture, he must meditate on the fire; but he must not think of the grass or other embers below, nor of the smoke rising above, nor of the colour or other properties of fire, as that it is warm; he must fix his mind on the clear fire in the centre, and reflect that the fire in his own body is of a similar nature, flickering and inconstant. The different names of fire must be repeated, such as páwaka, kanhawattani, játawéda, utásana, and téjo.

4. *Wáyo Kasina.*—In the practice of wáyo-kasina, he who has performed the exercise in a former birth may take as the sign a grove of bamboos or sugar-cane, when agitated by the breeze. But he who has not previously performed the exercise must seat himself at the root of a tree, or in some other convenient place, and think of the wind passing through a window,* or the hole of a wall; and that the wáyo in his own body is as inconstant as the wind that strikes upon the person when the breeze is felt to blow. After this he must meditate on the different names by which wind is known, wáta, máluta, anila, and wáyo. In other respects, the same form that is attended to in pathawi-kasina is to be observed.

5. *Níla Kasina.*—In níla-kasina flowers, a garment, an altar covered with flowers, or a gem, of a blue colour, may be taken as the sign. When the observance has been attended to in a former birth, it will suffice to look upon a tree covered with blue flowers; but if it has not been thus attended to, a vessel must be filled with flowers of a blue colour, but the pollen or the stalks are not to be seen; or a blue garment may be tied over the mouth of a vessel, tight, like the skin stretched upon a drum, which must be covered with flowers. The colour must be like that which is obtained from the rust of copper or from antimony; or a circle of a blue colour may be made upon the wall. The priest must then fix his mind

* In India this aperture is literally a window, without glass, or even a lattice-work, as in Turkey. In the north of England it is still called windur, probably from wind-door, as was conjectured by Skinner. The houses of the Anglo-Saxons appear to have been open in a manner that those who are accustomed to the conveniences of modern times can scarcely understand. The address of the aged thane to Edwin, king of Northumbria, when the subject of Christianity was brought before the witan, is well known; but it is too beautiful not to bear repetition. "When," said he, "O king, you and your ministers are seated at table in the depth of winter, and the cheerful fire blazes on the hearth in the middle of the hall, a sparrow perhaps, chased by the wind and snow, enters at one door of the apartment, and escapes by the other. During the moment of its passage, it enjoys the warmth; when it is once departed, it is seen no more. Such is the nature of man. During a few years his existence is visible: but what has preceded, or what will follow it, is concealed from the view of mortals."—Lingard's Anglo-Saxon Church.

upon that which he has chosen as a sign, and reflect that the sky also is of the colour of the sapphire; in other things proceeding as in the kasinas already described.

6. *Píta Kasina.*—The exercise of píta-kasina is the same as that of níla, the only difference being in the colour. A priest in the Situlpaw wihára took as the sign a throne ornamented with patangi (sappan, or log-wood) flowers, by which he was enabled to receive nimitta.—In the exercise of lóhita-kasina, the circle may be made with vermillion; and in ódáta-kasina, a vessel of lead or silver, or the orb of the moon, may be taken as the sign.

7. *Alóka Kasina.*—In álóka-kasina the sign may be a hole in the wall, a key-hole, or a window. If the same kasina has been observed in a former birth, it will suffice to take the light passing through a hole in the wall, or the sunbeam as it falls upon the ground through an opening in the thick foliage of a tree, or an aperture made among the leaves by which a hut is covered; but if it has not been exercised previously, the names of light, such as óbhása and álóka, must be thought of and repeated. Yet as a circle made by the sun or moon soon passes away, it will be better to take an earthen vessel, with a hole made in its side, in which a lamp must be placed; and then if it be put near a wall, the light from the hole will fall thereon, and the priest will be able to meditate upon the circle thus formed a greater length of time than if it were made in the manner first mentioned.

In the exercise of parichinnákása-kasina the sky must be looked at through a hole in the roof of a hut or through a hole of the prescribed dimensions made in a skin.

By the practice of pathawi-kasina the priest will receive the power to multiply himself many times over; to pass through the air or walk on the water; and to cause an earth to be made, on which he can walk, stand, sit, and lie. By ápo-kasina he can cause the earth to float; create rain, rivers, and seas; shake the earth and rocks, and the dwellings thereon; and cause water to proceed from all parts of the body. By téjo-kasina he can cause smoke to proceed from all parts of the body, and fire to come down from heaven like rain; by the glory that proceeds from his person he can overpower that which comes from the person of another; he can dispel darkness, collect cotton or fuel and other combustibles, and cause them to burn at will; cause a light which will give the power to see in any place as with divine eyes; and when at the point of death he can cause his body to be spontaneously burnt. By wáyo-kasina he can move as fleetly as the wind; cause a wind to arise whenever he wishes; and can cause any substance to remove from one place to another without the intervention of a second person. By the other kasinas respectively, the priest who practises them in a proper manner can cause figures to appear of different colours; change any substance whatever into gold, or cause it to be of a blood-red colour, or to shine as with a bright light; change that which is evil into that which is good; cause things to appear that are lost or hidden; see into the midst of rocks and the earth, and penetrate into them; pass through walls and solid substances; and drive away evil desire.

Those who are of both sexes cannot accomplish the exercise of kasina, nor the inhabitants of Uturukuru, nor Mára; and there are many others, among whom are the sceptics, that are similarly situated. Those only who have wisdom, determination, and the other powers, can practise this rite with success.

There are fourteen different ways in which the kasinas are to be exercised:—

1. *Kasinánulóma.*—This is to be practised in the following manner. First, pathawi-kasina is to be accomplished; then, in regular order, the ápo, téjo, wáyo, níla, píta, lóhita, and ódáta kasinas. Thus, the commencement must be made at the root, and from thence in regular progression to the end.

2. *Kasinapatilóma.*—In the exercise of this kasina the order must be the reverse of the former; it must be from the end to the root, from ódáta to pathawi.

3. *Kasinánulóma-patilóma.*—In this the order is from the root to the end, from pathawi to ódáta; and then again from ódáta to pathawi, from the end to the root.

4. *Dhyánánulóma.*—In this the order is from the first, to the second, third, and fourth dhyánas; then to ákásánancháyatana, ákinchanyáyatana, and néwásanyánásanyáyatana.

5. *Dhyánapatilóma.*—In this the order is the reverse of the mode just mentioned, being from néwásanyánásányáyatana, by retrogression, to the first dhyána.

6. *Dhyánánulóma-patilóma.*—In this the order is from the first dhyána to néwásanyánásanyáyatana, and then again from this to the first dhyána.

7. *Dhyánánukhantaka.*—In this the order is the same as in dhyá-

nánulóma, only missing one each time. The beginning must be made with pathawi-kasina, and then the dhyánas, &c., must be taken alternately, as from the first dhyána to the third, then to ákásánancháyatana, and so on to the end. When this is concluded the beginning must be made from ápo-kasina, and the order continued as before.

8. *Kasinánukhantaka.*—In this the order is from pathawi-kasina to the first dhyána, then again from téjo-kasina to níla and lóhita kasina, taking the alternate kasinas and dhyánas, until the whole are concluded.

9. *Dhyánakasinánukhantaka.*—In this the order is from pathawi-kasina, along with the first dhyána; téjo-kasina, along with the third dhyána; níla-kasina, with ákásánancháyatana; and lóhita-kasina, with akinchanyáyatana.

10. *Angasankantika.*—In this the order is from pathawi-kasina to the second dhyána.

11. *Arammanasankantika.*—In this the order is from pathawi-kasina, along with the first dhyána, to ápo, téjo, wáyo, níla, píta, lóhita, and ódáta kasina, and each dhyána is to be taken with all the kasinas in regular order.

12. *Angárammanasankantika.*—In this the order is from pathwi-kasina, along with the first dhyána; ápo-kasina, with the second dhyána, téjo-kasina, with the third dhyána; wáyo-kasina, with the fourth dhyána; níla-kasina, with ákásánancháyatana; píta-kasina, with winyánan cháyatana; lóhita-kasina, with akinchanyáyatana; and ódáta-kasina with néwásanyánásanyáyatana. Thus an outward rite and an inward meditation must be exercised alternately.

13. *Angawawattápana.*—To the first dhyána there are five angas; to the second dhyána, three; to the third dhyana, two; to the fourth dhyána, one; there is also ákásánancháyatana, &c. This is what is meant by angawawattápana.

14. *Arammanawawattápana.*—The reflecting that this is pathawi-kasina; this, ápo-kasina; this, téjo-kasina, &c.

When the whole of these fourteen exercises are not accomplished, the power of irdhi cannot be acquired, unless they have been practised in former ages. To him who has not exercised kasina in former ages its accomplishment is exceedingly difficult. Among those who have not thus exercised it, scarcely one succeeds in its acquisition, out of a hundred or a thousand who may attempt it. Even to those who accomplish the exercise of kasina, the acquirement of nimitta is exceedingly difficult; scarcely one in a hundred or a thousand is successful to this extent. Even to those who acquire nimitta, it is equally difficult to acquire arppana. Even to those who acquire arppana, it is equally difficult to discipline the mind in the fourteen modes that are prescribed. Even to those who have thus disciplined the mind, it is equally difficult to obtain the power of irdhi. Even to those who have acquired the power of irdhi, it is equally difficult to obtain khippanisanni. Even to those who have acquired khippanisanni, it is equally difficult to obtain parama-pratishtábháwa, or rahatship. In this way, by a process so long and difficult, is the rahatship to be received. As the potter gradually prepares and tempers his clay, that he may be able to make with it such vessels as he designs, so the mind of the priest must be gradually softened, in the way that has been prescribed, that he may acquire the power at which he aims.

As the baker, when making bread, adds the flour by degrees, and as the ploughman adds furrow to furrow, so the priest who exercises kasina mentally enlarges the circle from an inch to a span, gradually increasing it until it encompasses the whole court of the wihára, the village, the kingdom, the earth, the sakwala, and even a greater space. Again, as the jawana-hangsha, from its first taking wing, gradually increases the distance of its flight, until it can travel to the sun or the moon; so the priest who exercises kasina passes in mind from one to another of the rocks, hills, and rivers of the earth, until the whole seem to pass away and become flat, like the skin of a bull fastened down to the ground by a thousand pins.

When a priest has thirty-two houses in the walk or round in which he goes to receive alms, he sometimes receives as much at the first house as is sufficient for two houses; he therefore omits the second house, and goes to the third. The next day he may receive sufficient at the first house for three; he therefore omits the second and third houses and goes to the fourth. The following day he may receive as much at the first house as is sufficient for the whole round; he therefore goes to no other house. In like manner, in the exercise of bháwaná, samádhi, &c., when the benefit of two rites in the series is obtained by the observance of one, the second may be omitted, and when the benefit of three has been obtained in the same way, the second and third may be omitted.

The priest must exercise ákásánanchàyatana-bháwaná, the benefit of which is hereby declared. Assaults, stripes, and disputes arise from the possession of rúpa, or the body; but they do not exist in the arúpa world, and the destruction of rúpa is therefore to be desired. In order that this may be accomplished, the priest reflects upon the evils proceeding from rúpa. The man who has escaped from a serpent that he met with in the forest, when he afterwards sees a mark on the floor, a picture, a crevice in the ground, a rope, or the branch of a palm-tree, is afraid, and he therefore turns from the object with abhorrence. Or, if a man has an enemy in the village, from whom he or his property is in danger, he removes to another village; and if in that village he sees any one who has a voice or countenance like his enemy, he turns away from him in alarm. In like manner, he who receives pratibhága will regard the rúpa with aversion, and endeavour to escape from it. When the dog that has been bit by a boar in the forest afterwards sees in the twilight a vessel of rice upon the fire, he runs away from it in fear. And when a man who has been frightened by seeing the sprite called a pisácha afterwards sees in any lonely place a prostrate tree, he falls down in a fit from terror. In like manner, when the priest who exercises this mode of bháwaná sees into the evils connected with rúpa, he is afraid, and he therefore seeks to obtain release from it, or to destroy it.

By the same exercise the priest arrives at néwásanyánásanyá-samápatti. Under these circumstances the rúpa is not, and yet is; it exists, but in a manner the most subtle and attenuated. What is meant by these expressions may be learnt from the following comparisons. A sámanéra novice rubs a little oil in the inside of an alms-bowl; after which a priest asks for something to eat from the same bowl. The novice says, "I cannot do so, as there is oil in it." The priest then tells him to pour the oil into a cruse; but he says, "I am not able, as there is no oil in it." The truth is, that there is a little oil rubbed on the inside, but not enough to pour out. Again, two priests were walking together, when one said to the other, that he must take off his sandals, as there was water. The other then said, "If so, go and fetch my loose robe, that I may bathe;" but the first priest replied, "You cannot bathe, as there is no water." There was sufficient water to require the priest to take off his sandals, but not enough for him to bathe. Again, a brahman saw some one with a vessel, and he asked him to give him something to drink; but the man replied, "There is toddy in the vessel, I cannot." Then the brahman told him to give some toddy to another person who was near; but he said, "There is no toddy; I am not able." It was a toddy-vessel, so that he could not offer it to the brahman; but there was no toddy in it at the time, so that he was not able to give any to the man, as was requested. In like manner, that upon which this form of bháwaná is exercised, though it is, becomes as if it were not.

These exercises must be carried on with a calm and even mind, or the end that is aimed at cannot be attained.

When the unwise bee is about to prepare honey for its cell, it is too anxious to obtain the pollen, and so comes with such haste to the tree, that it is too exhausted to collect it; and when it comes a second time, the pollen has all fallen to the ground, and is useless. Another bee, moderately wise, comes at the proper time, but collects both the good pollen and the bad. And a third is all too late, so that the pollen is entirely gone. But the wise bee knows when the flowers bear the richest pollen; he comes at the proper time, and in a proper manner; collects as much as he requires, makes it into honey, and thus lives on the most delicious food. The surgeon's assistant (who learns to open veins by cutting the stalk of the lotus as it grows in the water) strikes so hard, that the instrument passes through the stalk to the other side, or the flower is driven under the water; or, on the other hand, he fears even to touch it, lest he should fail. But the skilful surgeon has a sharp instrument, and he knows exactly where to strike, and how to strike, because he has learnt to excel in his profession. The king offers a reward of four thousand pieces of gold to any one who will bring him a spider's web four fathoms long. A skilful man finds a web of this description, and he goes quickly and takes it. An unskilful man finds one, but he is afraid to take it lest it should break; though the other man has succeeded in taking the web he found, and has wrapped it round a reel, perfect from end to end. The skilful mariner hoists his sail when there is a strong breeze, and makes a short voyage. The unskilful mariner takes down his sail, even when there is no more than a moderate breeze, and remains in one spot; the other mariner hoists his sail to the breeze, and when it is high reefs it, thus arriving quickly at the destined port. The skilful novice, when directed by a superior priest, pours oil into a vessel without spilling a drop. But the unskilful novice is afraid, and is therefore unable to pour out the oil, though the other pours it out with the utmost ease. In like manner, the priest who would exercise bháwaná so as to arrive at arppana nimitta, must not, on the one hand, be too proud and confident; nor, on the other, careless and indifferent; he must possess an even, tranquil mind, free from agitation.

The goldsmith, when about to exercise his craft, erects a furnace, carefully tempering the clay; he then watches the metal to see whether it be properly melted; at one time blows, and at another sprinkles water; and when the metal is ready, he makes whatever kind of ornament is wanted. In like manner must he act who exercises bháwaná, in attending to the ordinances that are prescribed.

When these exercises are rightly performed equanimity is produced, as a natural consequence; so that the mind becomes entirely free from all that would agitate it, and even from all that would in any way attract its attention.

When a bullock unaccustomed to the yoke is fastened to a waggon, it runs hither and thither, in any direction, whether there be a road or not. The husbandman therefore takes a grown-up calf from its mother, and fastens it to a pillar; and though at first it attempts to get away, and is restless, it is not able, and it is made to eat and sleep near the pillar, until its wildness is overcome. So also the mind of the priest who does not exercise the various ordinances of meditation wanders after that which he sees, and is never at rest; but when he fastens his mind to áswása and práswása, or the inspirated and expirated breath, by the cord of wisdom, it is restrained, and is no longer attracted by sensible objects.

The áswása and práswása are caused by the hita, or mind, but cannot exist without the body. As the smith causes the bellows to open and shut, and the wind to proceed therefrom, and both the smith and the instrument are necessary to produce this effect, so for the existence of áswása and práswása there must be the rúpa, the hita, and the chétaná, or thoughts of the hita.

When a man jumps from an eminence, or carries a heavy burden upon his head, his breathing becomes violent; but when he goes into the shade, or drinks water, or places something cold upon his breast, it becomes more gentle. In like manner, by the exercise of meditation the breathing is tranquillised, as well as by entering upon the dhyánas.

There is no áswása or práswása to the child in the womb; to him who is drowned; to him who is born in the Asangignyátala-lóka; to the dead; to him who has accomplished the fourth dhyána; to those born in the arúpa worlds; or to those who have attained nirwána. Those in the womb or the water have not the necessary space; some have them not, because they have no chétaná; and to others it is the natural state. Some think that they may be overcome by a person's own exertions; but they will continue to all who are not included in one or other of the classes just mentioned. Gótama said that he spoke not of these things except to the wise, as the practice of them is exceedingly difficult. He who makes an embroidered zone must have a very small needle, with an eye still smaller; so he who performs this exercise must have a mind like the needle, and wisdom like the eye.

This exercise is connected with asubha bháwaná. It is said in the Milinda Prasna, that he who rightly perceives that all continued existence is sorrow, choosing the root of some tree in a solitary part of the forest, sits under it with his feet bent up and his body straight; then collecting his thoughts, with a calm mind he makes an inspiration and an expiration of the breath. Drawing a long breath through the nostrils, he notices, I have thus drawn a long breath. Breathing a long spiration from the nostrils, he notices, I have thus breathed a long spiration from the nostrils. Drawing a short breath through the nostrils, he notices, I have drawn a long spiration through the nostrils. Reflecting that the beginning, the middle, and the end of every kind of breath is from the body, he resolves, with a wise mind I will draw an inspiration; with a wise mind I will breath out an expiration. In a manner so as not to fill the cavity of the nose, restraining the violence or magnitude of his breath, he makes an inspiration, and noticing, I thus make an inspiration, he disciplines his mind; then making an expiration, he notices, I thus make an expiration. Reflecting on the joy connected with the exercise of the first dhyána, and causing its production, he thus makes an inspiration and an expiration. In the same way reflecting on the advantages connected with the exercise of the third dhyána, and causing its production, he thus makes an inspiration and an expiration. Indulging comprehensive thoughts, he makes an inspiration and an expiration. Restraining comprehensive thoughts, he makes an inspiration and an expiration. Reflecting on the manner of the fourth dhyána, he makes an inspiration and an expiration. Rendering his mind joyful by reflecting on the manner of samádhi, he makes an inspiration and an expiration. Collecting his mind, after the manner of the first dhyána, he makes an inspiration and an expiration. As in the fourth dhyána, freeing his mind from witarka, wichára, príti, sukha, and dukha, he makes an inspiration and expiration. Reflecting on the impermanency of the five khandas, he makes an inspiration and an expiration. Reflecting on the various forms of evil desire, he makes an inspiration and an expiration. Reflecting that by the destruction of all the elements of existence nirwána will be seen, he makes an inspiration and an expiration. Reflecting that by the abstract meditation called wipasénà, he may, as it were, leap to nirwána, he makes an inspiration and an expiration. Thus in sixteen different ways he exercises anápána-sati-bháwaná, and at each exercise disciplines his mind, or brings it into subjection. When he sees a dead body, fearful to look upon, thrown into the cemetry, or any other place, he reflects, my body is of the same nature as this. When he sees a dead body surrounded by blue-bottle flies, presenting blue putridity, like the body of a rat-snake, he makes the same reflection; and he repeats it when he sees the offensive juices oozing in many different ways from the various apertures of the body; when he sees a body torn to pieces amidst the combats of crows, kites, and other birds of prey; when he sees a body near the place of execution, decapitated, or with its hands and feet cut off, a frightful trunk; when he sees a body mangled by the weapon resembling a crow's foot; when he sees a body at the place of torture all covered with blood; when he sees a body in the cemetry, with worms creeping out of the nine apertures, and with worms all over, one that is too disgusting to look upon, one that by looking upon it would cut off all desire for the repetition of existence; and when he sees a body with the putridity gone, the flesh, blood, and veins all gone, so that it is a mere skeleton:—in all these instances he reflects, My body is of the same nature; and thus exercises karmmasthána-bháwaná. After this he exercises affection towards all creatures; he reflects that when the wise man sees any one in distress, he sympathises with him, and desires that his sorrow may be removed and entirely destroyed; when he sees any one invested with great glory or happiness, he approves of it, and rejoices in it; he regards all indifferently, without partiality or favour; he rejects all relationship, friendship, wealth, and pleasure, knowing that life is hastening to the mouth of death; and he reflects that the body is composed of the filth that proceeds from the nine apertures, and of the thirty-two impurities.

When the husbandman has done ploughing, he takes the oxen to a place where there is plenty of grass, and there lets them loose. When he wishes again to catch them, if he be at all skilful, he does not go to the forest to seek them; but he takes the reins and a goad, and sits down near the place where they are accustomed to drink. By and bye the oxen come to the water, and he catches them with the reins, after which he drives them along with the goad, and sets them again to the work of the plough. In like manner, the priest fixes his mind exclusively upon the nostrils by which are the issues and entrances of the breath, with a mind like the reins, and wisdom like the goad. The exercise must be continued until he arrive at mimitta pratibhága. This nimitta is not to all persons of one and the same kind. To some it brings much satisfaction; it is like cotton, or the wind. To others it is like the light of a star, a gem, a pearl, a cotton-seed, or a needle made of firm wood. To others it is like a thread upon which to string valuable beads, a garland, a mist, a cloud, a water lily, the wheel of a chariot, or the orbit of the sun and moon. In this manner, a number of priests assemble to hear bana. When the discourse is concluded, one asks another in what way the sútra appeared to him. Some will say that it appeared to them like a river falling from a high rock; others that it was like a forest with many flowers, or like a tree laden with fruit and presenting a cool shade. The same sútra will appear in a different manner to different persons; and it is the same with the reception of nimitta. This meditation on the inspirated and expirated breath, is called anápána-sati-karmasthána.

Relative to this subject the king of Ságal said to Nágaséna, "Is it possible to destroy the áswása and práswása?" Nágaséna replied, "It is possible." Milinda: "In what way?" Nágaséna: "Did you ever notice how a person snores when going to sleep after a plentiful meal?" Milinda: "Yes." Nágaséna: "Though he thus snores, is he alive?" Milinda: "Yes." Nágaséna: "The individual has not attained to the first dhyána or to wiwéka; he does not practice the prátimóksha and other sílas; he has not entered the paths; he is still under the influence of evil desire; he he is unwise; and whilst he yet has life, he snores. But the wise priest, who acts in a manner the reverse of all this, attains the dhyánas, and so destroys the áswása and práswása;" as the tranquillity of the mind increases in proportion to the diminution of the grossness of the body.

The word dhyána is said to mean, "that which burns up evil desire, or the cleaving to existence." It is sometimes used in the sense of meditation, and at other times is allied to samádi; in some places it is a cause, and in others an effect.

There are five principles that are connected with the dhyánas. With these five they are perfect, as when we speak of the four divisions of an army, or five kinds of musical instruments, or eight directions. They are witarka, wichára, príti, sepa, and chitta-ekangakama.

The dhyánas are divided into five sections, called pratamadhyána, dwitiyadhyána, tritiyadhyána, chaturtadhyána, and panchamadhyána; or first, second, third, fourth, and fifth dhyánas.

To the first dhyána belong witarka, attention; and wichára, investigation.

To the second dhyána belong príti, joy; sepa, comfort; and chitta-ekangakama, mental restraint.

When the third dhyána is accomplished there is the possession of upékshá.

When the fourth dhyána is accomplished there is an entire destruction of the cleaving to existence.

In the exercise of the first dhyána the mind is like the waves upon the water, when there are some large and some small; there is no clearness; that which is the subject of contemplation is like a fish seen in the water; and the samádhi that is attained is of an inferior character. In the second dhyána the samádi becomes more pure, as the mind recedes further and further from witarka and wichára. There is a degree of upékshá possessed in the first and second dhyánas, but it is not perfect; they are like a man who walks in a place covered with sharp stones, whilst the third dhyána is like a man who walks in an even road.

When the third dhyána has been entered, the mind, unless it be rightly subdued, will still go out after the príta it has abandoned, as the calf that is tied at a distance from the cow continually seeks to break away from its confinement, that it may reach the udder whence it has been accustomed to draw milk.

With the fourth dhyána there is connected the wédaná called upékshá-wédaná. When the husbandman wants to catch a refractory bull, he drives the whole herd into the fold, and then, letting the animals out one by one, by this means he catches the bull; in like manner, in order to discover this form of wédaná, all the sensations must be collected together, and examined one by one, when it will be perceived. It is exceedingly small, and scarcely to be discerned, as it is not connected with either pleasure or pain. When the mind is thus cleansed by upékshá it becomes exceedingly pure.

There is also that which is called tatramadyastópékshá ; it is like the moon ; wédanápékshá is like the night ; witarka and wichára are like the sun. When the sun shines, the beams of the moon do not appear, but they appear at night. In like manner, when witarka and wichára are in existence there can be no tatramadyastópékshá ; but when they are done away with, it becomes apparent.

According to the system of the brahmans the fifth dhyána is to be entered ; but according to Budhism it is to be avoided (as it leads only to attainments that are of inferior excellence, and sets aside the present reception of nirwána.) There was a priest called Kádéwala who entered the fifth dhyána, and he was afterwards born in one of the arúpa-brahma-lókas. After the accomplishment of the dhyánas, the Budhists seek to enter the paths.

There are some bridges that are formed of a single tree ; and there are others so broad and strong, that a number of loaded waggons placed abreast can pass over at one time. In like manner, there is a difference in the attainments of the sráwakas, and it is ruled by the manner in which they exercise the dhyánas.

The state of mind that is produced by the exercise of the dhyánas is called parikarmma ; and according to its character will be the power of the divine eyes that will be received, as they will be more or less clear, strong, extensive in the circle of their vision, and permanent in their existence. Unless there be the forming of the parikarmma, the power of the divine eyes will be lost ; in which case there must again be the exercise of the dhyánas, as at first.

They who practice the dhyánas have the power to visit the brahma-lókas, and it is only by them that the power is received.

When the prince Sidhártta was under the tree at the festival of the plough, free from wastu-káma and klésha-kama, as well as from rága, dwésa, and móha, but still under the influence of witarka and wichára, and having also the príti and sepa that arise from wiwéka, he exercised the first dhyána. Then, having overcome witarka and wichára, and arrived at tranquillity of mind, and having the priti and sepa that arise from samádhi, he exercised the second dhyána. Then overcoming all regard for príti, he received upékshá, smirti, and sampajána ; and with these endowments of the rahats he exercised the third dhyána. Last of all, having become free from sepa, dukha, and sowrmanasya, but retaining upékshá, smirti, and párisudhi, he exercised the fourth dhyána.*

At the time that the déwa Sekra paid his first visit to Budha, the sage was performing dhyána, so that the déwa was not permitted to see him. On his second visit he reminded Budha of the circumstance, who said that, though he was not seen, he heard the sound of the déwa's chariot wheels. Now when a person is performing dhyána, he could not hear though a conch were to be blown close to him. How then, it may be asked, could Budha hear the sound of Sekra's chariot? The answer is this, that before commencing the exercise, he had appointed to return to consciousness at the moment the chariot was passing.

The supernatural effects that are here represented as being produced through the influence of abstract meditation, are said, in other instances, to arise from the possession of príti, or joy. There is one kind of príti that is called udwéga. The priest Maha Tissa resided at the wihára of Panágal. It was his custom to worship at the dágoba belonging to this temple, and on a certain festival he looked towards the place where the principal relics were deposited, thinking thus within himself: "In former periods many priests and religious persons assembled here that they might worship;" and as he was in the act of making this reflection, he received the power of udwéga-príti, by which he was enabled to rise into the air, and pass at once to the sacred place. Near the Girikanda wihára there was a village called Wattakála, in which resided a respectable woman who was an upásikáwa devotee. One evening, when her parents were about to go to the wihára to hear bana, they said to her, "On account of your present situation it will not be proper for you to accompany us to the wihára; we will go alone, and hear bana, and whatever benefit we receive we will impart to you." Though exceedingly desirous to hear bana, as she could not disobey her parents she remained at home. As the wihára could be distinguished from the court-yard of the house, she looked towards it, and seeing the lights of the festival, and the people in the act of worship, whilst at the same time she could hear the voices of the priests, she thought within herself, "They who can thus be present at the festival are blessed." By this reflection udwéga-príti was formed in her mind, and in an instant she began to ascend into

* This paragraph is taken from Turnour's Mahawanso, and the one following it from the Pújáwaluja. The rest of the information contained in the prepreceding parts of this chapter is taken from the Wisudhi Margga Sanné and Milinda Prasna.

the sky, so that she arrived at the wihára before her parents, who, when they entered and saw her, asked how she had come, and she replied, that "she had come through the sky." And when they further asked how she had thus exercised the power of a rahat, she said, "I only know that I did not remain any longer in the same place after I felt the joy; I know nothing more." *

There is another miraculous energy, called Sacha Kiriya, which can be exercised either by the laic or the priest; but it is the most efficient when accompanied by bháwaná. A recitation is made of acts of merit done either in this or some former birth, and by the power of this merit, when the recitation is truthfully made, the effect intended to be produced takes place, however wonderful its character may be. The word sacha signifies true; and kiriyang, an action; but in this particular instance sacha appears to be regarded as equivalent to merit. The exercise is nearly allied to the mantra of the Hindus, in the power of which the Budhists believe; but although the word mantra is frequently met with in their writings, I do not remember an instance in which it is used in reference to the sacha kiriya. Its potency may be learnt from the following legends.

There was an upásaka devotee in Ceylon, whose mother was sick. As the flesh of a hare boiled was prescribed for her, the son went to a field and caught one in a trap; but when the animal cried out, he thought within himself, "Why should one life be saved by the destruction of another?" and set it free. When he went home, and told the family what he had done, his brother derided him; but he went to his mother and said, "I have never knowingly taken the life of any creature whatever, from my childhood until now; by the power of this sacha kiriya may you be healed." In an instant her sickness was removed.

There was a priest, Maha Mitta, whose mother was afflicted with a boil. Of this she sent her daughter to inform her son, that he might recommend some remedy. The priest replied, "I do not understand the virtue of roots, but I possess a power that is greater: I have never, since I entered the priesthood, broken the precepts; by this sacha kiriya may my mother be healed." At that moment the boil dried up and fell off.†

In the fourth year of the reign of Asóka, as this king was one

* Wisudhi Margga Sanné. † Ibid.

day conversing with his nobles, he said, "If I had lived in the same age as Budha, I would have offered to him the whole of Jambudwípa; had I been king of the déwas, I would have offered to him the whole of the heavens; but I was born at an after period, and mine eyes have not beheld him; is there any one now in existence who has seen the divine sage?" The nobles replied, "It is now 221 years since the dissolution of Gótama; it is not possible, therefore, that there can be any human being now alive who has seen him; but in the Manjarika world there is the nága Maha Kála, who has been in existence from the beginning of the kalpa, and seen four supreme Budhas; and he possesses the power of making a form appear, exactly like that of the lord of the three worlds." The king, on hearing this, caused a golden fetter to be made; and when he received it he said, "By virtue of this sacha kiriya, my firm faith in the three gems, may this golden fetter proceed to the residence of the nága Maha Kála, and bring to my presence the nága king." So saying, he threw the fetter to the ground, that it might fulfil his command. In an instant the fetter proceeded to the nága world, through a cleft that was formed in the earth, and fell at the feet of Maha Kála. The nága looked to see what was the cause of its appearance; and when he perceived the faith and power of the king, he hastened to the world of men, attended by 10,000 other nágas; and the king made an offering to him of flowers and lights. When this was concluded, Asóka said, "I am wishful to see the form of Budha; now cause a representation of the sage to appear." But the nága replied, "I am yet under the influence of evil desire; Budha was free from all impurity. I am under the power of error; he was all-wise. I am inferior; he was supreme. I am finite; he was infinite. There are equals to me; to him there is no equal. How, then, can I cause an adequate representation of him to appear?" But at the persuasion of those present he caused an image of Kakusanda Budha to appear, forty cubits high, surrounded by 40,000 rahats, to whom the king offered worship and gifts, saying, that the wish of his heart was now accomplished. There then appeared an image of Kónágama Budha, thirty cubits high, surrounded by 30,000 rahats; and afterwards an image of Kásyapa Budha, twenty cubits high, accompanied by 20,000 rahats. When the image of Gótama Budha appeared, eighteen cubits high, seated near the bó-tree, as when he had conquered Mára, the king and his 16,000 queens looked on in wonder, and made an offering to him of the whole of his dominions.*

When Gótama Bódhisat was born in a former age, as Sáma, son of the hermit Dukhula, he rendered every assistance to his parents, who had become blind when he was sixteen years of age. It happened that, as he one day went for water to the river, the king of Benares, Piliyaka, entered the forest to hunt, and as Sáma after ascending from the river was, as usual, surrounded by deer, the king let fly an arrow, which struck Sáma just as he was placing the vessel to his shoulder. Feeling that he was wounded, he turned his face towards the spot where his parents dwelt, and said, "I have no enemy in this forest; I bear no enmity to any one;" though, at the same time, he vomited blood from his mouth. Thus he reflected, "I have omitted the exercise of maitrí-bháwaná, and some one has sent against me an arrow; for what reason it can be I cannot tell, as my flesh is of no use, neither my skin; I must therefore make enquiry." After saying this to himself, he called out, "Who is it that has shot me?" and when he learnt that it was the king, he related his history to the monarch, and said that his greatest grief arose from the thought that his blind parents would now have no one to support them, and would perish. But when the king perceived the intensity of his grief, he promised that he would resign his kingdom, and himself become the slave of his parents, rendering unto them all needful assistance in the stead of their son. Soon afterwards Sáma fell down senseless from the loss of blood; but a déwi, who in the seventh birth previous to the present was his mother, having perceived that if she went to the spot important consequences would ensue from her interposition, left the déwa-loka, and remaining in the air near the king, without being visible, entreated him to go to the pansal and minister to the wants of the blind parents of Sáma. The king was obedient, and and went to the place, where he informed the hermit and his wife that their son was slain. On hearing of his death they uttered loud lamentations, and requested to be taken to the place where he had fallen. They were therefore brought to it, when the mother, on placing her hand upon his breast, perceived that it was warm; at which she rejoiced greatly, as she knew by this token that he was not dead. She therefore resolved upon repeating a sacha-kiriya for his restoration, and said, "If this Sáma has in any previous period

* Sadharmmálankáré.

obtained kusala, by the power of this virtue (sacha) may the consequences of this calamity be removed; if from the time of his birth until now he has been continent and true, supported his parents, and excelled in the acquisition of merit; if I have loved him more than my own life; if we, his parents, possess any merit whatever;—by the power of these virtues (sacha) may the poison pass away from the body of Sáma, as the darkness vanishes at the rising of the sun." On the utterance of these words, Sáma revived, and sat up; after which the déwi also said, "If I have loved Sáma more than any other being, by the power of this sacha may the poison of the arrow be destroyed." Then by the united sacha-kiriyas of the déwi and his parents Sáma was restored to perfect health. The parents also received their sight, and the déwi repeated the ten virtues of a king to Piliyaka, by attending to which he was enabled to reign in righteousness, and was afterwards born in the déwa-lóka, as Sáma and his parents were in the brahma-lóka.*

This accident may appear to contradict the teachings of the bana, that the exercise of bháwaná is a protection from all evil; but the Budhists endeavour to reconcile the two by the following arguments, so called. It was through the forgetfulness of Sáma, they say, that he was slain, as he neglected to exercise the power he possessed. Thus, a warrior, clothed in armour, enters into the battle, and remains unhurt amidst the pelting of the arrows; it is not by the man, but by the armour, that the arrows are warded off, and prevented from hurting him. Or, a man who holds in his hand a certain medicinal root, thereby renders himself invisible; but this virtue is attached to the root, and not to the man. Again, the man who is under the roof of a cave fears not the rain; but it is the overhanging cave, and not the man, that prevents the rain from producing inconvenience. So also, the power of averting evil is attached to the exercise of bháwaná, and not to the man; and if he does not exercise it, the benefit is lost.

The nature of the sachi kiriya will be further illustrated by the legend of Siwi, and that of the Fish-king, both of which have been translated by the Rev. D. J. Gogerly, and appear in the Ceylon Friend, vol. iv. page 138. They are taken from the Chariyá Pitaka, one of the fifteen books forming the Khudugot division of the Sútra Pitaka. The work is attributed to Budha, and is composed in Pali verse.

* Milinda Prasna.

"INTRODUCTION.

"All my transmigrations during four atsankyas and one hundred thousand kalpas have been to complete my preparation for becoming a Budha. Leaving my journeyings from birth to birth during the kalpas that are past, I will declare my transmigrations during the present one.

"LEGEND OF KING SIWI.

"I was once Siwi, king of Aritha, and sitting in my magnificent palace I thus thought:

"There is no kind of treasure possessed by men which I have not given in alms. Should any one beg from me my eyes, unhesitatingly would I give them to him.

"Sakraya, the chief of the gods, sitting amidst his heavenly attendants, and knowing my thoughts, spake these words;

"The king Siwi, endued with great super-human power, sitting in his magnificent palace, and meditating on the various kinds of alms, does not perceive one that he has not given.

"What are his feelings? I will ascertain immediately. Wait until I know his mind.

"He then assumed the form of a trembling, hoary-headed, wrinkled, decayed, and emaciated blind man, and approached the king.

"Having taken this form, with his clasped hands raised to his forehead, he said;

"Great and just sovereign, the author of your country's prosperity! the fame of your almsgiving has ascended up, both to gods and men; I have a boon to ask;

"I am become blind of both eyes; give me one of yours, and retain the other yourself.

"When I heard these words I immediately with a joyful and compassionate mind thus addressed the trembling one:

"Ah! acquainted with my reflections while sitting in my palace, thou hast come to solicit the gift of an eye:

"My desires are accomplished! my wish is fulfilled! I shall this day give alms to a supplicant which I have not given before.

"Come! arise Siwika, be not unskilful; hesitate not! pluck out both my eyes and give them to the supplicant.

"My slave Siwika being thus addressed, scooped out my two eyes and delivered them to the beggar.

"When I proposed to give, when I gave, and after I had given this gift, I had no other design than that of becoming a Budha.

"It was not that I had no regard for my two eyes; my body was not displeasing to me; but I delighted in becoming a Budha, and therefore gave my eyes.

"LEGEND OF THE FISH-KING.

"At another time I was a fish-king in a large lake; and during the summer the heat of the sun dried up the water of the lake.

"Then the eagles, the kites, the cranes, and the crows, descending by day and by night, devoured the fish.

"I then thought, by what means can I deliver my relatives from this affliction which has befallen them?

"Reflecting on virtuous acts I perceived truth,* and saw that established in truth I could rescue my relations from this destruction.

"Having thus reflected, I thought of the most noble doctrines of virtue which continue constantly in the world, and performed the satcha kiriya, (saying)

"From the first period that I can remember, up to the present time, to my knowledge, I am not conscious of having wilfully injured any single being.

"Through this true declaration, ye lightnings flash and thunders roar, and ye clouds pour down copious rains: deprive the crows of their prey; let them mourn, but let the fish be delivered from sorrow.

"Consentaneously with my powerful satcha kiriya, the clouds uttered their thunders, and instantly the rains descended, filling the depths and overflowing the land.

"Having performed this supreme truth-act, and by my most excellent perseverance, (in virtue) being established in the glorious strength of truth, I caused the clouds to rain.

"In the performance of the satcha I have no equal. This was my satcha paramita (the path of truth, one of the ten paths to be fully traversed before arriving at the dignity of a Budha.)"

We learn from the Commentary that when Siwi had become blind he abdicated his kingdom and became a recluse, without regretting the performance of his benevolent act. In this situation he was again visited by the ruler of the déwas, who addressed him in the follow-

* By the word satcha, truth, I apprehend the satcha kiriya is meant.

ing words: "Great king, almsgiving is not merely productive of benefits in a future state, but in the present state also. Therefore perform a satcha kiriya concerning (or on account of) the merit of your almsgiving, and by the power of that you will obtain eyes." In accordance with this advice he pronounced the following:

> "Have any come to beg,
> Supplicants of various castes?
> When any one begged from me, then
> He was delightful to my mind.
> By that true declaration.
> May an eye be produced to me!"

Upon this one eye was produced; after which he said:

> "Did any one come to me to beg (saying)
> Give an eye to the Brahman;
> To him I gave eyes,
> To the mendicant Brahman.
> Great was the joy I experienced:
> The delight was not small.
> By this true declaration
> May a second (eye) be produced to me!"

It is said by the learned translator* of these legends that we are not here to understand natural eyes, but a divine or spiritual vision, by which the whole world of sentient being became apparent; but in this case how did Siwi see when he had only one divine eye? Did he see one hemi-kosm only, and not the other? Or, did he see all beings, but only by halves? Or, did he see the whole of all beings, but in a sort of purblind manner? These are grave questions for the Budhist schoolman.

Another legend, taken from the same source, will complete our notice of the sacha kiriya. There was once a courtezan, Bindumati, who turned the course of the mighty Ganges by the force of this spell, founded upon the manner in which she exercised her base vocation. "The king" according to the original authority, "hearing the rushing sound of the refluent river, being greatly astonished, enquired of his chiefs; Friends, why does the current of the great Ganges flow backwards? They replied: Great king, the courtezan, Bindumati, has recited the satcha kiriya, in consequence of which the Ganges flows back to its head. The astonished king hastened to the courtezan, and said: Is it true that by the satcha kiriya, you have turned the course of the Ganges? When she replied: Yes,

* The Rev. D. J. Gogerly; Ceylon Friend, vol. ii. p. 146.

your majesty: he asked: Whence have you that power? Who will receive your declaration? By what power can an insignificant person like you cause the stream of the Ganges to flow backward? she replied: Great king, I caused the stream to flow back by the power of truth (satcha). The king said: What power of truth have you, a thief, vile, immodest, sinful, an overstepper of all restrictions, one who leads astray the blindly lascivious? The courtezan confessed that she was all the king had named, but said that it was by the following truth-spell she had turned the stream of the Ganges, and that by the same power she could overturn the heavens; 'Does any one give me wealth, be he a prince, a brahman, a merchant, a labourer, or of any other tribe; whatever they may be, I receive them equally: the prince is not preferred, the labourer is not despised: contented, and free from regarding pleasure or pain I follow the owner of wealth.'" According to this principle, beings the most degraded may obtain the power to work the most stupendous miracles; and acts of the grossest iniquity may be done without guilt, if the mind be unmoved during their commission.

XXII. NIRWANA: ITS PATHS AND FRUITION.

As the subject upon which we now enter is one of the quæstiones vexatæ of Budhism, and is in itself of deep interest, a larger space will be required for its elucidation; and as no western opinion will be regarded as of any authority, we shall confine ourselves almost entirely to extracts from native writers. In the former pages of this work we have received nirwána as meaning simply, the cessation of existence.

1. *The Paths.*—There are four paths, margga, an entrance into any of which secures, either immediately or more remotely, the attainment of nirwána. They are:—1. Sowán, 2. Sakradágámi. 3. Anágámi. 4. Arya. Each path is divided into two grades:—1. The perception of the path. 2. Its fruition, or enjoyment, margga-ph'ala.

(1.) The path sowán, or srótápatti, is so called because it is the first stream that is entered before arriving at nirwána. It is divided into twenty-four sections, and after it has been entered, there can be only seven more births between that period and the attainment of nirwána, which may be in any world but the four hells.

(2.) The path sakradágámi is so called because he who enters it will receive one more birth. He may enter this path in the world of men, and afterwards be born in a déwa-lóka; or he may enter it in a déwa-lóka, and afterwards be born in the world of men. It is divided into twelve sections.

(3.) The path anágámi is so called because he who enters it will not again be born in a káma-lóka; he may, by the apparitional birth, enter a brahma-lóka, and from that world attain nirwána. This path is divided into forty-eight sections.

(4.) The path arya, or aryahat, is so called because he who enters it has overcome or destroyed, as an enemy, all klésha. It is divided into twelve sections.

When the fruit-tree is cut down, the latent fruit that is in it, which has not yet appeared, but which would appear in due time if it were permitted to remain, is destroyed. In like manner, by margga-bháwaná the klésha is destroyed that would otherwise have continued to exist and would have brought forth fruit.

They who have entered into any of the paths can discern the thoughts of all in the same or the preceding paths. Thus, he who has entered the path sowán can know the thoughts of any being in the same path, but not those of any one in the three other paths. He who has entered the path sakradágámi can know the thoughts of any being in the same path or in sowán, but not in the two other paths. He who has entered the path anágámi can know the thoughts of any being in the same path, or in sowán and sakradágámi, but not the thoughts of one in the fourth path, or the rahat. The rahat can know the thoughts of any one, in any situation whatever.

The wisdom necessary for the reception of the paths is called gótrabhu-gnyána. When the paths are entered the wisdom that is received by those who have made this attainment is called gnyána-dassana-sudhi. A man goes at night to watch the conjunction of the moon and certain stars; he looks up, but the moon is hid by clouds; then a wind arises and drives away the clouds, so that the moon becomes visible. The klésha that darkens the mind is like a cloud; the anulóma-chitta is like the wind; the looking up is like the sight of nirwána; the moon is like nirwána itself; and the passing away of the clouds is like the revealing of nirwána by the wisdom called gótrabhu-gnyána. The wind has power to disperse the cloud, but it cannot see the moon; so the exercise of anulóma drives away darkness from the mind, but it is insufficient for the seeing of nirwána. The man who looks at the moon can see it when the clouds have passed away, but he has no power to disperse the clouds; in like manner, it is gótrabhu-gnyána that reveals nirwána, but it has no power to disperse the klésha that darkens the mind. When nirwána has been revealed, gótrabhu-gnyána is of no further use; it is like the guide who is dismissed at the end of the journey.

The rahats can receive no further birth; they cannot be born again, either as déwas, brahmas, men, yakás, prétas, or asúrs; the power by which conception is received is entirely broken; the path of successive existence is destroyed; all cleaving to existence is cut off; all the sanskháras, the elements of existence, are destroyed; merit and demerit are destroyed; the winyánas are closed; and as the principle of life in the seed is destroyed when exposed to the influence of fire, so, in the rahats, the principle of evil desire is eradicated; all connection with the world is completed and done.

To say that any one has "seen nirwána," is to say that he has become a rahat.

The difference between him who has rága, or desire, and him who has not, is this — the first is ajjhósita, or cleaves to existence; the second is anajjhósita, he does not cleave to existence. As regards eating and drinking they may both appear to enjoy that which is good and reject that which is evil; but when the former eats food he distinguishes that which is bitter or pungent, avoids it, and prefers that which is sweet and agreeable; the latter also distinguishes one flavour from another, but he does not desire one description of food more than another.

There are some persons who obtain the rahatship instantaneously, whilst others can only obtain it by a slow process; they must give alms, make offerings, study the bana, and exercise the necessary discipline; but this difference arises from the merit obtained by the former class in previous births. Thus, one man has a field already prepared; he can sow his seed at once; he need not make ditches or fences, or spend his time in any similar work; but there is another man, who has no field prepared, and before he can sow his seed there is much labour to be undergone. Again, there are mangoes on a lofty tree; a rishi can take them at once, by coming through the air; but a man who has not this power, must wait until he has cut down sticks and creepers and made a ladder. Again, a strong man at once executes his lord's commands, but where there is not this strength there must be the united labour of many individuals. In like manner, some ascetics obtain the rahatship at once, whilst others are unable to obtain it without first attending to the various exercises that are enjoined.

In the time of Budha there was a novice who was unable in the space of many months to learn a single stanza of bana; in consequence, his preceptor, who was his own uncle, sent him away from the wihára. But the uncle, who was exceedingly sorrowful on account of having thus to dismiss his nephew, was met by Budha, who enquired why he was so sad. When informed of the cause, he told the uncle that in a former age, during the time of Kásyapa Budha, his nephew had derided a priest who was saying bana, which now prevented him from learning it; but that in another birth when he was a king, he was one day riding through the city, with his attendants, and as his face perspired freely he wiped it with his robe, reflecting at the same time on the impermanence of the body. For this act of merit he would now be enabled to become a rahat; and Budha therefore directed that he should look towards the sun, and call out "Rajoharanang, rajoharanang; may the dust (of evil desire) pass away!" At the moment in which the direction of Budha was carried into effect, the sage caused a piece of cloth to appear, that the nephew might be enabled to wipe his face therewith; and by this means he became a rahat.

The king of Ságal said to Nágaséna, "You have declared that when a laic becomes a rahat, he must, on the same day, either enter the priesthood or attain nirwána; now we will suppose that a laic becomes a rahat, but there is no one qualified to repeat the Kammawáchan, the formulary used at the ordination of a priest; and there is no alms-bowl or robe to be presented; could such a one admit himself to the priesthood, or would he remain a laic, or would some rahat possessing the power of irdhi come through the air to ordain him, or would he attain nirwána; how would it be?" Nágaséna replied, "He could not ordain himself, as this would be contrary to rule; nor could he remain a laic; so that either some one must come to admit him to the priesthood, or he must attain nirwána." Milinda: "Why is it so?" Nágaséna: "There are many evils connected with the state of a laic; it is therefore a state of weakness; and on this account the rahat must at once either become a priest or attain nirwána. But no blame can on this account be attached to the rahatship; it arises from the weakness of the state of the laic. In like manner, a man eats to repletion of good food, and because he cannot digest it, dies; in this case the fault is not to be attributed to the food, but to the want of power in the faculty of digestion. Were a large stone to be suspended by a slender cord, it would break; but no one could say that it was the fault of the stone. Again, were a man to be made king whose personal prowess was inferior, who had no powerful retainers, who was neither of the royal caste nor a brahman, of mean birth, and destitute of merit, it would only lead to his destruction, as he would not be able to uphold the dignity of his elevated position; but the fault would be in the man, not in the royal office. It is the same with the rahat; he cannot remain a laic, because that state is one of weakness and evil; it is insufficient to bear the weight of the greatness with which the rahat is invested."

There are five great powers, called abhignyáwas, attached to the rahatship; but not possessed by all rahats in an equal degree. 1. Irdhiwidhágnyána, or ásrawakshayagnyána; the power of irdhi. 2. Diwyásrotagnyána; the power to hear all sounds, whether distant or near, whether made by déwas or men. 3. Chétopariyagnyána, or parachittawijánagnyána; the power to know the thoughts of other beings. 4. Púrwéniwásánusmertignyána; the power of knowing what births have been received in former ages. 5. Satwayangé-chatuppatignyána; the power of knowing what births will be received in future ages.

The divine eye of the rahat can see that which cannot be perceived by the eye of flesh, as it can see any being whatever, whether in hell, upon earth, or in a déwa-lóka. The manner in which it acts is entirely different to the vision of those who have not entered the paths. It is not possessed to the same extent by all beings, but differs in degree, in proportion to the attainments of its possessor. There are many things that are too subtle or fleet to be perceived by one being with this gift, that may nevertheless be seen by another who is endowed with it in a superior degree. The lowest power is to be able to see things that are in existence at the time when it is exercised; but the being who possesses this power may not be able to see that which has only existed at some previous period, and has passed away or been destroyed; and he may not be able to discern objects at the very instant of their formation, from their being so exceedingly minute or momentary. It will perhaps be said that this degree of power is of no benefit; but its value is great, as it enables the possessor to see the thoughts of others, and to know the consequences of any course of action, whether it be good or evil, so as to be able to tell what kind of birth will be next received.

They who possess divine eyes are enabled rightly to learn the evil of demerit, from seeing the torments that are endured by the beings in hell, and by them alone can this evil be properly appreciated.

They who have overcome successive existence know that they will not be reborn, because they know that the cause of birth, which is the cleaving to existence, has been destroyed; even as the husbandman knows when he has reaped his grain, that his storehouse is full.

All beings who possess this wisdom, when they look at the past, do not see the same number of previous births. The extent of the number seen varies according to the merit of the individual. The Budhas can see any birth, of any being whatever; the tirttaka unbelievers can see only a few. The exercise of this faculty is not therefore like that of the sense of sight, which merely distinguishes colours, as to whether they be red, or blue, or yellow. It can only be acquired by him who practises the dhyánas; and the acuteness of the power will be in proportion to the manner in which attention is paid to these and other ascetical exercises.

The power of hearing in him who is pure, is freed by determined resolution and meditation from the evils produced by bile, phlegm, and wind. By this means it becomes perfect, as the grain flourishes when sown in ground free from grasses and weeds; and the power to hear any sound may thus be obtained, from the roaring of the lion to the gentlest whisper, whether near or at a distance.

The king of Ságal (in reference to the supernatural powers of the rahats), said to Nágaséna, "Can any one who has the fleshly body of a man go to Uturukuru, or to the other great continents, or to the déwa and brahma-lókas?" Nágaséna replied, "It is possible for one who has a body composed of the four elements to visit the places you have named." Milinda: "In what way can this be done?" Nágaséna: "Can you, at your will, leap from the ground, say to the height of a span or a cubit?" Milinda: "With ease I can leap eight cubits high." Nágaséna: "How do you do this?" Milinda: "I determine to leap; through this determination my body becomes as it were buoyant, and I rise from the ground." Nágaséna: "Just so the priest who has the power of irdhi determines to go to such a place; by the determination of his mind his body becomes as it were imponderous, and he is enabled thereby to pass through the air."

Again the king of Ságal said to Nágaséna, "Can a rahat lose his memory, or become bewildered?" Nágaséna replied, "He may become lost in abstraction, or from syncope; but he cannot in any other way lose his senses." Milinda: "Can he do that which is wrong, ápatti?" Nágaséna: "Through want of attention he might eat after the turning of the sun, and thus transgress the precept wikála bhójana, &c., in which case he would have to go to some priest who was free from blame, and sitting on his heels and putting his hands to his forehead, he would have to declare that it was not his intention thus to transgress in future; by which act he would become free from censure. Into such faults as these a rahat may fall." Milinda: "Is it from want of respect for the precept that he falls into this error?" Nágaséna: "No; it is not from this cause." Milinda: "Then it must be that he loses his memory." Nágaséna: "The faults that are committed among sentient beings are divided into two classes, lókawadda and pragnyaptiwadda. The first class includes such transgressions as the taking of life, the saying of that which is not true, and scepticism; there are ten in all, called the dasa-akusal. The second class includes such transgressions as can be committed by the priests alone. Thus, it is not forbidden to the laity to eat after the turning of the sun, nor to root up grass and trees, nor to make sport when bathing; but these things are forbidden to the priests. There are some priests who are suska widarsaka, of dry discernment; they are unable to acquire the power of comprehending all things. Such a rahat, though free from all evil desire, may not know the name of a man or woman whom he has not seen before; he may mistake a road with which he is not acquainted; he does not possess the sadabhignyá, or five modes of supernatural knowledge. A rahat of this description may commit a fault that is pragnyapti; but he cannot commit any of the ten crimes forming the class called lókawadda. It is only the supreme Budhas and Pasé-Budhas that are entirely free from every kind of ápatti; all other classes of rahats are liable to the commission of the faults that are called pragnyapti."

The rahats are subject to the endurance of pain of body, such as proceeds from hunger, disease, &c.; but they are entirely free from sorrow or pain of mind. For this reason: that which is the cause of the endurance of pain (food) by the body, still continues, or its use is not intermitted, and therefore bodily pain continues; but that which causes the endurance of pain (evil desire) by the mind, is destroyed, and therefore mental pain is destroyed. The same truth was declared by Budha.

On another occasion Budha said, that all sentient beings are afraid of punishment, and that all have a dread of death; but when he said this, those who have become rahats were excepted, as he declared at another time that the rahats have entirely overcome fear. In like manner, the chief of a village commands all his people to be called together near his house, and when they are assembled he is told that all are come; nevertheless the sick, the lame, the women, and the slaves are not there: though it is said that all are come, it is understood that many are absent.

It may still be asked, If there be the endurance of bodily pain, why is not nirwána attained at once? This is the reply: the rahats know neither desire nor aversion; they do not desire to live, nor do they wish to die; they wait patiently for the appointed time. This was the declaration of Seriyut:—"I am like a servant awaiting the command of his master, ready to obey it, whatever it may be; I await the appointed time for the cessation of existence; I have no wish to live; I have no wish to die; desire is extinct."

The 500 rahats who accompanied Budha, when he was attacked by the elephant in the street of Rajagaha, all fled away on the approach of the animal; but it was not from fear; neither did they wish to leave the great teacher to his fate. They intended thereby to give Ananda the opportunity of displaying his devotion, as he went to encounter the elephant alone, until commanded by Budha to retire. The earth, when it is ploughed, or its surface is broken, or from the seas, rocks, and mountains it bears, is unmoved by fear, because it has nothing through which fear can be produced. It is the same with the rahats. They have nothing through which fear can be produced; the instrumentality by which alone it can work is destroyed. Were a hundred thousand men, armed with various weapons, to assault a single rahat, he would be unmoved, and entirely free from fear.

The king of Ságal said to Nágaséna, "You have declared that the rahats feel no pain of mind, though they are still subject to pain of body; but does not the mind subsist because of the body? Is the rahat without authority, mastery, or supremacy over the body?" Nágaséna replied, "Great king, it is even so." Milinda: "But this does not appear to be right; even the bird exercises the lordship over its own nest." Nágaséna: "There are ten things that in every birth accompany the body; colour, heat, hunger, thirst, feces, urine, sleep, disease, decay, and death: over these things the rahat exercises no peculiar power." Milinda: "Will you explain to me how it is that this occurs?" Nágaséna: "Because of the earth all beings exist; but the earth cannot be commanded or con-controlled by these beings. In like manner, because of the body the mind exists; but the mind cannot command or control the body." Milinda: "How is it then that others have pain both of body and mind?" Nágaséna: "Because there has been no accomplishment of widarsana, and the other exercises by which the mind is brought into subjection. There is a hungry bull that is tied only by a small withe, which it breaks in its anger, and then runs away. In the same way, when the mind is not under discipline, it becomes irritated, breaks away from restraint, and disturbs the body, and then there is crying, fear, and the voice of sorrow; thus there is pain both of body and mind. But the mind of the rahat is under proper discipline; it does not disturb the body; it is bound as to a pillar by samádhi and other exercises; it is filled with the pleasure of nirwána; and the rahat is therefore free from pain of mind, whilst he is still subject to pain of body." Milinda: "But would it not be a thing to be esteemed as a wonder if, when the body is disquieted or agitated, the mind were to remain tranquil? Explain to me how this can be." Nágaséna: "The branches of a tree are shaken by the storm; but the trunk remains unmoved. In like manner, as the mind of the rahat is bound to the firm pillar of samádhi by the cord of the four paths, it remains unmoved, even when the body is suffering pain."

Upon another occasion Nágaséna related to Milinda the characteristics of the five gradations of being; and from his details we are enabled to learn more clearly the specific difference that is supposed to exist among the various orders of men, as regards their state of preparedness for the reception of nirwána.

(1.) There is the unwise being, who is under the influence of klésha, or evil desire, and of enmity, ignorance, and impurity; he has not attained to the fruition of the paths; he has not attended to the precepts, by which he might overcome impurity; his mind is not disciplined to the exercise of the tranquillity of samádhi; he has not received the wisdom produced by abstract meditation. The mind of such a being is therefore gross, slow, because he is not accustomed to the more profound exercises of abstraction. Thus, there is a clump of bamboos that as they grow embrace each other and become entangled; they have many knots, and the branches are twisted together into one mass. Now, if one of these trees be cut down at the root, the process of pulling it away will be slow. Why? Because the leaves, knots, and branches are all entangled together in such confusion that they cannot be extricated. In the same way, when any one is under the influence of the errors that characterise the unwise man, his mind is heavy, slow. Why? Because it is entangled in the meshes of evil desire. This is the first gradation.

(2.) There is the being who has entered the path Sowán, unto whom the doors of the four hells are shut; he has maintained the true profession, and entirely approves of the doctrines of the great teacher; he has thus arrived at the fruition of the first of the paths; he also rejects the error called sakkáya-drishti, which teaches, I am, this is mine; he has no doubts as to the reality of the Budhas; and he sees that the practices enjoined by the Budhas must be attended to if nirwána is to be gained; so that as regards these three doctrines his mind is free, not bound, but light, quick; yet, as to the other paths it is still slow, gross, entangled. Thus, in three degrees it is pure; but in all others it is yet under the influence of impurity. How? When the bamboo that has been cut down is cleared for the space of three knots, it might be pulled away to this distance with ease, were it not that it is entangled by the upper branches that yet remain. In the same way, the being that has entered Sowán is free as to the three doctrines that have been mentioned, but he is slow, heavy, and entangled as to the rest, which he has not yet embraced. This is the second gradation.

(3.) There is the being that has entered the path Sakradágámi (from sakrat, once, and ágámi, came), so called because he will once again receive birth in the world of men; he has rejected the three errors overcome by the man who has entered Sowán, and he is also saved from the evils of káma-rága, and the wishing evil to others. Thus, in five degrees his mind is pure; but as to the rest it is entangled, slow. How? When five knots of the bamboo have been cleared, it might easily be drawn thus far, were it not held by the upper branches that are yet entangled. In the same way, the man who has entered the path Sakradágámi is free as to the five particulars; but as to the rest, he is still bound, heavy, dull. This is the third gradation.

(4.) There is the being that has entered the path Anágámi (from an, negative, and ágámi, came); he does not again return to the world of men; he is free from the five errors overcome by the man who has entered Sakradágámi, and also from the five sanyójanas (so called because the being who is subject to further repetitions of existence is bound to them), evil desire, ignorance, doubt, the precepts of the sceptics, and hatred. Thus in ten degrees his mind is pure; but as to the path he has not yet entered, the rahatship, it is still slow, heavy, dull, entangled. How? It is like the tree that has ten knots cleared, but the rest allowed to remain. This is the fourth gradation.

(5.) There is the being who has entered the fourth path, and become a rahat; he has destroyed the four ásrayas (káma, bhawá, drishti, and awidya); he is free from the impurity of klésha, and has arrived at the fruition of the four paths; he has vomited up klésha, as if it were an indigested mass; he has cast it away as if it were a burden; he has arrived at the happiness which is obtained from the sight of nirwána; he is no longer subject to the repetition of existence; he is endowed with the four supernatural powers of the rahats; he has arrived at the most exalted state of the sráwakas: and in consequence of these attainments his mind is light, free, quick towards the rahatship, and all that precedes it; but heavy, bound, dull, as to that which is peculiar to the Pasé-Budhas. This is the fifth gradation.

(6.) There is the being called a Pasé-Budha (in Pali, Pratyéka-Budha); he has attained the high state of privilege that he enjoys, by his own unaided exertions, as he has had no teacher, no one to instruct him; he is called pratyéka, severed, or separated, and is solitary, alone, like the unicorn; thus his mind is light, pure, free towards the Pasé-Budhaship; but dull, heavy, bound, towards the state of the supreme Budhas; he has learnt that which belongs to his own order, but he understands not the five kinds of knowledge that are perceived by the supreme Budhas and by no other being; he knows not the thoughts of others; he has not the power to see all things, nor to know all things; in these respects his mind is heavy. Thus a man whether by day or night, arrives at the brink of a small stream, into which he descends without fear, in order that he may pass to the other side. But at another time he comes to a river that is deep and broad; there are no stepping-stones by which he can cross; he cannot see to the opposite bank; it is like the ocean; in consequence of these obstacles he is afraid to venture into the water, he cannot cross the stream. In the same way the Pasé-Budha is free as to that which is connected with his own order, but bound as to all that is peculiar to the supreme Budhas. This is the sixth gradation.

(7.) There is the being who knows all things; he is endowed with the ten powers; he has the four waisáradyas, viz. he has attained the supreme Budhaship, he has entirely overcome evil desire; he has ascertained all the hindrances to the reception of nirwána, and he knows fully all that is excellent and good; he has the eighteen properties of the Budhas; he has destroyed the infinite klésha; he can perform the wonderful prátiháryas; he is the supreme Budha, and towards all that belongs to the supreme Budhaship his mind is swift, fleet, quick. Thus, there is a garment made of the finest silk or cotton, or of hair; if against this garment a sharp, straight arrow is shot, from a bow that requires a thousand men to pull it, will it not most certainly be pierced, and this with the greatest ease? Why? Because of the fineness of the cloth, the sharpness of the arrow, and the strength of the bowman. In the same way, the mind of the supreme Budha is swift, quick, piercing; because he is infinitely pure. This is the seventh gradation of mind.

2. *Nirwána.*—Nirwána is the destruction of all the elements of existence. In this way. The unwise being who has not yet arrived at a state of purity, or who is subject to future birth, overcome by the excess of evil desire, rejoices in the organs of sense, áyatana, and their relative objects, and commends them. The áyatanas therefore become to him like a rapid stream to carry him onward toward the sea of repeated existence; they are not released from old age, decay, death, sorrow, &c. But the being who is purified, perceiving the evils arising from the sensual organs and their relative objects, does not rejoice therein, nor does he commend them, or allow himself to be swallowed up by them. By the destruction of the 108 modes of evil desire he has released himself from birth, as from the jaws of an alligator; he has overcome all attachment to outward objects; he does not regard the unautho-

rised precepts, nor is he a sceptic; and he knows that there is no ego, no self. By overcoming these four errors, he has released himself from the cleaving to existing objects. By the destruction of the cleaving to existing objects he is released from birth, whether as a brahma, man, or any other being. By the destruction of birth he is released from old age, decay, death, sorrow, &c. All the afflictions connected with the repetition of existence are overcome. Thus all the principles of existence are annihilated, and that annihilation is nirwána.

In the Asangkrata-sútra, Gótama has set forth the properties of nirwána. It is the end of sangsára, or successive existence; the arriving at its opposite shore; its completion. Those who attain nirwána are few. It is very subtle, and is therefore called súkshama; it is free from decay, and therefore called ajaraya; it is free from delay, the gradual developement of events, and therefore called nisprapancha; it is pure, and therefore called wisudhi; it is tranquil, and therefore called kshánta; it is firm, stable, and therefore called sthirawa; it is free from death, and therefore called amurta; its blessedness is great, and it is therefore called siwa; it is not made or created, but supernatural, and therefore called abbhúta; it is free from government or restraint, and therefore called aníti; it is free from sorrow, and therefore called awyápaga; and it is free from the evils of existence, and therefore called tána.

It cannot be predicated of nirwána that it has ceased to be, or that its existence is past; it is not a thing accomplished, or a relation to past time; nor is it a substance.

The man who has not attained nirwána may nevertheless become acquainted with its character. In this way. It may be known that those who have their ears, noses, hands, and feet cut off, suffer great pain, by those who have not undergone the same amputation of the limbs, from their tears and the cries that they utter. In like manner, from the joyful exclamations of those who have seen nirwána, its character may be known by those who have not made the same attainment.

All sentient beings will not receive nirwána. But if any one attain the knowledge that is proper to be acquired; if he learn the universality of sorrow; if he overcome that which is the cause of sorrow; and if he practise that which is proper to be observed; by him the possession of nirwána, nirwána-sampatti, will be secured.

Nirwáwa is dharmmá bhisamaya, the end or completion of religion; its entire accomplishment.

One day, in order to know what would be the reward of the king of Kósala, on account of the alms he gave at the request of the queen Mallika, the prince Sumana went to the Jétáwana wihára, and said to Gótama, " Sire, there are two of your disciples, equal in purity, wisdom, and the observance of the precepts; but the one gives to others of the food he eats, and the other does not; should both be born in a déwa-lóka, what will be the difference in their position?" Budha replied, "There will be a difference in five ways; the charitable disciple will have a longer life, and greater splendour, beauty, enjoyment, and honour." The prince enquired, " How will it be if they are born in the world of men?" Budha said that it would be the same. He then enquired, " How will it be if they both become priests?" And the sage replied, "The one will receive all that he requires without toil or effort in the same way as Bakkula, Síwali, and other priests." The prince then said, " How will it be if they become rahats and see nirwána?" and Gótama replied, " There will be no difference whatever."

There were two priests who were brothers. One of them, on a certain occasion, having said bana, went to his own residence, with the other priests. Whilst in the hall of ambulation he saw the full moon shining from a cloudless sky; and as he thought within himself that thus pure was his own mind; he asked, " How long shall I continue thus?" He then enquired if the priests had seen any one attain nirwána. Some replied that they had seen the rahats attain nirwána whilst seated upon a chair or couch; and others that they had seen it attained whilst the rahats were sitting in the air. The priest said that they should now see it attained in a different manner; and having made a mark in the path along which he walked, he said, that when he reached that place it would be attained. And it so happened, that when he arrived at that spot, in walking from one end of the hall to the other, he attained nirwána the moment that his foot touched the mark he had made upon the ground.

The king of Ságal said to Nágaséna, " There are some things in the world that are called karmmaja, as they come into existence because of karmma; others that are called irtuja, as they come into existence because of the season or time; and others that are called hétuja, as they come into existence because of hétu; now is there anything that is neither karmmaja, irtuja, nor hétuja?" Nágaséna replied, " Space and nirwána are neither karmmaja, irtuja, nor hétuja." Milinda: "Do not say that which is contrary to the teaching of Budha, nor reply without thought." Nágaséna: "Why do you speak to me thus?" Milinda: "You say that nirwána is akarmmaja, ahirtuja, and ahétuja. But has not Budha, in a hundred thousand different ways, declared to the sráwakas that an entrance into the árya-margga (the fourth path, that of the rahats), secures the accomplishment of nirwána (or is to be attained for that purpose)? Then how is it you say that nirwána is neither karmmaja, irtuja, nor hétuja?" Nágaséna: "Budha has said this: but he has not said that for the production of nirwána there is any hétu." Milinda: "Venerable sir, you say that Budha has declared that the árya-margga is the cause, hétu, of the accomplishment of nirwána, and yet you say also that nirwána is without a cause, ahétuja; I am confounded; I go from darkness into deeper darkness: I am in a forest; I go from an entangled thicket into a thicket more entangled; if there is a cause for the attributes or accompaniments of nirwána, there must also be a cause for the production of nirwána. The son must have a father; that father must have had another father. The scholar must have a teacher; that teacher must have had another teacher. The bud must have a producing seed; that seed must have had another producing seed. In like manner, if there is a cause for the accomplishment of nirwána, there must also be a cause for its production." Nágaséna: "Nirwána is not a thing that can be produced; and therefore it has not been said by Budha that it has a cause." Milinda: "This may be true; but explain to me how it is." Nágaséna: "Then bend your ear in a proper manner, and pay attention. Can a man, by his natural strength, go from this city of Ságal to the forest of Himála?" Milinda: "Yes." Nágaséna: "But could any man, by his natural strength, bring the forest of Himála to this city of Ságal?" Milinda: "No." Nágaséna: "In like manner, though the fruition of the paths may cause the accomplishment of nirwána, no cause by which nirwána is produced can be declared. A man may, by his natural strength, go in a ship to the other side of the sea; but he cannot, in the same manner, bring the sea to Ságal. In like manner the path that leads to nirwána may be pointed out, but not any cause for its production. Why? Because that which constitutes nirwána, nirwána-dharmma, is beyond all computation, asankyáta, a mystery not to be understood." Milinda: "Is it because nirwána is produced by neither merit nor demerit that it is beyond comprehension?" Nágaséna, "Yes; as nirwána is not produced by either merit or demerit; as it is not produced from any hétu, like trees and other similar things; as it is not caused by irtu, season or time, like the rocks, Maha Méru, &c. it is called asankyáta. As it is entirely free from evil desire, wána, it is called nirwána. It is not caused by Sekra, Maha Brahma, or any other being. It cannot be said that it is produced, nor that it is not produced; that it is past, or future, or present; nor can it be said that it is the seeing of the eye, or the hearing of the ear, or the smelling of the nose, or the tasting of the tongue, or the feeling of the body." Milinda: "Then you speak of a thing that is not; you merely say that nirwána is nirwána; therefore there is no nirwána." Nágaséna: "Great king, nirwána *is;* it is a perception of the mind; the pure, delightful nirwána, free from ignorance, awidya, and evil desire, trishnáwa, is perceived by the rahats who enjoy the fruition of the paths." Milinda: "If there be any comparison by which the nature or properties of nirwána can be rendered apparent, be pleased thus to explain them." Nágaséna: "There is the wind; but can its colour be told? Can it be said that it is blue, or any other colour? Can it be said that it is in such a place; or that it is small, or great, or long, or short?" Milinda: "We cannot say that the wind is thus; it cannot be taken into the hand, and squeezed. Yet the wind *is.* We know it; because it pervades the heart, strikes the body, and bends the trees of the forest; but we cannot explain its nature, or tell what it is." Nágaséna: "Even so, nirwána *is;* destroying the infinite sorrow of the world, and presenting itself as the chief happiness of the world; but its attributes or properties cannot be declared."

Again, the king of Ságal said to Nágaséna, "Will all who obey the precepts attain nirwána, or are there some who are not able?" Nágaséna replied, "Those who are born as quadrupeds, prétas, or sceptics, are unable (in that birth) to attain nirwána; as well as those who commit the five great sins; those who leave the doctrines of the Budhas and embrace those of the tirttakas; those who force a priestess; those who have the opportunity of hearing bana but neglect it; those who are carried away by the objects of sense; and children who are under seven years of age." Milinda: "The rest may be all right, but why cannot children attain nirwána? Are they not free from the three evils, rága, dwésa, and móha; as well as from pride, scepticism, passion, and evil reasoning? Then why are they excluded?" Nágaséna: "If the child were able to understand that which is right, and reject that which is wrong, he might attain nirwána; but his faculties of thought are weak; he cannot with a mind so limited comprehend that which is vast and endless. In like manner, no man, by his natural strength, can root up Maha Méru; nor can the whole of the extended earth be irrigated by a few drops of water, nor the whole world be illuminated by a firefly."

Again, the king of Ságal said to Nágaséna, "Is the joy of nirwána unmixed, or is it associated with sorrow?" The priest replied that it is unmixed satisfaction, entirely free from sorrow. Milinda: "This declaration I cannot believe: and for this reason. He who seeks nirwána is subject to pain, both of body and mind; in all situations he is pursued by sorrow; pain is communicated by every organ of sense; and he sees that he has to leave much wealth, and many relatives and friends. Those who possess the advantages of this world are thereby rendered joyful; there are things pleasant to the sight and other senses; and in this way regret is caused, when they have to be left; on which account I think that the joy of nirwána cannot be unmixed." Nágaséna: "It is nevertheless true that the joy of nirwána is unmixed. Is there not such a thing as the enjoyment of royalty, and is it not unmixed with sorrow?" Milinda: "There is." Nágaséna: "But a king is displeased with the people who live on the limit of his dominions; he pursues them that he may punish them; whilst thus engaged he suffers much from flies, musquitoes, cold, wind, sun, and rain; he must fight, and his life will be exposed to danger. How then is it you say that the enjoyment of royalty is unmixed?" Milinda: "The dangers of the warfare are not an enjoyment; but its trials are endured in seeking the kingdom, or in defending it. Princes seek the kingdom in sorrow, and when it is attained receive the enjoyment of royalty; on this account it is that the enjoyment of royalty is an unmixed satisfaction. The toil of the warfare is one, the enjoyment of its result another." Nágaséna: "In the same way, the happiness of nirwána is unmixed, though those who seek it are subject to sorrow; the sorrow is one, the happiness another; the two states are entirely distinct. Or, you may receive another comparison to the same effect. A disciple sets himself to the attainment of knowledge, and for this purpose places himself under the care of a preceptor; the knowledge he acquires is an unmixed good, but he has great pain and sorrow in acquiring it; and it is the same with those who seek the happiness of nirwána."

Again, the king of Ságal said to Nágaséna, "You speak of nirwána; but can you show it to me, or explain it to me by colour, whether it be blue, yellow, red, or any other colour; or by sign, locality, length, manner, metaphor, cause, or order; in any of these ways, or by any of these ways, or by any of these means, can you declare it to me?" Nágaséna: "I cannot declare it by any of these attributes or qualities (repeating them in the same order.") Milinda: "This I cannot believe." Nágaséna: "There is the great ocean; were any one to ask you how many measures of water there are in it, or how many living creatures it contains, what would you say?" Milinda: "I should tell him that it was not a proper question to ask, as it is one that no one can answer." Nágaséna: "In the same way, no one can tell the size, or shape, or colour, or other attributes of nirwána, though it has its own proper and essential character. A rishi might answer the question to which I have referred, but he could not declare the attributes of nirwána; neither could any déwa of the arúpa worlds." Milinda: "It may be true that nirwána is happiness, and that its outward attributes cannot be described; but cannot its excellence or advantages be set forth by some mode of comparison?" Nágaséna: "It is like the lotus, as it is free from klésha, as the lotus is separated from the mud out of which it springs. It is like water, as it quenches the fire of klésha, as water cools the body; it also overcomes the thirst for that which is evil, as water overcomes the natural thirst. It is like a medicine, as it assists those who are suffering from the poison of klésha, as medicine assists those who are suffering from sickness; it also destroys the sorrow of renewed existence, as medicine destroys disease; and it is immortal, as medicine wards off death. It is like the sea, as it is free from the impurity of klésha, as the sea is free from every kind of defilement; it is vast, infinite, so that countless beings do not fill it, as the sea is unfathomable, and is not filled by all the waters of all the rivers; it receives Seriyut, Ananda, Maha Kásyapa, and other most exalted beings, as the sea contains the Timi, Timingala, Timira, Pingala, and other large fishes;* and it is filled with the perfume of emancipation from existence, as the surface of the sea is covered with flower-resembling waves. It is like food, as it promotes age, as food increases the length of life; it increases the

* Some of these fishes are said to be many thousands of miles in length.

power of the rishis, as food increases the strength of men; it increases the virtues of those who receive it, as the reception of food adds beauty to the body; it overcomes the weariness produced by klésha, as food destroys the weariness of the body; and it drives away sorrow and pain, as food destroys hunger. It is like space, as it is not produced (by any exterior cause); it has no living existence; it does not die; it does not pass away; it is not reproduced; it cannot be collapsed or furtively taken away; it has no locality; it is the abode of the rahats and Budhas, as space is the habitation of birds; it cannot be hid; and its extent is boundless. It is like the magical jewel, as it gives whatever is desired; it also imparts joy, and by the light it gives is a benefit or assistance. It is like red sandal-wood, as it is difficult to be procured; its perfume is also peerless, and it is admired by the wise. It is like ghee, as it increases the beauty of the colour, its perfume is universally diffused, and its taste is delightful. It is like Maha Méru, as it is higher than the three worlds; it is also firm; its summit is difficult to be attained; and as seeds will not vegetate on the surface of the rock, neither can klésha flourish in nirwána; and it is free from enmity or wrath."

Again, the king of Ságal said to Nágaséna, "You declare that nirwána is neither past, future, nor present; and that it cannot be said that it is produced, nor that it is not produced; then does the being who acquires it attain something that has previously existed, or is it his own product, a formation peculiar to himself?" Nágaséna: "Nirwána does not exist previously to its reception; nor is it that which was not, brought into existence; still, to the being who attains it there is nirwána." Milinda: "There is much doubt in the world relative to nirwána, so I trust you will answer my questions in a clear and decisive manner, that my mind may be no longer agitated respecting it." Nágaséna: "As the disciple receives wisdom from the preceptor, so the being who is pure receives nirwána." Milinda: "What is nirwána? How is it?" Nágaséna: "It is free from danger, safe, without fear, happy, peaceful, the source of enjoyment, refreshing, pure, delightful. When a man who has been broiled before a huge fire is released therefrom, and goes quickly into some open space, he feels the most agreeable sensation; and it is the same with the man who, released from ignorance, hatred, and other evils, attains nirwána. The fire is ignorance, hatred, &c.; the man exposed to the fire is he who seeks to attain nirwána; and the open space is nirwána. Again, when a man who has been confined in a filthy place where there are the dead bodies of snakes and dogs, is released therefrom and goes without delay to some open space, he also feels the most agreeable sensation. The filth is pancha-káma; the man confined in the filthy place is he who is seeking nirwána; and the open space is nirwána. Again, when a man is exposed to danger from a band of enemies armed with swords, he is in great fear, and struggles violently to release himself, and then goes to some place where he can be free from fear and at rest. The place that is free from fear is nirwána." Milinda: "How does the priest who seeks nirwána receive it? How is it effected, or brought about?" Nágaséna: "The man who seeks nirwána carefully investigates the properties of the sanskháras; by this he sees that they are connected with decay, sorrow, and death; thus he discovers that there is no satisfaction attached to successive existence; that there is no such thing as permanent happiness. The man who sees a bar of iron that has been heated to the highest possible degree can discover no way whatever in which it will be desirable to hold it; and it is the same with him who contemplates the evils of successive existence; he can see no form whatever in which it is to be desired. Like a fish caught in a net; like a frog when attracted to the mouth of a serpent; like a bird in the claws of a cat; like a nayá in the beak of a garunda; like the moon in the mouth of Ráhu; he struggles to obtain release from existence. As the man who has gone to a distant country, when he sees the road that leads to his native land, thinks it will be well if he returns by that road; so the wise priest strives to gain an entrance into the fourth path, that he may attain nirwána."

Again, the king of Ságal said to Nágaséna, "Is nirwána in the east, south, west, or north; above, or below? Is there such a place as nirwána? If so, where is it?" Nágaséna: "Neither in the east, south, west, or north; neither in the sky above, nor in the earth below; nor in any of the infinite sakwalas, is there such a place as nirwána." Milinda: "Then if nirwána have no locality, there can be no such thing; and when it is said that any one attains nirwána the declaration is false. For the production of grain, there is the field; for the production of perfume, there is the flower; for the production of the flower, there is the forest; for the production of fruit, there is the tree; for the production of gold, there is the mine. If any one wishes for flowers or fruits, he goes to the place where they may be procured, and there meets with them; therefore, if there were such a thing as nirwána, it would have a locality; and if there be no such place, there can be no nirwána; the déwas and men who are expecting it will be deceived." Nágaséna: "There is no such place as nirwána, and yet it exists; the priest who seeks it in a right manner will attain it. Fire may be produced by rubbing together two sticks, though previously it had no locality; and it is the same with nirwána. The seven treasures of the chakrawartti have no locality, but when he wishes for them they come; and it is the same with nirwána." Milinda: "Be it so: but when nirwána is attained, is there such a place?" Nágaséna: "When a priest attains nirwána there is such a place." Milinda: "Where is that place?" Nágaséna: "Wherever the precepts can be observed; and there may be the observance in Yawana, China, Miláta, Alasanda, Nikumba, Kási, Kósala, Kásmíra, Gandhára, the summit of Maha Méru, or the brahma-lókas; it may be anywhere; just as he who has two eyes can see the sky from any or all of these places; or, as any of these places may have an eastern side."

Again, the king of Ságal said to Nágaséna; "Does the all-wise (Budha) exist?" Nágaséna: "He who is the most meritorious (Bhagawat) does exist." Milinda: "Then can you point out to me the place in which he exists?" Nágaséna: "Our Bhagawat has attained nirwána, where there is no repetition of birth; we cannot say that he is here, or that he is there. When a fire is extinguished, can it be said that it is here, or that it is there? Even so, our Bhagawat has attained nirwána; he is like the sun that has set behind the Hastagiri mountain; it cannot be said that he is here, or that he is there; but we can point him out by the discourses he delivered; in these he still lives."

The two preceding chapters may appear to possess little interest, if they be glanced at only in a cursory manner; but they are not without importance when we regard themt cleologically, as presenting a view of the brightest aspirations to which many millions of men are professing to adhere as their final hope.

It can scarcely be disputed, if the statements herein made are allowed to be a correct exposition of Budhism, that according to this system all sentient beings are called upon to regard the entire cessation of existence as the only means by which they can obtain a release from the evils of existence. This can only be accomplished by cutting off the moral cause of its continuance, viz. the cleaving to existing objects. This sensuous adherence may be got rid of by getting free from the efficient cause of its continuance, which is karma, or the united power of kusala, merit, akusala, demerit, and awyakratya, that which is neither one nor the other. In order that this may be attained there must be an entrance into one of the paths leading to nirwána.

But when we thus make a distinction between the moral cause and the efficient, it must be borne in mind that it is merely to make the subject more readily understood by those who have been accustomed only to western modes of thought, as in the sequence of existence propounded by Gótama they are not coeval but consecutive causes, in a chain composed of many links. The entire chain, one link naturally and necessarily producing the sequent link, is as follows: ignorance; merit and demerit; the conscious faculty; the sensitive powers, the perceptive powers, the reasoning powers, and body; the six organs of sense; contact, or the action of the organs; sensation; the desire of enjoyment; attachment; existence; birth; decay, death, and sorrow in all its forms.* Thus, the process is rather like the undulations of a wave, one producing the other and flowing into it, than the independent links of a chain.

The method by which the paths are gained is extremely intricate, and contrasts most strongly with the simplicity of the terms upon which salvation is offered in the gospel of Jesus Christ. Unless there has been a concurrence of favourable circumstances in previous births, the ascetic of the present age may give up the pursuit in despair; which is acknowledged to be the existing position of all Budhists, as no one now dares to hope for an immediate reception of nirwána.

Of the full perplexities of the system, however, little idea can be formed from the preceding translations, as I have arranged the paragraphs in a manner entirely different from that in which they appear in the MSS. whence they are taken, in order that the reader may be enabled to arrive, by successive stages, at the principal gradations that are regarded as being connected with the privileges of the Budhist. But in consulting the works by which I have been enabled to

* Gogerly's Essay on Budhism; Journal Ceylon Branch Royal As. Soc. i. 15.

arrive at these conclusions, I have had to wade through a mass of philologic and dialectic lore, so formidable in its extent, so minute in its classifications, and so subtle in its distinctions, that I should scarcely have had courage to undertake the task, could I have foreseen at the commencement the labour it would involve. In one or two instances, as at page 261, an example is presented from which the rest may in some degree be understood.

We learn from the statements herein made, that the sramana who sets himself to overcome the evils of existence retires from all intercourse with the world, and either exercises meditation, simply, or joins with it the practice of kasina, by which he is enabled to attain to nimitta, which is represented as being a mental illumination that brings with it, in various degrees of perfection, the state of mind called samádhi. This result of profound meditation includes undisturbed tranquillity, an equanimity the most entire; and in its superior degree it produces unconsciousness. "Budha has distinguished me," said Maha Kásyapa, "by comparing me, in thought, to the imperturtability of the air, though a hand be waved through it." When one of the monarchs of Ceylon was improving a certain tank, a priest was observed to be in the act of samádhi meditation, and as no one was able to rouse him from that state of abstraction, he was covered with earth, and buried in the embankment.* At another time some thieves mistook a priest in this state for a pillar, and heaped around him the booty they had obtained; but when he came to himself, and began to move, they fled away in extreme terror.

The exercise of the dhyánas leads to similar results; but when the fourth dhyána is accomplished, the rahatship is attained, and the ascetic arrives at the most propitious state in which it is possible for any sentient being to be placed. The rahat is entirely free from the effects of karma. As the awidya, ignorance, whence merit and demerit are produced, has entirely passed away from his mind, the succeeding stages in the sequence of existence are set aside; the effect ceases, as the cause no longer exists. When the present birth of the rahat ends, at his death the last undulation of the wave has rolled upon the shore; the echo has ceased; the light has become for ever extinguished.

The Budhist supposes that the acquisition of merit includes an accumulation of physical power. Although all events are homogeneous, being produced from one and the same series of causes, and

* Turnour's Mahawanso.

the word supernatural cannot be used of any event with strict propriety, there is a difference in the manner of their manifestation. I have not met with any graduated scale of either moral purity or concurrent energy that can be regarded as complete or perfect. In the lower stages of the sramana's attainments, his privileges and powers seem to run into each other; sometimes the ethical seems to be in excess, and at other times the physical; and it does not appear that the possession of any given degree of purity necessarily includes a proportionate degree of energy, unless, in addition to the acquisition of the purity, there has also been an attention to the appointed exercise by means of which the energy is attained. But as the exercise of the fourth dhyána, when properly conducted always leads to the possession of rahatship, it uniformly produces the most exalted effects. Yet even all rahats have not the same power. This will be seen by a reference to the knowledge they are supposed to possess relative to the circumstances of their previous states of existence. The following extract, in illustration of this topic, is taken from Budhagósha's Commentary on the Pitakas:—"The tirttaka unbelievers have the power of revelation over forty kalpas, and not beyond, on account of their limited intelligence. The ordinary disciples of Budha have the power of revelation over a hundred and a thousand kalpas, being endowed with greater intelligence. The eighty principal disciples have the power of revelation over a hundred thousand kalpas, The two chief disciples over one asankya and a hundred thousand kalpas. The inferior Budhas over two asankyas and a hundred thousand kalpas. Their destiny is fulfilled at the termination of these respective periods (being the term that has elapsed from the epoch of their respectively forming their vow to realise rahatship to their accomplishment of the same.) To the intelligence of the supreme Budha alone there is no limitation."* In a dialogue cited from the Vedas, one of the interlocutors, Jaigishavya, asserts his presence, and consequent recollection of occurrences, through ten renovations of the universe.†

The miracles ascribed to the earlier priests are so numerous, that the narrative parts of the sacred books may be said to contain an unbroken series, and many of them are of the most wonderful description. The recital of a single instance may suffice to expose the absurdity of their character. "The emperor Asóka said to the

* Turnour's Pali Budhistical Annals; Journ. Bengal As. Soc. Aug. 1838.
† Colebrooke's Miscellaneous Essays, i. 241.

priest Moggaliputta-tissa, 'Lord, I am desirous of seeing a miracle performed.' 'Maharája, What description of miracle art thou desirous of witnessing?' 'An earthquake.' 'Is it the whole earth that thou desirest to see shake, or only a portion thereof?' 'Of these, which is the most miraculous?' 'Why, in a metal dish filled with water, which would be the most miraculous, to make the whole water quake, or half?' 'The half.' 'In the same manner, it is most difficult to make only a portion of the earth quake.' 'Such being the case, I will witness the quaking of a portion only of the earth.' 'For that purpose, within a line of demarkation, in circumference one yojana, on the eastern side, let a chariot be placed, with one of its wheels resting within the line. On the southern side, let a horse stand, with two of his legs resting within the line. On the western side, let a man stand with one foot resting within the line. And on the northern side, let a vessel filled with water be placed, the half of it projecting beyond the line of demarkation.' The rája caused arrangements to be made accordingly. The théro priest having been absorbed in the fourth dhyána, rising therefrom, vouchsafed thus to resolve: 'Let a quaking of the earth, extending over a yojana in space, be visible to the rája.' On the eastern side, the wheel of the chariot that rested within the line only shook. In the same manner, in the southern and western sides, the feet of the horse, and the foot of the man, together with that moiety of their body resting within the line, shook. On the northern side, the half of the vessel also, together with the portion of water appertaining to that moiety which rested within the circle, shook; the rest remained undisturbed." *

Among the Brahmans also there are different classes in the same order of ascetics, and some of the rites that they perform are similar to those of the Budhists. "The sages, or yogi," it is said in the Vishnu Purana, as translated by Professor Wilson, p. 652, "when first applying himself to contemplative devotion, is called the novice or practitioner; when he has attained spiritual union, he is called the adept, or he whose meditations are accomplished. Should the acts of the former be unvitiated by any obstructing imperfection, he will obtain freedom, after practising devotion through several lives. The latter speedily obtains liberation in that existence (in which he receives perfection), all his acts being consumed by the fire of contemplative devotion. . . . . Endowed with the prescribed merits,

* Turnour's Pali Budhistical Annals; Journ. Bengal As. Soc. Sept. 1837.

the sage, self-restrained, should sit in one of the modes termed bhadrásana, &c., and engage in contemplation. Bringing his vital airs, called prána, under subjection, by frequent repetition, is thence called pránáyáma, which is as it were a seed with a seed. In this the breath of expiration and that of inspiration are alternately obstructed, constituting the act twofold; and the suppression of both modes of breathing produces a third. The exercise of the yogi, whilst endeavouring to bring before his thoughts the gross form of the eternal, is denominated álambana. He is then to perform the pratyáhára, which consists in restraining his organs of sense from susceptibility to outward impressions, and directing them entirely to mental perceptions. By these means the entire subjugation of the unsteady senses is effected; and if they are not controlled, the sage will not accomplish his devotions. When by the pránáyáma the vital airs are restrained, and the senses are subjugated by the pratyáhára, then the sage will be able to able to keep his mind steady in its perfect asylum." It is said, in a note to the Purána, "that pránáyáma is performed by three modifications of breathing: the first act is expiration, which is performed through the right nostril, whilst the left is closed with the right hand; this is called rechaka: the thumb is then placed upon the right nostril, and the fingers raised from the left, through which breath is inhaled; this is called púraka: in the third act both nostrils are closed, and breathing suspended; this is khumbaka: and a succession of these operations is the practice of pránáyáma." The same ceremony is thus described by Ward, in his Account of the Hindoos:—"The yogi must in the first instance by medicines reduce the appetites of the body and increase its strength; he must then learn the proper posture for the ceremony: this posture may be various, but a particular one is here enjoined—the yogi is to put his legs across in a sitting posture, and to hold his feet with his hands crossed behind him. The next act of austerity is that of learning to inhale and discharge his breath; in doing which he is to take a piece of cloth fifteen cubits long, and four fingers in breadth, and swallow it repeatedly, drawing it up and taking it down his throat, drinking water at intervals. He must next choose a seat on some sacred spot, at the bottom of a vutu tree, at some place frequented by pilgrims, near an image of an uncreated linga, or in any place peculiarly pleasant to a yogi, but it must be a secret one. That on which he must sit may be either kusha grass, or the skin of a tiger or a deer, or a blanket; but he must not sit on wood, nor on the earth, nor on cloth; his back, neck, and head, must be exactly erect: and he must remain motionless, his eyes fixed on his nose. The devotee must first with his thumb and fingers prevent the air from issuing from his eyes, ears, nostrils, and mouth, and with his feet bind up the two other avenues of respiration. This he is to practise by degrees till he is able to exist without inspiration and respiration. He who is thus far perfected will be able to subdue his passions, and to disrelish all the pleasures of the senses."

But although the same terms and rites are used by both Budhists and Brahmans, there is a difference in the meaning of the terms, and in the intention for which the rites are performed. "The meditating sage," according to the Vishnu Purána, "must think he beholds internally the figure of Vishnu. . . . When this image never departs from his mind, whether he be going or standing, or be engaged in any other voluntary act, then he may believe his intention to be perfect. . . . . .This process of forming a lively image in the mind, exclusive of all other objects, constitutes dhyána, or meditation, which is perfected by six stages; and when an accurate knowledge of self free from all distinction, is attained, by this mental meditation, that is termed samádhi." The six stages that belong to dhyána are: 1. Yama, acts of restraint and obligation. 2. Asana, sitting in particular postures. 3. Pránáyáma, modes of breathing. 4. Pratyáhára exclusion of all external ideas. 5. Bháwaná, apprehension of internal ideas. 6. Dháraná, fixation or retention of those ideas. The result of the dhyána or samádhi is the absence of all idea of individuality, when the meditator, the meditation, and the thing or object meditated upon, are all considered to be but one. According to the text of Patanjali: Restraint of the body, retention of the mind, and meditation, which thence is exclusively devoted to one object, is dhyána: the idea of identification with the object of such meditation, so as if devoid of individual nature, is samádhi.*

The Brahmans believe that Brahm is the only entity in the universe; and that there cannot, by any possibility, be any other being existent, of any kind or degree whatever, created or uncreated, visible or invisible, known or unknown. The world, with all that it contains, is only a manifestation of the supreme spirit; it is part and parcel of his own individuality. The soul of man partakes of the

* Notes to the Vishnu Purána, by Professor Wilson.

same essence; it is not a separate monad, but a portion of the deity. Nevertheless, as it is under the influence of awidya, ignorance, from being connected with prakriti, matter, it knows not its real nature, and supposes that it is a distinct and separate existence. The erroneous notion that self consists in what is not self, and the opinion that property consists in what is not one's own, are said to constitute the double seed of the tree of ignorance. "Travelling the paths of the world for many thousands of births," Késidwaja is made to say, "man attains only the weariness of bewilderment, and is smothered by the dust of imagination. When that dust is washed away by the bland water of real knowledge, then the weariness of bewilderment sustained by the wayfarer through repeated births is removed. When that weariness is relieved the internal man is at peace, and he obtains that supreme felicity which is unequalled and undisturbed. This soul is (of its own nature) pure, and composed of happiness and wisdom. The properties of pain, ignorance, and impurity, are those of nature (prakriti), not of soul. There is no affinity between fire and water, but when the latter is placed over the former in a caldron it bubbles and boils, and exhibits the properties of fire. In like manner when soul is associated with prakriti it is vitiated by egotism and the rest, and assumes the qualities of grosser nature, although essentially distinct from them, and incorruptible. Such is the seed of ignorance. . . . . Where could man, scorched by the fires of the sun of this world, look for felicity, were it not for the shade afforded by the tree of emancipation? Attainment of the divine being is considered by the wise as the remedy of the threefold class of ills that beset the different stages of life, conception, birth, and decay, as characterised by that only happiness which effaces all other kinds of felicity, however abundant, and as being absolute and final. It should therefore be the assiduous endeavour of wise men to attain unto god. The means of such attainment are said to be knowledge and works." *

The Budhists deny the existence of any such entity as Brahm. They are not pantheists but atheists. With the Brahmans they deny also the existence of a separate ego, a self; but "the Brahman idea is this, that . . I . . is Brahm; the Budhist, that . . I . . is a nonentity." In the circle of sequence, inserted above, it will be seen that no individuality is introduced; nothing that can be regarded as the man: there is the body, and there are various powers.

* Wilson's Vishnu Purána.

such as the conscious, the sensitive, the perceptive, the reasoning, and the sensuous; but there is no mention made of any conscious, sensitive, perceptive, reasoning, or sensuous entity. There are attributes, and there are facultives, active and passive; but there is no concrete source from which these powers are derived, or to which they belong. The Budhist, therefore, does not seek for absorption, but for annihilation. This subject belongs rather to the psychology of Budhism, or it would not be difficult to prove that in all these errors the system is consistent with itself; materialism, atheism, and the entire cessation of existence, stand or fall together; if the two former could be proved, the third would follow as a matter of course.

An explanation of what is intended by bhawo, which in the circle of sequence is translated existence, or state of existence, will render it the more probable that nirwána is literally annihilation. Absorption it cannot be, as there is no locality in which it can take place, no existence into which the sentient being can be merged. "Bhawo," it is said, "is two-fold; consisting of moral causative acts, and the state of being. Of these, what is kamma-bhawo, or what are moral causative acts? They are merit, demerit, and the thoughts of those in the corporeal (arúpa) worlds; and all those actions which lead to existence. Of these, what are the states in which beings are produced (or come into existence, whether by birth or otherwise)? 1. The state of sensual pleasures or pains, káma-bhawo (including the places of torment, the earth, &c. and six heavens.) 2. The brahma-worlds, rúpa-bhawo (where there are no sensible pleasures, and no pains, the enjoyments being intellectual, although there is bodily form). . . . . They are sixteen in number, and the duration of existence in them increases from one third of a kalpa to 16,000 kalpas. 3. The incorporeal worlds, arúpa-bhawo, where there is no bodily form. They are four in number, and the period of existence is from 20,000 to 40,000 kalpas. 4. A conscious state of being, including all except the asanyasattá. 5. An unconscious state of being, asanyasattá. 6. A state neither fully conscious nor yet altogether unconscious, néwasanyánásanyá-bhawo (the last of the incorporeal worlds, and the nearest approximation to nirwána.) (These states of existence may be) with one, with four, or with five of the component parts of a sentient being. The greatest number which any being can possess is five, viz. body, sensation, perception, the reasoning powers, and the conscious faculty. These five are possessed by the inhabitants of the earth, the déwa-lokas, and fifteen of the brahma-lokas; four of them (omitting body), by the inhabitants of the four incorporeal worlds; and only one by the asanyasattá, viz. body."* From this extract we learn that nirwâna cannot be a state of sensuous enjoyment; nor of intellectual enjoyment; nor of incorporeality; nor of consciousness; nor of unconsciousness; nor a state that is neither conscious nor unconscious. It must, therefore, be a non-entity; and the being who enters this state must become non-existent.

XXIII. THE MODERN PRIESTHOOD.

In nearly all the villages and towns of Ceylon that are inhabited by the Singhalese or Kandians, the priests of Budha are frequently seen, as they have to receive their food by taking the alms-bowl from house to house. They usually walk along the road at a measured pace, without taking much notice of that which passes around. They have no covering for the head, and are generally bare-footed. In the right hand they carry a fan, in shape not much unlike the hand-screens that are seen on the mantel of an English fire-place, which they hold up before the face when in the presence of women, that the entrance of evil thoughts into the mind may be prevented. The bowl is slung from the neck, and is covered by the robe, except at the time when alms are received. When not carrying the bowl, they are usually followed by an attendant, with a book or small bundle.

The exact number of priests that there are now in Ceylon cannot be ascertained; but I should think that it will not average more than one in four hundred of the whole population. This would give, for the island, about 2500 priests. This proportion is much less than in Burma, where again the priests are fewer than in Siam, though the temples are more numerous. According to Howard Malcom there is one priest to thirty inhabitants among the Burmans; and the same author informs us that, in the province of Tavoy, the number of priests is estimated at 400, with about 50 nuns. Be-

* Gogerly's Essay on Budhism; Journ. Ceylon Branch Royal As. Soc. i. 16. This enumeration will enable the reader to understand some of the terms not hitherto explained, that appear on the 261st page.

sides the great temple in Rangoon, there are more than 500 smaller ones, occupying as much space as the city itself, if not more. There are more than a hundred temples in Canton, of which the most considerable portion belongs to the Budhists. The whole number of the priests in the same city is estimated at 2000. The largest monasteries belonging to the Singhalese are in Kandy; but even in them there are not more than from twelve to twenty priests. In many of the village pansals only one priest is resident. But it is stated by Fa Hian that, at the time of his visit to Ceylon, there were 5000 ecclesiastics in one of the monasteries at Anurádhapura, and that upon a mountain not far distant (probably Mihintala) 2000 priests were resident. From the reports of the people he gathered that there were 50,000 or 60,000 priests in the whole of Ceylon. In some of the monasteries upon the continent of India he met with 3000 priests. In the inscription at Mihintala more than one hundred persons are separately mentioned as connected with the temple, including a secretary, a treasurer, a physician, a surgeon, a painter, twelve cooks, twelve thatchers, ten carpenters, six carters, two florists (who had to supply 200 lotus flowers monthly), and twenty-four inferior menials.

With this account it may be interesting to compare the number of persons attached to the monasteries of the west. According to William of Malmesbury the monastery of Bangor contained 2100 monks, who maintained themselves by the produce of their own labour. In the times of the Anglo-Saxons the monks in one monastery were also more numerous than in more recent periods; at Winchelcomb there were 300, and 600 in the united monastery of Weremouth and Yarrow.* The usual number was from five to twenty resident brethren; but to this there were many exceptions. At Tewkesbury there were 38 brethren and 144 servants. The abbey of St. Albans was limited to 100 brethren. In 1381 the establishment at Sallay Abbey consisted of the lord abbot and prior, nearly thirty monks, including novices, and forty-five or forty-six servants.† In the abbey at Whalley were a lord abbot, a prior, about twenty monks, besides an uncertain number of novices, twenty servants belonging to the abbot, and seventy in the general service of the house.‡ In the abbey of St. Edmund's Bury there were thirty-two officers under the abbot and 142 servants, in various departments.

* Taylor's Index Monasticus. † Whitaker's History of Craven.
‡ Whitaker's History of Whalley.

besides the officiating chaplains, the monks, and their servants. Before the dissolution of the cathedral priory of Norwich, the establishment consisted of the following persons:—The lord prior, sub-prior,* sixty monks, sacrist, sub-sacrist, cellarer or bursar, sub-cellarer or butler, camerarius or chamberlain, almoner, refectorer, pittancier, chaplains, precentor, sub-chantor, infirmarer, choristers, and keeper of the shrines; with the following lay officers: prior's butler, clerk of the infirmary, miller, cooper, maltster, carpenter, porter of the cellar, porter of the fish-house, caterer, woodherds, gardener's men, more than sixty servants for the monks, janitor, keeper of the sanctuarium, keepers of the garners, tokener, grooms, stallarius, provendarius, swanherd, gaoler, grangers, servants of the larder and of the kitchen, carters, scullions, &c., &c.† In Sumner's Antiquities of Canterbury there is a list of forty persons who were attached to the cellarer of the monastery of St. Augustine. In 1174 there were sixty-seven monks in the abbey of Evesham, with three nuns, three paupers at command, and three clerks, who had equal privileges with the monks. They had fifty-nine servants: five attended in the church, two in the infimary, two in the chancery, five in the kitchen, seven in the bakehouse, four in the brewery, four in the bath, two as shoemakers, two in the pantry, three as gardeners, one at the gate of the cloister, two at the great gate, five in the vineyard, four waited on the monks who went abroad, four as fishermen, four in the abbot's chamber, three in the hall, and two as watchmen.‡

The countenances of the priests in Ceylon are frequently less in-

* In some instances there was a fourth and fifth prior, and the general arrangement of the household differed from that of the priory of Norwich. The magister operis was the master mason; the eleemosinarius had the oversight of the alms; the pitantiarius had the care of the pietancies or pittances, which were extra allowances upon the usual provisions; the sacrista, or sexton, had the care of the vessels, books, and vestments belonging to the church, accounted for the oblations at the altars and images, and provided bread and wine for the sacrament; the camerarius, or chamberlain, had the care of the dormitory; the cellerarius, or cellarer, procured the provisions, and had the care of the kitchen; the thesaurarius, or bursar, received all rents and revenues, and paid all common expences; the precentor had the care of the choir, provided the music-books, parchment, ink, and colours, had the custody of the seal, and kept the chapter-book; the scriptores, or writers, transcribed the missals and books for the use of the library, for which they had frequently grants from pious individuals; the hostilarius, or hospitilarius, attended to the strangers; the refectiorarius provided vessels and servants for the refectory; and the infirmarius had the care of the infirmary, provided medicines, and prepared the dead for burial.—*Burton's Monasticon.*

† Taylor's Index.

‡ Tindal's History of Evesham, from Stevens's Appendix

telligent than those of the common people; indeed there is often an appearance about them of great vacancy, amounting almost to imbecility, and they seldom appear cheerful or happy. But there are exceptions to this rule, and a few whom I have seen exhibit an exact personification of the quiet and gentleness by which their system is characterised. The same appearance of mental inertness has been noticed by nearly all those who have travelled in countries where Budhism is professed. Howard Malcom says, that a more stupid set could not be picked out in all Canton, than the priests who officiate at the Budhist temple in the suburb of Honan. He had previously remarked this characteristic of the Budhist priesthood in other countries, and was confirmed in the belief of its being attributable to the character of their religion and the nature of their duties. Sir J. F. Davis says, that to judge of its effects on the priests, the practice of Budhism appears to have a most debasing influence, as they have nearly all of them an expression approaching to idiotcy. With this agrees the testimony of Bishop Smith, who says that the greater part of these wretched men saunter about with an idiotic smile and vacant look, and appear little removed in intellect above the animal creation, only a few seeming to be raised by mental culture above the generality, and exhibiting a refinement of mind and manners.

When not treated with disrespect, the priests of Ceylon rather court intercourse with Europeans than otherwise. I was frequently visited by them; especially by one old man, who had travelled through Bengal, Burma, Siam, and many other countries, and who prided himself upon being able to make calomel much better than the European doctors, as his preparation did not cause the falling out of the teeth, soreness of the mouth, or salivation. He learnt the secret from an ancient sage that he met with in a forest on the continent of India, and he was the only person alive who possessed this knowledge. Often when listening to him was I reminded of the mysteries and crudities of the alchemists, who during so many ages vainly sought for the elixir vitae and the philosopher's stone. In travelling through unfrequented parts of the interior, as was once my wont and my delight, I usually took up my abode at the pansal, and seldom was I refused a night's lodging or a temporary shelter during the heat of the day. The priests would bring out the alms-bowl, when they saw that I was hungry, and stirring about the contents with the bare hand, exhibit them before me, to tempt me to partake of them; or they would bring tobacco or some other luxury, to express their satisfaction at my visit. All that I had with me was a wonder to them, from the mechanism of my watch to the material of my hat. The paper of the tracts or Scriptures I gave them was supposed to be the leaf of some English tree. When I have taken off my ordinary clothes and put on my dressing-gown, they have told me that I now looked respectable; but that they could not at all admire me in my other dress. It was to my knowledge of their language I was in a great measure indebted for the welcome I received, as I was in most cases the only European with whom they had had the opportunity of entering into familiar conversation; and some were too indolent and indifferent, and others too confident in the truth of their own system, to feel enmity to me as the teacher of another faith. At the commencement of the Wesleyan mission, the priests of one village requested the use of the school-house in which to read bana, and could scarcely be brought to understand the motives upon which it was refused.

There is generally a school attached to the pansal, and the priests are much assisted by the boys whom they teach, in such offices as the bringing of water and the sweeping of the court attached to the wihára. But in forming an image of the eastern school, we are not to picture to ourselves the order and regularity of our own places of instruction. The children do not all attend at the same period of the day; as they have leisure, they go to the pansal, repeat their lesson, and then return home, or go to their employment in some other place. The school is a mere shed, open at the sides, with a raised platform in one corner, covered with sand, on which the letters are traced by the finger of the child when learning to write. The lessons are usually repeated aloud, and are recited in a singing tone, several boys frequently joining in chorus. On common occasions there is heard a low monotonous murmuring, interrupted at intervals by a general shout; as I have noticed the waves of the sea on a calm day, lazily rolling to the shore, with an occasional billow that by its deep booming breaks almost startlingly upon the previous silence. When strangers approach, the children scream out their tasks at the full pitch of their voices, and the din is for a time most unpleasant.

The letters of the Singhalese alphabet are classed and enunciated after the model presented by the Déwa-nágara, the vowels appearing first, and then, in order, the guttural. palatal, lingual, dental, and labial consonants. They are fifty in number, though not all in common use, and present a perfection not seen in the modern alphabets of Europe, as each letter has one uniform and definite sound. The long and short vowels are also distinguished; and at the first sight of a word, if the alphabet has been properly acquired, its exact pronunciation may be known. From the number of the letters, the learning of the Singhalese alphabet is rather a formidable undertaking, and the child is many weeks and sometimes, years, before he accomplishes this task; his improvement of course depending in part upon his own diligence, or the attention of the priest. An additional difficulty is created by the circumstance, that when the vowels are not initial, they are represented by a symbol attached to the consonant, which sometimes varies its form to adapt itself the more readily to the shape of the consonant with which it is connected. The first vowel has no symbol, but is to be considered as inherent in every consonant that has no symbol attached to it, similar to the short e supplied in Hebrew. It may have been during their residence in Babylon, when they would have the opportunity of communicating with the sages of the further east, that the Israelites adopted the use of the points, as it would be at this period the want of them was first more powerfully felt.

The hódiya, or alphabet, is usually copied upon tal leaves, ten in number, with the letters upon both sides, and two lines upon one page. The pupil is thus equally independent of the bookbinder, stationer, and publisher, as he has only to ascend a tree in order to procure his book, upon which he might write with a thorn from the bramble. There are a few compound letters, that are not included in the alphabet given to children. When the hódiya is properly mastered, the pupil proceeds to what is called pillan, the union of the vowels and consonants. Retaining the same tal leaves in his hand, he reads the word Swastisidham, May there be prosperity or success, which is always written at the commencement of the alphabet; repeating the characters letter by letter, and showing in what way they are united together, with their phonic power. He then proceeds to the first letter, a, saying, this is a; written with an elapilla (the symbol for á) it is á (long); and thus he proceeds through the whole, naming the symbol and telling the power of the letter when the symbol is prefixed, incorporated, or postfixed, as the case may be.

In the pansal schools, no work is used that is of a similar character to our Reading-made-Easy. After mastering the alphabet, the child writes the letters in sand, repeating the pillan as his finger traces the letters. In the left hand he holds a piece of wood, with which he erases the letter when its name and power have been pronounced, and an even surface is presented for the formation of the next letter. The entire course of reading includes the following works; and as the list was received from the most learned priest in Kandy at the time, it may be considered as correct:—1. Nampota. 2. Magul-lakuna. 3. Wadan-kawi-pota. 4. Gana-déwa-sælla. 5. Budha-gaja. 6. Nawaratna. 7. Wæsakára-sataka. 8. Namástaya. 9. Anurudha-sataka. 10. Budha-sataka. 11. Súrya-sataka. 12. Werttamála-sataka. 13. Werttamála-kyáwa. 14. Amarasingha.

1. Nampota, or name-book. This is the first book read at the pansals, and contains a collection of the names of villages, countries, temples, dágobas, déwálas, islands, caves, &c. some of which are in Ceylon and others fabulous, the names being strung together without any order of arrangement.

2. Magul-lakuna. An enumeration of the various signs and beauties upon the person of Budha.

3. Wadan-kawi-pota. A book in Singhalese or Elu verse, containing stanzas in honour of Budha, the Truth, and the Priesthood; of the three conjoined; of déwas, the host of heaven, emperors, kings, &c. There are also a few instructions on the powers of letters, grammatical rules, &c.

4. Gana-déwa-sælla. Stanzas containing an account of the birth of Ganesa, the Hindu déwa of wisdom, with prayers addressed to the same. It is written in Elu, and is merely read to accustom the tongue to the utterance of letters and combinations that are difficult to pronounce.

5. Budha-gaja. Stanzas in praise of Budha, written in a mixed style of Elu, Pali, and Sanskrit. It is understood only by the most learned of the priests, but is one of the most popular books that the Singhalese possess, as he who can read or repeat it is considered as a learned man.

6. Nawaratna. A description and eulogy of the nine most precious things in the world, the principal of which is Budha.

7. Wæsakára-sataka. One hundred (as the word sataka denotes) stanzas, written by a rishi called Wásana, in Sanskrit, with a sanné or explanation. It contains a collection of maxims, or proverbs, of which the following may be taken as a specimen; but there are

some that are of an evil tendency, and one at least that is too indelicate to be repeated.

"Though a man be of low caste, if he have wealth, he is honoured by the people of the world, but if he have no wealth, though of the race of the moon, he is despised.

"The pearls and gems which a man has collected, even from his youth, will not accompany him a single step towards the future world; friends and relatives cannot proceed a step further than the place of sepulture; but a man's actions, whether they be good or bad, will not leave him, they will follow him to futurity.

"The affliction that cometh in its appointed season none can prevent, even as no one can hinder the withering of the lotus flower at eventide.

"As drops of water falling into a vessel gradually fill it, so are all science, and instruction, and riches to be acquired.

"A benefit given to the good is like characters engraven on a stone; a benefit given to the evil is like a line drawn on water.

"Neither live with a bad man, nor be at enmity with him; even as, if you take hold of glowing charcoal it will burn you; if of cold charcoal it will soil you.

"A good action done in this world will receive its reward in the next; even as the water poured at the root of a tree will be seen aloft in the fruit or the branches.

"The evil man is to be avoided, though he be arrayed in the robe of all the sciences, as we flee from the serpent though it be adorned with the kantha jewel." This jewel is thought by the natives to be formed in the throat of the nayá. It emits a light more brilliant than the purest diamond; and when the serpent wishes to discover anything in the dark, it disgorges the substance, swallowing it again when its work is done. It is thought to be possible to obtain the jewel by throwing dust upon it when out of the serpent's mouth; but if the reptile were to be killed to obtain it, misfortune would certainly fellow.

"We must be deaf in hearing the evil of others, blind in seeing the imperfection of others, as those without members in committing sin, and as those without a mind in thinking to do wrong.

"Destruction cometh upon those who are at variance with the great, as the tusks of the elephant are broken when he tries to split the rock.

"To him who sits after eating there will be corpulence; to him who stands, strength of body; to him who walks, length of years; to him who runs, death will run.

"Be not friends with a man who has no hair on his breast, nor with one who has no whiskers.

"He who eats with his face towards the east will be long-lived; he who eats with his face towards the south will be rich; he who eats with his face towards the west will be famous; do not eat with the face towards the north.

"Though the good have only a little wealth, like the water of a well, it is useful to all; though the bad have much wealth, like the salt water of the sea, it is useful to none."

Some of these maxims are sufficiently foolish; but they are not without interest, as showing the kind of lore taught in the pansal schools and the modes of imparting instruction that are most popular in the east.

8. Námástaya. Stanzas in honour of Budha, written in Sanskrit. with an explanatory sanné.

9. Anurudha-sataka. Stanzas in Sanskrit, containing the names of the last twenty-four Budhas who have appeared, with the particular tree sacred to each, and concluding with praises addressed to the same.

10. Budha-sataka. Stanzas in praise of Budha written in Pali by Chandrabháwati, a brahman, who studied Budhism at Cotta, near Colombo, under Rahula, a very learned priest, and afterwards composed these verses.

11. Súrya-sataka. Stanzas in Sanskrit, in honour of the regent of the sun.

12. Werttamála-sataka. Stanzas written by Chandrabháwati, in Sanskrit, on the management of the voice in recitation, the peculiar tone in which the natives read.

13. Werttamála-kyáwa. Stanzas in Pali, in honour of Budha.

14. Amarasingha. The well-known Sanskrit dictionary, written a few years before the Christian era. "As it was the custom with all ancient oriental writers to write on every subject in metre, the Amarasingha is in poetry, and contains about 1500 slókas, or stanzas. When in Sanskrit only, it forms a volume of about 120 puskola pages. But there is a Singhalese commentary, and when this is added it increases the size of the work to two volumes, with 330 pages in each, of the largest kind of puskola. The language of the

commentary is so very high as to be intelligible to a very few of the readers of the work." *

The reading of these works completes the curriculum of a Singhalese student, unless he be intended for the priesthood or the medical profession; and it must be evident that there are few boys who can command the time requisite for passing through the entire course. It is to be lamented that so many precious moments are lost in the pursuit of that which is useless or pernicious, at an age when the native mind exhibits its greatest intelligence. The children of Indian parents, up to a certain period, are quicker than children of the same years living in more temperate climes; but when this age is past, they either become contented with their attainments, or sink into comparative inanition; whilst the mind of the fairer child still pants after new accumulatons, and seeks the zest of existence in the thick coming of thoughts—

> "Whose very sweetness leaveth proof
> That they were born for immortality."

The individual is the type of the race; and they live from generation to generation with as little change as is heard in the song of the bird or seen in the cell of the bee. Their precocity of mind and subsequent inferiority have indeed been thought to be allied to instinct, which, at once perfect in its degree, admits of no after-improvement; but the difference is in a great measure to be accounted for by the position in which the child of the Asiatic is placed; nor can we doubt that if he were insulated from the depressing influences to which he is subject, and an object worthy of his ambition were placed before him, the battle between the two races for the prize of intellectual superiority would be much more evenly contested.

The explanation of these works to their pupils, with the instructions imparted to the novices, occupies a considerable portion of the time of the superior priests. In some parts of the island medicine is practised by the priests to a considerable extent, and they are much in repute for their skill. The Walgam priest, who succeeded the learned Karatot as maha-náyaka, or principal priest of the district of Matura, in 1827, owed his elevation entirely to his celebrity as a medical man. Some of their compounds are very complicated, having even a greater number of ingredients than were used in the Salernian school in the eleventh century, when in one prescription

* Clough's Account of the Books in the Oriental Library purchased for the Wesleyan Mission from the estate of the late W. Tolfrey, Esq.

there were sometimes more than fifty items. Like the Egyptian physicians they depend much upon asterisms and exorcisms. A few of the priests employ their leisure moments in copying books, but in this department the energy that they exhibit is small; as very few of the pansals contain a good assortment of books, and where more numerous collections are found, they have usually been handed down from the priests of former times. They are less excusable in this respect than the ancient monks, as the material of which their books are fabricated costs only a trifle when compared with the price of parchment in the middle ages, or of papyrus in more remote periods. The pansal is the usual place of gossip for the men of the village, more especially in places where the demon that accompanies the spread of British influence, the sale of intoxicating liquors, has not found its way. In some instances priests, whilst yet wearing the yellow robe, give instruction in Singhalese and Pali to English gentlemen.

In no part of the island that I have visited do the priests, as a body, appear to be respected by the people, though there are individual exceptions in which a priest is popular, either from his learning, his skill in medicine, the sweetness of his voice, or his attention to the duties of his profession. I feel unwilling to make any positive statement as to their moral conduct, as it was generally described to me by interested persons. It may be inferred, in some measure, from their position as constrained celibates, in a country where the people pay little regard to the most sacred bonds. But when I have heard them spoken against, it has been rather on account of their rapacity than their licentiousness; though I have sometimes, and especially in certain districts, heard them accused of a great crime. In many places the people stand in awe of them, as they suppose that they have the power to inflict various calamities upon the subjects of their wrath. This fear is, however, by no means of universal prevalence. In 1839, some females went with brooms in their hands to the pansal at Raddalowa, near Negombo, and requested the priest to leave the place immediately, threatening in case of his refusal to use the brooms upon his back. The quarrel arose from an attempt of the priest to overcome the virtue of a young woman who had brought some cakes as an offering to Budha. The virtuous indignation of the broom-bearers triumphed; and the priest was obliged to leave the village. In the same year five men went one evening to a temple, and requested the priest to allow them to remain there for the night. This request was granted; but after it was dark they seized him, bound together his hands and feet, making bands of his own robe, and having thus secured him, bound also the servants that were residing with him, and then took away whatever they found that was of value. Instances are known in which priests have been found murdered in their pansals.

Under the native monarchs the priests possessed many privileges, and received the most distinguished honours. The yellow robe was sometimes assumed in order to escape from the punishment of crime; but not always with impunity. About A.D. 974 there was a revolt against Uddaya III. the leaders of which sought security by becoming priests. They were, however, seized and decapitated, after which their heads were thrown into the street; but the populace rose against the king, and subjected a number of his courtiers to the same fate. It is stated by the Abbe le Grand, in his continuation of Ribeyro's History of Ceylon (as translated by Lee), that the priests, up to the time of Raja Singha, received almost the same honours as the king himself; the impunity granted them being the more dangerous, as they were frequently engaged in conspiracies against the prince; and as they influenced the minds of the people according to their own will, they became very formidable opponents to the sovereign. In consequence of their disaffection Rája Singha abolished the exemption from punishment they previously enjoyed. Since the British took possession of the island, instances have not been wanting in which the priests have manifested a disposition to emulate the acts of their predecessors in their intrigues against the established government.

There are many of the wiháras that have no lands attached to them that would come under the denomination of glebe, unless we include the garden near the priest's residence, in which there are generally cocoa-nut and other fruit-trees. But in some instances, as we have previously noticed, the temples are rich in lands, and some of the most productive vallies in the interior belong to the wihára in Kandy called the Málagáwa, from its having been connected with the palace. The temple service is popular, on account of the perquisites that can be gained. The various hands through which the produce has to pass affords a favourable opportunity for peculation, as each person retains a large share, and the actual receipts of the priesthood are comparatively small; but this is principally when the temple is at a distance from the ecclesiastical domain, and the collecting of the produce has to be entrusted entirely to laics. After the conquest of the interior of Ceylon, in 1815, by the British, the king of England succeeded to the rights and privileges of the Kandian monarch, as head of the Budhist and Brahmanical churches; by which means acts were continually presented on the part of our professedly Christian government that must have been greatly offensive in the sight of Him before whom idolatry is "the abominable thing," utterly hated. This unholy alliance is now happily dissolved. The possession of lands by the priesthood, and the disputes that continually arise between the incumbents and their retainers, cause the priests to be frequently seen in the courts of law, which has had a tendency to bring them into disrepute with the more thoughtful of their adherents. They cannot possess lands as their own personal property, nor can they make over to others the property of the temples; but in many cases, the evils of nepotism are presented; and it would appear that in this way the revenues of many of the temples are scattered, as they are known to be rich in lands; and yet the sacred buildings are allowed to fall into ruin, scarcely an effort being made to prevent their destruction by the elements that in Ceylon lay waste the goodliest edifices with a might and rapidity never witnessed in more temperate climes.

The privileges granted to, or assumed by, the western monks, were of varied character and great importance, Like the sramanas of Budha they sometimes released criminals on their way to execution, by throwing over them the cowl. As the will of the monarch or noble was law, their interposition, when placed between the irritated chief and his innocent victim, would, in some instances, be beneficial; and the more so, as the rescued prisoner was commonly required from that time to submit to the restraints of monastic discipline. In the letters patent granted by Richard II. to the monks of Fountain's Abbey, A. D. 1387, we have a summary of their principal rights and immunities, which include "sac, soc, toll, team, and infangenetheoff, with the courts of all their tenants, and the cognizance of all transgressions in their lands, with the assize of bread and ale; the nomination or removal of their own bailiffs and servants, with all the fines and forfeitures within their premises; exemption from the assize of the county, riding, and wapontake, from danegeld, aids, scutage, pontage, pedage, and carriage; from tolls for repairing castles, clearing fosses, stallage, and taillage;

and no man could arrest any person within their premises, without the abbot and convent's leave." * Under the native monarchs, the tenants and retainers of the Budhistical establishments, when convicted of an offence before a chapter of the sangha, were either mulcted or required to execute some laborious work for the benefit of the fraternity. To have inflicted corporal chastisement, however slight, would have been regarded as a breach of the sacred code. The superior priests, though they could punish their predial servants, never sat as judges in other courts of law.

The priests who are attached to the smaller wiháras, when overtaken by the infirmities of age, and unable to carry the alms-bowl, are sometimes neglected by their followers, and have difficulty in obtaining a supply of food. I have noticed this particularly in the border districts, between the villages that have embraced Christianity, and those that are yet in heathendom. After their death, the bodies of the priests are burnt. In the year 1827, I witnessed the ceremony of the burning of the body of a young man, about twenty-two years of age, who had expired the preceding evening. It took place at Walgam, about two miles from the fort of Matura. The body was placed in a palanquin, and then carried to the spot where it was to be burnt, preceded by banners and tomtoms. About twenty priests followed in procession, among whom was the venerable uncle of the deceased, who had educated him, under the supposition that he would have succeeded to the temple over which he presided. On account of his great age and infirmity he had to be supported by the younger priests, and appeared to be much affected. The procession marched once round the pile, which was composed of a great heap of wood, laid in regular layers, and surmounted by a canopy made of the tender leaves of the cocoa-nut tree. The body, divested of its robes, was placed with its face downwards, in the centre of the pile, to which the uncle applied the torch, and the whole was soon in a blaze that spread its glare far and wide. Pieces of cloth were distributed to the poor; but no form was read, nor was any address delivered to the people. A rude monument is generally erected over the ashes of the priests, on the summit of which a bó-tree is planted.

The ceremonies practised in Burma, upon the same occasion, are much more expensive and imposing. As soon as the priest has expired, his corpse is opened in order to extract the viscera, which

* Burton's Monasticon Eboracense.

are buried in some decent place, and it is then embalmed after the fashion of the country. The body is swathed with bands of white linen, wrapped many times round it in every part, and upon these is laid a thick coat of varnish. To this succeeds a covering of gold, that adheres to the varnish; and in this manner the body is gilded from head to foot; after which it is put into a large chest, and exposed to the veneration of the people. Upon this coffin great care and expence are bestowed, the superior priests being accustomed to have it made several years before their death, so that its beauty is frequently such as to cause it to be admired by foreigners as well as natives. It is usually gilded all over, and adorned besides with flowers made of polished substances, sometimes even of precious stones. Placed in this superb receptacle, the body is exposed in public for many days, or even entire months, during which time there is a continual festival; bands of music are always playing, and the people flock in crowds to offer presents of money, rice, fruits, or other things necessary for the ceremony, by which the expences of the funeral are defrayed. When the day for the burning of the body has arrived, it is placed upon a large car with four wheels, to which is affixed a number of ropes, that the people may drag it to the cemetery. As the people divide themselves into two bodies, and strive with the greatest earnestness who shall have the honour of conveying the corpse to its destination, the vehicle is pulled first to the one side and then the other, until one party gains the advantage, and bears it off in triumph. Fireworks are let off near the pile, and beams of teak-wood are bored to receive a mixture of saltpetre and pounded charcoal. Great quantities of wood, gunpowder, and other combustibles, are heaped about the coffin, and the ceremony is concluded by setting fire to this pile, which is done by an immense rocket, guided to it by a cord.* When the deceased priest has maintained a character for peculiar sanctity, a part of his remains is not unfrequently preserved from the flames and retained as valuable relics.

Bishop Smith, in his account of the monastery at Honan, says, "We were conducted to the place where, in a kind of oven, the bodies of the deceased priests are consumed by fire. Near to this was the mausoleum, in which the ashes of the burnt bodies are deposited on a certain day in each year. Adjoining to it was a little

* Sangermano's Burmese Empire.

cell, in which the urns containing the ashes are temporarily placed till the periodical season for opening the mausoleum."

During the visit of Fa Hian to Ceylon, he was present at the burning of a priest's body at Anurádhapura. The ceremonies that took place were similar to those already described, except that, in the place of gunpowder, odoriferous woods and costly perfumes, provided at the expence of the king, were burnt upon the occasion.

The priests of Ceylon trace their origin from a remote period, as, according to the native legends, Budhism has there been professed more than 2000 years. In the 236th year after the demise of Gótama Budha, or B.C. 307, the reigning monarch, Déwánanpiya-tissa (or Tissa, the delight of the Déwas), sent ambassadors with magnificent presents to Asóka, the great promoter of Budhism, who reigned at Pátaliputra, the Palibothra of Megasthenes. The voyage occupied seven days, and seven more were occupied, after landing upon the continent, before the great city was reached. They were received graciously by the king, and on their return they were accompanied by other ambassadors from the Indian court, bearing valuable gifts, who were instructed to say to Déwánanpiya-tissa, in the name of the king. "I have taken refuge in Budha, his Truth, and his Priesthood; I have become an upásaka in the religion of Sákya. Ruler of men, embuing thy mind with the conviction of the truth of these supreme blessings, with unfeigned faith do thou also take refuge in this salvation."

In the same year, after the conclusion of the third great council of the Budhists, several priests were deputed as missionaries to different countries, among whom was Mahindo, the son of Asóka, who had renounced the world twelve years previously to this event. Accompanied by four priests and a novice, and a layman named Bhandu, he came through the air to Lanká, and alighted on a hill not far from the city of Anurádhapura, which was at that time the capital of the island. Upon the same day the king went to hunt, and was attracted by a déwa, who had assumed the appearance of an elk, to the spot where the priests had alighted; upon which Mahindo approached the king, and calling him simply Tissa, informed him of the object of their visit. The king enquired how they had come, and he replied, "I have not come either by land or by water;" after which the priest, to try the capacity of the king, thus addressed him, "Have you any relations?" The monarch replied, "I have many." Mahindo: "Are there any persons not thy relations?" The king: "There are many who are not my relations." Mahindo: "Besides thy relations, and those who are not thy relations, is there, or is there not, any other being?" The king: "There is myself." Mahindo: "Sádhu, ruler of men, thou art wise." By this means the priest discovered that the king was sufficiently gifted to understand the doctrines he had come to teach, upon which he recited to him one of the discourses of Budha; and the monarch, with the 40,000 followers by whom he was accompanied in the chase, embraced the religion of Budha. Soon afterwards the novice was commissioned to go to the court of Asóka, by Mahindo, whence to procure relics of Gótama, and the dish he used at his meals; and after procuring these he was to go to the déwa-lóka of Sekra, to procure the right collar-bone of the sage. All this was accomplished in the course of one single day. For the reception of the collar-bone the dágoba called Thúpáráma was erected; and on the day of its erection 30,000 persons entered the priesthood.

The princess Anulá, daughter of the monarch of Ceylon, declared her intention to renounce the world, but there was no one who could admit her to profession, as it was not lawful for any but a chapter composed of females to perform the ceremony. Accordingly, Arittho, the nephew of the king, was deputed to go to Pátaliputra, and invite Sanghamittá, sister of Mahindo, who had also embraced the life of a recluse, to come over to Lanká, to aid in the propagation of the faith; and at the same time the messenger was directed to request a branch of the bó-tree under which Sidhártta became a supreme Budha. Upon the same day as his departure he arrived at the court of Asóka, who, on hearing his message, was unwilling to part with his daughter; but she said, "Great king, the injunction of my brother is imperative; and those who are to be ordained are many; on that account it is meet that I should repair thither." By this means she overcame the reluctance of her royal parent. The king also consented to send the right branch of the bó-tree; but as he knew that it would be irreverent to cut it with an instrument, he went himself to the tree, attended by a thousand priests, and a great retinue of people, and making a streak with vermillion from a golden pencil, he said, "If this supreme right bó-branch, detached from this tree, is destined to depart hence to Lanká, let it, self-severed, instantly transplant itself to the golden vase I have prepared for its reception." The branch detached itself at once from the tree, and entered the vase, where it put forth a hundred shoots. Sanghamittá was accompanied by eleven priestesses and the ambassador, Arittho. The vessel in which they embarked was assailed by the nága snake-gods, that they might obtain possession of the bó-tree, though the ocean did it homage by remaining calm to the distance of a yojana around it, and the winds were equally respectful, causing music to be heard in the breeze, but by the supernatural power of the great priestess it was rescued from this danger, and brought in safety to Ceylon. The king rushed into the sea to receive it on its approach, and it was taken to the capital with all due ceremony. Arrived at the place where it was destined to flourish so long as Budhism shall be professed, it sprang into the air, self-poised, and ascended to the brahma-lóka, remaining there until the setting of the sun, when it returned to the earth and set itself in the ground, instantly putting forth roots, branches, and fruit.

However absurd these legends may appear, they are received as true both by priests and people. They throw a halo of so much brightness about the origin of the priestly order, that they are unwilling to examine whether they be a mere deception, caused by the length of the vista through which they are seen, or a grand reality under which their ancestors were permitted to rejoice. But although in this they may be led astray, they have cause of lawful exultation in the stand that their forefathers have made against the encroachments of the continental invaders. They did not say, as the pusillanimous Britons, under similar circumstances, are reported to have done, "the barbarians drive us into the sea, and the sea drives us back on the barbarians." The faith of Gótama was preserved; but it has not retained its hold upon Ceylon because it has had no powerful enemy with which to contend. The struggle was continued century after century; and if the warriors of Lanká had had an adequate historian to record their deeds, there are many places amidst its rice-clad hills that would have been magic names, vying in interest with Marathon or Thermopylæ. The Singhalese can point to a succession of 185 kings, from B. C. 543, and can rightly maintain that they are not a catalogue sprung from the brain of of some old chronicler, who had only to write down syllables, and thus create a line of monarchs. Whilst the nations of Europe have been again and again broken into fragments, and re-constructed under many different forms, all more or less heterogeneous, Ceylon has retained its almost primeval identity; and can exhibit its language, its religion, and its sacred monuments, as triumphant evidences of the fact. It is a problem worthy of investigation, how it has come to pass that the Budhist nations have preserved their individuality a longer period than any other people, if we except the nomadic tribes, upon the face of the earth. There is no country in either Europe or Asia, beside those that are Budhist, in which the same religion is now professed that was there existent at the time of the Redeemer's death.

The upasampadá succession was several times lost during these wars. It was last renewed in the reign of Kirtti Srí, who, however, consented to an arrangement that produced a great innovation upon orthodox Budhism. A decree was issued that ordination should be conferred only upon members of the gowi or agricultural caste, this being the principal caste in the island; and it was also established as a rule that the privilege should not be conferred anywhere but in Kandy, the residence of the king. At the same time the priests were divided into two communities, generally known by the name of the Malwatta and Asgiri establishments. The maha-náyakas, or principal priests of both establishments, reside in Kandy. They have equal authority; and the one is not in any way subordinate to the other. The priests under them believe precisely the same doctrines, and are bound by the same canons, so that they are two independent and co-equal communities of one and the same faith. It is difficult to discover in what way the distinction at first arose, unless the king may have wished to appoint a favourite to office without displacing the legitimate hierarch. Nearly all the priests in Ceylon belong to one or other of these establishments; but not in equal proportions, the Malwatta having a greater number of wiháras under its authority. There appears likewise to be a territorial division of the island, the Malwatta having authority over the temples towards the south of Kandy, and the Asgiri over those towards the north; but in some instances I have noticed that the priests of adjoining villages belong to different establishments.

The unauthorised regulation of Kirtti Srí naturally produced great dissatisfaction among the inferior castes. There is a caste called the chalia, or halágama, the members of which affirm that they came originally from India for the purpose of weaving cloth of gold, though by others a different origin is ascribed to their race. In more recent times they were employed by the successive European governments of the island in cutting cinnamon and preparing it for exportation, which being a profitable source of revenue, gave them considerable influence and importance. They are an enterprising race, with more of daring in their character than the rest of the Singhalese, and are strong in their attachment to Budhism. About the beginning of the present century, Ambagahapitya, a priest of this caste, accompanied by five other sámanéras, visited various countries wherein Budhism is professed, with the intention of receiving ordination, that he might have the power to confer this privilege upon other members of the same caste on his return to Ceylon. From the observations that he made in the course of his travels, he inferred that Budhism was professed in the greatest purity by the Burmans, which induced him to remain in that country until he had qualified himself for ordination. It is said that he was well received by the king of Burma and by the priests; and on his return, in 1802, after he had succeeded in the object of his wishes, he was accompanied by five Burman priests and by the sámanéras, all of whom had become upasampadá. These envoys had with them a sandésa,* or missive, from the principal priest in Burma to the sangha rája of Ceylon.

These priests, on their arrival, began to exercise the power they had received; by which means another community was established, in contradistinction to the Malwatta and Asgiri establishments of Kandy. At first it was not joined by any but the chalias; but it is now more extended in its influence, and includes priests of all castes. The more ancient establishments are called the Siam society, from the succession having been received from that country, whilst the other is called the Amarapura society, from its having originated from Burma. "The two parties thus formed," says a native writer, "are great competitors, and deny nirwána to each other; and as much animosity is to be seen among them as is to be found between two sects of any other religion. Their animosity is so great that they do not salute each other when they meet, and call each other duk-sílayas, or priests without sanctity. The object of of the Amarapura priests is to bring back the doctrines of Budhism to its pristine purity, by disentangling them from caste, polytheism, and other corruptions to which it has been subject for ages; and these priests, how difficult soever the task may be, have made a considerable progress in this reformation in the low countries, but especially in Saffragan, which may at present be regarded as the

* A Translation of this Letter appears in the Ceylon Friend for Jan. 1845, by Mr. Z. de Zoysa.

seat of this reformation, and where the difference in the tenets and principles of the two sects is greater and wider than anywhere else."* The same writer observes that the Amarapuras differ from the others on the following points:—1. They publicly preach against the doctrines of Hinduism, and do not invoke the Hindu gods at the recitation of pirit. 2. They give ordination to all castes, associating with them indiscriminately, and preach against the secular occupations of the Siamese priests, such as practising physic and astrology. None of their fraternity are allowed to follow such practises on pain of excommunication. 3. They do not acknowledge the authority of the royal edicts, that they have anything to do with their religion; neither do they acknowledge the Budhist hierarchy, nor the sanctity of the símas connected with the Malwatta and Asgiri wiháras, as they ordain in any síma provided it is set up according to the precepts of Budha. 4. They do not follow the observances of the Pasé-Budhas, unless sanctioned by Gótama. They do not, therefore, recite a benediction at the receiving of food or any other offering. 5. They do not use two seats nor employ two priests when bana is read, nor quaver the voice, as not being authorised by Budha. 6. They expound and preach the Winaya to the laity, whilst the Siamese read it only to the priests, and then only a few passages, with closed doors. 7. They perform a ceremony equivalent to confirmation a number of years after ordination, whilst the Siamese perform it immediately after. 8. They lay great stress on the merits of the pán-pinkama, or feast of lamps, which they perform during the whole night, without any kind of preaching or reading; whereas the Siamese kindle only a few lamps in the evening and repeat bana until the morning. 9. The Amarapuras differ from the Siamese by having both the shoulders covered with a peculiar role of robe under the armpit, and by leaving the eyebrows unshorn. As Pali literature is very assiduously cultivated by the Amarapuras, in order that they may expose the errors and corruptions of their opponents, it is expected that the breach between the two sects will become wider as time advances.

Another sect arose about the year 1835, originating in a discussion that was carried on between a priest at Bentotte, called Attadassa, and a few followers, on the one side, and the majority of both the Siam and Amarapura fraternities on the other. The prin-

* Mr. Adam de Silva; Ceylon Friend, Sept. 1845.

cipal object of dispute is respecting the day of the month on which the ceremony called wass ought to be commenced; reminding us of the controversies that existed in the fourth and sixth centuries relative to the mode of reckoning Easter. There is also some difference of opinion about the sánghika dána. The Bentotte priest puzzled his adversaries by his superior astronomical knowledge; but he has few supporters.

With these diversities of opinion and practice as exhibited by the Budhists belonging to one of the smallest among the nations of the world, we may infer that greater differences will exist between the Budhism of one country and that of another. There appears to be a general similarity between the religions of Ceylon, Burma, Siam, and China; but about the Adi Budhas of Nepaul, the lámas of Tibet, or the dairis of Japan, the Budhism of Ceylon knows nothing.

Throughout Burma monasteries are seen near every village, however small, and generally in situations that are beautiful or romantic in their character. These secluded sites may have been chosen by the priests as favourable to study and meditation; but Crawford saw many sacred places that had been abandoned, and was told that it was on account of the numerous gangs of robbers, who paid little respect to the priests. At the time of his visit there was no crime more frequent among the Burmans than sacrilege, though it was frequently followed by the infliction of a cruel death.

The Budhism of Burma, as illustrated by Sangermano, Buchanan, and Judson, appears to be identical with that of Ceylon in its principal rituals and ceremonies; but there are a few observances to which I have met with nothing similar in the customs of the Singhalese priests. One of the novices carries a piece of leather for the priest to sit upon when he goes abroad, whilst in Ceylon a piece of white cloth is always provided for this purpose by the people. The priests are obliged almost every moment to go through the ceremony called akat, which signifies a presentation or oblation. Thus, whenever one of them has occasion for anything, he says to the novice, "Do what is lawful;" upon which the novice takes up the thing he may want, and presents it to him, saying these words, "This, sir, is lawful." The priest then takes it into his own hand, and eats it or lays it by, as may suit his convenience. In performing this ceremony the priest must stand at the distance of a cubit from his disciple, otherwise he is guilty of a sin; and if what he receives be food, he commits as many sins as he receives mouthfuls. After covering their hands with a handkerchief, the priests have no scruple in receiving very large sums in gold and silver; and they are said to be insatiable in their lust after riches, and to do little else than ask for them. The prohibition not to touch a woman extends to the priest's own mother; and even if it should happen that she falls into a ditch, he may not pull her out; but, if no other aid be near, he may offer her his robe or a stick; at the same time he must imagine that he is pulling out only a log of wood. He may not caress a female child, however young, nor may he touch a female animal.

Eastward of Ramree there is a considerable sect, the members of which maintain that there is one eternal God, who has manifested himself in the different Budhas. They deny the doctrine of transmigration, and affirm that at death the future state of every human being is eternally fixed. They worship images of Gótama, merely as images, to remind them of deity. They have, however, temples and priests, and conform to all the Burman usages; but they are rejected as heretics by their countrymen.*

In Arrakan candidates for the priesthood are received without any regard to their country, caste, or previous religion. If the age of the postulant does not exceed fifteen years, he is appointed to the performance of menial duties, and gradually instructed about the duties he will afterwards be required to attend to, until he arrives at 20 years of age, the period appointed for ordination. It is not unusual for young men to enter the order for a limited period, that they may acquire merit or expiate some crime. The children of the laity are educated at the monasteries, no distinction being made between the rich and poor; and no remuneration is received by the priests beyond their usual allowance of alms. Some of the boys are allowed to go home to their meals; but they are obliged to sleep in the monastery, as the lessons they have learnt during the day are repeated in the evening, or at daybreak on the following morning.

About fifty years ago a class of metaphysicians arose in Ava, called Paramats, who respect only the Abhidharmma, and reject the other books that the Budhists consider as sacred, saying that they are only a compilation of fables and allegories. The founder of the sect, Kosan, with about fifty of his followers, was put to death by order of the king.

For an account of the Budhism of Nepaul we must turn to the

* Howard Malcom's Travels in South-Eastern Asia.

writings of Brian Houghton Hodgson, B.C.S., a gentleman to whose varied acquisitions, unwearied zeal, and munificent liberality, the interests of oriental literature and zoology are laid under the most weighty obligations. The following description appears in a small volume printed at Serampore, in 1841, entitled "Illustrations of the Literature and Religion of the Buddhists." It was written by an old man resident at Patna, in answer to the question, "How many castes are there among the Banras?" the word banra being defined as a corruption of bandya, "the name of the Buddhamárgí sect (because its followers make bandana, i. e. salutation and reverence to the proficients in bódhijnána)." "According to our Puránas," says this venerable authority, "whoever has adopted the tenets of Buddha, and has cut off the lock from the crown of his head, of whatever tribe or nation he be, becomes thereby a bandya. The Bhotiyas, for example, are bandyas, because they follow the tenets of Buddha, and have no lock on their heads. The bandyas are divided into two classes; those who follow the Váhya-charya, and those who adopt the Abhyantara-charya—words equivalent to the Grihastha ásram and Vairági ásram of the Bráhmanas. The first class is denominated bhikshu; the second, vajra áchárya. The bhikshu cannot marry; but the vajra áchárya is a family man. The latter is sometimes called, in the vernacular tongue of the Néwars, gúbhál, which is not a Sanskrit word. Besides this distinction into monastic and secular orders, the bandyas are again divided, according to the scriptures, into five classes: first, arhan; second, bhikshu; third, sráwaka; fourth, chailaka; fifth, vajra áchárya. The arhan is he who is perfect himself, and can give perfection to others; who eats what is offered to him, but never asks for anything. The bhikshu is he who assumes a staff and beggar's dish (khikshari and pinda pátra) sustains himself by alms, and devotes his attention solely to the contemplation (dhyána) of Adi-Budha, without ever intermeddling with worldly affairs. The chailaka is he who contents himself with such a portion of clothes (chilaka) as barely suffices to cover his nakedness, rejecting every thing more as superfluous. The bhikshu and chailaka very nearly resemble each other, and both (and the arhan also) are bound to practise celibacy. The vajra áchárya is he who has a wife and children, and devotes himself to the active ministry of Buddhism. Such is the account of the five classes found in the scriptures; but there are no traces of them in Nepaul. No one follows the rules of that class to which he nominally belongs. Among the Bhotiyas there are many bhikshus, who never marry; and the Bhotiya Lamas are properly arhans. But all the Buddhamárgis are married men, who pursue the business of the world, and seldom think of the injunctions of their religion. The Tantras and Dháranís, which ought to be read for their own salvation, they read only for an increase of their stipend, and from a greedy desire of money. This division into five classes is according to the scriptures; but there is a popular division according to the vihárs, and these vihárs being very numerous, the separate congregations of the bandyas have been thus greatly multiplied. In Pátan alone there are fifteen vihárs. A temple to Adi-Budha, or to the five Dhyáni-Budhas, called a chaitya, is utterly distinct from the vihár, and of the form of a sheaf of dhánya. But the temples of Sakya and the others of the Sapta Buddha Mánushi, as well as those of other chief leaders and saints of Buddhism, are called vihárs. . . . In short, if any bandya die, and his son erect a temple in his name, such structure may be called such an one's (after his name) vihár. With this distinction, however, that a temple to an eminent saint is denominated maha vihár, one to an ordinary mortal simply vihár."

To this account Mr. Hodgson has appended the following note:—"Of course, therefore, the Bauddhas of Nepaul have not *properly* any diversity of caste; that is, any indelible distinction of ranks derived from birth, and necessarily carried to the grave. *Genuine* Budhism proclaims the equality of all followers of Buddha; seems to deny to them the privilege of pursuing worldly avocations, and abhors the distinction of clergy and laity.* All proper Bauddhas are bandyas; and all bandyas are equal as brethren in the faith. They are properly all ascetics—some solitary, mostly cœnobitical. Their convents are called vihárs. The rule of these vihárs is a rule of freedom; and the door of every vihár is always open, both to the entrance of new comers, and to the departure of such of the old inmates as are tired of their vows. Each vihár has a titular superior, whose authority over his brethren depends only on their voluntary deference to his superior learning or piety. Women are held equally worthy of admission with men, and each sex has its vihárs. The old Bauddha scriptures enumerate four sorts of bandyas, named arhan, bhikshu, srávaka, and chailaka, who are correctly described

* The author of this work has stated, page 12, the reasons why he does not agree with this sentiment.

in the text, and from that description it will be seen that there is no essential distinction between them, the arhan being only segregated from the rest by his superior proficiency in bódhijnán. Of these, the proper institutes of Budhism, there remains hardly a trace in Nepaul. The very names of arhan and chailaka have passed away—the names, and the names only, of the other two exist; and out of the gradual, and now total, disuse of monastic institutes, an exclusive minister of the altar, denominated vajra áchárya, has derived his name, office, and existence in Nepaul, not only without sanction from the Bauddha scriptures, but in direct opposition to their spirit and tendency. Nepaul is still covered with vihárs; but these ample and comfortable abodes have long resounded with the hum of industry, and the pleasant voices of men and women. The *superior* ministry of religion is now solely in the hands of the bandyas, entitled vajra áchárya, in Sanskrit; gúbhál, in Newari: the *inferior* ministry, such bhikshus as still follow religion as a lucrative and learned profession, are competent to discharge. And these professions of the vajra áchárya, and of the bhikshu, have become by usage hereditary, as have all other avocations and pursuits, whether civil or religious, in Nepaul. And as in the modern corrupt Buddhism of Nepaul there are exclusive ministers of religion, or *priests*, so are there many Bauddhas who retain the lock on the crown of the head, and are not bandyas. These improper Bauddhas are called udás; they never dwell in the vihárs, look up to the bandyas with a reverential respect derived from the misapplication of certain ancient tenets, and follow those trades and avocations which are comparatively disreputable (among which is *foreign* commerce); while the bandyas, who have abandoned the profession of religion, practise those crafts which are most esteemed. Agriculture is equally open to both; but is, in fact, chiefly followed by the udás, who have thus become, in course of time, more numerous than the bandyas, notwithstanding the early abandonment by the bandyas of those ascetical practices which their faith enjoins, the resort of the greater part of them to the active business of the world, and their usurpation of all the liberal, and three-fourths of the mechanical, arts of their country; for the bandyas have the exclusive inheritance of thirty-six professions and trades; the udás, that of seven trades only. The vajra áchárya and bhikshu are the religious guides and priests of both bandyas and udás. All bandyas, whatever be the profession or trade they hereditarily exercise, are still equal; they intermarry and communicate in all the social offices of life—and the like is true of all udás—but between the one class and the other growing superstition has erected an insuperable barrier."

The Budhism of Tibet is a still greater departure from the observances of the original institute. It was introduced into this country in the seventh century. The superior priests who are called lámas, are regarded as incarnations of Budha, and possess so large a share of political authority that they can depose the sovereign of the country, and substitute another in his stead. It is said that formerly they were themselves the supreme rulers of the country, until one of the royal family, at the death of the principal láma, declared that the spirit of the deceased hierarch had entered into his body, by which he regained the power that had been usurped by the priests. The dress of the grand láma is yellow; that of other lámas of superior rank, red; and as these dignitaries wear broad-brimmed hats, their costume closely resembles that of the cardinals of Rome. In addition to the existence of monastic establishments for both sexes, the acknowledgment of a supreme infallible head of the whole religious community, and the adoption of pageantry in public worship, still further assimilate the Budhism of Tibet to the characteristics of the Romish church. Under its restraining influence the terrific Moguls and other Tartars are said to have been comparatively a mild and peaceable race. Celibacy is equally professed by the lámas, who are regarded as the secular clergy, and by the gelums, or monks, and anis, or nuns. The number of ecclesiastics and recluses bears an enormous proportion to the bulk of the community. Moorcroft (Trans. Royal As. Soc. 1824) states that nearly two-thirds of the productive lands are appropriated to the support of the priesthood.* A writer in the Athenæum, who recently visited this country, says:—"The sacred cradle of Shamenism, Tibet, is governed by an hierarchy possessed of the most absolute sway, and supported by an army, not of soldiers, but of monks. In every habitable spot throughout the country monasteries and nunneries rear their heads in stately grandeur; while the mass of the inhabitants seem contented with the honour of contributing towards the support of this priestly system. A life of laziness is looked on as the highest bliss; labour for daily bread is a disgrace.. . . . The capital of Tibet, Lhasga, the principal residence of the dalai láma,

* Thornton's Gazetteer, art. Ladakh.

with a population of 30,000 souls, contains many splendid monastic establishments, and is a place of considerable commercial importance." Csoma Körösi, who died of fever at Darjeeling, in Nepaul, in 1842, explored Great Tibet, and published a mass of information relative to its literature and religion, principally in the Journal of the Asiatic Society of Bengal. "The different systems of Budhism derived from India, and known now to the Tibetians," says this most enterprising traveller, "are the following four:—Vaibháshika, Santrántika, Yógácharya, and Medhyámika. The first consists of four principal classes, with its subdivisions. They originated with Shákyás four disciples, who are called in Sanskrit, Ráhula, Káshyapa, Upáli, and Kátyáyana:—1. The followers of Ráhula were divided into four sects, and wore on their religious garb from twenty-five to nine narrow pieces of cloth. The distinctive mark of this class was a water-lily jewel and tree-leaf, put together in the form of a nosegay. 2. The followers of Káshyapa, of the brahman caste, were divided into six sects, and wore on their religious garb from twenty-three to three pieces of narrow cloth. They carried a shell or couch as a distinctive mark or their school. 3. The followers of Upáli, of the sudra tribe, were divided into three sects. They wore on their religious garb from twenty-one to five pieces of narrow cloth. They carried a sortsika flower as a mark of their school, and were styled 'the class which is honoured by many.' 4. The followers of Kátyáyana, of the vaisya tribe, were divided into three sects, and wore the same number of narrow pieces of cloth as the former class. They had as their mark the figure of a wheel, and were styled 'the class that have a fixed habitation.'" I am not aware that the existence of these sects is known to the Budhists of Ceylon. They probably arose from some local dispute upon the subject of caste.*

The most interesting account of the priests of China that I have met with is presented in Bishop Smith's "Missionary Visit to China, 1844-46." From this source we learn that many of the priests of that country are fugitives, outlaws and bandits, who have been driven by want or fear to seek an asylum in the monasteries; though it is probable that some of them may have been led to seek solace in these retreats from the sorrows of life, prompted by a purer motive. The priests of Honan, near Canton, are generally a low set of men, only a few being versed in the native literature. The in-

* Journal Bengal As. Soc. Feb. 1838.

mates of the monasteries are only bound to a life of celibacy so long as they remain attached to the sacred community. For the most part they adhere to this mode of life from necessity, as they have no other mode of obtaining a livelihood; yet it is considered disreputable for them to return to the world that they profess to have abandoned. They may be seen standing at the entrance of the temples, leading an idle, sauntering life, "distinguished more by their bare shaven crowns, than by their manners or demeanour, from the surrounding crowds of idlers." An old priest, above eighty years of age, who resided at Teen Tung, confessed that the priests who came thither from a distance had almost invariably fled from home on account of the commission of some crime. "Here," says the bishop, "these wretched specimens of humanity live together in idleness. No community of interest, no ties of social life, no object of generous ambition, beyond the satisfying of those wants which bind them to the cloister, help to diversify the monotonous current of their daily life. Separated by a broad demarkation from the rest of society, and bound by vows to a life of celibacy and asceticism, they are cut off from the ordinary engagements of our world, without any well-founded hope of a better life." A gentleman who recently visited the temple of Koo Shan, near Foo-chow-foo, thus describes the manners of the priests in a more northern district of the celestial empire:—"I was led," he says, "to the kitchen and dining-room. When it is remembered that upwards of 100 priests get their meals daily here, it may be easily imagined that these places are worthy of a visit. The dining-room is a large square building, having a number of tables placed across it, at which the priests sit and eat their frugal meals. At the time of my visit they had just sat down to dinner. They appeared a strange and motley assembly. Most of them had a most stupid and unintellectual appearance—these were generally the lower orders of the priesthood. The abbot and those who ranked highest were intelligent and active looking men; but all had a kind of swarthy paleness of countenance which was not agreeable to look on. Many of them rose as I entered their dining-room, and politely asked me to sit down and eat rice. The wonders shown the visitors in the kitchen are some uncommonly large coppers in which the rice is boiled." *

The Budhism of Japan, in having a visible representative of Gó-

* Athenæum, Oct. 20, 1847.

tama, possessed of unlimited power, resembles that of Tibet. There is another resemblance in the fact, that as in Tibet the four sects there existent are supposed to have had their origin from men of four different castes, so in Japan it is supposed that the four first pontiffs, after the death of Gótama, belonged to the four great castes of India in their regular order. The legends known to the Japanese evince that the historical portions of their sacred records have been derived from the same sources as the Budhism of Ceylon and the continental nations professing the same faith ; but beyond this I have no means of ascertaining the identity of their respective tenets. The palace of the daïri, or supreme pontiff, in the spiritual metropolis, Miako, is said to form in itself a town of considerable size. The temples are extramural, being built upon eminences that command the most delightful prospects. In the largest, called the temple of Daï Bud, or the Great Budha, resting on ninety-six columns, there is a gilt statue of the sage, of the usual form and appearance, but so immensely large, that according to the Japanese, "six persons can squat, without inconvenience, on the palm of his hand," and his shoulders reach from pillar to pillar, a space measuring from 30 to 32 feet.

The Burmans, Siamese, Nepaulese, Tibetans, Chinese, and Japanese, are the principal nations, in addition to the Singhalese, who now profess Budhism. Once predominant throughout India, it is now nearly unknown in that vast region, except as seen among the Jainas, who appear to profess either a spurious Budhism, or a kindred faith derived from the same original source as the tenets of Gótama. It does not comport with the plan of this work to enter upon the historical, the psychological, or even the ethical features of this great system ; but as the character of the priesthood cannot be rightly understood, without a deeper insight into the general system than it is possible to derive from the statements contained in the preceding pages, a few additional remarks are here presented, for the information of any reader who may be unaccustomed to oriental research.

All that we can now know of the doctrines of Budha is from indirect sources, as he left nothing in writing ; and the works that profess to record his discourses commonly include legends that can have only a very slight foundation in truth. Thus it is utterly impossible that Budha himself can have laid claim to the wonderful powers that are ascribed to him by his followers ; unless we suppose that he was either labouring under an aberration of intellect or that he was a wilful deceiver of the people. The miracles with which his name is connected, have been, during many ages, one principal support of the system; but when it comes to be philosophically considered, they will prove one of the readiest means of its destruction. We must reject almost entirely the accounts we have of the personal history of Budha, in all perhaps but the bare outline of his life, such as his family, the age in which he lived, the names of his contemporaries, and the places of his residence. All the rest is either allegory, as his battle with Mara; exaggeration, as the accounts of the honours he received and the acts he performed; or absolute falsehood, as the fable of his journey, at three steps, to the déwa-loka of Sekra. The doctrines he taught, apart from the effects they are said to have produced, may have heen handed down with greater precision, as there was here less temptation to pervert the simple truth.

The doctrines now current under the name of Budha, are essentially atheistic, in the usual acceptation of the term. There is a supreme power, but not a supreme Being; or if Budha is regarded as supreme it is only in a modified sense, as this is not the name of a single entity, but of many entities; not indeed existent, at least in their full potentiality, at the same period; but all resembling each other in a much more perfect manner than is possible under the ordinary circumstances of men. The supreme power is karma, the merit and demerit of intelligent existence. It is this that controls all things, sometimes acting in an aggregate capacity, as in the general economy of the universe; but more clearly seen in the effects it produces upon the individual being. From its consequences there is no escape, except under peculiar circumstances; and even the blessings conferred by Budha were declared to be the effect of merit produced in previous stages of existence. It was this merit that placed the different persons who became his disciples in a situation favourable for the reception of his assistance; and unless there was this previous merit the advantages that he could confer were comparatively small.

The Budhists teach that when Gótama Budha ceased to exist, near the city of Kusinára, he did not enter upon a future state of being; his existence was not renewed in another world; at that time he for ever ceased to be, as really and truly as the light of a lamp ceases to be when its flame is extinguished. He is therefore in no sense an object of personal trust or confidence ; the affections cannot be placed upon him; his guidance cannot be sought, nor his sympathy received ; and when his name is invoked, it is under the supposition that by some latent process, which cannot be explained, the prayer addressed to him will be answered, without the intervention of an intelligent cause. This will be more clearly seen when it is remembered that in the threefold protective formulary called the tun-sarana, Budha is placed in exactly the same position as his doctrines and the associated priesthood. The second class of this series can in no wise be intelligent, nor can we conceive of the third as exercising an influence apart from the members of which it is composed. Yet this is the only reufge of the Budhist ; a being annihilated ; a law non-intelligent, and an idea non-existent, a mere abstraction.

The doctrines of Budha relative to the individual man partake of the same character of withering scepticism. There is no such thing as an immortal soul. Every being, until nirwána, or extinction, is attained, necessarily produces another being, unto whom are transferred all the merit and demerit that have been accumulated during an unknown period by an almost endless succession of similar beings, all distinct from each other, never contemporaneous, but all bound by this singular law of production to every individual in the preceding link of the chain, so as to be liable to suffer for their crimes or be rewarded for their virtues. Yet though the effects of karma are infallible as to the consequences they produce, they are by no means certain as to the period or person upon whom they fall. A man may be the inheritor of the foulest crimes, committed during the three or four generations of being immediately preceding ; and yet on account of some virtue performed by the being preceding him in the fifth generation, he may live in happiness, without a cloud to darken his prosperity during any part of his present existence, and may leave the consequences of these crimes, and his own added to them, to be endured in all their bitterness by the being he himself will produce, or by some more distant being in the same series. We think that no one can deny these inferences who has had the opportunity of studying the system, although it must be confessed that the popular notion upon the subject approaches rather to transmigration, as that idea is usually received.

With these errors at the foundation of the system, no purity in its moral code can be of much avail; but as the subject is one of great importance, we will pursue it a little further, and briefly examine that part of Budhism which is supposed to constitute its greatest excellence. It is evident at once that the denial of an intelligent conservator of the universe shuts out the possibility of the existence of one great class of virtues, and these the noblest that arise in the human breast. Other virtues are by the same means entirely changed in their character, though the name may be retained. As an instance, we may notice submission; in the believer, a confession of the righteousness of the dispensations appointed by the Supreme Being, even in the utmost extremity of human agony, with an acquiescence in their infliction; but in the sceptic, mere stoicism, a sullen endurance of that which cannot be prevented. Again, obedience in these two different persons must be an act essentially dissimilar in all its aspects. In the one case, the law is considered as paramount in its claims, from the supremacy of the Being by whom it is promulgated; in the other, there can properly be no law, and the transgression of what is so called is merely an error or inconvenience, not accompanied by guilt. Hence there can be no right sense of "the exceeding sinfulness of sin," nor any true contrition. Yet we have taken law under its lowest character; and have not considered that the law of revelation is not only promulgated by a Being supremely great, but by One who is also infinitely just and good, and to whom man in particular is laid under unceasing obligations for the reception of countless blessings.

It is not the name alone that is to be regarded, but the interpretation that is put upon the several terms. For instance, almsgiving in itself is a most excellent virtue, but by the Budhists it has been converted into a mercenary act, and its purpose has been entirely vitiated; inasmuch as its obligation and rewardableness rise in magnitude, not with the wretchedness of the person to whom the gift is imparted, but with the elevation of the recipient individual in the scale of Budhistical excellence. Why should the destitute be succoured, when they are only reaping the reward of their crimes, and any aid granted to them would only be like sowing seed upon the rock?

Whatever man is, he has made himself, according to Budhism, by his own unaided energy; he is the maker of his own fortune; he is indebted to no one for his present position. All that he now enjoys is the result of merit he has acquired in previous ages and births. But in the prosperous man this idea must necessarily lead to pride, of a kind that cannot possibly be entertained by a believer in an intelligent Supreme Cause; and in the unfortunate man it must lead to despair, as he sees that he has no resource in himself, and that it is in vain to look for it elsewhere.

It will be said, perhaps, that there are the moral precepts, almost word for word the same as those of the decalogue, and that here, at least, Budhism is to be regarded in a more favourable light. To this we again reply, that it is not the simple command that is to be taken; but the interpretation that is put upon it by authorised expounders.

The first of the dasa-sil, or ten ordinances binding upon the priest, prohibits the taking of life. As all life is homogeneous, we should infer that it must be an equal crime to kill an animal as to kill a man; but the proportion of the offence rises according to the merit of the being whose life is taken. Now we shall ever find that in all cases similar to this, where the equipoise of truth is lost, and a law is carried beyond its right limit, consequences are produced the very reverse of what was intended. Thus, when the life of a man and that of an animal are in any way regarded as of similar value, it will not occur that the animal is raised from its natural level to be equal with the man, but that the man will be depressed from his real dignity to an equality with the brute. In all countries where these sentiments are prevalent, there is great recklessness relative to human life; and if it were not that they are usually accompanied by a timidity with regard to personal suffering, consequences the most deplorable would be the result of this law, which at first may appear to be more excellent than the simple prohibition of murder. It will be seen, by even a slight attention to this subject, that when the existence of a Supreme Deity is denied, and the doctrine of transmigration is believed, scarcely one of the common arguments against murder is of any power.

The third of the dasa-sil entirely forbids all sexual intercourse; but this precept does not apply to the householder, he being only prohibited from approaching the woman who is the property of another, which includes married women and wards. In the case of the priest, there is the same unnatural strictness that we have noticed relative to the taking of life; but in the application of the precept to the great mass there is a lamentable defectiveness in its requirements. As among the Greeks and Romans, it is not the act that is in itself a crime; its criminality arises from the injury it does to another person's property. The injury that the woman herself sustains appears to be regarded as nothing, unless she have a protector. Budha was married, and had a son born on the day he left his family and became an ascetic; but besides the princess Yasódhará-déwi he had many thousands of concubines, according to the exaggerated legends of his life; and his father, Sudhódana, king of Kapila-wastu or Kimbulwat-pura, was married to two sisters at the same time, this being a common custom of the Sákya race from its commencement. The practices of the courtezan did not incapacitate her from receiving the highest privileges held out by Budha to his followers, nor did he require, in order to their reception, a previous course of penitence; indeed these practices are, in some instances, regarded as meritorious.

The other precepts are all, in a similar manner, either of too rigid a character to secure the possibility of observance; or are so loose in their requirements, as defined in other parts of the system, that they are deprived in a great measure of the claim they would otherwise have upon our regard. They all, in a greater or less degree, bear evidence of the earthliness of their origin, and are rather an ineffectual attempt to teach men the way of rectitude than a perfect law.

Another defect in Budhism is its principle of selfishness, whilst at the same time it has the appearance of great benevolence. The ascetic is taught to exercise this wish, "May all the superior beings in the universe be happy; may they all be free from sorrow, disease and evil desire; may all men, whether they be priests or laics, all the déwas and brahmas, all who are suffering the pains of the hells, be happy; may they all be free from sorrow, disease, and evil desire!" A wish most enlarged and benevolent; but not an effort is the ascetic required to make towards its accomplishment. There are many beautiful sentiments, set forth with a child's simplicity, yet full of the most touching poetry, by which the excellence of equanimity is taught; but when taken in connexion with other parts of the system, with which they must necessarily be conjoined, it will be seen that they are either mere verbiage, or that the principles they inculcate are little more than indifference to all things, the good as well as the evil, whatever may be the meaning of a few sentences detached from the more essential doctrines.

It is the aim of Budhism to overcome all emotions, all preferences, all that would disturb the quiet repose of the mind. It seeks to destroy the passions, not to regulate them. But however imperfect it may be as a system, when compared with other religions it will be seen that there are parts of it entitled even to praise. We think that much caution is required as to the terms in which Christians speak of it, especially when conversing with the natives by whom it is professed. When we say to a Budhist, in just so many words, "Your religion is false;" his mind, if he be a man of any thought or information, will instantly reflect thus:—"How can that be, when there are so many things in it exactly the same as in the Bible? Does not my religion also teach me not to steal, or to lie, or to commit murder? If my religion be false, Christianity must be false as well." We must therefore carefully explain to him that there are certain principles common to all religions, in a greater or less degree, without which they would not be received as such by mankind; but that only one of these religions can have been taught by an all-wise Being. This one religion is to be received by all, implicitly, in its entirety; and other religions can only be so far true as they approach towards this standard. When, therefore, we say that Budhism is a false religion, we do not mean to say that every part of it is equally false, but that it is not divinely inspired; it was formed by a man or men, who were liable to err, and have erred, in innumerable instances; consequently it cannot teach the way of purity or peace, or save from wrath and destruction.

The doctrines of Budhism are not alone in the beauty of many of their sentiments, and the excellence of much of their morality. "It is not permitted to you to render evil for evil," was one of the sentiments of Socrates. One of the triads of Druidism was to this effect:—"The three primary principles of religion are, Obedience to the laws of God, concern for the welfare of mankind, suffering with fortitude all the accidents of life." Confucius taught that men should "treat others according to the treatment which they themselves would desire at their hands." Similar extracts might be multiplied to an indefinite extent; but it may suffice to repeat the caution, though it be well known, made by Sir William Jones, in 1794, in the Eleventh Discourse delivered before the Asiatic Society, "On the Philosophy of the Asiatics."—"If the conversion of the Pandits and Maulavis in this country shall ever be attempted by Protestant missionaries, they must beware of asserting, while they teach the gospel of truth, what those Pandits and Maulavis would know to be false: the former would cite that beautiful Arya couplet, which was written at least three centuries before our era, and which pronounces the duty of a good man, even in the moment of his destruction, to consist not only in forgiving, but even in a desire of benefiting his destroyer, as the sandal tree, in the instant of its overthrow, sheds perfume on the axe which fells it; and the latter would triumph in repeating the verse of Sadi, who represents 'a return of good for good' as a slight reciprocity, but says to the virtuous man, 'confer benefits on him who has injured thee;' using an Arabic sentence, and a maxim apparently of the ancient Arabs. Nor would the Mussulmans fail to recite four distichs of Hafiz, who has illustrated that maxim with fanciful but elegant allusions:—

> 'Learn from yon orient shell to love thy foe,
> And store with pearls the hand that brings thee woe:
> Free, like yon rock, from base vindictive pride,
> Imblaze with gems the wrist that tears thy side:
> Mark, where yon tree rewards the stony show'r
> With fruit nectareous, or the balmy flow'r:
> All nature calls aloud; Shall man do less,
> Than heal the smiter, and the railer bless?' "

We only stop for a moment to notice the expression, "*If* the conversion of the Pandits and Maulavis *shall ever be attempted* by Protestant missionaries!" It strikes upon the ear like a sound all strange; but what an interesting comment might be made on the events that have taken place since it was written!

It would have been well if Budhism, in aiming at too much, had gone to the furthest limit of possible good; but that this has been accomplished no one can assert. Its inherent defects have prevented it from reaching the end it has seen in the distance, but has never been able to approach. How could it be otherwise, when man is left to his own unaided efforts in the great work of freeing himself from the defilement of evil! It is like the throwing of a pebble into the Ganges to arrest its mighty stream. The Budhist knows nothing of an atonement; he reels under the weight of his sin, but he cannot rid himself of the burden. The voice that promises him rest is only a sound; it has no living existence, no substantiality. In the wilderness to which he is driven no cross does he see, no river of blood, no fountain of life with the cheering words inscribed upon the rock that overhangs it, "Whosoever will, let him come, and drink freely, and live!" He hears of salvation, but he discovers no Saviour. Thus mocked with delusive promises, his disappointment is severe; the best affections of his heart are destroyed; and if he still pursues the system, he is converted into a harmless being, silent, and full of abstract thought that seeks its own annihilation, so that even of thought there may be none.

XXIV. THE VOICE OF THE PAST.

It has long been known that monachism was rife in the east, some ages previous to its adoption in Europe; but the history of its origin was involved in the same obscurity as the source of the mighty streams upon the banks of which the first ascetics commenced the practice of their austerities. By some of the fathers it was thought that its most intense manifestation was peculiar to Christianity. "Who is there," asks Athanasius, "but our Lord and Saviour Christ that has not deemed this virtue (of virginity) to be utterly impracticable (or unattainable) among men; and yet he has so shown his divine power as to impel youths, as yet under age, to profess it, a virtue beyond law?" "None of the ancients, none before the time of Christ," says Chrysostom, "were able to addict themselves to the ascetic practice of virginity." * But that these sentiments were utterly incorrect is abundantly proved by the facts recorded upon the preceding pages; unless the fathers intended simply to assert that the pretensions of the barbarians to purity were vain and unfounded.

It is not in my power to pass the veil that shrouds from observation the origin we wish to trace; but we are able, now, to make nearer approaches towards it than were possible before the history of Budhism was known. That Gótama Budha effected a great change in the social polity and religious institutions of the inhabitants of India cannot be denied; but how much of the system that bears his name was originally propounded by himself, or how much of that which he really propounded was the product of his own unaided intellect, will remain an unanswered problem to the end of time. It is maintained by the Budhists that he was entirely *αὐτοδιδακτος*. The wisdom that he manifested was the outbeaming

* Taylor's Ancient Christianity.

of a self-enkindled flame, not an inspiration from any exterior source; nor was it the result of any process of thought or reason. To whatever object he directed his intellectual vision, whether it were near or remote, whether past, present, or future, he saw it in a moment, intuitively, and yet in a manner the most absolutely perfect.* Though the sramanas believe that there has been, and ever will be, an endless succession of Budhas, they maintain that previous to the manifestation of a Budha, all knowledge of the former Budhas, and of the doctrines they taught, is entirely lost, and that all we now know of the Budhas previous to Gótama has been discovered by the intuition of the sage and that of his disciples. By these unwarranted assumptions a mystery has been thrown around the real character of Gótama, which defeats the aim of the historian who would examine it by the canons of truth.

At the very onset of our researches, we meet with difficulties of the most formidable description, as there is little co-eval light from any other source than the sacred books of the Budhists; and these records abound so much with absurdities, that in many instances it would require the powers of a rahat to separate the true from the false. We may, however, collect from these venerated documents that there were both recluses and societies, communities, or schools, previous to the age of Gótama. But the recluses were not in communities, nor did the communities practise the austerities of the recluse. The originality of Gótama's system of discipline appears to have consisted in the more perfect combination of the two classes into one order, so that in this respect he rather resembled the Pachomius than the Anthony of the west. In the legends of the Budhists there are numerous allusions to other societies, consisting of

* "The omniscience of Budha is not the knowledge of all things, but the power of knowing whatever he wishes to know. In opposition to other teachers, who deduce their doctrines from certain previously assumed principles, and who may err either in the data, or in the deductions from them, Budha affirms of himself that the complete field of truth is before him, that the eye of wisdom to perceive it was obtained by him when he became a Budha; and whatever he desires to know he perceives perfectly, and at one glance, without any reasoning process."—Rev. D. J. Gogerly, Ceylon Friend. The following extract is from P. Molinæus de Cognit. Dei, quoted by Howe, Bless. Right. cap. 6. "A man, conveniently placed in some eminent station, may possibly see, at one view, all the successive parts of a gliding stream; but he that sits by the water's side, not changing his place, sees the same parts, only because they succeed; and those that pass, make way for them that follow, to come under his eye: so doth a learned man describe the unsuccessive knowledge of God." I have some recollection of having seen a similar figure applied to the knowledge of Budha, but cannot at present refer to the passage.

men and women who were leagued together for some common purpose; but in those instances in which religion is concerned there appears to be little more than the usual bond between the master and his disciple; and whenever we see evidences of a closer union the character of the association appears to be collegiate and not coenobite, philosophical and not religious. The tirttakas were the most formidable rivals of Gótama; but we are not sufficiently acquainted with the facts of their history to decide in what degree their discipline approached to the regularity of a monastic order.

Further researches may cause these conclusions to be modified. But if it be so, if it be proved that there were other monastic orders in existence, and that Gótama was not the institutor of the system, it will place in a more striking view the greatness of his genius, in having established an order that has long survived all contemporaneous systems; and that now, more than two thousand years after its promulgation, excercises a potent influence over many millions of the human race, in regions at a considerable distance from the source of its dissemination. No philosopher of Greece was able to secure for his sect so decided a pre-eminence; and although in an age of darkness Aristotle maintained a paramount sway in the halls of the schoolmen, it was only as an instrumentality by which mistaken men hoped to illustrate more clearly the system that had emanated from Israel.

The practice of austerities is so interwoven with Brahmanism, under all the phases it has assumed, that we cannot realise its existence apart from the principles of the ascetic. At an early period of the present era of manifestation, Dhruva, the son of Uttánapáda, the son of Menu Swáyambhuva, who was "born of, and one with, Brahma," began to perform penance, as enjoined by the sages, on the banks of the Yamuná. "Whilst his mind was wholly absorbed in meditation, the mighty Hari, identical with all natures (took possession of his heart). Vishnu being thus present in his mind, the earth, the supporter of elemental life, could not sustain the weight of the ascetic. As he stood upon his left foot, one hemisphere bent beneath him; and when he stood upon his right, the other half of the earth sank down. When he touched the earth with his toes, it shook with all its mountains, and the rivers and the seas were troubled, and the gods partook of the universal agitation.

"The celestials called Yámas, being excessively alarmed, then took counsel with Indra how they should interrupt the devout exercises of Dhruva; and the divine beings termed Kushmándas, in company with their king, commenced anxious efforts to distract his meditations. One, assuming the semblance of his mother Sunítí, stood weeping before him, and calling in tender accents, 'My son, my son, desist from destroying thy strength by this fearful penance. I have gained thee, my son, after much anxious hope; thou canst not have the cruelty to quit me, helpless, alone, and unprotected, on account of the unkindness of my rival. Thou art my only refuge; I have no hope but thou. What hast thou, a child but five years old, to do with rigorous penance? Desist from such fearful practices, that yield no beneficial fruit. First comes the season of youthful pastime; and when that is over, it is the time for study; then succeeds the period of worldly enjoyments; and lastly, that of austere devotion. This is thy season of pastime, my child. Hast thou engaged in these practices to put an end to existence? Thy chief duty is love for me; duties are according to time of life. Lose not thyself in bewildering error; desist from such unrighteous actions. If not, if thou wilt not desist from these austerities, I will terminate my life before thee.'

"But Dhruva, being wholly intent on seeing Vishnu, beheld not his mother weeping in his presence, and calling upon him; and the illusion, crying out, 'Fly, fly, my child, the hideous spirits of ill are crowding into this dreadful forest with uplifted weapons,' quickly disappeared. Then advanced frightful rakshásas, wielding terrible arms, and with countenances emitting fiery flame; and nocturnal fiends thronged around the prince, uttering fearful noises, and whirling and tossing their threatening weapons. Hundreds of jackals, from whose mouths gushed flame, as they devoured their prey, were howling around, to appal the boy, wholly engrossed by meditation. The goblins called out, 'Kill him, kill him; cut him to pieces; eat him, eat him;' and monsters with the faces of camels and crocodiles and lions, roared and yelled with horrible cries, to terrify the prince. But all these uncouth speeches, appalling cries, and threatening weapons, made no impression upon his senses, whose mind was completely intent on Govinda. The son of the monarch of the earth, engrossed by one only idea, beheld uninterruptedly Vishnu seated in his soul, and saw no other object.*

* This narrative would suit the history of almost any recluse, in any age. If, apart from the influence of the cross, all men are ever to be made one, it must be by asceticism, as no other principle or prejudice can at all compete with it in its powers of assimilation.

"All their delusive stratagems being thus foiled, the gods were more perplexed than ever. Alarmed at their discomfiture, and afflicted by the devotions of the boy, they assembled and repaired for succour to Hari, the origin of the world, who is without beginning or end; and thus addressed him: 'God of gods, sovereign of the world, god supreme, and infinite spirit, distressed by the austerities of Dhruva, we have come to thee for protection. As the moon increases in his orb day by day, so this youth advances incessantly towards superhuman power by his devotions. Terrified by the ascetic practices of the son of Uttánapáda, we have come to thee for succour. Do thou allay the fervour of his meditations. We know not to what station he aspires: to the throne of Indra, the regency of the solar or lunar sphere, or to the sovereignty of riches or of the deep. Have compassion on us, Lord; remove this affliction from our breasts; divert the son of Uttanápáda from persevering in his penance.' Vishnu replied to the gods: 'The lad desireth neither the rank of Indra, nor the solar orb, nor the sovereignty of wealth, or of the ocean: all that he solicits I will grant. Return, therefore, deities, to your mansions as ye list, and be no more alarmed: I will put an end to the penance of the boy, whose mind is immersed in deep contemplation.'

"The gods, being thus pacified by the supreme, saluted him respectfully and retired, and, preceded by Indra, returned to their habitations: but Hari, who is all things, assuming a shape with four arms, proceeded to Dhruva, being pleased with his identity of nature, and thus addressed him: 'Son of Uttánapáda, be prosperous. Contented with thy devotions, I, the giver of boons, am present. Demand what boon thou desirest. In that thou hast wholly disregarded external objects, and fixed thy thoughts on me, I am well pleased with thee. Ask, therefore, a suitable reward.' The boy, hearing these words of the god of gods, opened his eyes, and beholding that Hari whom he had before seen in his meditations, actually in his presence, bearing in his hands the shell, the discus, the mace, the bow, and scimetar, and crowned with a diadem, he bowed his head down to earth; the hair stood erect on his brow, and his heart was depressed with awe. He reflected how best he should offer thanks to the god of gods; what he could say in his adoration; what words were capable of expressing his praise: and being overwhelmed with perplexity, he had recourse for consolation to the deity. 'If,' he exclaims, 'the lord is contented with my devotions, let this be my reward, that I may know how to praise him as I wish. How can I, a child, pronounce his praises, whose abode is unknown to Brahma and to others learned in the Vedas? My heart is overflowing with devotion to thee: oh, lord, grant me the faculty worthily to lay mine adorations at thy feet.' "

From this narrative we learn that the practice of asceticism is supposed by the Brahmans to have commenced at a very early period; and that it leads to the possession of an energy the most mighty. The Hindu ascetics of more recent times are in many instances those who have fulfilled their supposed destiny as men, and then retire into the wilderness, that instead of assuming another form at their death they may be prepared for re-absorption in the supreme essence. In abstaining from animal food the Brahmans are stricter than the Budhists; but the followers of Gótama never knowingly take life, and therefore regard the pasuyajna or aswamédha, a sacrifice supposed by the Brahmans to be highly efficacious, with great abhorrence.

The principal allusions to India that are found in the fathers of the church have been collected by Cave, in his Life of Pantænus, catechist of Alexandria, who was sent to these regions as a missionary, about the end of the second century. "Having arrived in India he set himself to plant the Christian faith in those parts, especially conversing with the Brachmans, the sages and philosophers of those countries, whose principles and way of life seemed more immediately to dispose them for the entertainment of Christianity. Their children as soon as born they committed to nurses; and then to guardians, according to their different ages, who instructed them in principles according to their capacity and improvement; they were educated with all imaginable severity of discipline, not suffered so much as to speak, or spit, or cough, while their masters were discoursing to them, and this till they were seven and thirty years of age. They were infinitely strict and abstemious in their diet, eat no flesh, drunk no wine or strong drink; feeding only upon wild acorns, and such roots as nature furnished them withal, and quenching their thirst at the next spring or river; and as sparing of all other pleasures and delights. They adored no images, but sincerely worshipped God, to whom they continually prayed: and instead of the custom of those eastern nations of turning to the east, they devoutly lift up their eyes to heaven; and while they drew near to God took a particular care to keep themselves from being defiled with any vice or wickedness, spending a great part of both night and day in hymns and prayers to God. They accounted themselves the most free and virtuous people, having hardened their bodies against all external accidents, and subdued in their minds all irregular passions and desires. Gold and silver they despised, as that which could neither quench their thirst nor allay their hunger, nor heal their wounds, nor cure their distempers, nor serve any real or necessary ends of nature; but only minister to vice and luxury, to trouble and inquietude, and set the mind upon racks and tenters. They looked upon none of the accidents of this world to be either good or evil; frequently discoursed concerning death, which they defined to be, a being born into a real and happy life. In short, they appeared in most things to conspire and agree with the stoics, whom therefore they esteemed of all sects to be the most excellent philosophers."* The ancients who wrote of India seldom made a proper distinction between the Brahmans and Budhists. Of the above description, some parts will apply to the former class, and others to the latter. Too high a character is here given of the religious life of the Hindus, but their customs would appear profoundly impressive to a Christian who had imbibed the ascetic principles that were even then in existence; and when it is remembered that Pantænus was the preceptor of Clemens Alexandrinus, and taught in the school at Alexandria after his mission to the east, it will be seen that his visit to India may have produced a greater influence upon the church than has yet been given to it by the historians who have written of that period.

In the extensive regions between India and Syria, where stood the mighty cities of Nineveh and Babylon, and along which the tide of conquest was rolled by Dionysus, Osiris, and Sesostris, the traces of asceticism are few. It might be said that the people were too strong in their attachment to pleasure, and had too many of its appliances within their reach, to be readily induced to abandon the world; were it not that an excess of luxury frequently generates the ascetic element, by the principle of antagonism that manifests itself in the working of all human institutions.

* Cave's Lives of the most Eminent Fathers of the Church. His authorities are :—De Brachman. Morib. et instit. vid. inter alios Alexand. Polyb. de Reb. Indic. ap. Clem. Alex. Stromat. l. iii. c. 7. Strab. Geogr. l. xv. p. 1038. Bardesan. Syr. l. de fat. ap. Euseb. Præp. Evang. l. vi. c. 10. Plutarch de vit. Alexand. Porphyr. περ. ἀποκης. l. iv. s. 17, 18. Pallad. de Bragman. Tract. de Orig. et Morib. Brachman. inter Ambrosii oper. ad Calc. Suid. in voc. Βραχμανες. Euseb. Hist. Eccl. l. v. c. 10. Hier de Script. in Pantæn.

It has been noticed, relative to the Greeks, that "the century between 650 and 500 B. C. appears to have been remarkable for the first diffusion and potent influence of distinct religious brotherhoods, mystic rites, and expiatory ceremonies, none of which find any recognition in the Homeric epic." * This was precisely the age of Gótama; and the coincidence is striking. The Greeks were as free from the ascetic element as any people we can name, but even among them there was one nation that was apart from the rest; and if we examine the causes of its idiosyncracy we shall see that they arose from the more powerful development of this principle. It is said that Lycurgus, in his wanderings, penetrated as far as India; and we can discover many points of resemblance between the precepts promulgated by Gótama and the laws of the Spartans. The submission of the young was strictly enforced in the code of the Spartan legislator, and great respect was paid to the aged; there was a community of property; nearly all distinctions of rank were abolished; the education, dress, and food of all classes were the same; the diet was of the simplest kind; the use of gold and silver was forbidden; ointments were not allowed; only one garment was used; the beds were of reeds, from the banks of the Eurotas; all were taught to endure the greatest hardships unmoved; theatrical exhibitions were discountenanced; commerce was prohibited, and even agriculture; and there was a public mess. The young were set free from the restrictions under which they had previously laboured when twenty years old, the same age at which the sámanéra novice was admitted to ordination. But the Spartan annihilated self that he might become a patriot; the Budhist ascetic, that he might become non-existent.

The Orphic brotherhood tasted no animal food but the flesh of the consecrated ox, and wore white linen garments. The Orpheotolists used to come before the doors of the rich, and promise to release them from sin; but it was by songs and sacrifices. The Pythagoreans had a community of goods; they took their meals in common, and were strictly temperate; they forbore the use of sumptuous garments, and restrained anger, maintained a constant serenity, and cultivated powers of endurence. As neither Pythagoras nor Lycurgus committed his laws to writing (another resemblance to Gótama), their history is involved in too deep an obscurity to allow of much reliance being placed upon any exhibition of their

* Grote's History of Greece, iii. 114.

character; yet there is a unity about our accounts of the institutions bearing their name that pleads for their consistence with truth, either as the result of previous influences upon the individual or as produced by the gradual development of events. The Cynics, when in the strictness of their first severity, appear to have more nearly resembled the ascetics of the east. Antisthenes wore only a coarse cloak, full of holes; he carried a wallet; and confined himself to the simplest diet. The expression, "I had rather be mad than sensual," would not be out of place in the mind of a Budhist; but the snarling propensities that won for him the name of "The Dog" would have been entirely discountenanced by Gótama. The property of Diogenes consisted in a cloak, a wallet, and a staff; he ate his meals in public, and slept in his famous tub or the porticos of public buildings. He too sought to annihilate the body, but the means he took for this purpose were not such as Budhism approves, nor would this system hold in any estimation whatever a man who revelled in filth and practised indecencies.

The vow of the Nazarite was the only ascetic custom of which we have any notice in the sacred Scriptures, as existing among the children of Israel; and, as in the case of blood-revenge, the regulations given by Moses may have been intended rather to restrain the pernicious effects of a custom already established, than to introduce a new principle among the people of God. It was a sacrifice of the whole man, body and mind, to the Lord; and as the procreation of children appeared to the Israelites to be a duty, and not a degradation, there was no inconsistency in the mother of Sampson becoming a Nazarite that she might have a son. The Rechabites, who are called by Jerome "patres monachorum," refrained from wine and the erection of substantial dwellings, but the aim of their observances appears simply to have been, to maintain their nationality and independence.

The first order of recluses, for the knowledge of whose practices we have to go exclusively to the records of extra-Indian literature, is that of the Essenes. The Pharisees were more nearly allied to the Brahmans of India, whilst the Sadducees partook of the scepticism of the Budhists, and the Essenes of their asceticism. The Essenes gave themselves up to a contemplative mode of life, avoided the ordinary pleasures of existence, and repudiated marriage; they despised riches, and had one common fund; commerce was avoided; they took their meals in common, each person having a loaf of bread set before him, with a single plate of one kind of food, and they drank only water; their garments were not renewed until worn out; they abstained from conversation on ordinary topics, endeavoured to maintain a perfect tranquillity of mind upon all occasions, and were unmoved amidst the most cruel tortures; a noviciate of three years was required before any one could enter into the order, after which they took an oath that they would obey the commands of the elders, and conceal nothing from the community; they had villages of their own, or when in cities lived apart from the rest of mankind; and they rejected sacrifices, offering only gifts or self-consecration at the temple. Like other communities of a similar kind, they were frequently joined by those who were suffering from remorse of conscience, by those who were disgusted with the vanities of the world, and by the aged. Near Alexandria, on the shores of lake Moeris, resided an order of recluses called Therapeutae, who are supposed to have been a branch of the Essenes; but this opinion is controverted. They were shut up in separate cells, lived on bread and water, and ate only in the evening.

The earlier heretics, in many instances, distinguished themselves by the course of self-denial they enjoined upon their disciples. Of this kind were Saturninus, Marcion, Bardisanes, Tatian, Severus, Manichaeus, and Hierax. The followers of these misguided men macerated their bodies by repeated austerities, and shunned every kind of indulgence with rigid pertinacity. They denounced wedlock, as being a great hindrance to the Christian principle; and held abstinence and meditation in high esteem. The followers of Tatian substituted water for wine in the administration of the eucharist. They were called encratitae, the temperate, and hydroparastatae and acquarii, water-offerers. It was supposed by Severus that wine and women were produced by the evil principle, as they are the cause of the chief miseries of man. The Marcionites admitted none to baptism who were married, and none to the eucharist who did not renounce wedlock. On the other hand. Elxai despised continence, and obliged his followers to marry. The Ebionites, who were supposed to be so called from their poverty, with some other of the heretical sects enumerated above, held that it was wrong to possess anything beyond that which is absolutely necessary for daily subsistence, as the present world, in its very nature, apart from its abuse, is the exclusive possession of Satan, and therefore all communion with it must be more or less connected with sin.

But, although the principal ascetics of heathendom and heresy have now passed under our review, all their mortifications and abstractions appear to be feeble and effete, when compared with the manifestations of the same principle that are seen among the myriads of India. The system towered to the loftiest height in the place of its birth; and it was here that it assumed the most formidable majesty and exercised the most extended influence.

There is in all men a yearning after something that is beyond the limits of the visible world; and although this feeling may too generally be overpowered by the pressure of toil and the strife of passion, there are times when the solemn thought will present itself that a higher destiny is intended for man than that which he now inherits. By some minds, a divinity is communicated to the simplest objects of creation; and a pebble, a flower, a cloud, or a rill, becomes an instrument of music from which are sent forth strains of sweet harmony or lofty measure: this type of mind forms the poet. In other minds there is dissatisfaction with the common affairs of life, a moodiness which scowls at all that is connected with refinement and luxury, and would turn away from the sight of the brightest gem that ever adorned a coronet to contemplate the lack-lustre sockets of a skull: this type forms the recluse. By other minds the attention is directed to voices unheard by the busy multitude; they realise the objective presence of some superior intelligence, to whose influence they implicitly resign themselves, or they lose their own consciousness in the mute contemplation of its more glorious attributes: this type forms the mystic. And there are other minds that seek only to dive into the mysteries of the future, or to gain possession of miraculous energies, either by an increase of their own inherent powers or by allying themselves with the spirits of other spheres: this type forms the soothsayer and the magician.

All these types of mind are united in the recluse of India; but he has thoughts and sympathies that are peculiar to his own order. When he would become a poet, he makes his pebble into a mountain and his rill into a sea; when a recluse, he rejects not only the pleasures of earth, but the enjoyments of heaven; when a mystic, he would lose his very being, as well as his consciousness; and when a soothsayer or a magician, he invokes not the aid of other intelligences, as he can stretch forth his hand and the universe becomes plastic to his touch, and he can summons eternity to present itself to his vision. Though the thoughts he loves best to cherish are vast even to utter extravagance, he allows not the tranquillity of his mind to be ruffled by their presence; in its inner depths his spirit is still placid; thus resembling rather the thick-ribbed ice of the lake, which the rock that has toppled from the summit of the overhanging mountain cannot move, than its limped water that the gentlest breeze will ripple. Hence, when he would assume to himself a supernatural power, he utters no spell; he seeks no voice of incantation; he asks for no mystic strain from the minstrel's harp. A clod of earth or a basin of water, and deep silence, are all that he requires to enable him to work the mightiest miracles. Even these simple signs can be dispensed with, when he proceeds to the higher stages of the exercise. In the twenty-second chapter of the Vishnu Purána we have a representation of one mode of dhyána, in which the conception of a thing is attempted to be rendered more definite by thinking upon its types; or in which, at least, the thoughts are more readily concentrated by being addressed to a sensible emblem instead of an abstract truth. Thus the yogi says to himself, "I meditate upon the jewel on Vishnu's brow, as the soul of the world; upon the gem on his breast, as the first principle of all things," and so on: and thus through a perceptible substance proceeds to an imperceptible idea.* But the rahat only needs the emblem in the preparatory rite; when once he has received an inner evidence that the power he seeks is gained, he can ever afterwards exercise it by an act of volition, without any supernumerary aid.

The entrance of the spirit of asceticism into the Christian church was affected at an early period. Its progress was at first slow. Those who have seen the approach of the lion know well that every limb of the animal's body, and almost every hair, seems to be instinct with a separate life, the object of which is, to deprive its advance of all appearance of motion; and then there is the bound, the seizure, and the conquest absolute. Thus stealthy, and thus fatal, was the approach of the ascetic spirit; and it was this that enabled it to gain a hold so mighty upon the early professors of the

* Wilson's Vishnu Purána.

faith. Satan became transformed into a sylph of light, very beautiful in appearance, and too diminutive to be supposed capable of working harm. By this means the capitol had been taken before the enemy was discovered; and the principle in question was too congenial to human nature to allow of any prolonged resistance when its evils became apparent.

At an after period, when the advocates of the system were called upon to defend it from the attacks of its opponents, precedents were sought in the Scriptures. Jerome (Ep. 49) cited Elias and John the Baptist as the fathers of monachism, and referred to the sons of the prophets, who dwelt in the fields and solitudes, and "erected for themselves tabernacles near the Jordan;" and also to the Rechabites, "who drank no wine nor strong drink, and dwelt in tents." It was supposed, from a misconstruction of Exod. xiii. 2, that the first-born who were sanctified to the Lord embraced perpetual virginity, and that Mary was one of the temple virgins thus consecrated. The Carmelites were so specific in their assertions as to maintain that Elias was the first of their own order, and that he was called "bald-head" because he had adopted the tonsure. By some writers it was argued that there was a regular succession of hermits upon mount Carmel from the sons of the prophets to the time of Christ; and that these hermits, having at an early period embraced Christianity, continued the succession to the twelfth century, when the order was introduced into Europe. The community of goods, for a time adopted by the apostolic converts, was adduced in defence of another branch of their peculiarities.

As the ascetic principle is universally prevalent in the heart of man, and requires scarcely any encouragement to call it forth to activity, it is in vain to enquire how it arose in the church of Christ, or in what form it was first manifested. There are many virtues essential to the evangelic life, that, if carried to excess or perverted from their original intention, would each do something towards the advancement of this specious delusion. Of this kind are humility, the non-resistance of injuries, chastity, fasting, prayer, almsgiving, abstraction from the world, and communion with God. There is not one of these graces that the recluse does not imagine he fulfils in a better manner than other men; and upon this he founds his claim to superiority of holiness upon earth, and to a greater degree of glory throughout eternity.

The high estimation in which celibacy was held by many members of the primitive church was probably of spontaneous origin. It would at first be commended by those pastors of the church in whom there had been a departure from the simple doctrines of the gospel, as enunciated by the apostle Paul, Rom. iii. 38. Among those who listened to their instructions would be many who had received as much light as was necessary to enable them to discover their own wretchedness, but not enough to lead them to the cross as the source of brighter expectations. These mistaken neophytes, glad to discover any course that held out a prospect of deliverance, would be ready to embrace the ascetic principle, and put it to the test. The pastors, receiving these convictions as the evidence of a divine attestation to the truth of their words, would be induced to give greater prominence to this principle in their public addresses; and the multitude, ever ready to look at the outward and visible form, rather than the inward and spiritual grace, would begin to regard the celibate with peculiar reverence, causing a class of persons to arise whose pernicious influence upon the church was like that of the palmer-worm among the vine-leaves or the locust in the cultivated vale. The order of development might be thus:—Occasional continence, 1 Cor. vii. 5, would pass into perpetual abnegation; and chastity would pass into celibacy. The motive would be at first concealed, then avowed, followed by the applauses of the crowd and the sanction of the church. The avowed celibates would cling to each other from similarity of position; in their mutual intercourse certain observances would be regarded, and then a code of laws would be formally drawn up, and an association known by some particular name would be organised. In the beginning, admission would be open to nearly any candidate whatever; but a period of probation would afterwards be appointed and restrictions would be placed upon the privilege of membership. The members would at first carry on their own concerns; and then the rulers of the church would interfere. There would, at the commencement, be a simple acknowledgment of the excellence of celibacy; and then vows to maintain it inviolate, at first whilst connected with the association, and then until death, would be made. No change in the mode of dress would at first be insisted upon; but in process of time a particular habit would be adopted. Instruction might at first be given to the celibates or virgins at separate hours, after which a separate place would be assigned to them in the churches. The next step was, to leave entirely the habitations of men, and reside in the wilderness; and at last, to erect monasteries, in which the recluses could be assembled, whether from the city or the forest, and be leagued together as one family, apart from the world. The way to the desert had been previously thrown open, by men who fled thither from persecution, and who, from the advantages they found in a life of retirement, were induced to make it their permanent abode.

By common consent, the title of the father of monachism (among Christians) is given to Anthony, who in the Decian persecution took refuge in the mountains of Egypt, and there adopted a course of the most rigid self-denial. After living twenty years in solitude, amidst the vivid associations that could not fail to be presented by the ruined tower in which he dwelt, he began a more active career; and proclaiming to others the privileges of the anchoret, he established two settlements to which many resorted for the love of God. But the institutor of the conventual life was Pachomius, who founded the first cloister in the island of Tabenna, on the banks of the Nile, A. D. 340. Until this period each monk performed his exercises alone, not far from his own village; but Pachomius gave to the recluses by whom he was joined a system of rules, and subjected them to control, by this means forming the associations that had formerly existed without discipline or inspection into a regularly constituted order. These examples were soon followed in other parts of Christendom. The names of Ammon, Paul the Simple, Hilarion, and Simon Stylites will ever be renowned, unless the time should come when men will have too many objects of present interest to allow them to contemplate the follies of the past. Eusebius, bishop of Vercelli, about A. D. 350, retained the clergy of his diocese in his own dwelling, that he might instruct them in the duties of their profession, and by this means introduced a form of monastic observance that is supposed to have given origin to the institution of regular canons.* Basil, an eloquent writer, and one of the most eminent men of his age, introduced monachism into Pontus and the neighbouring provinces, A. D. 378. By Athanasius, it was introduced into Rome; by Benedict, into the other parts of Italy; by Martin and Cassian, into Gaul; and by Boniface, into Germany.

* The canons were a middle order between the monks and secular clergy. They adopted the monastic discipline and manner of life, having a common dwelling and mess; but they did not take upon themselves any vows. They were appointed to discharge ministerial functions in certain churches. In some monasteries there were both canons and monks.

The strong hold that monachism, about the same period, gained upon the church, may be inferred from the eminence of its supporters, and the wide expanse over which they were spread. Among its advocates, in addition to the names already mentioned, were Ambrose, in Italy; Gregory Nazianzen and Chrysostom, in Constantinople; Jerome, in Syria; Epiphanius, in Cyprus; and Augustine, in Italy. It is said * that Pachomius had 1300 monks in one convent, and more than 7000 in other places, under his inspection. In another convent, in the Thebais, there were 5000 monks, and in the single city of Nitria there were fifty convents.

The priests of the different countries where Budhism is professed appear to have a greater resemblance to each other than we see among the various orders of Christendom; and there has been in general less departure from the precepts of the institutor of the system. The monks not having, like the Budhists, a code of laws that they regarded as given by inspiration, any one was at liberty to establish a fraternity and give to it whatever laws he pleased. The anomalies presented from this source were nowhere more apparent than among our own countrymen. Without mentioning the differences between the British, Scotch, and Roman monks, there were the various rules of St. Patric, St. Congal, St. Columb, St. Molva, St. Columban, &c. among the Irish and Scotch; and St. David, St. Asaph, St. Cuthbert, St. Adhelm, &c. among the Britons and Saxons. Even in Alfred's time there were "diversi generis monachi;" and after the conquest, at the general visitation of the houses, A. D. 1232, there were not, among the Benedictines, two monasteries that lived after the same manner.† The different gradations of authority that now exist in the monastic hierarchy were formerly unknown; its provincials, generals, chapters, and congregations, are comparatively a recent addition to the institute.‡ Each founder of a monastery legislated for his subjects, uncontrolled by the opinions or commands of a superior. Although this diversity of operation was generally lamented, Bernard pleaded that the principle was correct, as "there must be in the church a variety in external forms and modes of life, in order to adapt it to the various necessities and circumstances of mankind; but that since the several members were united by the spirit of love, these differences could be no cause of schism."§ But innovations

* Giesler's Text Book. † Tanner's Notitia Monastica.
‡ Lingard's Anglo-Saxon Church.
§ Neander's Life of St. Bernard, by Matilda Wrench.

did not cease with the foundation of the convent, as each succeeding abbot modified, by addition or retrenchment, the discipline previously established, sometimes borrowing from the rules of other monasteries, and sometimes framing new constitutions in his own right. By this means the peace of the fraternity was sometimes destroyed, although in other cases the authority of a definite rule would be a great advantage. About 1223, a contention having arisen between the abbot of Evesham and the rest of the community, relative to some almost obsolete regulations, all the ancient customs, before traditional, were collected and written down by the abbot, and afterwards submitted to the pope for his approbation.* The great number of different orders that arose rendered it necessary that a stop should be put to the practice, and Innocent III. decreed that no new order should be established. Gregory X. issued a similar decree relative to the mendicants. In the index to Hospinian's valuable work on the monks there are the names of 203 different orders, and some account is given of each order in the text. The interference of the popes, however, was sometimes exercised in a pernicious manner, by relaxing the severity of the original rules; and by glosses and explanations further changes were effected, through which more rapid strides were made towards corruption.

The diversities of practice among the monks present themselves under almost every form to which we may direct our attention.

By some fraternities ignorance was accounted as a virtue, and to others we are indebted for the preservation of nearly all we know of antiquity, including the record of divine revelation. The first monks being laymen would almost necessarily be ignorant, and from their previous habits would despise all kinds of literature, whether sacred or secular. Thus, the monks of Citeaux, leading an ascetic life, in silence, prayer, and manual labour, were regardless of literary occupations; whilst those of Premontré, who were nearly coeval in their foundation, combined with these exercises an assiduous attention to intellectual pursuits.† There was in Italy a particular order calling themselves Brothers of Ignorance, who all took an oath not to know anything or learn anything. "All the monks, in reality," said Luther, "belong to this order." That the earlier priests of Budha were ignorant we may infer from the fact

* Tindal's History of Evesham.

† Berrington's Literary History of the Middle Ages.

that their sacred institutes were not committed to writing until upwards of 500 years after the death of their founder; and if they had been men of general intelligence it would not have been possible to palm upon them so great a mass of absurdities and inconsistencies as is contained in the records they profoundly venerate.

The changes that took place throughout the Roman empire soon after Christianity was generally received have been too exclusively referred to the inroads of the barbarians. The reading of the ancient classics would be discouraged by the pastors of the church, lest they should lead the young student to admire with pernicious intensity the system that a little time before had held in the same regions an unlimited sway. We who are of more recent times can peruse the myth or the legend; we can listen to the rythm that has never been surpassed in the pleasantness of its cadence, or to the periods that are unequalled in the majesty of their roll; we can contemplate the manifested conceptions before which the mightiest sages have bowed down in lowly reverence; and the only effect they produce is one that is æsthetic, and not religious. But it was not so in the earlier centuries of the Christian era. The student then beheld around him the monuments of a superstition that might yet have some hold upon his affections; here was the mighty shrine, still beautiful, that had been erected by his own ancestors; there the very statue,

> "which, if made
> By human hands, *seem'd* not of human thought,"

before which his mother or some other beloved relative had been accustomed to worship; from his playmates in the country or the slaves with whom he was most familiar among the domestics at the city residence of his parent, he would hear many a tale of nymph or of dryad; and the barbarous words or pleasant echo of many an ancient invocation would be impressed upon his memory, as he listened to it over the blazing faggot or in the stillness of the moonlight. Hence it came to pass that the scholars in the medi-æval monastic establishments were commanded to look upon all heathen authors with suspicion; the only use to be made of them being to learn therefrom "the rules of grammar, the quantity of syllables, and the laws of metre." In some foundations, as in that of Isodore, the perusal of heathen authors was entirely forbidden. Justinian, by an edict, imposed a perpetual silence upon the schools of Athens, under the idea that heathenism was still inculcated in the lectures of its professors.* Nor let it be said that these fears were groundless. We may see the power of ancient associations, even when the tenets of a better faith are professed, in the bardic poetry of our own country, and in the great number of old customs having a pagan origin that are still clung to with a tenacity that proves their strength, when even the death-struggle has long been carried on. There is also, in countries where heathenism is still professed, a danger lest the toil of the student or the care of the controversialist should be received as an act of homage to the excellence of the works over which they pore. When these dangers had passed away, the monks of some of the fraternities embraced the advantages of their position, and freed themselves from the trammels, now become comparatively useless, by which their predecessors had been properly bound. Basil and his companions, in their retirement on the banks of the river Iris, spent a considerable portion of their time in the study of the Scriptures, in which they availed themselves of the assistance of the commentators, and especially of Origin. Benedict enjoined his disciples to read, copy, and collect books. In the sixth century the recluses of both sexes were enjoined by the founders of the monasteries in which they lived to employ a certain portion of their time in reading the works of the fathers. Libraries were established, and to the more feeble of the monks was assigned, although not to them exclusively, the duty of copying manuscripts. In the next century the times for study were regularly appointed, and public examinations and discussions were held, that it might be seen whether the students had turned to good account their opportunities of acquiring knowledge. Upon the character of the abbot much would depend, both as to the nature of the studies, and the diligence of the transcribers. John Whethamsted, abbot of St. Albans, caused more than eighty books to be written during his abbacy; and by the care of one of the abbots of Glastonbury fifty-eight were written. In 1305 the monks of Bolton gave thirty shillings, the price of two good oxen, for the Book of Sentences, by Peter Lombard; "but," says Dr. Whitaker, their historian, "I can only discover that they purchased three books in forty years." The library of the Grey Friars, London, built by Sir Richard Whittingdon, was 129 feet long, and 31 feet broad, and was well filled with books. There were 1700 MSS. in the library at Peterborough Ingulf tells us that when the library at Croyland

* Hallam's Literature of Europe. Giesler's Text-Book.

was burnt the monks lost 700 books. The ecclesiastics were sometimes assisted by the munificence of laymen. William, son of Richard de Perci, gave three ox-gangs of land, with five tofts, at Dunesley, to the chauntor of the abbey church at Whitby, to make and write books for the church; and Richard de Paston granted a rent-charge of twelve pence per annum to the convent at Bromholm, to keep their books in repair. Two water mills were assigned to the precentor of Bury Abbey to find parchment and ink for the convent. The literary labours of some of the monks, since the invention of printing, more particularly of those forming the congregation of St. Maur, are too well known to require more specific notice.*

The priests of Ceylon are entitled to a share of the praise received by the western recluses. When the literature of the island was nearly annihilated by the ravages of the continental kings, they set themselves to copy and translate the principal works connected with their religion, which they procured from Burma and Siam. But they have written very few original works; and those they possess abound so much in repetitions from each other, that it becomes a tedious exercise to read them, after one or two of the more celebrated have been perused.

The advancement of Christianity will have an effect upon the literature of Asia, similar to that which was produced upon the study of the classics, when the gospel first began to grapple successfully with the ancient religions of Greece and Rome. In India, the supreme power being in the hands of Christians, the native pundits receive comparatively little encouragement; the pastors of the church discountenance the reading of the ancient books by their converts, unless it be by a few, for the purpose of refuting their arguments or exposing their absurdity; and in a little time, more especially with Pali literature, the most active of its students will be men of another land and a different creed. And as the oriental scriptures, when their contents are known, possess no such fascination as that which will ever attract men of taste to the perusal of the relics of Greece and Rome, it is not improbable that many of the books written in Sanskrit and Pali will in time be entirely un-

* Neander's Bernard. Hallam's Literature. Berrington's Literary History. Burton's Monasticon. Taylor's Index Monasticus. Whitaker's History of Whalley. Tanner's Notitia Monastica. Whitaker's History of Craven. Hospinianus de Monachis.

read, and perhaps their style unintelligible. This process of decay is already apparent in Ceylon. There being no outward stimulus to exertion, the priests exhibit no enthusiasm of study, and many of them are unable to read at all. In China these effects are still more apparent, as it is said that few of the priests in that country understand Pali. Its peculiarities preclude its being written with alphabetical accuracy in the Chinese character, so that it degenerates into a complete jargon, wherein the sound is but imperfectly preserved, and the sense not at all. But the people of the east have immense advantages over those of the west when in the same state of transition. Our forefathers did not fight merely for the settlement of local institutions, however wide their immediate influence may extend. They wrote, and spoke, and bled, for the establishment of principles. These principles and institutions, with all the improvements that experience has taught us are necessary, are taken to the inhabitants of India, and in the vigour of their energy are at once presented for their imitation, or authoritatively promulgated for their adoption. They may sometimes mistake our meaning, as when the people of some parts of the Company's territory, at the time trial by jury was introduced among them, complained that, after they were compelled to give the government so many lacs of rupees annually for the administration of justice, they should be obliged, after all, to administer it themselves. But it requires only a little experience to enable them to see the greatness of the boon they have received. As their language will remain unchanged, they have another advantage over the west. It was in the period when the Latin language became unintelligible to the mass of the people, and the modern languages were not fully formed, that the torpor was presented which seemed to paralyse the powers of the intellect to so great a degree that, during several ages, there was little improvement in either art, science, or the literature connected with sacred truth.

The monks were not all bound by an inviolable oath; as among the priests of Budha, the obligation to further obedience was sometimes a voluntary act. In the number of recluses addressed by James, of Nisibis, there were some who had dedicated themselves to continence by a vow, and others by resolution. Philip Neri forbade any of his disciples to bind themselves to the community by oath or vow. The bond of union was to arise from mutual affection and respect. The French Oratorians, founded by Peter de Berulle, are a congregation of priests who live in voluntary poverty and obedience. They can of their own accord leave the congregation. On this account they are said not to be "religious men;" but their title to belong to the order would have been allowed in more ancient times.

There was no uniformity in the practices of the various orders of monks, as to the nature of their employments, or the manner in which they spent their time. Upon some of the monks manual labour was enjoined as a duty. In the Regulations ascribed to Basil (Basil. Regula, c. 37), there is this declaration:—"Since our Lord Jesus Christ says not generally that every man, but that the *workman* is worthy of his meat, and since the apostle directed us to work with our own hands, in order that we may give to him who hath need, it followeth, that to work honestly is a manifest duty. For we should neither make use of religion as a pretext for idleness, nor as a means to escape labour." Basil said also, that those trades should be preferred that did not interfere with a tranquil and peaceable life, that occasioned little trouble either in preparation or disposal, that require little intercourse with others, and that did not minister to vanity. Chrysostom relates that the monks of Egypt imitated the zeal of the apostles, passing the night in sacred hymns and vigils, and the day in prayer and the work of their hands. Cassian tells us that the monks laboured in order that they might support those who were suffering from famine, and those who were in prison. Augustine records that the monks of Syria and Egypt, from the produce of their labour, sent ships laden with provisions to distressed districts. Among the trades that were followed we see smiths, weavers, builders, &c., who devoted the avails of their labour to relieve the indigent.* The followers of Anthony and Pachomius made mats and baskets. The patriarch of the western monks enjoined his followers to devote at least seven hours a day to manual labour. But this command was followed with less exactness when the circumstances of the church had become different in their character. The accession of wealth rendered labour unnecessary as the means of obtaining a subsistence; and the lower motive for its continuance having passed away, the higher one soon followed. It was seen that the monks could employ themselves more pleasantly, as well as more usefully, in literary pursuits. The language employed in the exercises of religion had

* Neander's Life of Chrysostom, by Stapleton.

ceased to be spoken in the lands where it was once the most powerful testimony to the greatness of the Roman power; and even in Rome itself it was fast giving way to the mellifluous dialect by which it was succeeded. The priests of Budha have never exercised any trade, or become artisans. All kinds of manual labour, except agriculture, are regarded in the east with great contempt; and it would be far easier to persuade men of the higher castes to undergo a severe penance, than to induce them to saw a plank, or forge a nail, or weave a web. The sacred books being written in Pali, the same necessity existed among the sramanas to study this language that there was among the monks relative to Latin; and the assiduity with which they have set themselves to this task is seen in the number and extent of the grammars they have written, and in the glosses and comments by which they have explained the text of their scriptures. The obligation they are under to seek their food by carrying the alms-bowl from door to door, frequently gives employment to nearly the whole of the morning; and they afterwards teach the novices or write books upon the leaf of the talipot. In the practice of medicine they sometimes employ their time to a good purpose, though this course is not sanctioned by the institute. From some of the employments that engaged the attention of at least the higher orders of the monastic fraternity the priests of Budha are entirely free. The yellow robe has never been covered by the coat of mail, nor has the voice of the sramana been heard amidst the din of the battle. In 1075, William the Conqueror ordained that no abbot should judge any man to the loss of life or limb, or give his vote or countenance to any others for that purpose; but in 1264, sixty-four abbots and thirty-six priors sat in the English parliament.* The disciples of Gótama have sometimes been engaged in intrigues, both at the court of the monarch and at the hall of justice; but they have never become judges or legislators. In their temples there are no chantries, "instituted and endowed with possessions, that masse might there bee songe for the sowle of the founders and their kindred," nor were lands ever granted to them "to saye masse and oder service for ever, for ye (donor's) sowle and for fader and moder, and for all christen sowles."

Relative to diet, there was also considerable diversity of practice. By some orders animal food was entirely prohibited, whilst the

* Burton's Monasticon. Taylor's Index Monasticus.

excess of good cheer enjoyed by others of the monks brought the system into general disrepute. Even in the same age the monks of one country differed from those of another in their dietetic observances. When in Wittemberg, the usual food of Luther and his brethren was bread and herrings; but when he arrived on the banks of the Po, in his journey towards Rome, the consequences of which were so momentous, he beheld the table at the Benedictine monastery covered with every delicacy; and though he said indignantly that the church and the pope had forbidden such things, his reproof produced no reformation. The average consumption of food in the abbey of Whalley, when in the zenith of its prosperity, was 200 quarters of wheat, 150 quarters of malt, 8 pipes of wine, 132 oxen and cows, 120 sheep, 60 calves, and 30 lambs, three-fifths of which appear to have been expended at the abbot's table, and two-fifths at the inferior tables and in alms-deeds. The resident population of the monastery amounted to 120 souls, exclusive of visitors and mendicants, who were daily partakers of the monastic hospitality. In 1381, the estabishment at Sallay abbey consumed 70 head of cattle annually, or nearly a beast to every person. The establishment at Bolton consisted of a prior, 15 canons and 2 conversi, besides certain armigeri; 30 free servants inter curiam, from 70 to 80 servants extra curiam, and a number of domestic slaves, of whom more than 20 must have been attached to the abbot; in all more than 200 persons. In one year they consumed, wheat flour, 319 quarters; barley meal, 112 quarters; oatmeal for pottage, 80 quarters, and for dogs, 39 quarters; provender for horses, 411 quarters; oats malted for ale, 636 quarters; barley, 80 quarters. Besides venison, fish, poultry, &c., they slaughtered annually 64 oxen, 35 cows, 1 steer, 140 sheep, and 69 pigs; and consumed 113 stones of butter; with spiceries in abundance, viz. 200 lb. almonds, 72 lb. rice (for which 9*s.* were paid), 19 lb. pepper (for which 21*s.* 7*d.* were paid), 4 lb. saffron, 25 lb. cummin, maces 1 quartern, figs and raisins 1 rase. And in one year they purchased 1800 gallons, or at least 8000 bottles of wine.* Were a bill of fare to be presented from any of the eastern pansals, though it were one in which the priests were not remarkable for their abstemiousness, it would bear a very different aspect, as its items would be almost exclusively confined to rice, fruit, vegetables, and spices. But we are not from this to argue their superior sanctity, as little

* Whitaker's Histories of Whalley and Craven.

else than vegetable aliment is used by the people among whom they live.

In other arrangements there has been a greater similarity among the laws and customs of the different orders of ascetics.

The Pythagoreans were commanded, before they arose in the morning, to call to mind the actions of the previous day. They were to try to remember the first action of the day, and then to go on through each succeeding period; and to call to mind the nature of the conversations they had held, and with what persons. Upon many of the monks a similar exercise was imposed; and the novices among the Budhists are enjoined to be very particular in their attention to this duty. Ephrem, of Edessa, advised his disciples to examine themselves strictly every morning and night, as the trader casts up his losses and gains. But the disciples of Gótama have no acts of worship similar to the canonical hours of the monks, as in the rule of Benedict,* who, in allusion to Psalm cxix. 62, 164, appointed the horae canonicae to be the nocturnae vigilae, matutinae, tertia, sexta, nona, vespera, and completorium.

In the fourth century the *βοσκοι* are mentioned as wandering about in companies. About 360, the Messalians appeared, wandering beggars, who imagined that prayer alone was necessary for the blotting out of sin, and despised all public worship. Benedict mentions (Reg. c. 1) a kind of monks called Gyrovagi, "semper vagi et nunquam stabiles," who committed great excesses; and says that it is better to be silent about them than to speak of their iniquities. They were worse than the Sarabitae, who are mentioned by Jerome (Ep. 22) in terms similar to those usually employed in describing pretenders to piety; he tells of their "coarse garments and abundant sighs," not forgetting "the detraction of the clergy." Both monks and nuns are mentioned by Augustine (De Opere Monach. c. 28) as leading an unsettled life, at one time stationary, and at another wandering; some sold the relics of martyrs, and others imitated the Pharisees in the ostentation of their dress.† It was not unusual with the monks of the middle ages to travel even to distant countries, with the professed object of finding a suitable place in which to live secluded from the world; but in many instances it was the mere love of adventure that led to these perilous

* Giesler's Text-Book.

† Hospin de Monachis. Riddle's Ecclesiastical Antiquities.

wanderings. There is extant a poem called the pilgrimage of St. Brandon. This ecclesiastic, with a number of monks, set out in quest of a place of retirement, where they could carry on their devotions unmolested. In the course of their memorable voyage they visited an island supposed to be one of the Canaries. Among the Mahomedans there are itinerant dervishes, Sayyat, the most remarkable of whom are the Calendars, who are bound not to remain long in one place. Many attempts were made to check the wandering propensities of the monks. By both popes and synods they were forbidden to leave the monastery without the abbot's consent, or to ramble from one monastery to another. In 1478, thirty-one monks were allowed to make excursions from the abbey of Whalley; and in 1521, only five, on account of the expense. They were also charged not to leave the congregation to which they belonged, and out of vanity or ambition to seek a new cell, or commence a fraternity. In some instances there was a communion of privilege between different monasteries, as between those of Malmsbury and Evesham, by virtue of which, if any one, by the suggestion of the devil or his own depraved will, should leave his proper residence without leave of absence, he was to be allowed refuge in the other; and if he afterwards repented and made satisfaction, he might be reconciled to his own foundation and restored to it, unless his fault were such as deserved deprivation." * It was natural for them to wish to indulge their curiosity relative to the world without; and to preserve them in patient obedience to the ordinations of restraint was a work of difficulty. It is said, in a petition presented to Henry VI. by the monks of Whalley, that "dyvers that been anchores and recluses aforetime contrary to theyre own oth and professyon have broken owte of the plase where they are reclusyd and departyd therefrom wythout any reconsilyation;" and they especially complain of one Isold of Heton, who was not "willyng nor entendyng to be restoryd agayn, and so livyng at her own liberte by this two yere, and more like as she had never bin professyd." † Among the injunctions to the nuns of Nun Appleton, in 1489, were these: that none of the sisters use the ale-house, or the water-side, where the course of strangers daily resort; and that "the prioress license no sister to go a pilgrimage, or visit their friends, without a great cause, and then to have a companion." ‡ In some

* Tindal's History of Evesham. † Whitaker's Whalley.
‡ Burton's Monast. Ebor.

instances, however, the opposite principle was carried to extravagance. Speed and Stow relate that at the burning of the city of Meux, by William the Conqueror, there was an anchorite residing within the walls of the Church of Our Lady, who preferred to suffer martyrdom, rather than break the vow he had made never to quit the place of his retirement.*

In the earlier records of the Budhists there are frequent instances of large numbers of priests wandering about from place to place, generally in search of some convenient spot in which to perform the ceremonies of their religion that require solitude and seclusion for their proper exercise. The spread of Budhism into different countries was facilitated by this spirit of restlessness, and it would appear that some of the regions that are situated at a distance from the birth-place of Gótama are indebted to it for their knowledge of his doctrines. To the travels of Fa Hian we have frequently had to refer. Accompanied at first by a number of companions, but afterwards permitted to pursue his journey alone, he travelled about 1200 leagues by land, and more than 2000 by sea, and visited thirty kingdoms. In 502, Soung-yun and Hoeï-seng traversed many of the same regions, and about a century afterwards Hinan thsang visited almost every part of India. In 964, the emperor of China sent forth 300 priests to collect relics of Budha and copies of the sacred books.† From other countries similar pilgrimages have been commenced, and embassies of almost equal magnitude have been undertaken. Yet the priests have not been prompted to these extended wanderings by the restraints of the wihára, as they are under an obligation to pass its limits every day, and they may be seen abroad at almost all hours. I have sometimes been visited by them at night; but it was regarded as contrary to rule to be absent from the monastery at such a time, unless it were for the purpose of reading bana upon some public occasion. "The intimate connection," says Humboldt, in his Cosmos, "which existed amongst the different Budhist sacerdotal establishments contributed its influence to diffuse a great variety of vegetable forms. Temples, cloisters, and burying-places were surrounded by gardens, adorned with exotic trees, and covered by variegated flowers of different forms. Indian plants were early diffused over China, Corea, and

* Taylor's Index.

† Sykes's Notes on the State of Ancient India, Journal Royal As. Soc. No. xii.

Nisson. Siebold was the first to draw attention to the cause of the mixture of the flowers of remotely separated Budhist lands." This interesting result is strictly in accordance with the habitudes of the priests, in all ages of which we have any record; and if the native works were more specific in details of a similar kind, it is probable that we should be able to trace many other existing affinities to the same source.

When the Hindu yogis are about to perform dhyána, they are in the first instance to reduce the appetites of the body by medicines. I have not met with any custom of this kind in the works I have read, as practised by the Budhists. There are many regulations relative to the sick diet of the priest; but they are to be observed in times of disease, and not as a moral appliance. The spare food of the priests, and their rule not to eat anything solid after mid-day (though liquids may be taken without a breach of the command), preserves them in the enjoyment of health, and they frequently live to a great age. But in the west there has been a greater tendency towards the practice of the Hindus, rendered necessary, we may suppose, by the gross diet and uncleanly habits of many of the monks. The monks of Citeaux were obliged to submit to a regular bleeding, in February, April, June, and September, for the purpose of subduing the flesh more effectually; and the sum of £6 18*s*. in silver money was granted to the monastery at Evesham to be annually and for ever divided among those monks "who are let blood, for defraying their expences in blood-letting." *

In nearly all the monastic orders, to whatever religion they may belong, there are persons of various grades, upon whom obligations are enforced in proportion to the sanctity of the class. In some orders, as in the tertius ordo de Paenitentia of Francis, there were members who observed the rules without withdrawing from the world. In the monasteries there were monachi laici, who formed a middle order between the clergy and laity, the position in which the monks themselves stood until the tenth century. Even after the monks received ordination, the distinction was kept up with the utmost strictness between the regulares and the clerici saeculares, who were priests with the cure of souls. Stephen, a nobleman of Auvergne, instituted a new species of monastic discipline in 1073. His followers were divided into two classes, clerks and converted brethren, upon the former of whom he imposed the observ-

* Neander's Bernard. Tindal's History of Evesham.

ance of an uninterrupted silence. Attached to the more celebrated orders there were individuals called fratres adscripti, among whom were many nobles, and even monarchs, who thereby received the right to assume the monkish habit at the approach of death. The Jesuits, after a noviciate of two years, take the simple vow of scholars, binding themselves to chastity, poverty, and obedience, in the presence of the domestics of the establishment in which they reside. The professed Jesuits, when their studies are completed, make their vows again, in public, after which they cannot be dismissed but by the order. There is another vow, to undertake any mission enjoined by the pope, which is taken by some, but is not binding upon all; in this case they are called spiritual coadjutors; but when the fourth vow is not taken, temporal coadjutors.* In Budhism there are properly only the sámanéra novices and the upasampadá priests. All are required to observe the ten obligations and the precepts of the Pátimokkhan; but in addition to these, there is a great multitude of observances that are represented rather as being beneficial than as absolutely binding; and as each individual is permitted to practise as many of them as he chooses, there may be an almost endless variety of classes. It was the adopting of a distinction of this kind that first led to the idea that there are gradations of merit in the church, which was followed by the still more fatal error of works of supererogation.

The exhibition of a republican spirit is another feature in which nearly all orders of monks are agreed. The doors of the monastery have ever been open to all who were willing to enter; and from the aids presented by the system, many a low-born peasant has worked his way to the honours of the abbacy or the episcopate. By the rule of Benedict, the superior of each monastery was chosen by the suffrages of its inmates. In the establishments belonging to this order no distinction was shown to the novices or monks on account of birth or rank; all the residents were equally required to practise the severities of the rule, and take their share in manual labour. It was the granting of exemptions to respectable individuals, under the pretence of health, that first caused a relaxation of monastic discipline. The monks of La Trappe not only obey the superiors, but also the lay brethren, although they know that they are in the wrong. Thus, a monk having an imperfect model set before him that he was to copy, followed the model implicitly, though he knew

* Alban Butler's Lives.

that by so doing he set the music of all the church books wrong. The abbot of Evesham was required to preserve entire the number of monks, and was neither to receive nor to reject any one, either for a time or for a perpetuity, without consent of the convent, or of its greater and wiser part, assembled in chapter; nor was he to confer any estates, or dismiss the tenants and husbandmen, without the consent of his brethren. The same principle is acknowledged in India. The missionary Rhenius says in his Journal, "There are four candidates for the office of high-priest (among the Jainas); one of whom the people are now assembling to elect. This election of priests by the majority of voices, is a curious circumstance. The Jainas appear to be thorough republicans, not in religious matters only, but also in civil." Among the Budhists there is an almost unlimited admission of postulants; nor are any to be rejected, unless, as we have noticed, the candidate be deformed, diseased, or the servant of another. When admission has been obtained, and the rite of ordination been passed through, there is perfect equality among all the members, as regards the reception of privilege and the exercise of power. It was a mighty achievement that was accomplished by Gótama, when in India, where the fetters of caste are riveted with the greatest strength, he successfully instituted an order that sets its restraints at open defiance, and joined the rája, the brahman, the sudra, and the outcaste, in one common brotherhood. Among the persons who were first admitted to the priesthood by Gótama, according to an ancient legend, were several princes of high rank. Upon a festive occasion they stole away to a private place, having previously agreed upon the course they would pursue, and taking off their ornaments gave them to the barber Upáli.* The barber reflected that if it would be a gain to the princes to become recluses, it must be a much greater advantage to him to embrace the same mode of life; and he at once resolved to follow their example. The princes consented that he should accompany them, and when they came to the village in which Budha was residing at the time, they requested, as a mark of their sincerity, that the barber should be ordained first. They thought that, as they would have to worship him because of his prior admission, their return to the world would be thereby prevented, as it would be impossible for them to brave the ridicule of

* The barber afterwards became a priest of some consequence, as will be seen by a reference to pages 175 and 336.

their relatives, who in that case would say, "What, is it you who worshipped the barber?" Budha approving of their design, the barber was admitted first to ordination, and was worshipped by the princes.*

There is no order among the Budhists distinct from that of the presbytery, the sangha being a congregation of théros, or elders, presided over by a moderator, who is strictly primus inter pares. Whilst maintaining the necessity of a succession, the power is regarded as being resident in the association, and not in the individual. The idea of a succession is not lightly treated by the Budhists, inasmuch as they consider that there can be no true sangha unless its members have been admitted to the order by a previous sangha, of legal constitution; and carrying back the same thought another step, they do not consider any sangha to be legally constituted, unless there has been, in the same manner, a succession of regular appointments, from the commencement of the order. When in any country the succession has been lost, no attempt has been made to create a spontaneous sangha. When better times have come, application has been made to some other country for a renewal of the authority. And even when certain classes have been illegally shut out from the reception of the order, they have in no instance that has come under my notice regarded themselves as forming a perfect church, until the succession was legally received. The confession of sin being made to the priests when assembled in chapter, and not to an individual, is another proof of the popular spirit that runs through the system. It is also worthy of remark, that if all the priests in any given temple or district, though regularly ordained, were to be guilty of some misdemeanour requiring absolution, it would be out of their power to hold a legal sangha, until they had been absolved by some priest who was free from the same impediment; and although the absolving priest were to be guilty of some other, and even greater misdemeanour, it would be no bar to his exercise of the power of absolution. In the ancient church confession was made openly to the whole assembly of the faithful; but as this course led to great evils, the power to receive confession was confined to the clergy, by which the exercise of discipline was in time perverted from its legitimate uses. The struggle

* Pújáwaliya. I omitted to say, in the fifth chapter, that when any one was admitted to the priesthood by Gótama, he simply said, "Come hither, mendicant!"

for superiority that we see among all classes of men was exhibited in this particular. After the commencement of the mendicant orders, a controversy arose as to whether it was lawful to confess to any other than the parish priest, as it was declared by many that even the pope himself had not this power without the priest's consent. But Boniface VIII. decreed that application should be made to the bishop, when it was desirable that any friar should administer the sacrament of penance; and if the bishop refused the request, application might be made to the pope, who, if he thought fit, might grant it "by the plenitude of his power."

Among all ascetics there is a tendency to superstition, which in weaker minds generates the consequences that arise from melancholy and fear, and leads stronger or more daring minds to form unwarranted assumptions relative to the powers that may be acquired by means of the privileges of their position. When a schoolboy I had sometimes to pass the abbey of Kirkstall, at night, and alone; and from the impression then made upon my mind, I can easily suppose in what manner the ancient monasteries might become the birth-place of unearthly imaginations and supposed supernatural appearances. There would be the hooting of owls, the beating of the air by the bat's broad wing, and the cry of the rook as the blast of the storm shook the tree to which its nest was attached; noises would be heard in every part of the edifice, now in the roof, and now in the crypt, as the wind rushed through the apertures of the tower and along the aisles; the passage from the dormitory to the chapel, when the monk was just aroused from sleep, and then the wild appearance and tremulous intonations of some of the more fervent of the brethren, would render him susceptible of the most agitating impressions; the images and pictures of the saints would sometimes seem to smile, and at other times to weep, as the moonbeam or the dim light from the waxen taper fell upon their features; when the banners above were moved by the breeze, it would seem like the rushing of the wings of spirits come to watch them at their orisons; in instances not a few, deeds of darkness would have been done by one or other of the inmates, or upon the same spot; near the altar would be relics; the monuments upon the walls would tell that the dead were near, and the cemetery would add its associations to increase the force of these terrors. By these agencies the imagination would be most powerfully wrought upon; whilst in such places there would be little of the light of science or of scriptural truth to prove the unreality of the fears that had been raised; and in the silence and solitude of the cloister ample time would be afforded for dwelling upon these ideas in their sternest form. To many of these phantoms the recluse of the forest is a stranger; but there is no scene upon earth that the darkness cannot people with "the children of an idle brain." Abroad there may be the screaming of the bird of prey, the roar of the wild beast, as he seeks his victim or rejoices in its blood, and the mystic voice of the waterfall; and in the shade of the rock, or the gloom of the cave, when the silence is broken only by the dull fall of the water-drop that has percolated through the roof, or the overhanging branches assume to themselves shapes of gibe and threat as they wave in the breeze, the spirit of even the bravest will not be entirely unmoved. The trees too have a voice, only to be equalled in its terribleness by the ocean's roar; and there are times when the storm seems to stir the very depths of the forest in its anger, and every blast is like the shout of defiance from some invisible power preparing itself for the fatal onslaught.

But in India an influence is presented that can exist in no other region of the world to the same extent; and it is this that gives to the asceticism of the Hindus a congruity, and invests it with a dignity that cannot be obtained in other lands. The warmth of the climate enables the recluse to remain abroad nearly the whole of the year with comparatively little inconvenience. Other associations are produced besides those that turn the mind back upon itself, and make its thinkings an eating into its own vitality. The smile of the moon, the twinkling of the stars, the span of the rainbow, and the gathering of the clouds, seem here to assume even more than their wonted magnificence. It is unnecessary to state, that in many places the expanse of the horizon is almost limitless to the east, the west, and the south; and that towards the north it is bounded only by the most sublime range of mountains upon which the eye of man ever rested. We may learn from Humboldt the nature of the inspiration inhaled in such a scene. It was when wandering "amidst the Alpine landscapes of tropical America and the dreary steppe-lands of Northern Asia," that the mind of this great man, whose science I venerate, but over whose religious sentiments I deeply mourn, was led to determine to write a work that should elaborate his view of created things, whether on earth or in celestial space. We need not wonder, therefore, at the vastness of the ideas presented in the religious systems that have emanted from India. The starveling recluse of Europe bears a similar relation to his elder brother of India, that the stunted exotic does to the gigantic tree in its primitive forest, rich in foliage, but wanton in its wildness and terrible in the majesty of its presence.

To aid in the perfecting of a system like that of the Vedas or the Pitakas, India presents other advantages. The system of caste, with all its evils, has had one favourable result; it has prevented much bloodshed. The people of the lower castes are comparatively indifferent as to what government they live under; if it be beneficent, it brings to them no boon; if it be oppressive, no additional curse. The village in which they reside is frequently surrounded by the abodes of men of other castes, with whom they have little intercourse; and political intrigue is no more to them than to the timid fawn that crosses their pathway as they traverse the forest. The great events of the age are disregarded, or perhaps entirely unknown. It is recorded of India, by Robertson, that whilst hostile armies have been fighting a battle in one field, the peasants of the country have been ploughing or reaping in the next field. This statement is not to be received literally, but in its main features it agrees with fact, and confirms the view I have given of the social position of the Hindus. The yogi, in consequence, lives within a world of his own; the aspirations that have been awoke within him are the result of his own thoughts, and he gives them to one single object. Robert Hall says, that "the power of fixing the attention is the most precious of the intellectual habits;" and it has been said by Archimedes, that "he had the power and habit of intense and persevering thought, without which other intellectual gifts are comparatively useless." For the acquirement of this power of mental insulation the Hindu has pre-eminent advantages; and his thinkings have an intensity, a continuity, and an amplitude that are peculiar to himself. Were he willing to set out from some simple truth as the starting point, and then to pass on by regular induction to other truths, his uninterruptedness of thought might lead to results of unspeakable benefit to mankind; but instead of this, he lets his imagination only take wing, and bids all his other faculties remain in abeyance that they may silently watch its flight into the outer darkness.

It was from these causes that the extravagance of pretension put forth by the Hindus originated. "According to the Sánkya system," we are told by Colebrooke,* "power is eight-fold: consisting in the faculty of shrinking into a minute form, to which everything is pervious; or enlarging to a gigantic body; or assuming levity (rising along a sunbeam to the solar orb); or possessing unlimited reach of organs (as touching the moon with the tip of a finger); or irresistible will (for instance, sinking into the earth, as easily as in water); dominion over all beings, animate or inanimate; faculty of changing the course of nature; ability to accomplish anything desired. . . . . .One of the four chapters of Patanjali's Yóga-sastra (the third) relates almost exclusively to this subject, from which it takes its title. It is full of directions for mental and bodily exercises, consisting of intensely profound meditation on special topics, accompanied by suppression of breath and restraint of the senses, while steadily maintaining prescribed postures. By such exercises, the adept acquires the knowledge of everything past and future; remote or hidden; he divines the thoughts of others; gains the strength of an elephant, the courage of a lion, and the swiftness of the wind: flies in the air, floats in the water, dives into the earth, contemplates all worlds at one glance, and performs other strange feats." The powers attributed to the rahats are equally wonderful; far greater than any that the wizards, the sorcerers, or the genii of other lands have dared to assume; and the silent abstraction of the sage is more potent than all the circles, rings, spells, incantations, and talismans by which man has endeavoured to control the invisible world. The Greeks who like Orpheus visited Hades, were either themselves divine, or were specially assisted by some divinity. It is said of Melampus † that one day when he was asleep under an oak tree, some serpents came and cleansed his ears with their tongues; and when he awoke, he was surprised to find that he could understand the language of birds, and knew all the secrets of nature: but his powers would not be regarded as at all wonderful in India. The miracles attributed to Apollonius Tyaenus were of a similar character. He knew the language of birds, and could render himself invisible, evoke departed spirits, utter predictions, and discover the thoughts of other men; but in the fables that are related of him, it is said that he was an incarnation of the god Proteus, or that his supernatural powers were

* Miscellaneous Essays, i. 251.
† Thirlwall's and Grote's Histories of Greece.

imparted to him by the good spirits with whom he held communion.* The power to become invisible has been pretended to by the Basilidians, the Cabbalists, and many others; but as in the case of Gyges, it is usually attached to a ring or some other object.

A rite bearing some resemblance to the kasina of the Budhists was practised by the Romans. Theodorus, the secretary of Valens, having had a tripod erected for him by the soothsayer (Zosim. iv. 13) which was so contrived as to exhibit the letters of the alphabet, saw in the magic circle the characters Θ. E. O. Δ.; from which he supposed that he was destined to wear the imperial purple. The Arabs had a gem of crystal, to which they ascribed many wonderful properties, as they supposed that they could behold in it any scene whatever that they wished to witness. The astrologers of England, in the time of their ascendancy, made great use of these gems; and even in our own day attempts have been made to impose upon the credulity of the public by men who have pretended to the possession of similar assistances. In Thompson's Castle of Indolence,

> "One great amusement of their household was,
> In a huge crystal magic globe to spy,
> Still as you turn'd it, all things that do pass
> Upon this ant-hill earth."

The hydromancy of the Greeks differs from ápo-kasina, as the mirror they made use of was not still water, but the eddy of the whirlpool, into which a stream was continually falling. The Jews, Arabs, and Syrians had a similar superstition, as they also were accustomed to look into the basin of rocky pools in order to discover hidden events; and the pool called the Devil's Glen, in the county of Wicklow, is an evidence that even nearer home the circular cavity made by the rush of the cataract is regarded as a spot where spirits love to sport.

The miracles attributed to the saints approach more closely towards the wonders of the east; but even these venerated personages must yield the palm of power to the Hindu sages; and the common events that are recorded of them, such as the speed of Paulus, when, by a divine energy "he flew like a bird to inter the body of Anthony;"—the preservation of Martin when he lay down in the midst of the flames that he might extinguish the fire that had kindled around him in the night;—the walking upon water by Marus when he went to save his fellow-monk, Placidius, who had

* Encyclopædia Metropolitana, x.

fallen into a lake;—the finding of the key at Rome, by his own servant, in the belly of a fish, with which Egwin, first abbot of Evesham, locked his fetters, and then threw into the Avon, saying that they should not be unlocked except by that very key, or by divine inspiration;—or even the raising of Peter to life by Stanislas, when it was disputed whether the said Peter, previous to his death, had given his lands to the church; *—are not worthy to be named as wonders in the presence of the rishi or the rahat.

In the lives of the saints there are, however, several relations so strikingly similar to the effects ascribed to udwéga-priti, page 272, that the coincidence is worthy of remark. When James of Sclavonia was once at prayer, he was seen by a fellow-friar to be raised in body from the ground. Philip Neri was sometimes seen raised from the ground during his devotions, at which time his countenance appeared shining with a bright light. Ignatius Loyola was sometimes seen raised in prayer two feet above the ground. Teresa was subject to similar elevations, though she endeavoured to resist them. The same occurrence is related of Dominic, Dunstan, Cajetan, and many others. Richard, chancellor to Edmond, archbishop of Canterbury, one day opening softly the chapel door, saw the prelate raised high in the air, with his knees bent, and his arms stretched out. Calmet knew more than one saint who was sometimes involuntarily raised in the air, and remained hanging in it without any support.† But these saints, as well as the Greek sophist, Eunapius, of whom the same story is told, were only raised a few feet from the ground, and did not pass through the air like the disciples of Gótama, that they might visit other worlds.

It is well, when examining an error, however absurd it may be, to try to discover the truth from which it may have originated. The germ of ascetic pretension seems to lie in the simple fact, that a temperate mode of living renders the mind clearer in its perceptions, more capable of continued thought, and more energetic in the exercise of its will. Hence the supposition that if abstemiousness be carried to its utmost limit, and other analogous appliances are added, the mind will become omniscient in its power to know, and omnipotent in its power to act. By Schlegel it is called "a species of arrogated omnipotence," "the self-potency of obstinate and tenacious thought." It has been said,‡ that it is one of the maxims of

* Alban Butler's Lives. Bibliotheca Sacra. Tindal's History of Evesham.
† Alban Butler, April 20, May 26. ‡ Mosheim's Ecclesiastical History.

ancient philosophy, that "in order to the attainment of true felicity and communion with God, it was necessary that the soul should be separated from the body, even here below, and that the body was to be mortified and macerated for this purpose." And it has been said again,* that the Grecian philosophers taught, that "the end of philosophy is to free the mind from encumbrances, which hinder its progress towards perfection, and to raise it to the contemplation of immutable truth;" and to "disengage it from all animal passions, that it may rise above sensible objects to the contemplation of the world of intelligence."

The philosopher and the ascetic here yield to a common impulse. Of Epimenides, who was regarded as "a purifying priest of superhuman knowledge and wisdom," it is reported that he received his food in a supernatural manner, and that his soul could leave the body at any time he wished, and be made to return to it again.† Empedocles, who flourished soon after Gótama Budha, said of himself, that he was "an immortal god, and no longer a mortal man." He celebrated the religion of some one (though it was not known to whom he referred, whether Pythagoras or Parmenides), who, "possessed of the richest mental and intellectual treasures, easily perceived everything in all nature, whenever with the full energy of his mind he attempted to do so," and he made a distinction between "knowledge obtained through the senses and knowledge obtained through reason," saying "that we are not to trust to our eyes or ears, or any part of our body, but to aim at a knowledge of things by thought."‡ Epicurus, who lived about a century after Empedocles, asserted that he was perfectly independent of all his predecessors, and prided himself upon being, as we have said of Gótama, αὐτοδιδακτος; he asserted that the criteria which guided him in his search after truth were derived "from sensuous perceptions combined with thought and reflection." § It was fabled of Democritus that he blinded himself in order that his mental vision might be rendered more clear and acute; but although the necessity of deep thought was thus acknowledged, yet knowledge derived from reason was not, in his opinion, specifically different from that acquired by the senses.‖ The philosophy of Plato, upon these subjects, partakes much less of an oriental character. He taught

* Enfield's History of Philosophy.
† Professor Adolf Stahr; Smith's Biographical Dictionary.
‡ Professor Brandis. § Dr. Schmitz. ‖ Adolf Stahr.

that "philosophy springs from the impulse *to know;*" but in what he said * relative to self-intellection, the sources of our knowledge, "the impulse to become like the Eternal," and the nature of the soul, "that it is not an harmonious union and tuning of the constituents of the body," he was opposed to the system of Gótama.

The systems of the philosophers who appeared after the introduction of Christianity into the world exhibit more clearly the ascetic element, in its self-confidence and claim to subjective potency. In the system taught by Ammonius Saccas it is declared that "faith is derived from inward perception," and that by the practice of an austere discipline it is possible so to refine the faculty of the mind that receives the images of things as to render it capable of holding communion with invisible spirits and of performing miracles by their assistance.† Plotinus, the originator of the new Platonic system, who had joined the expedition of Gordian into the east that he might learn the philosophy of Persia and India, believed, it is said, in the power of calling up spirits by intense meditation, and of working upon them at a distance by magic. When invited by Amulius to join with him in a sacrifice he said, "those gods of yours must come to me, not me to them." Porphyry asserts that during his own intercourse with him he had, "by a transcendant energy of soul," four times risen to a perfect union with God. He taught that the soul, "by virtue of its innate intuition, can explain the hidden fulness of the original being, and by virtue of its peculiar striving can get it, as it were, out of itself, and so separate in itself the soul and the spirit." ‡ "Unconditioned Being, or the Godhead," he said, "cannot be grasped by thinking or science, only by intuition." The word here rendered intuition is by G. H. Lewes called immediate presence. "To attempt to know the Infinite by reason is futile; it can only be known in immediate presence, *παρουσια*. The faculty by which the mind divests itself of its personality is ecstacy. In this ecstacy the soul becomes loosened from its material prison, separated from individual consciousness, and becomes absorbed in the infinite Intelligence from which it emanated. In this ecstacy it contemplates real existence; it identifies itself with that which it contemplates." As to the means by which this state of mind is to be obtained, it is said that "everything which purifies the soul, and makes it resemble its primal simplicity,

* Charles Peter Mason. † Mosheim's Ecclesiastical History.
‡ Professor Brandis.

is capable of conducting it to ecstacy."* It was said also by Origen, who had attended the lectures of Ammonius Saccas, that "human souls were originally altogether of a similar frame with all higher spirits;" and that "it is the destiny of the soul that it should, being purified, again raise itself up to that life, in the pure immediate intuition of God."†

The Gnostics joined together the old oriental system, the Platonic, and the new Platonic. In this heresy there are many divisions, but nearly all its disciples appear to have the same end in view, "by searching to find out God;" but their wanderings too frequently end in an opposite result. As they cannot in this manner discover the Infinite, they put themselves in the place of God, and dream away existence in the vain thought that by austerities and exercises of the intellect they have attained to a participation in divinity. The Gnostic believed himself to be "neither in heaven nor on earth, but to have entered into the pleroma;" he was better according to his own account, "not only than all men, but than all gods." Basilides, one of the most eminent of the Gnostics, taught that the faith of the elect finds out doctrines without any demonstration, by means of a spiritual comprehension, or intellectual sight. In Montanism—the founder of which exhorted Christians to a more strict ascetic life, and used to fall into a kind of transport, during which, without consciousness, but as the passive influence of a higher power, he made oracular announcements—we have another exhibition of the same principle.‡ The Montanists bear a nearer resemblance to the Brahmans, and the Gnostics to the Budhists, of India.

The next apparition of these ever-living principles was among the schoolmen. We can discover the same features, though the tones of the voice are a little varied, and a much greater deference is paid to the word of God. As one development after another passes in review, the general resemblance is so striking as to make us ask, for the moment, if the doctrine of transmigration be not true. Even after mature thought we are led to the conclusion that the tenet is at least founded upon fact. There is a metempsychosis of the errors that are generated from man's brain; but not of the individual generator. The disciples of Duns Scotus spoke of their great master as the Budhists had previously spoken of their greater

* Biographical History of Philosophy, by G. H. Lewes, ii. 196.
† Neander's History of the Christian Religion, ii. 300. ‡ Ibid.

Gótama; and said that he arrived at truth rather with the readiness and certainty of intuition than by the doubtful process common to other minds. The same sentiments relative to the possession of creative potency are seen in both systems. The schoolmen taught* that all the attributes of God are communicated to the creature, except the ascitas (the not having anything that comes from elsewhere), and consequently that it is possible for a creature to be eternal, à parte ante et è parte post, and infinite as to knowledge, power, local presence, justice, goodness, &c. if the argument be carried out to its legitimate conclusion. They said that by the obediential powers creatures are susceptible of the faculty of operating all sorts of miracles, and also of the power of creating. Even the oriental doctrine of absorption had a scholastic avatar. The Thomists, with whom the Scotists did not disagree on this particular, taught that the divine essence is itself immediately united to the intellect of the blessed in ratione speciei intelligibiles, so as that there is no place for any intervening likeness or representation. They assert concerning the species intelligibiles, in general, that they have not locum objecti, intellectionem terminantes; and that the understanding so acts by them, as fire by its proper form. Cajetan affirms that the intellect and the intelligible species are more one than the matter and form in the compositum: for matter is not turned into the form, nor è contra, but the intellect, which is in itself mere power, in genere intelligibili, turns into its very intelligible object; and the intelligible object itself is after a manner imbibed in the intellect. Beside this immediate union of the divine essence itself with the intellect, they assert a lumen gloriae, an accident superadded, without which the vision cannot be performed; though this addition is rejected by the Scotists. Some, though they admit it, think the vision may be without it, and that it does not imply a contradiction that there should be a beatific vision without the lumen gloriae, as it is received immediately from God. Whether there be any verbum creatum, the product of intellection, the Thomists are themselves divided. Their more common opinion is, that there is none. The principle and term of the vision of the blessed are owned to be nothing else but the simple divine essence. Concerning the formal act itself, it is much disputed, whether the creature's intellect do at all effectually concur to it, or whether God himself be not the only efficient or agent in this vision. Some do

* Bayle's Dictionary, art. Agreda.

not hesitate to affirm the latter, and say plainly, that the action of the inferior agent wholly ceases, and the superior only acts; the same thing that D. M. Casauban, in his Enthusiasm, charges Maximus with, who in a work entitled Theological Headings writes thus: that the soul taken into immediate union with God, loses all its knowing power.* Between these subtleties and the doctrine of absorption there is little difference.

Among the monks, the most learned and the most ignorant were equally in danger of trusting too much to individual illumination, derived from the exercise of silent thought: and of supposing that by meditation they could learn hidden truths, and acquire knowledge that was not to be obtained either from the word of God or any other source of general revelation. It was asserted by Bernard that what he understood of divine things, he had acquired by contemplation and prayer, especially in forests and fields, and that he had had no other teacher than beeches and oaks.* The Beguines taught that man ought to be guided more implicitly by instinctum interiorum than by evangelical truth.

In some of these speculations, more particularly of those which emanated from the Alexandrian school, we have the nucleus of much that has recently been enunciated by the German metaphysicians. That which Plotinus called ecstacy was by Schelling called intellectual intuition. "With Schelling," it is said by Morell, "the great organ of philosophy is intellectual intuition (intellectuelle anschauung), by means of which faculty, he supposes, we have an immediate knowledge of the absolute. This intellectual intuition is a kind of higher and spiritual sense, through which we feel the presence of the infinite both within and around us; moreover, it affords us a species of knowledge, which does not involve the relation of subject and object, but enables us to gaze at once by the eye of the mind upon the eternal principle itself, from which both proceed, and in which thought and existence are absolutely identical. Before the time when creation began, we may imagine that an infinite mind, an infinite essence, or an infinite thought (for here all these are one) filled the universe of space. This, then, as the self-existent One, must be the only absolute reality; all else

* Howe's Blessedness of the Righteous, cap. 3. The note whence these illustrations are taken is worthy of being examined by those who may not have other means of reference to the speculations of the schoolmen upon this subject.

† Hagenbach's History of Doctrines, by Carl W. Buch, i. 433.

can be but a developing of the one original and eternal being; and intellectual intuition is the faculty by which we rise to the perception of this, the sole ground and realistic basis of all things." "Fichte compressed everything," says Blakey, "within the ego—the human soul. This placed philosophy in a prison house; she could have no liberty nor expansive faculties. Her sphere of action must be enlarged; and for this purpose another principle must be brought into play. This principle is the intellectual intuition, by which we obtain an immediate knowledge of the absolute. This intellectual intuition is a lofty and spiritual faculty, by which we are able to recognize the infinite both within and without us; and we are thus enabled to withdraw our contemplations from the narrow and contracted circle of subject and object, and direct them to that great and all-absorbing potency, from which everything in the universe is derived. All matter and thought now lie stretched out before us; the imprisoned faculties of man are set at liberty; and we are in a position to test every power and agency in nature, and discover those relations and ties which they have with the self-existent One, who fills all space, and exists in all time. Schelling having got this new principle fairly launched, began to make active use of it. In the first place, he descanted loftily on its great dignity and importance. The intellectual intuition contained within itself the elements of its own creative energy. It was not, as some philosophers conceived, a simple substance, with the two properties of extension and thought; but an eternal, self-spontaneous, and self-developing mind; the living and perpetual vivifying soul of the universe. And we are told, moreover, that this august energy was sacred from vulgar participation; it was not to be gazed on by common mortals; it was only to be known and comprehended by the favourite few. Plotinus considered his ecstatic principle of philosophy capable of being communicated only to certain persons, and to them at uncertain intervals; so in like manner does Schelling confine the knowledge of his intuition of the absolute. It is not a mental power enjoyed by all men. Indeed it cannot be comprehended by them. And our philosopher expresses great contempt for the uninitiated, and accuses them of stupidity, for what, after all, is more their misfortune than their fault. Really we do not see, says he, why philosophy should pay any attention to incapacity. Better far that philosophy be isolated from the common routes of knowledge, so that they may not lead to it. Philosophy commences when ordinary knowledge ends." *

This is the old deception, partially modified. The evil spirit said unto man in innocence, "Ye shall be as gods;" † and unto man fallen he says, "Ye are gods." There is either in that spirit a great poverty of invention; or he knows that man is too heedless to listen to "the voice of the past," and that therefore it is not necessary for him to change his tactics. He gathers together the thickest darkness of Hades, and when he has extracted from it a still grosser residuum, he takes man into its midst, and tells him that now he is allied to infinity; he listens to the whisperings of all orders of being with whom he can hold communion, and taking a few truths and a few mystical words from each order, he mutters them to man, and tells him that he is now omniscient; he unfolds before his imagination that which he says is a world visible to none but the elect, in which all manner of energies, supernatural agencies, and creations, are exhibited; saying that *this* is the work of the initiated man, and that the perfected man has accomplished *that*, and then he concludes oracularly, "Thou art a man thus gifted; therefore, thou art omnipotent." The Brahmans have taught us an instructive lesson, the moral of which is applicable to the greater part of the tenets that have passed under our review. "Whilst Brahma formerly in the beginning of the kalpa," it is said in the Vishnu Purána, "was meditating on creation, there appeared a creation, beginning with ignorance, and consisting of darkness. From that great being appeared five-fold ignorance, consisting of tamas, obscurity; móha, delusion; tamisra, gloom; mahámoha, extreme delusion; and anhatamisra, utter darkness. They are the five kinds of obstruction, viparyyaya, of the soul's liberation, according to the Sánkhya philosophy. They are called in the Pántanjala philosophy the five afflictions, klésa, and are explained by awidya, ignorance; asmita, selfishness, literally, I-am-ness; rága, love; dwésha, hatred; and abhinivesa, dread of temporal suffering." ‡ There is this diffe-

* Blakey's History of the Philosophy of Mind, iv. 129.

† "Ye shall be as gods, *knowing* good and evil," or, "having knowledge of all kinds," as the Jews understand the passage.

> "Coveitise to konne
> And to know sciences,
> Putte out of Paradis
> Adam and Eve."—*Piers Ploughman*, l. 9724.

‡ Wilson's Vishnu Purána, p. 34.

rence between Brahma and the ascetic; the deity knew that darkness was darkness; but the ascetic takes darkness for light.

There is a sameness in the thoughts of all ages, whether we look at the legend or the myth, the offspring of man's imagination; at his ethical systems, the offspring of his conscience; or at his metaphysical speculations, the offspring of his intellect. Of the ethical and metaphysical affinities we have had a sufficiency of illustration in the preceding pages; and of the mythical, ample evidence might be adduced, were this the proper place for its presentation. Buttman has stated * that "the whole mythus of Hercules arose from the proud consciousness of power which is innate in every man, by means of which he is able to raise himself to an equality with the immortal gods, notwithstanding all the obstacles that may be placed in his way." "The similarity of the human faculty of conception," says W. von Humboldt, "leads to the same explanation of the same phenomenon; many similar myths may have very certainly risen, without historical connection, out of the similarity of man's poetical and speculative constitution." † Were it possible for a yogi and a rahat from India, a Greek philosopher from one of the schools holding the power of intuition, an ascetic from the wilds of Syria or the mountains of Egypt, a heretic from the school at Alexandria, a monk from one of the monasteries of Europe, a schoolman of the middle ages, and a modern German metaphysician of the school of Schelling to meet together; and were it possible for them to forget their sectarian subtleties and nice distinctions; they would find that there was a vast mass of speculation about the main principles of which they were agreed. They would be of one mind relative to the four following propositions. 1. That there is an objective potency of intellect. 2. That this potency can be rendered subjective by concentrated thought, ascetic exercises, or determined effort. 3. That this potency can only be acquired by the initiated. 4. That the initiated may enlarge this potency to a limitless extent. As to the efficient cause of the potency, there would be a difference of opinion; some would ascribe it to intuition alone, whilst others would attribute it to an alliance with higher spirits or with God; but of its existence there would be no doubt. From this uniformity of thought we are warranted in concluding that all men have sprung from one source, are moved by one impulse, and

* Leonard Schmitz; Smith's Biograph. Dict.
† Humboldt's Cosmos.

are subject to a control that is one in the manner of its exercise. The sameness of error may arise from the circumstance that the principles communicated to man, by his Creator, are so stern and unyielding that the powers of evil can only restrain or impel his inclinations, without being able to destroy them or alter their essential character; they can deceive man by presenting to him that which is merely a semblance of the truth, but they cannot change his homogeneity. We are also led to see that there is in all men a yearning to be delivered from the bondage of evil, either by the annihilation of existence or an union with God. "We witen," says an inspired apostle, as his words are translated by Wycliffe, "that eche creature sorwith and trauilith with peyne till yit:" Rom. viii. 22. Hence it follows, that if a remedy can be found for man's disease, it will be of universal application and efficacy. "The gospel," says the same apostle, "is the power of God unto salvation, to every one that believeth:" Rom. i. 16. Therefore, it is the duty of those who are in possession of the truth, patiently and perseveringly, with meekness, a sincere compassion, a sympathy the most tender, and thoughtful, and delicate, and a love that constantly exhibits an entire absence of I-am-ness, that it may spend and be spent for the rescue of those who are in mortal peril; to give to every man the means of reading the word of truth, and to impress its great message upon his attention. It is pleasant to think what a beautiful world ours will be, and what a noble being man will be, when these divine principles, "like a sea of glory," shall roll through every land.

The Budhists of modern times do not pretend to possess the power of working miracles, though they suppose that there are yet supernatural attestations to the truth of their system, one of which they think is presented by the appearance of what they call Budha's rays. This appearance is thus described by Dr. Davy. "There is a peculiar phenomenon," he says, "occasionally seen in the heavens, in the interior, that is deserving of notice. In January, 1820, it was witnessed in Kandy, and by European gentlemen as well as by natives. One of the former, a most respectable individual, in whose account I could put the firmest reliance, described it to me to be an appearance of rays or beams of light in motion, intersecting one another, faintly resembling the northern lights. It occurred when the atmosphere was clear, in the middle of the day, in mid-air, beneath the vault of the sky, unattended by any unusual circumstance of weather that might lead to conjectures respecting its cause and nature. The natives call it Budoo-rais (Budhoo-rays) and consider it ominous, boding ill in general, and auspicious only when it appears in the month of May. They imagine that it is never witnessed, excepting over a temple of Budhoo, from whence, as the name they have given the phenomenon implies, they suppose it to emanate."* I have been told by persons who have seen this appearance, that it is caused by the presence of masses of cobweb,† that from their lightness have been raised into the air, and there float, becoming visible when shone upon by the sun; but it is possible that it may be caused by the winged seeds that abound in some parts of the jungle, and at certain seasons are seen in great profusion, when wandering in search of a resting-place, and appearing like the tiny parachutes of some travelling fay.‡ It is somewhat singular that the rays should ever be regarded as ominous, such appearances being generally supposed to be eminently propitious in their character. They are met with among all people who are given to superstition, varying in their form with the notions of the time. Thus, it was supposed, even recently, that the lady Hilda occasionally rendered herself visible in the abbey of Whitby, where she once resided. In the summer months, in the forenoon, the sunbeams fall in the inside of the northern part of the choir, at which time those who stand on the west side of the churchyard, may imagine that they perceive, in one of the highest windows of this venerable ruin, the resemblance of a lady clothed in white. It is simply a reflection caused by the sunbeam; but it was thought to be St. Hilda, appearing in a state of glory.§

The purity of the motive professed by the monastic orders, the grandeur of the end at which they aimed, the extent of the philanthropy they have exercised, the important collateral benefits they

* Davy's Account of Ceylon, p. 71.

† No idea can be formed in England of the abundance or strength of cobwebs in a tropical country. A reverend friend of mine once excited the mirth of his brethren, in Ceylon, by telling them that he had been arrested in his course by the number of cobwebs carried across the pathway. The fact itself was not at all doubted; but the singularity of the circumstance arose from the massiness and muscle of the narrator.

‡ It is perhaps not unworthy of remark that this class of little personages, so frequently met with in western mythology, has no existence in the east. The Hindus have imagined beings that are hundreds of miles in size; but they have nothing that is wee or little.

§ Charlton's History of Whitby.

have been the means of conferring, the beauty of the localities and the splendour of the edifices in which they resided, and the great extent of the influence they once possessed, produce so powerful an effect upon the imagination, that after their progress has been traced, an intervenient pause is required, before the character of the system can be seen in the light of truth.

I am not about to pass an indiscriminate censure upon every part of the institute. It had some excellencies; under certain circumstances it presented advantages that are to be obtained from no other source; and some of its professors are worthy of all admiration for the extent of their learning, the assiduity of their labours, the disinterestedness of their exertions, the holiness of their lives, and the closeness of their walk with God. It would be a manifestation of an unwarranted one-sidedness were we to measure the primitive celibates by the standard of the present age, or to forget the peculiarities of their position. To act thus would be like examining the fire-fly under the meridian sunbeam of its native tropic, and then asserting that it emitted no light.

In order to know aright the benefit conferred upon the nations by Christianity, it would be necessary to have exhibited before our mental vision an exact picture of the moral state of the pagan world. When the child of a heathen parent enters upon the career of his existence he is assaulted by innumerable foes, as varied in their character as the avenues to his spirit by which their inroads are effected. Naturally prone to place his affections upon that which is "of the earth, earthy," he readily enters into an alliance with the evil one, and then almost every object within the circle to the limits of which he is spell-bound, becomes a power to lead him still further astray. He may watch the foam of the cataract, or admire the delicate pencilling upon the petals of the flower, or gaze upon the stars when the whole expanse of the heavens appears like one unbroken canopy of gems; but he knows not that these "declare the glory of God:" he regards them as the unlearned look upon the letters of some illuminated manuscript; they are beautiful, but without meaning. And when he turns away from the works of God to hold communion with man, the influences to which he is exposed are almost entirely adverse to his moral improvement. The exquisite taste of the Greeks and the refinement of the Romans did not exempt them from these perversions. When a youth of the seven-hilled city was in the company of his playmates, their conversation was interpolated with expressions that even the hardened libertine of a Christian land would blush to utter. When at home, the furniture of his parent's house, the pictures upon the walls, the common household utensils that he daily used, exhibited scenes the most vile and disgusting. When conversing with even the most respectable females of his acquaintance, an accident or a breeze of wind might expose ornaments they had about their persons of a shape the most grossly offensive. When passing through the street of the city his eye would oftentimes be met by the phallic symbol, with the motto, "Hic habitat felicitas;" but near it was the chamber of death. The school of the philosopher was open, but his words were clothed with no power; and who could tell, amidst the din of angry disputation, with whom was the certainty of truth? The public bath invited him to while away his time amidst the incense of its perfumes and the enervating luxuries of its numerous apartments, where he might have anything that earth could give to gratify his appetite or minister to his pleasure. The stream of population passing on with noise and jest, and all the manifestations of an intense excitement, would indicate the path to the amphitheatre; and there, amidst the dance, and the song, and the strife, he would be invited to drink more deeply of the fatal cup, until his brain throbbed, and his whole frame reeled, under the power of the maddening spell.

The white wing of the sea-bird moving beneath the blackness of the storm-fraught sky, the pearl in the ocean shell, the lotus-flower spread out in virgin purity over the mud of the morass, are emblems frequently used by the orientals to set forth the character of the virtuous man whilst living in the midst of the pollutions of the world; but the most appropriate object to which these beautiful images can be applied is the church of Christ at the period of its commencement. It is not to be wondered at that the convert from heathenism, when the light of heaven revealed to him the exceeding sinfulness of sin, rushed at once from the foul spectacle, and sought in solitude, or in communion with some kindred spirit, for that repose which was not to be found in the usual dwelling places of men. Of the sincerity of many of the earlier ascetics and later monks no one can doubt. The strong language used by Savonarola is in itself sufficient to convince us that the motive was frequently pure. On the 24th of April, 1475,* he took refuge in a

* Savonarola's Life and Times, anon.

Dominican monastery at Bologna, as a candidate for the vows. The next day he wrote a letter to his father, in which he gives his reason for the step he had taken. "The reason," says this resolute novice, "which induces me to become a monk is this: in the first place, the great wretchedness of the world, the iniquity of men, the violence, the adultery, the theft, the pride, the idolatry, the hateful blasphemy into which this age has fallen, so that one can no longer find a righteous man. For this, many times a-day, with tears, I chanted this verse, 'Heu, fuge crudeles terras, fuge litus avarum.' And this because I could not endure the great distemper of some of the people in Italy; the more also, seeing virtue extinct, ruined, and vice triumphant; this was the greatest suffering I could have in this world: therefore daily I entreated of my Lord Jesus Christ, that he would rescue me from this defilement. Continually I made my prayer with the greatest devotion, imploring God, saying, 'Show me thy path, for to thee do I lift up mine eyes.' Now God has been pleased in his infinite mercy to show it me, and I have received it, though unworthy of such grace. Answer me then, is it not worthy that a man should fly from the iniquity and filth of this wretched world, if he would live like a retired being, and not like a beast among swine? Indeed, would it not have been most ungrateful if, having asked God to show me the straight path in which I should walk, when he deigned to point it out to me I had not taken it? Oh, my Saviour, rather a thousand deaths, than that I should be so ungrateful, or so oppose thy will!" It was under circumstances of a different description that Luther resolved upon becoming a monk; but his motive was equally sincere. When on a journey to Erfurth, and not far from that city, he was overtaken by a mountain storm; the rapidity with which the pointed flame followed the thunder-crash told him that his danger was most imminent; and under the influence of the terror that arose in his mind, he knelt upon the tremulous ground, and solemnly vowed that he would abandon the world, and devote himself entirely to the service of God. Even in our own day the feeling of a similar impulse is not unfrequent. "I used often to lament," says Henry Moore, the biographer of Wesley, "that there were no Protestant monasteries; for I thought it impossible to live in the world, and be saved; and I am sure that, for several years of my youth, I would gladly have left all in the world for the hope of eternal life. Vain hope! to leave all the creatures, if that were possible, and yet retain my old, unchanged nature."* The same principle is to some extent acknowledged by some of the modern Missionary Societies, who insulate their converts from the world, that they may be preserved from the evils to which they would otherwise be exposed; with the additional advantage that they may have readier access to the means of grace, and be the more easily watched over by their pastors. The poet Cowper exclaims—

> " O for a lodge in some vast wilderness,
> Some boundless contiguity of shade!"

but it was merely that he might avoid the necessity of witnessing man's oppression of his fellow man, as he says upon another occasion,

> " Not that I mean to approve, or would enforce
> A superstitious and monastic course;
> Truth is not local, God alike pervades
> And fills the world of traffic and the shades,
> And may be fear'd amidst the busiest scenes,
> Or scorn'd when business never intervenes."

In the writings of the fathers, and of others who have come in contact with asceticism, or lived under its influence, there are passages worthy of the most enlightened mind. "The kingdom of God," says Clemens, "is not meat and drink, or a system of formal and visible observances, or of servile abstinences from ordinary enjoyments; but righteousness and peace; and it is the inner not the outward man, which God chiefly looks to." And again: "What—may not self-command be preserved under the conditions of married life? May not marriage be used, and yet continence respected, without our attempting to sever that which the Lord hath joined? . . . . The kingdom of God is not meat and drink; and in like manner as genuine humility consists in meekness of soul, not in the maceration of the body; so, and in like manner (true) continence is a virtue of the soul, and relates to that which is hidden (in the heart) not to the outward life.† . . . . Our Saviour does not command us, as many superficially suppose, to cast away our earthly property, but to banish from our souls the thoughts of money and desires after it—that sickness of the soul, the cares, the thorns, of this earthly life, which choke the seed of heavenly life. . . . . . . What is that which our Lord announces as something new, as the only source of life of which those of old knew nothing? What is this which is peculiar to him? What the

* Mrs. Smith's Life of the Rev. Henry Moore.
† Strom. lib. iii. vii. Taylor's Ancient Christianity.

new creation? He desires not that which is outward, which others have also done, but something higher, more divine, and more perfect, which is signified by this outward conduct; namely, that all which is foreign to the soul must be torn out by the roots, and banished from the soul. . . . . . For they who of old despised outward things gave away indeed their earthly goods, but they cherished within them far stronger desires; for they were filled with vanity, pride, and contempt of other men, as if they had done something above the reach of simple humanity. . . . . A man may have thrown away his earthly goods, and yet his desire for them being undiminished, he will be doubly disquieted by regret for his profusion, and by his deprivation of the necessaries of life. . . . . . How could one man impart of his goods to another, when all had nothing? And could this doctrine of our Lord escape being in contradiction with many other of his glorious doctrines? . . . The genuine Christian has the apostles for patterns; and, in fact, a man does not distinguish himself by choosing a solitary life, but he obtains a victory over other men, who stands fast as a husband and father, amidst all the trials which befall him by anxiety for wife and children, servants and fortune, without allowing himself to be withdrawn from his love to God. But he who has no household escapes many trials; as he has only himself to take care of he is below that man who, more disturbed in the care of his own individual salvation, still enters more into the intercourse of life, and really exhibits in miniature a likeness of Providence itself." * "How shall we escape our enemies," asks Chrysostom, "if some do not busy themselves about goodness at all, while those who do withdraw from the battle?" "You surely will not despise nature," says Synesius, "and pretend that, fixed to one spot, ye have the power of living solely for contemplation—as if ye were raised above all human affections—gods, only veiled in a body. Know, then, that ye are far from being gods, or even godly and wise men—rather, arrogant boasters." † In more modern times the same cautions have been given, in numerous instances. "It is not the tranquillity of the monastic solitude," says Alban Butler, "nor a distance from the busy scenes of the world, but the mastery over a man's domestic passions, and the government of his own heart, which is the source of that peace of mind which invites the Holy Spirit into a soul, and is the greatest blessing on this side heaven." And again; "The solitude that avails must be

* Neander's History of the Church, i. 313, 315.
† Neander's Chrysostom.

chiefly interior, that of the mind still more than of the place, by freeing and disengaging ourselves from worldly care and business, from the attachment to our senses, and from all those things and even thoughts, which soften, disturb, allure, or distract us, or which breed in us vanity or vexation. If we cut not off these things, under the name of retirement, we shall be more persecuted with a dissipation of thoughts, and the noise and cravings of our passions, than in the midst of the most active and busy life. How shall a Christian, who lives in the world, practise this retirement? By not loving its spirit and maxims, by being as recollected as may be in the midst of business, and bearing always in mind that salvation is the most important and only affair: by shunning superfluous amusements, and idle conversation and visits; and by consecrating every day some time, and a considerable part of Sundays and great festivals to the exercises of religious retirement, especially devout prayer, self-examination, meditation, and pious reading."

The arguments that are used in favour of the monastic institute are various; but the more powerful may be divided into two classes —those that plead for the greater *purity* of the state, and those that assert its superior *charity*. Each of these ideas is presented under two aspects; as to the effect it produces upon the monk himself, and as to the influence it exercises upon the world.

In my observations upon the superior purity that is claimed by the recluse, I am not about to rake up from their obscurity the numerous facts that prove the corruption of particular individuals or orders; but will here content myself with a passing notice of the conclusions to which men have come who have had ample opportunities to know the truth of what they affirm. Savonarola said, "The chastity of the cloister is slain." Luther speaks of "the hell of celibacy;" and on another occasion tells us that when some monks were taking a possessed man to the convent, the devil who was in him exclaimed in smooth tones, "Popule meus, quid tibi feci?" When Barromeo suppressed several monasteries in his district, he said, "Monialium non dicam collegia, sed amantium contubernia." When Sebastian Mayer, reader of the Franciscans, published a recantation of the Roman errors, he said, speaking of those who live in convents, in allusion to a passage * in Bernard: "These monks

* This passage is usually inscribed on some conspicuous part of the Cistercian houses: "Bonum est nos hic esse, quia homo vivit purius, cadit rarius, surgit velocius, incedit cautius, quiescit securius, moritur fœlicius, purgatur citius, præmiatur copiosus."—Whitaker's Whalley.

live more impurely (than other men), fall more frequently, recover themselves more tardily, walk more unsteadily, rest more unquietly, die more despairingly, are cleansed more rarely, and are condemned more severely." Nor is the vow of celibacy a whit more respected in our day, or more efficacious in its power of restraint, in those countries where the profession is the most common. A priest of Grenada stated to the Rev. J. Rule, and a numerous company of his parishioners who were present confirmed the fact, that no priest who does not steadily cohabit with a female is regarded as a man of decent moral character, unless he be aged.* The Rev. M. Hobart Seymour, in contrasting the Jesuits with the other religious orders, says: † "The others are inactive, lazy, indolent, and careless of everything. There are many exceptions—most honourable exceptions, among the members of those orders, amidst whom there are some whose activity, learning, and morals, would be an ornament to any body of men in the world; but these are too few to save the general character of the monks and friars of Rome, of the city of Rome; for those remarks are not intended to apply to those of other cities, and other lands, where I have had no means of observation. In the city of Rome the monks and friars, with the exception of the Jesuits, have no one characteristic to recommend them to the wise and good; and the absence of learning—the lazy indifference—the occasions of scandal, so unhappily characteristic of so many; has so strongly contrasted with the learning, the activity, and the moral lives of the Jesuits, that it may well be believed that the good character of one, is built in a great measure on the ill character of the others." The reformer Czerski, in a recent address to the Polish nation,‡ has dared to publish the following sentences, which would only have endamaged the cause he advocates, had they not been founded on fact. "The most ignorant peasant," he says, "of the present day, is well aware of what passes in the priest's dwelling; thoroughly understands the connexion between the saintly owner and his housekeeper; and can tell many a tale of the mysterious journeyings of the latter, and of the clerical children scattered hither and thither throughout the land, and severed from every tie of family or kindred. . . . . . Hence it is no uncommon thing to hear the laity theorising thus: It is a much easier, as well as happier, mode of life, to practise such a mode of life as the Roman priests do, than to marry; for clerical celibacy is not only the

* Rule's Mission to Gibraltar and Spain. † Mornings among the Jesuits.
‡ Evangelical Christendom, iii. 86.

most unshackled of all lives, but gives the fullest scope for enjoying the pleasures of the world. . . . . The poorest and most ignorant, when he comes out of the chapel to which habit alone attracts him, casts contemptuous and condemnatory glances on the vicarage, which he well knows to be the dwelling of vice, and shaking his head says to himself: I would not be a priest for all the ease and honour of his station. And whence this honest disgust, but from a knowledge of the vicious lives generally arising from priestly celibacy?" *

The monks, for the most part, have fewer opportunities of committing sin than the priests, from their stricter confinement, and the secrets of their prison-house may never be fully revealed until the day of eternity shall declare them; but in the lives of the ascetics disclosures are sometimes unwittingly made that bespeak the existence of a wantonness of imagination of which they who have been permitted the sanctities of marriage know nothing. Jerome had to fast whole weeks in order to overcome the assaults of the enemy; and the details of his struggles, as he carried "the miserable sack of his body" to the secret parts of the wilderness, the deep vallies, and the craggy rocks, afford a melancholy insight into the circumstances of the recluse. Even in old age it was necessary for Dorotheus, the Theban, to toil incessantly; and he would give his body no rest, saying, "This enemy would destroy me, therefore I am resolved to be beforehand with it, and keep it in subjection." Although the popes were ascustomed to excommunicate monks who appeared without their ecclesiastical dress, the same permission might in some cases be given to them that was received by the sramana; a monk might take it off "ut fureter occulto, vel fornicatur." †

The effect that is produced upon the public mind by the existence of the various orders of celibates is supposed to be eminently beneficial. "Who can measure," says the Spaniard, Balmez, "the salutary influence which the sacred ceremonies with which the Catholic church celebrates the consecration of a virgin to God must have exercised on female morals? Who can calculate the holy thoughts, the chaste inspirations which have gone forth from those silent abodes of modesty, erected sometimes in solitary places, and sometimes in crowded cities? Do you not believe that the virgin whose heart begins to be agitated by an ardent passion, that the

* It is just to add, that during a recent visit to Ireland I found that the priests were regarded as being free from the crime here charged upon their Polish brethren.

† Pascal's Provincial Letters, by Pearce, page 80.

matron who has allowed dangerous feelings to enter her soul, have not often found their passions restrained by the remembrance of a sister, of a relative, of a friend, who, in one of these silent abodes, raises her pure heart to heaven, offering as a holocaust to the Divine Son of the Blessed Virgin all the enchantments of youth and beauty? All this cannot be calculated, it is true; but this, at least, is certain, that no thought of levity, no inclination to sensuality has arisen therefrom. All this cannot be estimated; but can we estimate the salutary influence exercised by the morning dew upon plants? can we estimate the vivifying effect upon nature? and can we understand how the water which filters through the bowels of the earth fertilises it by producing fruits and flowers?"* These allusions are very poetical, but they are inaptly chosen. The nun is not like the dew of the morning, but, if pure, like the drop that is sometimes seen pent up in the crystal or gem; she is not like the light of heaven, but, if pure, like the solitary flame that guides the workman through the intricacies of the mine, unseen by all but himself, and except to him of no further benefit; she is not like the water that steals imperceptibly from cell to cell that it may give life to the lily or expansion to the rosebud, but, if pure, like the water of the tank or the pool in the deep glen, that the breeze or the sunshine can scarcely reach, and that slakes not the thirst of any living thing. We fear that the situatión of the recluse will rather be regarded as an expression of hopelessness or weakness. They who are at liberty will argue thus: If my friend had not known that it would be utterly impossible to preserve her purity whilst living in the world, she would not have abandoned it, and deprived us of the privilege of her presence. What am I, that I should hope to do better? I can only resign myself to my fate.—The state of morals in those countries where convents most abound is a sad comment upon the beautiful imagery of the Spaniard. Were his conclusions fortified by fact, it would be a glory we should have to share with the millions of Budhism; and would not infidelity be the more probable result, if it could be proved that the intensest glory of Christianity is only a something that was in existence many centuries previous to the Redeemer's advent?

The recluses are supposed to exhibit a nobler example of self-abnegation and charity than other men. Of the great mass of the

* Balmez; Protestantism and Catholicity compared: by Hanford and Kershaw.

monks in all ages this idea cannot be correct, as they were frequently gainers by the taking of the vow; there being places of profit and honour for the more respectable, whilst the poor were provided with a maintenance for life. It may assist us in our endeavour to form a right estimate of the privations and benevolences of the monks if we look at the circumstances in which they were placed. I have no new information to offer upon the subject; but the better known may be the more correct. The abbot of Clairvaux enjoyed episcopal honours, and had an income of 90,000 francs, with a superb country-house about half a league from the monastery. He had under his dependence eighteen abbeys and twenty-eight nunneries, forty-one abbies commendatory, and forty in foreign countries. In addition to his stipendiary revenues he received yearly more than 8000 bushels of wheat and 700 hogsheads of wine. He also enjoyed the revenues arising from the forges and forests, and the overplus of the corn and wine provided for the use of the monks.* In 1301, the monks at Kirtstall Abbey had 216 draught oxen, 160 cows, 152 yearlings and bullocks, 90 calves, and 4000 sheep and lambs.† In the priory of Norwich 1500 quarters of malt, more than 800 quarters of wheat, and other things in proportion, were used every year. The prior of Thetford had pasturage for 1500 sheep in Westwic and for 1000 sheep in Rushworth. The revenues of the monastery at Abingdon, at the dissolution, were valued at £1876 a-year. At the same period, the plate at Fountains' abbey amounted in value to £708, of which plate to the value of £519, consisting principally of chalices and crosses, was in the church, and to the value of £147, consisting principally of basons, ewers, and goblets, was in the custody of the lord abbot. In the church was a cross of gold, weighing 14 ounces, at £2 3*s*. per ounce, in which was "a piece of the holy cross," valued at £32 2*s*. so that the real cross went for nothing, so low had the value of relics then fallen. There belonged to the house 2356 head of horned cattle, 1326 sheep, 86 horses, 79 swine, 135 quarters of wheat, 40 quarters of rye, 136 quarters of oats, 90 quarters of barley and malt, and 392 loads of hay. At the time of the ecclesiastical survey, A. D. 1534, the most wealthy monastery in England was Westminster, the annual value of which, according to Speed, was £3977. The best endowed nunnery was that of the Brigettines,

* Translator's Preface to Neander's Bernard, by Matilda Wrench.
† Burton's Monasticon.

at Sion, the only house of that order in England; its revenue, according to the same authority, was £1944.*

In addition to the annual revenue of the monasteries, there were many other sources whence assistance was derived, a few only of which can here be noticed. In places that were famous for the possession of some particular relic or image, the sums received at the altar were considerable. During the period in which Thomas-a-Beckett was a popular saint, more than a thousand pounds were in some years presented to the church at Canterbury by the pilgrims. The singular proportion in which the gifts were presented is well-known. In one year there was offered, at Christ's altar, £0 0*s.* 0*d.*; at the Virgin's, £4 1*s.* 8*d.*; at St. Thomas's, £954 6*s.* 3*d.* Bequests like the following are not unfrequent:—"Hervey, son of Akarius, gave the ninth sheaf of all his corn growing upon his demesnes in Gudreston to the priory of Maryke, in the deanery of Richmond." In many instances it was the third sheaf that was given. In 1362, Henry, duke of Lancaster, granted in trust to the abbot of Whalley, certain cottages and lands, "to support two recluses in a certain place within the churchyard of the parochial church of Whalley, as also two women servants to attend them, there to pray for the soul of the said duke, his ancestors and heirs, to find them every week seventeen loaves of bread, such as are usually made in the convent, each weighing fifty shillings sterling, and seven loaves of an inferior sort and the same weight; also eight gallons of their better beer, and threepence for their food. Moreover, at the feast of All Saints yearly to provide them ten large stockfishes, one bushel of oatmeal for pottage, one bushel of rye, two gallons of oil for their lamps, one pound of tallow for candles, six loads of turf (no coal), and one load of faggots.†

The revenues received by the religious were not for their own maintenance alone. They were to be very charitable, and there were particular charities that they were required to exercise by the terms upon which they received their lands and hereditaments from the laity. In 1289, the commons of the realm of England represented to the king in parliament that "the bishoprics, abbeys, and other benefices were founded by the kings and people of England, to inform the people of the law of God, and to make hospitality, alms, and other good works of charity, for which end they were en-

* Taylor's Index. † Whitaker's Whalley.

dowed by the king and people of England."* Grants were not unfrequently made "ad vestitum monachorum, ad victum, ad luminaria, ad hospitalitatem faciendam, ad fabricam ecclesiæ, ad reparanda ecclesiæ ornamenta."† In some instances the monks themselves adopted rules for their guidance in the giving of alms. In 816, the Benedictines, in synod assembled, came to the following resolution: "ut de omnibus eleemosyna datis, tam ecclesiæ quam fratibus, decimae pauperibus dentur."‡ The friars of the order of the Holy Trinity for the Redemption of Captives devoted one-third of their revenues to the purpose implied in their name. Bequests like the following are frequently repeated: "Mathias Forestare gave to the monks at Fountains' abbey, one toft and croft, &c., for the support of the poor at the gate." At the priory of Thetford there was annually distributed to the poor, in alms, £8 10*s.* from bequests made for that purpose; and the monks of the same place, by the Cluniac rule under which they lived, fed eighteen persons daily, besides pilgrims.§ In 15 Edw. II. the Lady Mary Bassingburn made a benefaction of a messuage in Wykes, and several pieces of land and fen ground, to the prior and convent of Spinney, upon condition that they constantly maintained in the said messuage seven poor old men, with the allowance of one farthing loaf of bread, one herring, and one pennyworth of ale every day, and three ells of linen, one woollen garment, one pair of shoes, 200 dry turf, every year, to every one of them. The abbots and monks of Evesham had their corredy, or allowance, for a whole year after their death, in the same proportion as when they lived, which was bestowed upon some poor person for the good of their souls; and the cellarer of the same monastery allowed to each poor person who had been at the chapter-house at the Lord's supper, one loaf and three salted fishes, and as much ale as was necessary.‖ By the survey taken in 26 Hen. VIII. the revenue of Stoneley priory was certified to be £151 over and above all reprises; of which the sum of £4 5*s.* 4*d.* was then reckoned for the charge of eight quarters of rye, made into bread, at 5*s.* the quarter; three quarters of malt in beer, at 4*s.* the quarter; and 200 herrings at 20*d.* the hundred; all of which were given in alms to poor people at the washing of their feet on Maunday Thurs-

* Burton's Monasticon.
† Tanner's Notitia.
‡ Hospin. de Monachis.
§ Taylor's Index Monasticus.
‖ Tindal's History of Evesham.

day; and besides this the sum of £5 7*s*. 8*d*. per annum was charged for the relief of the poor.* The monks of Sallay gave in one year "pauperibus et mendicantibus" 5*s*. 3*d*. which Dr. Dunham Whitaker calculates was less than a thousandth part of the income of the house. In addition to the assistance rendered to the poor at the monasteries, there were also hospitals that partook somewhat of a monastic character. In St. Giles's hospital, at Norwich, in 1430, besides an establishment of canons, priests, chaplains, choristers, &c., eight poor bed-ridden persons were lodged and supported; thirteen persons daily dined and were refreshed at the fire after dinner; a certain number of pilgrims and strangers were received and lodged there every night; seven poor scholars who were received from the grammar school were to dine there daily; on the founder's anniversary 100 poor persons were fed with meat and drink; on the feast of Annunciation alms were distributed to 180 poor people; and a weekly allowance was made to twenty other poor persons, who prayed for the soul of bishop Goldwell; besides which most of the superannuated chaplains of the diocese were supported at that hospital.† St. Paul's hospital, in the same city, was established "for the relief and lodging of poor strangers and sick impotent persons," and for "the lodging of way-faring men and women." There was also an allowance to divers women called poor sisters of £28 7*s*. 1*d*. who were to pray daily for the souls of the founder, of Henry I, of King Stephen, and Queen Matilda.‡ About 1190, Hugh, eighth abbot of Reading, founded, without the gate of the monastery, a hospital for twenty-six poor people, and the entertainment of strangers and pilgrims who might be passing along the great western road. St. Bartholomew's hospital, at London, was originally endowed for the entertainment of poor diseased persons till they got well, of distressed women big with child, till they were delivered and able to go abroad, and for the maintenance (till the age of seven years) of all such children whose mothers died in the house.

The monasteries were subject to many impositions, besides the regular demands that were made upon their revenues by the inmates and the poor. King John once extorted above 1200 marks of silver from the abbey at Fountains, which obliged the monks to sell their plate and part of their sacerdotal vestments. Under the

* Fox's Monasteries. † Whitaker's Craven.
‡ Taylor's Index.

pontificate of Innocent III, 1198, the canons of the priory at Burlington complained that the archdeacon of Richmond, in visiting one of their churches, travelled with ninety-seven horses, twenty-one dogs, and three hawks, whereby he consumed more of their provision than would have maintained that house for a long time.* The following rule was observed in the convent of St. Edmund's Bury:—"When the abbot is at home he is to receive all guests of whatsoever condition he be, except religious, and priests of secular habit, and except their men, who on such pretence applied at the gate of the court-lodge; but if the abbot be not at home, then all guests of whatever condition are to be received by the cellarer, up to thirteen horses. But if a layman or clerk should come with more than thirteen horses, they should be entertained by the servants of the abbot, either within the court-lodge, or without, at the expence of the abbot. All religious men, even bishops if they be monks, are to be charged upon the cellary, and at the expence of the convent, unless the abbot will do him special honour, and entertain him in his own hall at his own expence." The usages connected with the hospitium were such as we might suppose a worldly-minded monk would covet; but they were not in harmony with his position, unless under stringent regulations. I have often been entertained in convents, where, however, I must do my kind hosts the justice to say, I never observed any improper compliance on the part of the monks, except upon one occasion in Cyprus; but I could see that the custom was open to serious abuses.

There were other institutions established by the monks, or of a monastic character, that were more in unison with the professed intention of the recluse. Of this kind was the congregation founded by Camillus de Lellis, a Neapolitan, who, grieved to see the sloth of hired servants in attending the sick, formed the project of associating certain individuals for the voluntary performance of this office. The members of this order were to go every day to the hospital to serve the sick, making their beds, and paying them every attention that was requisite; and the founder ordained that they should bind themselves to attend upon persons infected with the plague, and minister to the sick in any place where their services might be required. In nearly all the orders the monks were divided into classes, of which each in rotation, except the abbot, attended to the duties of the hospital. In instances without num-

* Burton's Monasticon Eboracense.

ber, members of the various orders, both men and women, have exhibited examples of the noblest charity, in exposing themselves to diseases of the most malignant type, and administering to the wants of the sick under circumstances the most repulsive.

We are unable in this division of our review to make any comparison between the monks of the east and west, as no heathen nation ever founded an establishment bearing the character of an alms-house or an hospital. The only exception with which I am acquainted is that of the Banyan hospital at Surat. "In 1772 this hospital," as we learn from Hamilton, "contained horses, mules, oxen, sheep, goats, monkeys, poultry, pigeons, and a variety of birds; also an aged tortoise, which was known to have been there seventy-five years. The most extraordinary ward, was that appropriated to rats, mice, bugs, and other noxious vermin, for whom suitable food was provided. In 1780 it consisted of a large piece of ground enclosed by high walls, and subdivided into several courts or wards for the accommodation of animals. In sickness they were attended with the greatest care, and here found a peaceful asylum for the infirmities of old age. When an animal broke a limb, or was otherwise disabled, his owner brought him to this hospital, where he was received without regard to the caste or nation of his master."* The natives of Ceylon build ambalams, that are places of accommodation for travellers, like the serais of the Mahomedans, or the choultries of the Hindus. They are erected to acquire merit, and the same motive might induce them to found hospitals, were it not that in all places where Christianity has not been received, man places no confidence in his fellow man. Hence the heathen never give money or lands *in trust*. They erect buildings, and like the Anglo-Saxons, "make folk-ways, with bridges over deep waters and miry places," as these require no permanent endowment. But the idea of an hereditary stewardship, in which the jus utendi does not belong to the person in possession, seems to be almost entirely alien to the pagan mind. When lands are given to the temples, the usufruct is in the right of the feoffee, and there are other members of the same corporation in a similar position, whose interest it is to see that their common property is preserved intact.

The history of monastic institutions, notwithstanding their many claims to our respect and veneration, is a confession of failures and

* Hamilton's East-India Gazetteer, art. Surat.

defects. Their avowed object has always been a reformation of manners, for the accomplishment of which each successive order began in poverty, but, gradually increasing in wealth, became alike corrupt, and a relaxation of discipline was the consequence. Each new institution arose from the degeneracy of its predecessor; and was an additional proof, to all who had eyes to see, or minds to understand, that the system itself had an inherent impotency, and was utterly unable to produce the consequences that were desired. Yet all innovations were guarded against by every possible means that human ingenuity could devise. "If any shall endeavour," said Canute, in his charter to the Benedictine monastery, at St. Edmund's Bury, "which God avert! by any means to subvert this liberty or change it . . . . may he be cursed with eternal captivity! may he never enjoy his liberty! may he be given up to the service of the devil! and, with him, may he be bound in inextricable chains! unless satisfaction should succeed his error, which we heartily desire."* The monks were charged by the people with impurity and selfishness, the two evils to which they were intended to be the most uncompromising antagonists. Even in our own day, the voice of popular tradition, in songs, and proverbs, and tales, reiterates the same accusation. Of the sentiments that were entertained in the fourteenth century, Piers Ploughman may be received as a correct exponent. It was the rapacity of the monks that called forth his bitterest invectives. Listen to his lay:

"Go confesse thee to som frere,
And shew hym thi synnes;
For whiles Fortune is thi frend
Freres wol thee lovye,
And feeche thee to hir fraternitee,
And for the biseke
To hir priour provincial
A pardon for to have,
And preien for thee pol by pol,
If thou be pecuniosus."—l. 6678.

"By my faith frere, quod I,
Ye faren lik thise woweris
That wed none widwes
But for to welden hir goodes.
Right so, by the roode!
Roughte ye nevere
Where my body were buryed,
By so ye hadde my silver."—l. 6716.

* Taylor's Index Monasticus.

"And how that freres folwede
Folke that was riche,
And folk that was povere
At like pris thei sette;
And no corps in her kirk-yerde
Nor in his kirk was buryed,
But quik he biquethe aught
To quyte with her dettes."—l. 8037.

"Freres and fele othere maistres,
That to lewed men prechen,
Ye moeven materes unmesurable,
To tellen of the Trinité
That ofte tymes the lewed peple
Of hir bileve doute.
Bettre it were to manye doctours
To leven swich techyng
And tellen men of the ten comaundments,
And touchen the sevene synnes,
And of the braunches that burjoneth of hem,
And bryngen men to helle.
And how that folk in folies
Mispenden hir fyve wittes,
As wel freres as oother folk
Foliliche spenden
In housynge, in haterynge,
And in to heigh clergie shewynge,
Moore for pompe than for pure charité,
The peple woot the sothe,
That I lye noght! loo!
For lordes ye plesen,
And reverencen the riche
The rather for hir silver."—l. 9741.

There can be no doubt that among the monks there have been, and are, many most holy men, who will have their reward. But, the constant round of ceremonies, some of them unmeaning, whilst others are contrary to the word of God, they are called upon to attend to, must have a deadening influence upon the best affections of the heart, and act as an incubus upon its efforts to free itself from evil. Hence, among all orders in which regular labour is not prescribed, there is a tendency to introduce repetitions into their acts of worship, the use of which is almost necessary under these circumstances, to prevent a greater evil; but as it brings the worshipper under the condemnation of Christ, who has said expressly, "Use not vain repetitions," it follows that in the system itself there must be some radical defect. The resemblance we have so often had to notice between Romanism and Budhism is here also presented. The Romanist prays thus:—

> "Heart of Mary, conceived without the stain of sin!
> Heart of Mary, full of grace!
> Heart of Mary, sanctuary of the Holy Trinity!
> Heart of Mary, tabernacle of the Incarnate Word!
> Heart of Mary, after God's own heart!
> Heart of Mary, illustrious throne of glory!
> Heart of Mary, perfect holocaust of divine love!
> Heart of Mary, abyss of humility!
> Heart of Mary, attached to the cross!
> Heart of Mary, seat of mercy! &c." *

After each repetition of an attribute, the worshipper says, "Pray for us!" There are similar litanies, addressed to the saints.

The first article in the twenty-first volume of the Tibetan Do is entitled "Buddha náma, sahasra pancha, sata chatur, tri panchasat," and is, as the name implies, the enumeration of 5453 epithets of a Budha, or Tatágata, each being descriptive of some fancied or real excellence, and being accompanied by a reverential formula. Thus:—

> "I adore the Tatágata, the universally radiant sun!
> I adore the Tatágata, the moral wisdom!
> I adore the Tagágata, the chief lamp of all the regions of space!

And so on, through 137 leaves.

From the professed design of monastic establishments we are led to suppose that the charge of selfishness will be the last that can be made against the monks; but when we examine more closely the position of the celibate, even under the most favourable circumstances, we see that it is not one that is likely to be germanent of a disposition inclined to the exercise of kindness or pity, or capable of feeling the softer and sweeter sympathies. It sets aside the wisdom of the lesson that is taught us by the apostle, relative to the ground of our confidence in the Redeemer's mercy, Heb. ii. 18; iv. 15; his argument being, that Jesus Christ is "able to succour," "touched with the feeling of our infirmities," *because* he has been placed in a situation similar to our own, in which he had the same trials to suffer, and the same temptations to bear. Notwithstanding all the cautions that are presented by history, we still cherish the idea that

* Horne's Mariolatry.

the monks were more gracious masters and more considerate landlords than other men; but Abelard says that in his day they generally oppressed their vassals far more cruelly than did the temporal feudatories; and Piers Ploughman says,

> "For-thi chastité withouten charité
> Worth cheyned in helle;
> It is as lewed as a lampe
> That no light is inne.
> Many chapeleyns own chaste,
> Ac charité is aweye;
> Are no men avarouser than hii
> When thei ben avaunced.
> Unkynde to hire kyn,
> And to all christene
> Chewen hire charité
> And chiden after moore;
> Swiche chastité withouten charité
> Worth cheyned in helle."—l. 836.

The priest of Budha, by the tenets of his religion, as well as by the economy of his institute, is taught to disregard all human woe; except, that in some of the exercises of meditation he may form the wish that all sentient beings may become happy. The sramana receives, but does not give; and the following description is unhappily too characteristic of the order. "We proceeded," says Bishop Smith, "into the centre of the Beggar's Square, in the suburbs of Canton, where numbers of idle vagabonds were pursuing their various methods of amusement or vice. A number of emaciated pale forms were also to be seen, partly covered with mats. Some were gasping for breath, and were scarcely able to move. Others were motionless, and seemed to be destitute of life. Numbers of poor mendicants, on the approach of sickness and disease, are brought hither by their relatives, and left to perish, in neglected and unpitied destitution. One poor youth, with a look that pierced my inmost soul, had just sufficient strength to stretch forth his hand for that temporal relief which was, alas! now unavailing. I counted four or five, close by, to all appearance dead. Desirous of assuring myself of the fact I stooped, and removing the scanty matting which partially obscured their pallid features, gazed on the ghastly spectacle of death. Within three or four yards of the corpses, a company of noisy gamblers were boisterously pursuing their nefarious vocation. Such is the baneful spell of paganism! Even within sight of Budhist altars, close by numerous temples dedicated to heathen gods; under the vertical beam of all the benevolence that paganism can be supposed to diffuse; we behold the spectacle of death and the dying, sinking into the grave because none will help them, and most of them perishing from actual starvation and neglect. The most corrupt form of Christianity knows no anomaly of this kind. The most feeble measure of Christian influence forbids hunger, penury, and disease to linger within sight, without making an effort to impart relief. But heathen priests permit the groans of the dying sufferer to ascend to the sky, as a testimony to that declaration of Holy Writ, The dark places of the earth are full of the habitations of cruelty."

As the monks are free from the usual cares of the world, their minds dwell with the greater intensity upon any subject to which they may direct their attention. Hence, whenever they have engaged in controversy, they have been warm partizans of the cause they espoused; and when they have become persecutors, as in the reign of Theodosius I. their fury has known no bounds. In the ninth century it was not unusual for them to take part in the tumults and seditions that arose in the towns and cities of the empire, until their audacity was restrained by repeated edicts from the imperial court.

The priests of Budha, however, manifest little hostility to the various religions that are professed around them. This indifference is easily explained, as, upon their own principles, all violent opposition, even to error, would be contrary to the precepts. For this reason, the annals of Budhism record fewer instances of persecution than those of any other creed. Truth is to be had in reverence, by whomsoever it may be professed. The bana alone contains pure, unmixed, perfect truth; but as in all systems there is a portion of truth, they are to be regarded as being less beneficial, rather than as an absolute injury, to be destroyed by fire and faggot. This principle is exhibited wherever Budhism prevails. When the British consulate was about to be erected at Foo Chow, the mandarins, of their own accord, introduced a clause into the agreement made with the building contractor, specifying that the masons and carpenters should never perform any work on the Sabbath-day, nor in any way interfere with the religious observances of the English. In the same spirit, the mandarins, before paying the consul a visit, frequently sent to see whether it was the Sabbath-day or not.* The priests of Ceylon are not alone in their willingness to show attention to men of another faith. "On some occasions," says a British officer, relative to Arrakan, "I have found a welcome in the wihára, when shelter was denied me elsewhere; and with that welcome the more substantial evidences of good-will in the shape of a repast prepared for myself and followers. I never left the monastery in prosecution of my journey without feeling grateful to those good monks, who had so charitably received the white stranger into their mansion." The mildness inculcated by the system to which the sramanas adhere, has sometimes led to singular results. Sri Sanghabó, monarch of Ceylon, A. D. 246, was greatly devoted to Budhism, and entirely prohibited the taking of animal life in his dominions. The greatest malefactors, though condemned to death, were secretly released at night by the king's order, and the corpses of persons who had died a natural death were exposed at the place of execution, as though they belonged to the delinquents. Thus the majesty of the law was upheld, without the infliction of mortal punishment; but the land fell into anarchy in consequence, and the king was deposed. Another monarch, Wíra Nissankha Malla, A. D. 1200, "considering that robbers committed theft through hunger, gave them whatever riches they desired, and thus relieved the country from dread."

The monks have made many professions of humility; but the situation of the recluse is one that is eminently calculated to foster sentiments of self-sufficiency and pride. It was a custom with the monkish writers to affix peccator to their name. Hence Jerome, in his life of Paulus, says, "Whosoever thou art that readeth this, I entreat thee to remember Jerome, a sinner." Francis would not suffer the monks of his order to be called Fratres, brethren, or friars; but Fratercculi, little brethren, or friars minor. Yet it is said † that when Martin, of Tours, was invited to a feast given by the emperor Maximus, at which the most illustrious men in the realm were present, near the middle of the entertainment, the king commanded that an attendant should present a goblet to the bishop, as was the custom. Maximus expected to receive it again from the hand of Martin; but the bishop, when he had drunk, gave it to his presbyter, as he thought there was no one more worthy to drink after him, and that it would not be right for him to prefer to his

* Smith's China. † Professor Emerson, Andover: Bibliotheca Sacra.

presbyter, either the king himself or any one else in the court. The encouragement given to the laity, at the approach of death, to put on the monkish habit, or the cowl, was the exhibition of a similar spirit. Even such men as king John were taught that by this means they would have an entrance into heaven; and many others there were—

> "Who, to be sure of paradise
> Dying put on the weeds of Dominic,
> Or in Franciscan thought to pass disguised."

The Brahmans speak of themselves as being "lords of all," and as "having feet for earthly kings to adore." They are all objects of worship, and have divine honours paid to them, especially the religious guides. The spiritual guide, in the estimation of the disciple, is literally a god.*

The pride of the Budhist priest is not from birth; nor yet is it alone from the class to which he belongs, as he supposes that he has a right to belong to the order from the merit he has acquired in former births, by which his self-consequence is increased to a degree that cannot be entertained by those who do not believe in the doctrine of transmigration. The sramana receives worship from the householder, and he forms part of the sangha in which all Budhists profess to take refuge, when they repeat the threefold formula of protection. The priests never make obeisance to any one, and never pay any outward mark of respect. In the books, they are represented as using the word *to*, a form of the second person singular that is offensively low, when addressing kings, or even deities; all other persons use the honourific form of the verb when addressing them, but they never use it in return; they receive honour from all beings, in all forms; but they never give it to any being, in any form. In the Pújáwaliya there is an account of a priest who was so intent upon gaining rahatship, that for the space of thirty years he did not wash his feet, and at last he became so offensive that the déwas could smell him more than a thousand miles off; but, notwithstanding his state of filthiness, at the end of that period Sekra, the ruler of one of the heavens, came and washed his feet, and thought himself honoured in being allowed to perform even this menial office for so holy a priest. It is said in the Bhikkhaparampará Játaka that when a king was once travelling in disguise he received a present of food from a nobleman, which he gave to a

* Ward's Hindoos.

guru who had come to the same place. The guru gave it to a hermit, and the hermit to a Pasé-Budha, who eat it, without uttering a single word. This excited the curiosity of the nobleman, who enquired why he had eaten it thus unceremoniously when the others had passed it by; and he replied, that as he was the most eminent person there, it was his right to receive the offering and enjoy its benefit. This self-importance of the priests induces them to despise all other men who are not in possession of the same dignity, and to look on them as being no higher in the scale of existence than the beasts of the field. Thus, on a certain occasion,* when Duttagámini, who reigned in Ceylon, B.C. 161, was seated upon his throne, he called to mind the countless lives he had sacrificed, and peace of mind was denied him. Whilst under this affliction he was visited by eight rahats, who said to him, "O, ruler of men! we have been deputed by the priesthood to administer comfort unto thee." Thereupon the rája thus replied, "Lords, what peace of mind can be left for me, when, under one plea or another, I have been the means of destroying great armies?" They replied, "From the commission of that act there will be no impediment in thy road to salvation; herein no more than two human beings have been sacrificed; the one person had been admitted to the pale of the salvation of the faith; the other had attained the state of piety which enabled him to observe the five precepts. The rest, being heretics and sinners, are on a par with wild beasts." They added, that as he was to cause the religion of Budha to shine forth with great splendour he was to subdue his mental affliction.

It is incumbent on the king of Siam to pay an annual visit to the temples, in procession. On entering one he takes off his shoes. After presenting the offerings, he makes three several profound obeisances, at each of which his head touches the backs of his hands. He concludes by making three similar obeisances to the superior, and making such gifts as are customary. The superior and the rest of the priests sit unmoved during the ceremony; but the king does not exhibit this humility more frequently than the prescribed rule requires, and avoids the ceremony whenever he can. When he goes abroad he uses the precaution to send heralds before him, to warn all priests to keep out of his sight, since, were he to meet one, the customary homage would be required.†

* Turnour's Mahawanso, cap. xxv.

† Capt. James Low; Asiatic Researches, vol. xx.

The respect with which the Burmans regard their priests, especially the superiors, and the honours they lavish upon them, are so excessive that they are almost equal to those they pay to Budha. Whenever a layman meets a priest in the street, he must respectfully move out of the way to let him pass; and when any one goes to visit a superior, he must prostrate himself before him three times, with his hands raised above his head in token of reverence, or rather of adoration, and remain in this posture during the whole of his audience.*

The nimbus that distinguishes the Greek and Romanist saints is of eastern origin; as Budha is said to have been attended by an appearance of glory, extending six cubits above his head; and his principal disciples are represented by the native painters as having a similar mark of eminence.

It is thus apparent that the leading features of asceticism are the same, whatever form it may have assumed, or to whatever religion it may have belonged; and it now only remains, in order to complete our imperfect notice of the system, to examine it under the aspect it presents in our own age. For this purpose we shall confine our scrutiny to the two countries in which religion is at present a more popular element than in any other land where Romanism is professed—Belgium and Italy. In the former it is the Romanism of activity and usefulness; in the latter, of ceremony and splendour.

"In mentioning," says a recent writer, "the revival, or, perhaps we should rather say, open reappearance of the more ancient religious orders, it is necessary to guard against the supposition that their identity with their prototypes of the middle ages extends to their internal organisation and course of life; whereas we must limit our conception of their oneness solely to their origin, combined energy, undeviating aim, and prevailing policy, apart from the mode in which their designs are carried out, which, with a wisdom too seldom evinced by "the children of light," is undeviatingly adapted to the circumstances of the age and sphere in which they are called to act. In accordance with this principle, but very few of even the oldest orders have retained their monastic character, in the strict meaning of the term; but, conforming to the practical bias of our day, have found for themselves new, and, for the nineteenth century, assuredly more efficient modes of influencing the

* Sangermano's Burmese Empire.

public mind, than vigils, fasts, and other monkish austerities. Thus, in a large proportion of those countless communantés, belonging to different orders, with which Belgium is covered, the original, ruling idea of monachism, viz. the promotion of a contemplative life, has given place to various plans of active usefulness, whether towards the rising or the failing generation; such as conducting educational seminaries for the young, or giving tendence on the sick, the infirm, the old, or the forsaken. Thus, for example, the four monasteries of the Annunciation, though originally founded for the exclusive cultivation of religious contemplation, in the strictest sense of the word, now possess three educational establishments in the diocese of Mechlin. . . . The recently founded religious orders (which, perhaps, might more fitly be denominated congregations), possess peculiarities deserving special notice. For example, though assimilated to the elder orders in many outward respects, such as residence, dress, manner of living, &c., they yet diverge from them in several most essential particulars. First, their entrance vow is binding for five years only; and an after, personal application to the bishop is requisite to their taking upon themselves that irrevocable engagement to the order, from which death alone can absolve them. Secondly, the vow of poverty is by no means universal among the modern religious communities; and, thirdly, pretending to no higher position in the church militant than that of auxiliaries to the secular clergy, they are professedly subordinate to the diocesan ordinary. . . . One order only, that of the Jesuits, forms an exception. Despite ceaseless conflicts and occasional defeats, that remarkable order still contrives to uphold its distinctive principles, and to maintain its autocracy unimpaired; and in Belgium, as elsewhere, abides by the unflinching principle of "aut Caesar aut nullus," embodied in Ricci's world-famed declaration, Sint ut sunt, aut non sunt. . . . Belgium contains twenty-two monasteries, among which, beside the ancient orders, such as the Benedictine, the Trappist, the Dominican, the Franciscan, and the Pré Montré brethren, may be noticed the comparatively modern foundations of les Frères de la Charité (with the houses scattered through the five dioceses.) les Ignorantins ou Frères des Ecoles Chrétiennes (with twenty-one houses); thirdly, the Josephites, or Frères de St. Joseph de Grammont (with seven houses), a peculiarly Belgian order, devoting itself to the education of youths, and specially those of the higher grades of society; its members are divided into three classes, viz.

priests, seminarists, and artisans. Fourthly, les Frères des bonnes œuvres de Renaix (with four houses), who take on themselves the care of the aged, the promotion of free schools for the poor, and of workshops (ateliers de Charité) for needy or decayed tradesmen. Fifthly, les Frères de Notre Dame de la Misericorde (with three houses) whose attention is specially directed to the imprisoned and the sick. Sixth and seventh, two several divisions of Frères Xaverians, of which one, surnamed de Vandale, devotes itself to education and nurse-tending in private houses; the other, surnamed de Miséricorde, fulfils a similar mission in houses of detention and correction. But numerous as are the male congregations of religious orders in Belgium, they fall far short of those occupied by female votaries. In proof of this assertion it may suffice to state, that the single diocese of Mechlin, though by no means the most conventual in the country, contains 33 orders of nuns, comprising 109 communantés. Of these last, eight only (belonging to the orders of the Annunciate, the Clarissite, the Carmelite, and the Capuchine nuns), are devoted to an exclusively contemplative life; all the rest devote their energies to the active promotion of objects similar to those aimed at by the male orders; as, for example, attendance on the sick, whether in private families or hospitals, the imparting of instruction in all its grades (from the free school of the poor to the pensionat for the highest class females in the land), the tendance of aged, infirm, or lunatic persons of their own sex (these last, generally speaking, in separately arranged establishments), the providing of funerals for the stranger and the indigent, the nurse-tending of poor lying-in women; the instruction of the deaf, dumb, and blind, the education of orphans, and the management of infant schools. . . . There exists not in Belgium a single household which has not contributed at least one member either to the regular or irregular clergy, to the monastery or the nunnery." *

As we approach the Alps, we exchange an activity that addresses itself to the wants and woes of mankind, for one that appeals almost solely to the imagination. For the information we now present relative to the monastic establishments of Italy, we are principally indebted to the interesting volumes published by the Rev. M. Hobart Seymour, M.A.†

* Evangelical Christendom, Aug. 1849.

† A Pilgrimage to Rome, third edition. Mornings among the Jesuits at Rome, second edition. Seeleys.

The events of the last two years have been more important, evangelically, than any that have taken place since Luther's contest with Rome. The absence of the pope is of little importance, when compared with the opportunity that was for a time presented for pouring into Italy the light of truth immediately from the Word of God, and for employing its presses in the multiplication of the Scriptures. Gigantic efforts have been made to get rid of priestly domination; and though they may appear for a time to be unsuccessful, it is only a momentary pause, that the blow hereafter to be dealt may fall with the deadlier force. Happy will it be for this beautiful land, if, when the hour of deliverance shall come, not man's madness, but God's truth, be the ascendant potency.

The late revolutionary movement in the canton Vallais arose from the dissatisfaction of the people with the exemptions claimed by the ecclesiastics. It is said that when any of the laity has made himself liable to the civil law, he has only to assume the cowl at some convent as a lay-brother, by which he becomes amenable only to the ecclesiastical law, and is exempted from the penalties to which he would otherwise have been subject. The monks and nuns, as well as the whole body of the priests, enjoy this privilege. Notwithstanding these advantages, the duties of religion are neglected; in the same canton there are whole villages in which not more than two or three persons are able to write, and the instruction imparted in some of the convents is scarcely worth the name. In Italy, not more than one monastic establishment in one hundred, whether of monks or nuns, takes the least part in the conduct of schools or the management of hospitals. The mendicant orders are generally composed of the lowest of the people, who are themselves unable to read. In an account of a religious service at Genoa, the monks are described as "chatting, laughing, and promenading with as much levity as the youngest and gayest of the congregation." Those in Rome are said to be denounced by the citizens as "idle, debauched, and licentious." In that city there is a priest, a monk, or a nun, for every six families, the whole number being about five thousand.

There are two classes of monasteries, one of which is designed for the higher grades of society. As it is not usual for the younger sons of these families to marry, they are usually attached to the church, which, however, does not imply ordination, but the becoming a member of some monastery. The mode of life in these convents is similar to that which is seen in the English universities. In one establishment visited by Mr. Seymour, there was appropriated to each of the twenty-two gentlemen of which it consisted, a suite of small apartments, consisting of a sitting-room, a sleeping-room, and a little study, all opening into another vacant apartment or gallery. The inmates of these establishments take the three vows of chastity, poverty and obedience; but they can leave the convent, frequent the coffee-houses, and visit their female friends, with few restrictions upon the freedom they are allowed to exercise. The other class of convents belongs to the poorer orders exclusively. The inmates are chiefly Franciscans and Capuchins, known by their coarse brown dresses, shaven crowns, sandaled feet, cord, and rosary. One establishment of this kind contains 170 monks, not more than half-a-dozen of whom are ordained. Each monk has a small room to himself, with a bed laid or spread on the floor, a table, a chair and a stool; but the dirt and stench are said to be beyond description, to be equalled only by the loathsomeness of the monks by whom they are inhabited.

Of the nunneries there is a similar division. In establishments of the more respectable class, the nuns have many privileges and comforts; they can employ themselves in needle-work or the education of the young; but in the great majority of the nunneries there is no occupation for either mind or body. The majority of the nuns of Rome are said to die of madness before they are five-and-twenty years of age. Notwithstanding all the precautions that are used, and all the misery that is induced in consequence, events are continually transpiring that tend to bring discredit upon the system; and yet it may be presumed that the instances of impurity that become generally known are few when compared with the actual transgressions. There are some convents in which the nun is not allowed, after admission, ever again to see her relatives; once a year, on an appointed day, she may hear their voices, and if she hears them not, she may suppose that they are dead.

It has been regretted by many persons that there are no societies or congregations among Protestants similar in purpose to the monastic establishments. "We might anticipate much good," says the Rev. S. Fox, rector of Morley, "from the revival of monasticism in close union with our branch of Christ's Holy Catholic Church; for it would be the means not only of remedying the defects which are felt to exist in promoting the temporal and eternal interests of mankind, but it would also be found a source of unspeakable comfort to many who would gladly avail themselves of the opportunity which would thus be afforded of retiring from the noise and tumult of the world, and spending their hours in meditation and prayer. . . . If monasteries were once more established, and adapted, not merely to the altered condition of the Anglican Church, but to the present state of the country, the people who now feel themselves despised and neglected, would at the gate of the monastery learn that their sufferings were not unheeded."* That some advantages would be gained by the establishment of monastic orders amongst us, no one can deny; and perhaps the same may be said of almost every form of social change that we can imagine. But it would argue a strange want of judgment, were we to look only at the minimum of advantage, and leave out of the account the multitudinous mass of evil that might be attendant upon the same course. The voice of the past, relative to this great subject, is one in its solemn utterance, and unless we intend to prove the existence of a metempsychosis of error by determining that, be its evils ever so many, it shall again and again be revived, we are called upon to give unto this voice our most earnest heed, and therefrom learn wisdom.

In all ages there have been men who have entertained right notions about the ascetic system, and have warned others against the errors that it generates; but their individual enlightenment has had no influence upon the church at large, nor even at all times upon their own conduct. In the earlier church Tertullian (Apologet. c. xliii.) could say, "We are no Brahmans, nor Indian gymnosophists; we are no dwellers in the woods, no men who have left the common haunts of life; we feel deeply the gratitude we owe to God, our Lord and Creator; we despise not the enjoyment of any of his works; we only desire to moderate this enjoyment in such a manner that we may avoid excess and misuse. We therefore inhabit this world in common with you, and we make use of baths, of shops, of workshops, and fairs, and all that is used in the intercourse of life. We also carry on, in common with you, navigation, war, agriculture and trade; we take part in your occupation, and our labour, when needful, we give to the public service." "No offering," said Bede, in the mediæval age, "though made to a monastery, could be pleasing to the Almighty, if it proceeded from an impure conscience." "The man who indulges his passion," said

* Fox's Monks and Monasteries.

the prelates in the synod of Cloveshoe, "in the confidence that his charities will procure his salvation, instead of making an acceptable offering to God, throws himself into the arms of Satan." In the modern church the eminently pious de Renty has said,* in addressing a lady of rank, "my design is not that you should demolish your walks, or let your gardens run into a wilderness; the ruins I speak of must be made in our own minds, not executed on things insensible. When I say we must set all on fire, my thoughts were to follow that admirable spirit of the apostle, who would that we have poverty amidst our riches, and divestment in the midst of our possessions; he means, that our spirit should be thoroughly purified, and separated from all creatures; and that there should not be, in our hearts, any other inclinations than those of Jesus Christ, who saw all this world without destroying it, but withal, without cleaving to it." Were the sound of the convent bell again to be heard in the vales of Britain, all the light arising from the millions of the Scriptures that have been distributed throughout the land, would be insufficient to prevent many from attempting to purchase heaven, either by gifts of money for the support of monasteries, or by a personal abandonment of the world; until the same melancholy tale had again been told that has been so often repeated, and men had learnt from experience what other modes of teaching fail to impress upon their minds.

The example of Jesus Christ is before us. We are unable to tell what was the manner of his conduct during youth. One little sentence is all we are permitted to listen to: "Is not this the carpenter?" But we may learn from it that the Lord of all did not disdain to engage in what the working classes of my neighbourhood call, in their own expressive language, hand-labour. And we may also infer, that as this was the first circumstance presented to the minds of the people of Nazareth in glancing at the past, it was the most prominent feature in the conduct of Jesus during his residence in their city. Nor is this all. If the son of the holy Mary had been different to other men, moody in his disposition, and mysterious in the manner of his speech; if it had been his wont to turn away from the light and beauty of the world, and court only the solitude of the forest or the gloom of the cave; these very eccentricities—such is man—would have made his fellow-citizens more ready to listen to his words and to receive him as a messenger from

* Alex. Knox's Remains.

heaven. When the exercise of his ministry commenced, all his modes of action were in perfect contrast to those of John, the preacher of the wilderness. Whatever insight we have into the mental individuality of Christ Jesus as man, is in congruity with the simple narrative of the evangelists, in all that they record of the circumstances of his life. "He *went about* doing good." When assailed by the great temptation, he was in the wilderness, but was driven thither by the Spirit.—Mark i. 12. There is a nameless something about the words of Christ that causes them to win their way into our hearts. It is this that makes them so admirably adapted to arrest the attention of the child; so that the little beings around us who are just doffing off their infancy know all about the domestic economy of the Jews at this period of their history. They have seen, and the hand that drew the picture was divine, the maid grinding at the mill, and the good housewife kneading her meal, baking her bread in the oven, putting the candle into its stick, pouring her wine into the bottles, and mending her old garments; they have had a peep into the treasure-store, and have seen the moth eating her raiment, and the rust corrupting her ornaments of metal; near the principal entrance to the house, they have pitied the poor beggar, whose sores the dogs were licking as he lay; in the garden they have seen the mint, the cummin, the anise, and the mustard, and the vine, the olive, and the fig; around the house they have noticed the hen gathering her chickens, and the sparrow near the house-top; in the street, they have watched the children at play, and men praying at the corners, or sounding a trumpet to tell of their alms-deeds; in the field, they have seen the grass and the lily, the grain in all stages of maturity, and the plougher, the sower, the weeder, and the reaper; in the wilderness, they have seen the hole of the fox, the stray sheep, and the coming of the wolf; and on the sea-shore they have watched the fisherman, either mending his tackle, casting his nets, or throwing the fish he has caught into the creel. The discourses of Christ are so eminently graphic, that some of them might be repeated by pictorial representations alone, without the aid of a single sentence of connexion or explanation; and every separate group in the varied scene tells of activity or of home. The beginning of his miracles was at a marriage; and the bidding, the procession, and the supper, are illustrated at large in his addresses. These facts are significant, and the course of action they inculcate is essentially non-monastic in its character.

The monachism that is pleaded for in our day is not that of the cell or the cloister; but the system as seen in active operation among the Romanists of Belgium. The greater amount of good that may be done by this method, the zeal and benevolence it will call forth, and the readier means it will afford to the church to grapple with the evils around it, are the arguments that will be urged why convents and nunneries should again be established. But we think that, where these considerations are presented, the good that is effected by less exceptionable means is too frequently overlooked. There is a prestige about all that Rome does, which gains from the unthinking a greater share of sympathy and admiration than is really due. The relation of a single instance may suffice. I was present at a ceremony of the Greek Church, in Jerusalem, when parts of the gospel were read in several different languages, to commemorate the introduction of the gospel to as many different nations. The Romanists have a still more imposing ceremony. Once in the year, on the day of the Epiphany, passages are read in about fifty different languages, in the theatre of the Propaganda, at Rome, for a similar purpose. With this we may contrast the declaration of the Bible Society, that it has printed the Word of God in 140 languages, and distributed upwards of twenty millions of copies of the Scriptures, in part or entire; or that of the Tract Society, which has printed tracts in 110 languages, and distributed five hundred millions of copies of different works, varying in size from a single page to a large volume, each of which contains a distinct enunciation of the method by which man may receive salvation. The poetry of the one is greater than that of the other; but in true sublimity, the simple declaration of the evangelical societies has immensely the advantage.

The exercises of charity that are brought into existence by the monastic institute are another plea for its re-establishment. But when this part of the system is narrowly examined, a great part of its apparent grandeur passes away. Many of the most splendid gifts that have been laid upon the altar of the monks have been presented to expiate some crime; and at present, in those places in which the system is the most popular, the most usual appeals for support are to a principle that is selfish and mercenary. The monks themselves have been merely the almoners of another's bounty.

We hesitate not to affirm that if the history of any village in England where the evangelical principle predominates could be fully known, it would be seen that in the patient endurance of hardships, the maintenance of an unshaken integrity, the display of a high sense of honour, the willingness to suffer rather than to sin, the offering of pecuniary contributions for benevolent purposes, and the calling forth of kindness and sympathy exhibited in such acts as the tending of the sick, succouring the distressed, and visiting the houses of the poor, the narrative would elicit universal admiration and vie in interest and beauty with anything that has been presented under any religious system whatever. Take the monk away from his own peculiar sphere, and he is nothing, or he lives for himself alone; whilst the man who takes the Bible for his guide is constantly moving in the midst of an extensive circle, scattering around him coruscations of beneficence that are pure as the glory that plays around the seraph when he returns from some mission of mercy to his wonted place in heaven.

We omit all reference to the fact that the great commands of the law cannot be obeyed by the recluse; and pass on to the argument, less acknowledged but equally conclusive, that the system loses sight, entirely, of the mighty privileges that are granted unto all men by the economy of the gospel.

It is matter of surprise to some persons that man has not the power to command the angelic spirits to do his bidding and reveal to him the mysteries of the other world. They long for the power to ascend into the heavens by the rainbow; they would soar in the cloud, dance in the eddy of the waterfall, outstrip the winds or the lightning in the swiftness of their speed, and rush past the visible stars to the spheres that like sand of gold seem to cover the shores of infinity. They ask for dreams, voices, revelations, and spells of power, that they may be enabled to uplift the veil that shrouds the throne of God from mortal ken, and live amidst the thunders of the divine presence. But the word of God sets at nought all these unhallowed aspirations. It says to the child of dust that he is to be simple, meek, docile, and lowly of heart; and that he is to set himself with all submissiveness to do his duty in that state of life in which he has been placed by a wise and good Providence. But it ennobles the man who thus lives, by telling him that when he eats, and when he drinks, and when he exercises the meanest acts of his existence, it is possible for him to "glorify God;" to be adding, by this means, to the brightness that fills the universe with its ineffable splendour; so that the throwing of the shuttle, or the rinsing of the cup, or the tilling of the ground may become an act as pleasing to the Creator as the awaking of the melody that undulates around his throne from the voices of the hosts celestial. We are warranted in making this assertion by what the apostle has said to the slave. "Servants, δουλοι, be obedient. . . . . as unto Christ; not with eyeservice as menpleasers; but as the servants of Christ, doing the will of God from the heart; with good will doing service, as to the Lord, and not to men. Knowing that whatsoever good thing any man doeth, the same shall he receive of the Lord, whether he be bond or free."—Eph. vi. 5. "Servants. . . . . whatsoever ye do, do it heartily, as to the Lord, and not unto men; knowing that of the Lord ye shall receive the reward of the inheritance; for ye serve the Lord Christ. . . . and there is no respect of persons." —Coloss. iii. 22. This is one of the cheering thoughts, so frequently presented by the Scriptures, that reconcile man to his lot, and enable him to live in the midst of even severe toil and trial with serenity upon his brow and gladness in his heart. The mind loves to linger over these incidents; and they are an additional testimony to the divinity of the record in which they are contained.

The volume of inspiration does not say to man, "Cease from the combat; flee away from the presence of the adversary; retire to the monastic shades." Other religions have thus spoken, and have thereby confessed their own earthliness and impotency; but the gospel of Christ asserts the high and holy source whence it originated in the majesty with which its commands are uttered. Disdaining to succumb, even for a moment, to the mighty phalanx that is enleagued against it; rejoicing in the conscious possession of a power that will one day render it universally triumphant; it says, with the stately dignity of truth, "Go, man, right away into the midst of the world; avoid even the appearance of evil, but in all that is needful for thy well-being eat, and drink, and act like other men; there is a power that can preserve thee in the midst of the corruptions that are around thee; bear about with thee an angel's blessedness, and let thy life be all praise, all sweetness, and all love,"

XXV. THE PROSPECTS OF THE FUTURE.

The sacred records of the Budhists contain a prophecy, in which it is declared that after the elapse of 5000 years (from the time of its establishment) their system will become extinct; and the gradual manner in which its destruction will be effected is set forth at length.

It is said * that there are five antardhánas, declensions, or disappearances, in the course of which all knowledge of the religion of Budha will cease to exist. This declension is divided into five different epochs.

1. The first epoch, called pratiwédha, extends to the period when the attainment of the paths to nirwána will no longer be possible. The means by which the four paths and their fruition may be gained, with the four attainments peculiar to the rahats, will first be lost, in retrogressive order. All will be lost to the path sowán; then in successive order to the níla kasina, the first dhyána, the manner of performing the kasinas, and the acquirement of the nimitta illumination.

2. The second epoch, called pratipatti, extends to the period when the observances of the precepts by the priesthood will cease. When those who have been able to attain the paths have disappeared, others will still exercise karmasthána, perform the kasinas, and practice the fourteen ways of subduing the mind, the irdhis, arppana-samádhi, the power of benefitting others, and the softening of the mental and moral faculties; but as the method in which these will be performed will be defective, they will not avail for the attainment of the paths. In some instances these exercises will be performed with diligence, in order that future benefit may be received; but when it is found that the possession of supernatural powers cannot be acquired by the exercise of kasina, it will be generally neglected, and the four sangwara síla alone will be observed. The priests will then think that as they have kept the precepts and exercised meditation without being able to attain the paths, this is not an auspicious period for the performance of these things. Faults will be committed, and at first confession will be made to the sangha of the priesthood; but afterwards this will be neglected, and that which is forbidden will be practised. Those who thus err will

* Sadharmmaratnákaré.

at first be reproved by the more faithful, but others seeing what is done, will follow the same example; and when all the faithful are gone, those who succeed them will become still more careless. Thus the observance of the precepts by the priesthood will be discontinued.

3. The third epoch, called pariyapti, extends to the period when the understanding of Pali, the language of the bana, will cease. In process of time the understanding of the tunpitakas will be unattainable. Whilst this exists, the attainment of the paths, the observance of the precepts, and a knowledge of Pali, will be continued; but when the attainment of the paths is lost, the sentient beings existing in the world of men will love evil, and hate that which is good, by which the affection of the déwas will be diminished. The sun, moon, the twelve rásis or signs, and the nekatas, or lunar mansions, will become unpropitious; the kings of the earth will gradually become oppressors; the nobles will become unjust; the chiefs of the people and the people themselves will become depraved; and on account of this general defection the déwas of the clouds and winds will cease to send the needful showers and seasons. The seasons for the work of the husbandman will be out of their regular course; the grain will not come to maturity; and a famine will ensue. As the people will not have it in their power to present the usual offerings, the priests will be unable to provide for their disciples, who being left to obtain the means of support in any way they can, will be under no restraint, and they will have no opportunity of receiving instruction. Then will be lost the means of understanding the deep Abhidharmma. This will be lost from the patthána prakarana to the dhammasangini, in retrogressive order. After this the understanding of the Sútra Pitaka and the Winaya Pitaka will be lost. Then the sányuttaka-níkáya will be lost, to the óghátarawa-sútra, in retrogressive order; the medum-sanghaya, from the indriya-bháwaná prakarana to the múlapariya-sútra, in the same order; the dik-sanghaya, from the dasottara-sútra to the brahmajála-sutra; and in this way the whole of the Sútra Pitaka will be lost. But the priests will still be able to study the Winaya Pitaka and the Játakas; of these the greater part will neglect the Winaya Pitaka; leaving that which is abstruse, from the idleness of their disposition they will study only the Játakas. In time even the Játakas will not be understood; the Wessantara Játaka will first be lost; then the ten principal Játakas, and thence in order to

the first, Apannaka; and thus the knowledge of Pali will be entirely lost. As long as there is a priest who can repeat only four stanzas of the original bana, the religion of Budha may be considered to exist; but at length a king who wishes to hear bana will place a vessel filled with golden coin upon an elephant, and will proclaim three times through the city that it will be given to the priest who can repeat a single stanza of bana, and such a priest will not be found.

4. The fourth epoch, called linga, extends to the period when the reception of the priesthood will cease. In process of time the priests will put on the robe in an improper manner, and place the hands and feet in a way contrary to rule, so that the faithful upásakas will be grieved. They will put the alms-bowl in a cloth or bag, and carry it suspended from the neck; they will then carry it in the hand, or suspended from some support, as the tirttakas carry their gourds. They will dye the robe in a manner different to that which is commanded in the Winaya Pitaka, of a colour only approaching to yellow, like the seeds of batu, or nightshade. They will then put on a robe that has been worked, or that is of different colours, but will still say that they are priests. They will also practise husbandry and merchandise. It was declared by Gótama to Ananda that until this period shall arrive, those who make offerings to the associated priesthood will receive merit, or be rewarded for that which they present. The priests will continue to degenerate; they will begin to take life, and to plough and sow. A piece of cloth will be tied to the person as a mark of the priesthood; but in time this will be thrown off, as they will say there is no benefit from such a distinction; and at last they will have houses of their own, and families. Thus the priesthood will cease.

5. The fifth epoch, called dhátu, extends to the entire disappearance of the relics of Budha. In 5000 years from the time of the commencement of Budhism, the faith of men in Gótama will be diminished; and as the relics will not receive the honours to which they have been accustomed, they will go to the places where Gótama in his lifetime performed religious acts. They will then be collected together at the Ruanweli dágoba, in Anurádhapura; after which they will go to the Rájáyatana dágoba, in the Nága-loka; thence they will go to the bó-tree at the foot of which Gótama attained the Budhaship. A throne will here appear, upon which they will place themselves, and will form an exact resem-

blance of the body of Gótama when alive. The déwas, brahmas, and demons, knowing that this will be the last opportunity they will have of paying honour to the relics of Gótama, will assemble from the 10,000 sakwalas, and present offerings. Then the relics will put forth rays of glory that will extend to the brahma-lókas. The brahmas and other beings will exclaim, "To-day the relics of Budha will become extinct!" They will tremble exceedingly, and with a sorrow equal to that which was manifested when Gótama attained nirwána they will cry out, "the religion of Budha has passed away; the glory of Budha is defiled; the commands of Budha are neglected; the fame of Budha is overshadowed!" Their thoughts will be carried forward to consider how long this darkness will continue, and when Maitri Budha will appear; after which they will respectfully circumambulate the relics three or four times, and return to their respective worlds. A flame will at length proceed from the relics, extending far, and by this they will be burnt. The déwas and brahmas, on perceiving this, will remain for a time in grief, and make no use of their festive couches and chariots; but in due course the remembrance of these things will pass away, and the inhabitants of the various worlds will return to their accustomed modes of existence, all knowledge of the doctrines of the Budhas having entirely disappeared from the earth.

It was a bold assertion of Gótama, to declare that the religious system he taught would continue for the space of five thousand years; yet it was singular that he should tell of its extinction at all. We trust that long before this period has been added to the age of the world, the prophecy of the sage will be fulfilled. The carelessness and indifference of the people among whom the system is professed are the most powerful means of its conservation. It is almost impossible to move them, even to wrath. As the battering-ram that would break down the mightiest wall is of little use against the rampart of earth; so the want of firmness in the minds of those to whom the truth is presented prevents them from being impressed by its influence. They appear to acquiesce in the propositions that are made to them; but it is merely an outward assent that they give, and not that of the understanding. But in countries where the messengers of the cross have laboured the longest, and with the greatest diligence, the sramana has been brought to acknowledge the power of the Word of God. Not long ago the high priest of the Budhists in Ceylon wrote to the monarch of Siam to solicit gifts, and informed his majesty, that unless he came forward liberally to support the cause of their common religion, it would soon be banished from the island by the efforts of Europeans to impress their own systems upon the minds of the people. This is a triumph of no common order, and it will afford a vantage-ground for the combat to those missionaries who are living in other countries where Budhism is professed. The ancient Romans said of their city,

> "While stands the Coliseum Rome shall stand,
> When falls the Coliseum Rome shall fall,
> And when Rome falls, the world."

And the Budhists of other lands have a similar supposition relative to the Budhism of Ceylon. They imagine that the isle of Lanká is sacred ground, from its being the spot in which the bana was first committed to writing; and that whilst their system flourishes there, it will flourish every where; but that when it falls there, it will fall throughout the world. The ancient fabric already totters; it will soon be swept from its base by the power that alone is resistless; and in its stead will be erected the temple of the Lord, in which all the earth will worship the Father Everlasting.

ERRATA.

Page 8 *line* 33, *for* Pariwána *read* Pariwára.
10 „ 25, *for* Sarmana *read* Sramana.
10 *note*, *for* Milanda *read* Milinda.
51 *note*, *for* Kámawachan *read* Kammawáchan.
57 *note*, *for* Malcolm *read* Malcom.
60 *line* 20, *for* sámadlhi *read* samádhi.
65 „ 34, *for* it *read* then.
75 „ 5, *for* ἀχυρται *read* ἀγυρται.
141 „ 29, *for* was *read* is.
212 „ 26, *for* upásikas *read* upásakas.
213 „ 20, *for* reflection *read* refection.
217 „ 17, *for* cupula *read* cupola.
270 „ 4, and 26, *for* samádi *read* samádhi.
270 „ 34, *for* prita *read* priti.
271 „ 17, *for* the paths *read* nirwána.
272 *note*, *for* Pújáwaluja *read* Pújáwaliya, *and dele* pre *at the end of the line.*
276 *line* 33, *for* sachi *read* sacha.
304 „ 33, *for* sages *read* sage.
308 „ 21, *for* arúpa *read* rúpa.
326 „ 19, *for* couch *read* conch, *and for* or *read* of.
357 „ 31, *for* affected *read* effected.

INDEX AND GLOSSARY.

TEXTS CITED OR ILLUSTRATED.